DIFFICULT NEIGHBORHOODS

DIFFICULT NEIGHBORHOODS

The Semiotics of Conflict in Culture,
Literature, and Language

EDITED BY

Sachiyo M. Shearman, Władysław Chłopicki,
Władysław Witalisz, and Linda G. Kean

PUBLISHED BY EAST CAROLINA
UNIVERSITY ACADEMIC LIBRARY SERVICES

Copyright © 2025 ECU Academic Library Services

All rights reserved

The publication of this book was made possible by the financial contribution of East Carolina University and the Excellence Initiative Program of the Jagiellonian University.

Suggested citation: Shearman, S. M., Chlopicki, W., Witalisz, W., & Kean, L. (2025). Difficult Neighborhoods: The semiotic of conflict in culture, literature, and language. Greenville: ECU Academic Library Services.

DOI: https://doi.org/10.5149/9781469696560_Shearman

ISBN 978-1-4696-9655-3 (paperback)
ISBN 978-1-4696-9656-0 (open access ebook EPUB)
ISBN 978-1-4696-9657-7 (open access ebook PDF)

Published by East Carolina University Academic Library Services
Distributed by the University of North Carolina Press

www.uncpress.org

CONTENTS

vii Preface

SECTION ONE
1   Conflict and Unity Across Borders

ONE
3   Borders, Brexit, and the Reconstruction of Europe – Gerard McCann

TWO
23 Borders of Perception in Estonian and Polish Cultural Narratives – Liisi Laineste and Dorota Brzozowska

THREE
43 (Un)Bordering Gibraltarian Literary Culture: Identity and Recognition – Rafael Vélez Núñez and Giordano Durante

SECTION TWO
57 Analyses of Messages Entailing Conflict Views

FOUR
59 #MoreThanAnAthlete: The Building of Community in a Divided Neighborhood – Linda Kean and Todd Fraley

FIVE
71 Unraveling Conflicting Attitudes Toward Rape: Victimization in Discourse and the Fine Line Between a Good and Bad Victim – Olga O'Toole

SIX
90 Voices of Outrage and Support: Understanding Public Reaction to the Larry Nassar Sentencing – Charles Meadows and Carrie Meadows

SECTION THREE
103 Examination of Messages in Russia

SEVEN
105 Russophobia Frame and Dysphemism in Russian Sports Discourse During Wartime – Daiki Horiguchi

EIGHT
123 A War Between Generations: The Generational Boundary in Contemporary Russian Drama – Elena Kurant

NINE

138 Intertextuality vs. Transtextuality: Political Cartoons on the Russian-Ukrainian War – Orest Semotiuk

SECTION FOUR

157 Conflicts in Classic and Modern Literature

TEN

159 From Victims to Survivors: The Impact of Migration on Women in Novels by Female Migrant Writers – Dorota Rygiel

ELEVEN

177 Kościuszko's Name in Byron's Poetry: Echoes of the News from Poland in *Don Juan* and *The Age of Bronze* – Monika Coghen

TWELVE

191 "What's in a Name?": Shakespearean References in the Case Law of the European Court of Human Rights – Michał Kowalski and Agnieszka Romanowska

THIRTEEN

209 Troy as a Metaphor of Conflict: Trojan Allusions in Public Discourse About the War in Ukraine – Władysław Witalisz

SECTION FIVE

223 Conflict in Interactions: Avoidance, Identity, Messages, and Consensus

FOURTEEN

225 Conflict Avoidance Experiences in Family and at Work: Narrative Analysis of Avoidance Motives, Strategies, and Impacts – Sachiyo Shearman and Kumi Ishii

FIFTEEN

241 GIFference Conflict?: The Use of GIFs Among Generations – Anita Buczek-Zawiła, Krzysztof Idczak, Emilia Januś, Eryk Kowalczyk, and Wiktoria Kozieł

SIXTEEN

264 Between Borders and Identities: (How) Arab EFL Learners Engage with Global English – Yousif Al-Naddaf and Romuald Gozdawa-Gołębiowski

SEVENTEEN

290 Difficult Neighborhoods: Consensus and Conflict in Academic Book Reviews – Monika Zasowska

315 List of Contributors

PREFACE

Welcome to the Across Borders X edited book titled *Difficult Neighborhoods: The Semiotics of Conflict in Culture, Literature, and Language*. This book examines the semiotics of conflict in culture, literature, and language, as we navigate the challenging neighborhoods where we reside. We live and work in a world with diverse perspectives. As we go about our daily lives, we face diverging views, values, and cultures. When these diverging views and values collide, we inevitably face conflicts, creating situations that require us to navigate a "difficult neighborhood."

We have numerous examples of difficult neighborhoods worldwide. According to the Council on Foreign Relations, there are 28 ongoing and active conflicts around the world, including frequently reported conflicts such as the war in Ukraine and the Israeli-Palestinian struggle, and less-frequently reported conflicts such as the internal conflicts in the Democratic Republic of Congo and the Civil War in Myanmar (Council on Foreign Relations, 2025). We want to believe that humans are more intelligent in the 21st century, following two global wars in the 20th century—World War I, which resulted in an estimated 8.9 million fatalities, and World War II, which resulted in 30.8 million fatalities (Herre et al., 2024). Unfortunately, however, we continue to face various conflicts around the world, causing destruction and various conflict-related causalities.

Our emphasis in this book is not just geopolitical conflict, but also conflict in various media messages, classic and modern literatures, and in human interactions. As we learn the dynamics of navigating conflicting views in various contexts, we aspire to understand their mechanisms, to deal with conflicts effectively, and to transform difficult neighborhoods into more collaborative and supportive communities, fostering mutual respect and shared goals.

The current book features original research studies that examine the semiotics and pragmatics of conflict in various discourses of borders and neighborhoods—geographical, political, ethnic, religious, and linguistic—as expressed in widely understood cultural texts. With this diverse scope in mind, we hope to cast a stone, suggesting that we understand and approach various conflicts in a more creative, humane, innovative, and objective manner.

This book consists of five subsections. In the first section, we include articles that explore conflict, cultural identity, and unity across borders. Scholars explore various contexts, including the European Union after Brexit, the cultural narratives of the Estonian and Polish borders, and the borders in the Straits of Gibraltar. In the second section, contributors examine various messages that convey conflicting opinions: opinions on athletes, opinions on rape victims, and opinions on criminals. In the third section of the book, academic and cultural analyses of messages in Russian are examined. The readers are to learn about generational struggles in Russian drama, Russophobia and dysphemism in Russian sports discourse, and the rhetoric used on Russian-Ukrainian war. In the fourth section, analyses of conflicts in classic and modern literature are presented. Authors provide compelling analyses of the experiences of female migrants' conflicts, examination of Kościuszko's name in Byron's poetry, inquiry of European Court on Human Rights referencing Shakespeare, and analysis of public discourse on the war in Ukraine.

In the final section of the book, interpersonal conflict analysis examines conflict avoidance, the use of GIF images in conflictual messages, intrapersonal conflict struggles related to identities, and consensus and conflict in academic book reviews. We hope that the readers will find this edited book valuable in learning how conflict has been addressed in challenging neighborhoods and how we can enhance our approach to navigating conflicting views and values.

The editors would also like to express our sincere gratitude to all the reviewers who contributed to the blind review process. All the reviewers' input provided to the editors and contributors of this book was invaluable in making this publication possible. We would like to thank Ms. Jaylin Thompson and Mr. Dan Elliot, who jointly designed the cover of the current book. Jaylin is a Master of Arts student, and Dan Elliot was a faculty member in the School of Arts and Design at the College of Fine Arts and Communication at East Carolina University.

Lastly, the editors would like to thank all the people who made the Across Borders X Conference possible. The biannual Across Borders conference started about two decades ago in the hope of establishing connections across borders to foster the exchange of scholarships in the arts, humanities, and social sciences. The connections were established in Europe but are now expanding to the rest of the world. The editors would like to thank everyone who assisted in establishing, supporting, and continuing the effort to sustain the Across Borders Conference. We, the editors, are thankful for its success, and we hope this effort continues.

References

Herre, B., Rodes-Guirao, L, & Roser, M. (2024). "War and peace" [online resource]. https://ourworldindata.org/war-and-peace

Council on Foreign Relations. (2025). *Global conflict tracker*. https://www.cfr.org/global-conflict-tracker/

SECTION ONE

Conflict and Unity Across Borders

CHAPTER ONE | GERARD MCCANN

Borders, Brexit, and the Reconstitution of Europe

Abstract

European political culture has changed significantly in recent years. Working through a global recession, a pandemic, and the outbreak of interstate war, countries have struggled to get a process in place which can pivot politics into an environment where stability and prosperity are again bedrocks of European polity. Within a volatile context, European integration has—again—come under question as a method of intergovernmental engagement, with various ideological forces across the continent seeking disintegration and political realignment. Arguably, the basis of the post–Cold War consensus on peacebuilding has been undermined. This chapter looks at the sociopolitical pressures that European states are facing, and with particular reference to the withdrawal of the United Kingdom (UK) from the European Union (EU), it will investigate reasons for the growth of euroscepticism. It will conclude by reviewing how the process of European integration has been compromised and examining points of intervention where European political life can reconstitute itself as a safeguarding entity for the diverse peoples of an increasingly polarized continent.

Keywords: Europe, integration, Brexit, populism, reconstitution

As a political and cultural entity, Europe has changed significantly over the past decade. Political turmoil, economic rebalancing, and demographic remapping have altered the continent in a manner not seen since the tumultuous conflagration at the close of the "First" Cold War. Questions over the free movement of people and the very nature of democracy itself have come to the fore, with shifting power balances and geopolitical disintegration all caught under the shadow of the most brutal war seen on European soil since 1945. Systemic changes and disruption in respect to governance, the (mis)management of borders and attempts at redefining the integrating process, have affected civil and political discourse alike. This article aims to analyze the backstory to this "reconstitution" of Europe with political divergence, populism, and border disputation at the fore. It will assess recent developments in political culture and survey how a language of borders and "othering" is changing our understanding of what modern Europe is or could be.

With specific reference to the United Kingdom's (UK) withdrawal from the European Union (EU), it will reflect on the rationale of "ever closer union" and will voice a caution on neglecting—that is, not addressing—communitarian and nationalistic reflections, where competition over difference and isolationism could ferment conditions for future instability and conflict (Martill & Staigerm, 2018, pp. 1–18). Finally, with a more positive outlook, the paper will address the reimaging of Europe in the interests of a common destiny shaped by a more conventional idea of an open European demos, where futures can be aligned and politics cohesive. A starting point is the comment by Robert Schuman that, "The European spirit signifies being conscious of belonging to a cultural family and to have a willingness to serve that community in the spirit of total mutuality, without any hidden motives of hegemony or the selfish exploitation of others" (Schuman, 1949).

Functionality vs. Process

The end of the Cold War played a significant role in the outworking of European integration. The period from mid-1989 onward witnessed the breakup of Central and Eastern Europe, marked by the consolidation of democratic cultures in some regions and the spiraling into conflict in others. The lifting of the borders following the Cold War facilitated an outward reach and interconnectivity across Europe which—at that point—accelerated efforts toward the harmonization of laws, merging economies, and a range of cross-border policy initiatives. In Strasbourg in December 1989, after witnessing the breakup of the Soviet Union, the European Community leaders issued a prophetic joint communiqué on the emerging political situation and the need for unity through uncertainty: "… the Community is and must remain as a point of reference and influence. It remains the cornerstone of a new European architecture and, in its will to openness, a mooring for future European equilibrium" (quoted in Urwin, 1995, p. 262; see also Rifkin, 2005, pp. 58–70). The challenges were evident from day one, with power becoming more fluid and societal tensions within member states increasingly accentuating differing visions of what Europe should look like. Even at this early configuration of a new European polity, there were diverging aspirations and understandings.

Going through the 1990s, the language and posturing around European integration shifted somewhat, but it did so within a multicomplex policy environment where the social market and welfare focus of Brussels had to try to accommodate competing assertions on national identity, sovereignty and digressions on fundamental freedoms. The dissolution of the Soviet Union on December 26, 1991, coupled with the speed of the reunification of Germany and the transition of Central European countries from command-state economies to market-driven systems, was laden with fault lines at every point (Swann, 2000, pp. 27–48). The transformation brought forward different notions of what integration actual meant, disrupting the Monnetian consensus that "Core"—Western—Europe had held since the 1950s. Political interests from the East centered around the opening up of economic opportunities in developing European regions, with the new vision coming through the lens of democratization with salient marketization—the free movement of people being the most impactful aspect of integration. The dismantling of the Iron Curtain brought with it ideological nuances which complicated the liberal bent of the EU as it had developed, with countries such as Poland, Hungary, and the Czech Republic (all joining in 2004) arriving with radically different solutions to the problems of the Community. There were disparate points of view emerging at a very move from aspirant member states, coupled with establishment resolve among the institutions in Brussels. John Gillingham, in his epic *European Integration 1950–2003: Superstate or New Market Economy?*, highlighted the political imbalances at this time and the stratification that had come to permeate the integration process:

> Their power and prestige suffered, strength turned into weakness, and governmental authority waned. Scope for independent action on the domestic front diminished. As a result, at the European level, summit after summit ended in discord, gridlock, or nothing at all. The word had to substitute for the deed, debasing political currencies on both sides of the former Iron Curtain and leading to disillusionment and division. (Gillingham, 2003, p. 305)

The new "order" may have extended the EU's reach and helped balance political and economic systems in most former communist countries, but it also complicated the composition of the continent as a liberal, cosmopolitan entity.

Post–Cold War European society had been characterized by a general optimism and the adoption of competitive market-based economies—albeit within a Keynesian/Monnetian model of economic integration. In the 1990s, for those on a path to membership of the EU, this was highly appealing. The EU established political and economic participatory obligations, such as those laid out in the Copenhagen Criteria of 1993, requiring new member states to adopt recognized standards and guarantees, democratic principles, fundamental rights, a compatible rule of law, and a functioning market economy. In return, they were welcomed into the largest economic bloc on earth with financial support to enhance commercial and financial integration. The functionalistic aspects of this "top-down" form of integration did not go unnoticed and, indeed, had been flagged up before. One voice of caution came from sociologist and renowned UK Peer, Ralf Dahrendorf, who anticipated tremors in the architecture of the Community in his early analysis *Plädoyer für die Europäische Union* (*Plea for the European Union*) (Dahrendorf, 1973, pp. 76–85), where he warned of the alienation of large numbers of people from the idea of "Union" if the system remained centralized and determinate. Very observantly, the process, with its fluidity, needed to take into account the nuances of difference and the desperate nature of European society, political culture needed to be recognized. The ubiquitous concept of Europe needed to be enhanced, but it also needed to be skillfully adaptively inclusive. There was an opportunity in the 1990s to reimagine this integrating Europe through the energy of eastern European people and their aspirations. The opportunity was there to capture the diverse, mercurial nature of European polity. At this point, it quite possibly missed a bridge to the processional aspects of integration, a moment which would have given space to alternative or reserved attitudes to the pace of change.

Furthermore, through its disjointed approach, the EU (paradoxically) saved the nation state as it had evolved postwar, flaws and all. Alan Milward, in *The European Rescue of the Nation State*, noted this feature of the confusion of a multispeed Europe. It was, in his view, "A part of that post-war rescue of the European nation state, because the new political consensus on which this rescue was built required the process of integration, the surrender of limited areas of national sovereignty to the supranation" (Milward, 2000, pp. 3–4; see also Rusmussen & Knudsen, 2009, pp. 85–99). Significantly, the Maastricht Treaty (1992) asserted the European Union's systemic and functionalist nature further while the push for deeper integration fueled Brussels' aim of globalization and its desire to compete on the global stage. Arguably, the Brexit juggernaut in the UK began at this point. As more nationalities joined the EU and its multicultural society began to anticipate greater cooperation, mobility, and connectivity—there surfaced a counterculture in which significant numbers of the EU's citizenry were ill at ease.

In *Europe as I See It*, Romani Prodi, the former head of the European Commission and one of the architects of the European Union going into the new century, let it be known that there was an awareness that functionality with a lack of subsidiarity could generate sociopolitical disintegration, "alienation," that would stack up problems for the future of an already stretched process of integration.

> In some ways, politics seem powerless to help in the face of these new problems that are shared by all European countries. Citizens accuse politicians of having lost contact with society and of taking decisions affecting the common good on the basis of oligarchical and inefficient practices. This poses the risk of the gradual alienation of individuals from their institutions and the generation of radicalism or apathy. (Prodi, 2000, p. 2)

From Values to Realignment

The shifting geopolitical map of Europe in the 2000s was increasingly reflecting the complexities of the post–Cold War world, pushing European countries to deepen all aspects of policy coherence in order to compete in a coordinated way on the global stage. It was believed that this would allow member states to leverage collective power to negotiate as a bloc with other global powers—particularly the United States and China (Eichengreen, 2007, pp. 406–413). Indeed, globalization made cooperation across borders essential, building a global role for the Community, but it also carried with it the price of further distancing Brussels' mechanisms of power from regional and local exigencies.

Political divergence could be seen in the efforts to create a European Constitution from 2001 onward (culminating in the signing of the Treaty of Lisbon on December 13, 2007), an attempt to make the EU more coherent and unified in response to ongoing "external" threats. While the Constitution failed to gain support in referenda in France and the Netherlands, thus collapsing the whole strategy, the Lisbon Treaty (coming into force on December 1, 2009) picked up its mantle to address some of the concerns about EU governance, its global role and decision-making structures. As a corollary to that, public debates over issues such as sovereignty, national identity, and indeed integration gained momentum and led to regional introspection on the very notion of European unity. This contributed to the existing obstacles facing integration, the further rise of euroscepticism generally and the UK's turmoil over a vote to "Leave" or "Remain" in the bloc. Treaty disputes flagged up recurring themes on regional and national difference. The Lisbon Treaty, arguably, accentuated recognizable fault-lines in European democracy that had been there, but were being continually glossed over. This was commented on as early as 2002 by Mikael af Malmborg and Bo Stråth in *The Meaning of Europe*:

> Established differences in national and macro-regional self-understanding influence attitudes towards European integration. Patterns of history are in no way deterministic, but Europhile versus Europhobe national discourses can predispose some nations to react mainly positively and others negatively towards the imposition of a European polity on the nation states. The 'Europeanization' of nation states is in part the outcome of deeply entrenched notions on Europe—as well as on the nation—is also deeply contested within the various national settings. (Malmborg and Bo Stråth, 2002, p. 13)

Post–Cold War society may have provided solid justifications for European integration, but it also had been vigorously contested, revealing stresses to the system and a prevailing, possibly elitist, concept of unity. The political shifts, the expansion of Westernized liberal democratic values and the rise of globalization were all key facets that drove European integration through to the signing of Lisbon, but it left as many contradictions in the process as solutions. Indeed, "storing up trouble for the future" has continually been a problem of design with flaws being embedded throughout the *acquis communautaire* since the emboldened days of Maastricht (Ludlow, 2009, p. 25). The process had been multifaceted, with differing ways of identifying national positions across European societies, bringing forward varying options on the speed and depth of what was shaped by Brussels. Nonetheless, the post–Cold War period signaled a slowly integrating, increasingly hard fought for, Europe polity.

Post–Cold War Europe emphasized human rights, the rule of law, democratic governance, peacebuilding and what the EU defined as a "Social Europe." The EU was presented as an actor in promoting pillars of stability both within and beyond Europe, with its enlargement policy ("widening" and "deepening") being shaped in a manner that would by intent strengthen democratic practices and protect the rights of minorities and marginalized groups. This period also witnessed the EU take a proactive role in foreign policy, supporting peacebuilding efforts in the Balkans and other post-Soviet regions. The conflict in the former Yugoslavia, in particular, was a pivotal moment, with a concerted voice from the member states of the EU seeking to promote stability through integration in the interests of peace. It became the default position on war that would reemerge with Ukrainian negotiations on EU membership during the struggle to liberate the country after Russia's illegal invasion on 24 February 2022.

Social Europe, one of the pillars of European integration, may have given a depth to the process but it also had myriad implications with respect to cultural difference and diversity (Hantrais, 2007, pp. 1–23). "… for all the disappointment experienced by the EC's social architects, some foundations have been laid down for a European house which is more than purely economic in character" (Wise & Gibb, 1993, p. 286). Over time, the idea of a unified Europe gained acceptance in many parts of civil society, particularly in Western Europe, where citizens had come to embrace the benefits and ideals of multiculturalism. Other regions of the EU, particularly in the Mediterranean periphery, which was struggling with people trafficking and illegal migration, were less sanguine. These reservations were to gain momentum as the crises over migration rolled out, with 2015–16 being a notable period of change in this regard. Challenges coalesced where immigration, economic inequality, xenophobia and a rise in populism across many countries provoked divergent and often disruptive political voices. In the round, the EU had to balance progress laden with identity politics and angry voices on national sovereignty, leading to tensions in member states and euroscepticism in just about every jurisdiction. Key values were being questioned for the first time since World War II, in a change of public attitudes.

Since the mid-2010s, dissident political movements had been emerging, engendering a significant rethink by many of the purpose and meaning of European integration and the nature of its unification. The causes of this shift had been rippling across the continent for many years, but a few reasons stand out. In the early 1990s, in *Single Market to Social Europe*, Mark Wise and Richard Gibb had registered a "schism" evident across Europe and highlighted a problematic deficit in the democratic system, with all the dangers that would entail:

> Indeed, there are sometimes signs that a dangerous gulf is opening up between political leaders who have adopted a European vision and their general publics which are still largely operating within purely national frames of thought … But if those with federalist ambitions fail, what alternative future can the peoples of Europe expect? All the old centrifugal forces in Europe, which have caused such massive destruction in this century, might easily be rekindled. (Wise & Gibb, 1993, p. 313)

Euroscepticism has not only been about criticizing the EU and its institutions; it has also been a manifestation of long-standing opinions on sovereignty, centralized economic control, and the perceived overreach of EU governance. As a result of this, all member states have witnessed a rise in new social movements that questioned or rejected the EU's authority and articulated rhetoric that sought to "regain" control over domestic politics. The consolidation of influence by political voices from this perspective within national legislatures—advocating a resetting of the postwar ideological consensus or calling for referenda "in" or "out"—became the norm in European political life. Furthermore, questioning the liberal democratic principles that shaped the EU became a destabilizing and disruptive feature, envisaging an emasculated integration process and a weakened institutional and legal base. It also marked the reemergence of a particularly assertive brand of nationalism which could use the integration process as a point of opposition. Many political theorists had warned about the possibility of emboldened neo-nationalism. By the 2010s, this ideology had been again mainstreamed across the European political landscape—with its central target being "ever closer union" (Hobsbawn, 1992, pp. 177–192; Anderson, 1991, pp. 5–7; Billig, 1995, pp. 60–92; Gellner, 1983, pp. 137–143; Puri, 2004, pp. 22–32).

Rebalancing Europe: The Brexit Effect

The most notable example of this process of de-Europeanization was dramatically witnessed with the success of the British "Brexiteer" movement. The UK's exit from the EU after the June 23, 2016, referendum was perhaps the most disruptive fulcrum in the history of the EU. For most, it was an unexpected shock:

> Despite the multiple crises in which the Union finds itself embroiled, neither publics nor authorities had fully comprehended the probability of 'Brexit'. Unprecedented in nature, the vote shook whatever remained of the once preponderant *telos* of European integration—encapsulated in the symbolic, if legally vacuous, Treaty commitment to 'ever closer' union—to the core. (Martill & Staiger, 2018, p. 1)

Driven by a combination of economic disruption, the ineffective management of immigration, and attacks on governmental leadership, the decision to leave frustrated the continent's historical settlement on integration. It also set the precedent for other populist "exit" movements in countries (notably in Italy, France, Poland, and Hungary) where Eurosceptic parties gained ground, advocating stronger sovereignty, reerecting borders by means contrary to the "open" Schengen Agreement, and demeaning the EU's liberal norms. Italy's Fratelli d'Italia and Rassemblement National in France, for example—as with the UK Independence Party (UKIP), politically profited from skepticism.

From that baseline, political movements could be built focusing on perceived national weaknesses and impoverishment, with Brussels to blame. Indeed, Hungary's prime minister, Viktor Orbán, leader of Fidesz, garnered a majority government as *the* most outspoken critic of EU policies, remaining at odds with EU institutions and pro-EU governments, yet paradoxically drawing heavily from EU structural support. With the emergence of euroscepticism, the digital revolution and advancements in communication technologies provided alternative means of media and communication, brokering new fronts over just about every aspect of European politics. The ability to marshal a lobby instantly across borders, linking in with like-minded advocates, for or against, combined with increased travel opportunities within the Schengen Area, fostered on one side a sense of European identity and interconnectedness, and on the other suspicion and discord. Working through from the Lisbon Treaty's roadmap for integration, the demarcation lines had been consolidated across the Union, certainly from the point where the Treaty was being ratified. The political battle around Brexit had been in place from this point onward, even though there had been a long history of suspicion of Brussels in British politics. Interestingly, while skepticism emanated predominantly from the Right (in particular, Margaret Thatcher through to Boris Johnson), there were also powerful voices from the Left of the spectrum—as can be seen from this December 29, 1974, comment in a letter to his constituents by Tony Benn, onetime grandee of the UK's governing Labour Party (a party which seemed integrationist throughout its history):

> British membership of the Community, by permanently transferring sovereign legislative and financial powers to Community Authorities, who are not directly elected by the British people, also permanently insulates those Authorities from direct control by the British electors who cannot dismiss them and whose views, therefore, need to carry no weight with them and whose grievances they cannot be compelled to remedy. (Benn, 1974, p. 40)

By the 2020s, populist/Eurosceptic movements had galvanized political discourse across many European nations. Lobby and single cause movements intertwined with nationalist actors to stress the need to protect national identity, close economies, and reject perceived threatening external influences. In this trajectory of politics, the EU became an easy target for the denigration of its policies and institutions.

There was also the resurgence of cultural sensitivities around the idea of multiculturalism and a growing fear of losing local, religious and cultural aspects of national life due to what some labeled "wokeism." There was the disjointed mess that became the management of EU migration policy, leading to a rise in "nativist," often xenophobic, rhetoric. The leaders of far-Right populist groups agitated on the difficulties between local identity and broader European unity, with the migrant crisis becoming a major trigger to accelerate the growth of these movements, with many political leaders—often from long established parties—expressing fears about (perceived) "threats" from "others." Multiculturalism could be framed as a challenge to "native" ways of life. The ideological nuances played a distinct role in strengthening exit-minded sentiments, where populist leaders were seemingly apoplectic in their opposition to EU-led immigration policies.

In the UK, immigration was repeatedly highlighted as the key reason for the way the Brexit referendum ended up, with the Leave vote eventually tipping the balance against a Remain vote. The surprise of this was that it went against every significant political, economic, cultural, educational, and security opinion in the UK at that time—June 2016. On the eve of the referendum:

- Every previous prime minister and opposition leader in the UK wanted to remain in the EU.
- Every parliamentary party—bar the small Northern Irish Democratic Unionist Party—wanted to remain in.
- All other 27 leaders in the EU wanted the UK to remain in.
- Barack Obama and the USA wanted the UK to remain in.
- All major business leaders wanted to remain in, including the Confederation of British Industries (CBI) and Institute of Directors (IoD).
- All university vice-chancellors wanted to remain in.
- All trade unions wanted to remain in.
- All security organizations (MI5/MI6) wanted to remain in.
- Even the bookmakers favored a Remain vote (predicting an 80% chance of a Remain win [William Hill]).

The arguments on behalf of the status quo were, most thought, undeniable. The emerging counterbalance, fixated on personality politics, scattered through social media bubbles, were peppered with repeated slogans ("Get Brexit Done," "Take Back Control," "Leave Means Leave") and arguments that a lot of the UK population seemed to be able to relate to. From a more intellectual position, Conservative Daniel Hannan, in *Why Vote Leave*, summed up why many in Britain were swayed into an anti-EU, anti-integration, anti-migrant position:

Instead of the rule of law, we have the imperative of political union: when the dots and commas of the treaties stand in the way of deeper integration, they are unhesitatingly set aside. Instead of parliamentary democracy, we're governed by unelected officials who reach their decisions in secret, often after being lobbied by vested interests. Instead of personal liberty, we have a mass of pettifogging regulation that makes us poorer as well as less free. (Hannan, 2016, p. xiv)

Economic factors have also been present throughout this political realignment of Europe. The Eurozone crisis, austerity measures imposed by EU institutions, and the uneven benefits of European regional policy led to widespread dissatisfaction, particularly in Southern European countries such as Greece, Spain, and Portugal. The rollout of the austerity measures that all governments imposed after the 2008 global financial crisis (which was notably severe in the UK) remained a live issue long after the recession was over. People felt the reduced standard of living with the resultant depreciation of the quality of life and were receptive to the politics of blame. Governmental policies were seen by critics as prioritizing fiscal discipline over national welfare, which in turn fueled anti-EU sentiment. Rational analysis was lost in the fog of social media, while national governments struggled to argue the case for Brussels. Furthermore, there was a growing belief that the benefits of EU integration were not being evenly distributed across Europe, where wealthier regions in Core Europe, comprising the triangle running from Frankfurt to London to Paris, were seen as benefiting from EU privilege, while poorer regions, the peripheries and southern regions, were facing recurrent economic stagnation, underinvestment and continual high unemployment. This led to a feeling among many of alienation and resentment, highly exploitable as political currency.

What seemed to be happening through the 2010s was that political realignments were intersecting with deeper social rifts. The EU's emphasis on multiculturalism and a quickly evolving human rights architecture, provoked push-back from parts of the population that felt these policies threaten traditional values. Cultural conservatism gained political traction against a highly assertive liberalism, the hegemony, with many exit movements drawing support from broader sensitivities and religious conservatism. This could be seen in regions of the EU where Christian churches, particularly in Central and Eastern member states, non-contrite or evangelical churches, registered resistance to the EU's advocacy of progressive social policies, including LGBTQ+ rights and religious and gender equality. These lobbies attracted historically placid apolitical demographic groups to rail against what they viewed as a "immoral" liberalism emanating from Brussels. Ironically, in the larger Western churches, there has always been a guarded approval of integration. Lécile Leconte, in *Understanding Euroscepticism* (2010), noted this paradox:

Churches certainly remain globally supportive of European integration ... leaving aside value-based Euroscepticism (which is mostly expressed by the Catholic clergy), church questioning about the role of religion in the integration process raises two important issues. First, they point to the risk that the EU may be increasingly perceived as a mere market ... Second, they raise the issue of a growing atheism and its impact on support for the integration process. Indeed, it has been found that, among younger Europeans especially, atheism is correlated with lower levels of support for European integration. (Leconte, 2010, p. 227)

While the political and cultural divides within countries and across the EU have become more pronounced, as reflected in voting patterns, another fracture became patently obvious. Urban areas, with their more diverse and cosmopolitan populations, tended to be more pro-European, while rural areas are more often than not Eurosceptic. This divide exposed geographic cultural shifts in Europe, where rural ways of life are confronted by urbanized, globalized values. This became very evident with the referenda on the European Constitution in France and the Netherlands as early as 2005 but can be seen in every election across the EU since. Cities with larger, more diverse population concentrations almost without exception support parties that are pro-EU, whereas rural areas have garnered support around the more populist and nationalistic parties (CISE, 2025; EU, 2025). This was very evident in the Brexit referendum, where London, Manchester and Liverpool—the biggest cities—were strongly Remain while the most rural of areas, the farming communities of the south-west and midlands, voted Leave. Birmingham as a large city, interestingly, bucked this trend by voting to leave by 1%, reflecting the peculiar socio-economic demographic makeup that that city faces—Birmingham is a "superdiverse" city, with a sizeable majority of the population coming from non-British backgrounds.

The response from Brussels to the success of the Brexit lobby was a mixture of disbelief and sadness, almost as if it was at the beginning of a process of reversal. While there was a window left open for a UK return to the fold at some point, a moment of reflection looked at why so many saw the EU project as unappealing or even damaging (the UK officially left on December 31, 2020, after a period of "transition"). The break in faith and the breach in trust did not go without comment. European Commission President Ursula Von Der Leyen, in a lecture titled "Old friends, new beginnings: Building another future for the EU-UK partnership," at the London School of Economics on January 8, 2020, commented:

But the truth is that our partnership cannot and will not be the same as before. And it cannot and will not be as close as before—because with every choice comes a consequence. With every decision comes a trade-off. Without the free movement of people, you cannot have the free movement of capital, goods and services. Without a level playing field on environment, labour, taxation and state aid, you cannot have the highest quality access to the world's largest single market. The more divergence there is, the more distant the partnership has to be. (Von der Leyen, 2020)

In fear of other exit movements, European leaders called for reforms to make the EU more attractive in the new world order, more flexible, responsive, and democratically aware—with Europeanization being the formal response to the rising tide of Euroscepticism. Suggested interventions aimed to address some of the concerns that fueled exit movements, without leading to disintegration. Ernst Hass, the American political scientist from Berkeley, made an interesting observation on the vacillating outcomes of this model of democracy which suggested—in the European context—that a reset in the product of integration would be prudent. He noted that, "The ontology is 'soft' rational choice: societal actors, in seeking to realize their value-derived interests, will choose whatever means are made available by the prevailing democratic order. If thwarted they will rethink their values, redefine their interests, and choose new means to realize them" (Haas, 2006, p. 439). Euroscepticism has been one of those means. As Europe grapples with its position in an increasingly polarized world, and with a second Cold War creating a new Iron Curtain across the continent, the tension between nationalism and the need for a renewed vision of Europe is likely to remain a defining cause for European politics into the foreseeable future.

The UK's decision to leave the EU also raised fundamental questions about interstate relations. Brexit sparked quite an angry debate about the future of the bloc, leading some countries to reconsider the benefits of deeper union while others still advocated for more federalism to avoid further fragmentation. For the first time since the Schengen negotiations, borders became an issue of intense debate. EU borders were invariably affected by the manner in which the UK exited, with an almost instant disruption to trade and investment (Solanke, 2023, pp. 442–452; Mindus, 2017, pp. 77–79). By design, the UK's withdrawal from the bloc created barriers to trade, new tariffs, regulatory hurdles, and the return of customs checks. Borders reemerged that had not been witnessed in a generation, with the Irish border region bringing forward the most awkward of mechanisms to find a solution, ending in the establishment of an Irish Sea border between Great Britain (England, Scotland, and Wales) and the EU, of which Northern Ireland remained as an integral part of the single market (The Windsor Framework; see also McAleese, 2017). It caused a reconfiguration of interstate relationships, especially among sectors wanting to "game" the single market. Problems with inflation, scarcity of produce, protectionism and key worker emigration all reverberated across regions linked to the withdrawn UK. London, which was previously a major financial hub within the EU, migrated significant financial activities to other European cities, with Dublin, Frankfurt, Paris, and Amsterdam benefiting from the outflow. Indeed, the Dublin government and its financial sector set up thousands of desks in anticipation of specialist worker "flight" from London. The outcome of this was that it served to weaken the integration of financial markets across Europe and not only the UK.

Historically, the UK was an important actor within EU governance, a power broker on a level with France and Germany, particularly in the design of policies relating to migration, trade, foreign affairs and regulatory frameworks. Its departure meant the EU had to adjust its policies without one of its largest and most influential members. In that, it forced the EU to reconsider how it functioned and how to maintain cohesion among its remaining members. One consequence was an increased push among the most vocal advocates of integration within the EU Council to deepen integration in certain areas (such as defense, tax harmonization, climate change mitigation, and digital technology), while others considered slowing the process to focus on internal state unity. An ironic effect of Brexit has been that progressive integration is back on the table for discussion: "This re-politicisation of the European project, and the opening up of public debate on the question of Europe's future, represent positive developments for European politics, wherever one lies on key ideological fault lines" (Martill & Stieger, 2018, p. 264). In the wake of Brexit, many EU leaders have used the opportunity to reaffirm the importance of European core values and the rationale for integration—with the war in Ukraine energizing many into the realization that the founding principles of the Union around sustainable peace and building prosperity were as relevant as ever. One of the post-Brexit trends has been a growing emphasis on European strategic autonomy. This has encouraged efforts to reduce reliance on external powers (including the US and China) and to develop a more cohesive European policy framework.

While Brexit was largely seen as an isolating event—the impact on the UK economy has been a warning to all. A recurrent fear in Brussels has been that it may embolden anti-EU sentiment and lead to further fragmentation. As a result of the divisions exposed by Brexit, some EU leaders have called for "differentiated integration" (DI)—a model where different countries participate at different speeds and varying levels of involvement in EU policies, with some opting out of certain areas of integration. Alexander Stubb, the former prime minister of Finland, argued the case for such a mechanism in that it could carry member states along at different paces, with borders dissolving absolutely in some cases and national sensitivities being retained to varying degrees in others. Stubb spoke of multispeed, variable geometry, and à la carte ways of being a member of the EU (Stubb, 1996, pp. 283–295). Such ideas reemerged post-Brexit under the banner of a two speed Europe. The concept was there to an extent previously, but a formalized structure around this could prove to be problematic in that it is exactly what the UK had—outside the Eurozone, outside Schengen, and recessionary support initiatives among other things—and it still left.

One unexpected result of Brexit was the level of political convergence among most member states at governmental level. The great disrupter of the integration process, the UK, was out of the conversation and those remaining could engage in what for a time post-Brexit became a very federalistic dialogue on the future of the EU. With Brexit, the EU also could increasingly focus on expanding its core of committed members, old and new, while distancing itself from more reluctant countries. Since Brexit, it has meant advancing accession negotiations with potential new member states, especially those in Central and Eastern Europe, and states which would be favorable to progressive integration (Ukrainian accession being of special interest). Problematically, as the core consolidated its base, a growing distrust of EU institutions and key figures promoting integration sparked onto the stage—with Ursula Von Der Leyen, Emmanuel Macron, and Angela Merkel becoming particular targets of criticism. Lack of subsidiarity remained a problem. Over the years, there had been a growing divide between EU institutions and ordinary citizens, with many feeling disconnected from key decision-making processes in Brussels. As suggested in the point on the urban/rural divide, subsidiarity has been left neglected by established politics. A lack of trust complicated the push for deeper integration, as people resisted the further consolidation of power at institutional level. Helen Wallace, in *European Integration After Amsterdam*, anticipated these systemic problems clearly:

> ... changes in the context and conditions for integration; variations in the objectives of actors; differences in the interests of the actors; controversies about which values and norms should be embedded in the process; debates about the feasible and desirable policy scope for shared regimes; and questioning of the institutional rules and practices through which to develop policy regimes. (Wallace, 2000, p. 178)

These problems still remain, yet Brussels has leverage enough to foster intercultural dialogue, a sociology of integration, if it had the political will to do so. Many European cities are global models for intercultural living, where citizens from different backgrounds integrate successfully, cultivating a sense of belonging, and as the EU slogan goes, creating "unity in diversity." EU initiatives invariably helped create understanding and diminish prejudice. And then there is the nuanced regulation of the media, which plays a crucial role in shaping public perceptions of other cultures and peoples, with the power to accentuate differences or engender interdependence. The growing presence of diverse media outlets—the anarchy of social media—and the representation of minorities in mainstream media can contribute to reducing stereotypes and promoting a more inclusive narrative differences or engender into a "hostile environment"—a term synonymous with Brexit.

Futures and Solutions

The concept of an "ever closer union" has once again been circulating around intra-community tensions, while the narrative on borders has shifted dramatically. Where once the priority was on removing barriers and obstacles to the harmonization of relationships, recent years have seen a renewed emphasis on sovereignty. Change is resonating in political rhetoric across the continent—coupled with varying degrees of "othering" against migrant communities and newcomers. For many, especially in the context of a new Cold War and the enforced migration of millions of Europeans westward, European integration can be seen as a key element in ensuring peaceful cooperation. The post-Brexit scenario has raised concerns about the potential destabilizing effects on European unity, particularly in terms of security, borders, the weaponization of refugees, and the importance of the EU as an international guarantor of peace and a diplomatic force.

Brexit and European integration emanated from the same political source, and both have had profound impacts on social and cultural perceptions on the continent. These two interconnected phenomena have shaped identities, relationships, and the everyday experiences for many individuals—especially in countries that joined the EU after the fall of the Berlin Wall, where EU membership became implicit to their sense of freedom. European integration offered a sense of belonging to a broader community, and the idea of a European identity became normalized. In the UK, alternatively, the EU was seen by many as an external force, as debates about Britishness versus Europeanization intensified. For the 48% of Britons who voted Remain and perceived themselves to be EU citizens, the way the vote went was a removal of their citizenship, negating the basic rights they held through the *acquis communautaire*: to live, work, and study across borders, or to live as citizens in other member states. For the 52% who voted Leave, their motives were essentially about "control" (on the legal implications, see Mindus, 2017, pp. 85–95).

Another effect of Brexit has been the accentuated divide between the UK's devolved regions, with tensions emerging over perceptions of inequality and feelings of economic marginalization and being left behind in the fight between London and Brussels (Birrell & Gray, 2017, pp. 778–779). In many deprived areas of England, in particular, Brexit was linked with a protest vote against what many believed to be Brussels depriving England of investment. In Scotland and Northern Ireland—devolved regions that were avidly Remain—the vote ironically sparked debates about the breakup of the UK, Scotland's independence from the UK, and the reunification of Ireland. The vote revealed deep regional divides within the UK, replete with sharp oppositions between different generations, cultural tensions, and competing social classes (McAleese, 2017). For example, older generations, who were often more nostalgic for a time before the EU, tended to favor leaving, while younger people, who had experienced opportunities through European mobility and multiculturalism, saw themselves as Europeans, and tended to support staying within the EU. In a twist of legacy, the UK's exit from the EU affected sectors of the economy that were usually the preserve of the young—study, mobility, research, arts funding, and educational exchanges such as the Erasmus + program. With the latter, a significant feature within higher education and opportunities for young people, mobility disappeared almost instantly. The upshot has been that musicians, artists, tech entrepreneurs, and students (predominantly preserves of the young) have expressed frustration over the increased bureaucratic and logistical barriers that limit their ability to participate in European cultural and educational life.

There is of course the rollercoaster of the European economic system which has been the stabilizing mechanism for peaceful intercommunity relations. Indeed, the Eurozone continues to evolve, moving toward deeper financial and fiscal integration. While economic disparities between richer northern states and southern Europe still exist, and while fiscal limitations imposed by EU rules continue to irritate smaller economies, the transfer of structural and regional funds has proved to be a rebalancing factor, which for the exit movement has was always a problem. Brexit was a serious shock to a system that may not have been perfect, but it was evidently developmental. Post-Brexit Britain still struggles with the highly visible benefits of EU membership— membership had been economically prudent for the UK.

> The wider impact of economic developments following Brexit is of much concern, especially the potential consequences for wages, employment, standards of living and particular important economic activities such as the agri-food industries and the associated well-being of rural communities. (Birrell & Gray, 2017, p. 779)

Ongoing economic recovery strategies from the Great Recession of 2008–2010 and adjustment post-COVID-19, as well as global economic uncertainties such as energy supply volatility, the climate crisis and Russian wars, will be significant tests for coordinating economic integration. That said, continued efforts to strengthen the EU's single market through innovation, developing the skills economy and investing in its digital economy could still act as drivers for stability. For most people in the EU, the ideal of a Social Europe remains alive, particularly for those who are marginalized or peripheral to economic activity. There have been significant risks with actual exit as we have seen, with effects showing realignment at all levels of EU polity, including the erosion of economic interdependence, breaking conventional political alliances, and cultural divergence. Importantly within the maelstrom of exiting, the principal of subsidiarity has been fundamentally compromised, with knock-on effects for social policy in terms of ensuring human rights-based approaches to policymaking, equal opportunities, labor rights, and social security. In hindsight and with the latter taken into account, increased transparency, genuine dialogue with citizens, along with reforms to EU institutions could help address concerns around Euroscepticism, advancing a more inclusive EU that listens to the voices of its citizens to reimagine integration.

Conclusion

The European integration process has always been a complex and dynamic entity, balancing diverse cultures, languages, and political histories. In the past decade, this tapestry of interests has undergone significant transformation, driven largely by political realignments and influenced by economic volatility. Among other things, these changes have brought forward questions about border security, democratic intent, and identity. Populism, as a renewed political force, has propelled these questions to the forefront of the Community discourse. To get a good appreciation of the backstory there is a need to constantly review Europe's constitutional basis—its rationale—and the principles which underlie integration, to assess how these developments are reshaping our understanding of Europe and its people. At its core it is about peace and prosperity, and quite possibly this mission has slipped. In an exceptional address to the Council of Europe on October 11, 2022, then Irish President Michael D. Higgins brought the dilemma of Europe's future into focus with reference to its past:

> Achieving a vibrant democracy requires that we engage citizens meaningfully, inclusively, comprehensively in an understanding and commitment to human rights. We need to anticipate challenges before they become crises and indeed before they become disasters, and use all the tools available, traditionally and currently, to us. How remarkable it is that in recent times we, given our European intellectual heritage, have enabled the neglect of philosophy to test our assumptions and indeed anthropology to inform us on diversity and difference. These disciplines have had the potential to offer us so much to our present circumstances in understanding and anticipating the crises of our contemporary times, including those sourced in ethnic, linguistic or historical bases. I put forward today the case for returning to the use of tools such as anthropology in Europe as … means of promoting a deeper understanding of diversity and cultural difference, and indeed anticipating potential conflicts … It is a time to make the case for solidarity, protection and possibilities. (Higgins, Council of Europe, 2022)

The end of the Cold War marked a new chapter for the peoples of Europe, characterized by the hope of integration and socioeconomic inclusion. For many, the EU became the symbol of a new era, acting in solidarity, growing from a regional economic community into a political and economic entity of unprecedented global reach. Early successes after the eastward enlargement, such as the introduction of the euro and the periodic accession of Central European countries, painted a picture of a continent moving steadily toward unity. The journey has, however, been meandering and challenged at every point, as can be seen with the legal patchwork that is the *acquis communitarie*. Indeed, Brexit, the greatest signal act of protest in the EU's 70 years, was as much a challenge to the ideal of a unified Europe as it was an advocation of an independent UK. Surviving this "shock" provides an insight into the resilience of the constitutional base and the process.

> International organisations "die" more often than may be imagined, but this is unlikely to be the fate of the EU. If the average age of an intergovernmental organisation is twenty-three years, the EU demonstrates a high level of good basic health:

at sixty, it has already outlived many international organisations. This is perhaps proof that it is indeed more than a traditional organisation under international law. (Solanke, 2023, p.63)

Understanding Europe's present and future requires reflection on its past. Historical memory plays a crucial role in shaping its political discourse. The lessons of the 20th century, particularly the dangers of nationalism and isolationism, must inform policymaking, Europe's history of conflict underscoring the importance of cooperation and unity. The wisdom and learning are in the history to be drawn from. On Wednesday, February 16, 2000, Václav Havel spoke to the European Parliament in Strasbourg:

> In my view, the main European values, as shaped by the turbulent spiritual and political history of Europe, and as adopted by other parts of the world, or at least some parts of the world, are obvious. Respect for the individual and for ... freedoms, ... rights and ... dignity, the principle of solidarity, equality before the law and the rule of law, protection of all ethnic minorities, democratic institutions, separation of the legislative, executive and judicial estates, political pluralism, respect for private property and free enterprise, a market economy and the development of the civil society. The form which these values currently assume naturally reflects countless modern European experiences, including the fact that our continent is becoming a main multicultural crossroads. (Havel, 2000)

The reintegration of Europe, its reimagining, faces both challenges and opportunities. While Europe has demonstrated resilience in the face of recent turbulence, such as the pandemic, the war in Ukraine, or Brexit, future reintegration depends on navigating political divisions, strengthening cultural ties and fostering equitable economic convergence. There is hope for a more united Europe, but it will require substantial effort to overcome current obstacles and adapt to new global realities. By reflecting on its history and embracing innovative approaches to integration, Europe can continue to evolve as a unified, yet diverse, entity. Recent history challenges us to rethink our understanding of the European project and to consider how best to navigate the complexities of a continent constantly in flux.

References

Anderson, B. (1991). *Imagined communities*. Verso.
Benn, T. (1974, December 29). The Common Market: Loss of self-government. Letter to the constituents of Bristol South East. In Martin Holmes (Ed.), (1996), *The Eurosceptical reader* (pp. 38–41). Macmillan Press.
Billig, M. (1995). *Banal nationalism*. Sage.

Birrell, D., & Gray, A. (2017). Devolution: the social, political and policy implications of Brexit for Scotland, Wales and Northern Ireland. *Journal of Social Policy, 46*(4) (Brexit Special Issue), 765–782. https://doi.org/10.1017/S0047279417000393

CISE. (2025). Dataset of electoral volatility in the European Parliament elections since 1979. https://cise.luiss.it/dataset/dataset-of-electoral-volatility-in-the-european-parliament-elections-since-1979/

Dahrendorf, R. (1973). *Plädoyer für die Europäische Union*. R. Piper.

Eichengreen, B. (2007). *The European economy since 1945*. Princeton University Press.

European Union. (2025). European election data. https://results.elections.europa.eu/en/tools/download-datasheets/

Gellner, E. (1983). *Nations and nationalism*. Cornell University Press.

Gillingham, J. (2003). *European integration 1950–2003: Superstate or new market economy?*. Cambridge University Press.

Hannan, D. (2016). *Why vote leave*. Head of Zeus.

Hantrais, L. (2007). *Social policy in the European Union*. Palgrave Macmillan.

Hass, E. (2006). Does constructivism subsume neofunctionalism?. In M. Eilstrup-Sangiovanni (Ed.), *Debates on European integration: A reader* (pp. 437–446). Palgrave Macmillan.

Havel, V. (2000, February 16). Speech to the European Parliament, Strasbourg.

Higgins, M. D. (2022). Reasserting the moral weight of the Council of Europe. Speech by H. E. President of Ireland, Michael D. Higgins, Council of Europe Parliamentary Assembly, Strasbourg, Tuesday, October 11, 2022. https://rm.coe.int/pace-october-plenary-address-president-michael-d-higgins/1680a91a51

Hobsbawm, E. J. (1990). *Nations and nationalism since 1780*. Cambridge University Press

Holmes, M. (1996). *The Eurosceptical reader*. Macmillan Press.

Leconte, L. (2010). *Understanding Euroscepticism*. Palgrave McMillan.

Ludlow, N. (2009). Value, flexibility and openness. In J. Baquero Cruz & C. Closa Montero (Eds.), *European integration from Rome to Berlin: 1957–2007*. P.I.E. Peter Lang.

Malmborg, M. af, & Stråth, B. (2002). *The meaning of Europe*. Berg.

Martill, B., & Staiger, U. (Eds.). (2018). *Brexit and beyond*. UCL Press. https://discovery.ucl.ac.uk/id/eprint/10041784/1/Brexit-and-Beyond.pdf

McAleese, M. (2017). Border lands: The trouble with Brexit. *The Tablet*. http://www.thetablet.co.uk/features/2/9648/mary-mcaleese-interview-border-lands-the-trouble-with-brexit

Milward, A. (2000). *The European rescue of the nation state*. Routledge.

Mindus, P. (2017). *European citizenship after Brexit*. Springer Nature. https://link.springer.com/book/10.1007/978-3-319-51774-2

Prodi, R. (2000). *Europe as I see it*. Polity.

Puri, J. (2004). *Encountering nationalism*. Blackwell.

Rasmussen, M., & Knudsen, A. L. (Eds.). (2009). *The road to a united Europe: Interpretations of the process of European integration*. Peter Lang.

Rifkin, J. (2005). *The European dream*. Tarcher Penguin.

Schuman, R. (1949, May 5). Speech at the signing of the statutes of the Council of Europe, St. James's Palace, London.

Solanke, L. (2023). *EU law*. Cambridge University Press.

Stubb, A. C-G. (June 1996). A categorization of differentiated integration. *Journal of Common Market Studies*, 34(2), 283–295. https://doi.org/10.1111/j.1468-5965.1996.tb00573.x

Swan, D. (2000). *The economics of Europe: From common market to European Union*. Penguin.

Urwin, D. W. (1995). *The community of Europe* (2nd ed.). Longman.

Von Der Leyen, U. (8 January 2020). "Old friends, new beginnings." Lecture at the London School of Economics. https://www.lse.ac.uk/Events/2020/01/20200108t1115vLSE/a-lecture-by-ursula-von-der-leyen

Wallace, H. (2000). Flexibility: Integration or disintegration?. In K. Neunreither & A.Wiener (Eds.), *European integration after Amsterdam*. Oxford University Press.

Wise, M., & Gibb, R. (1993). *Single market to Social Europe*. Longman.

CHAPTER TWO | **LIISI LAINESTE AND
DOROTA BRZOZOWSKA**

Borders of Perception in Estonian and Polish Cultural Narratives

Abstract

The contemporary buzzwords—globalization, transnationality, and fluid identities—stress the ephemerality of geographical and cultural borders. The present-day international relations give evidence of the blurring of borders between geographical and political regions, but at the same time the ever-present conflicts that arise at the ephemeral borders indicate that not much has changed in the attitudes of people. We are still sensitive to potential differences and at a constant lookout for danger that these might bring along. At the same time, it is clear that the notion of geographical location carries a slightly different meaning for people who live today than it did for people who lived 100 years ago. This paper will explore the limits of vernacular geographical perception in Poland and Estonia, focusing on their mutual neighbors and invaders: Germans and Russians. This will allow mapping both Estonianness and Polishness as well as the imaginary and actual borders of people inhabiting these countries.

Keywords: geographical location, folk songs, imaginary borders, Poles, Estonians, Germans, Russians

Introduction

Identities have been central to human existence through times, being linked to a sense of belonging and communities. In the present-day world, in the transnational and globalizing contexts, a crisis of identity has been announced, amid other crises. A crisis of belonging (reanimated recently by the American psychologist Geoffrey Cohen, see Cohen, 2022) means that people have lost meaningful social connections and that this is behind much of the sound and fury around identities today. Feeling excluded or wronged makes people bitter, susceptible to misinformation, and prone to lashing out and trolling, fueling a vicious cycle.

In examining the evolution of perception surrounding geographical borders, it becomes increasingly evident that the delineations that once seemed so concrete have shifted toward a more nebulous understanding in the contemporary world. Historically, country borders often served as definitive markers of identity, social categorization, and cultural belonging. People lived within relatively stable frameworks dictated by geographical proximity and the accompanying social customs. These borders were marked by stereotypes about the other nations and groups. This is most evident in the history of joking relationships, where clear patterns evolved, e.g., between neighboring countries. In jokes, the opposition of "us" and "them" is often accompanied with an evaluation. "They" are backward, old-fashioned, stupid, brutish, and uncivilized (Remmel, 2003; Oinas, 1979): generally speaking, they are strange and bad. "We," on the other hand, are civilized and generally good. In this process, the image of the positive self becomes hazy and unspecific, while the strangeness of others is stressed, nuanced, and exaggerated. Christie Davies (1990; 2002) has delineated models that account for most of neighborly joking relationships, claiming that we tend to laugh at groups of people who are similar and geographically close, but lay at the periphery of the area and are characterized by technical ineptness and an accent or dialect that sounds funny to the joke-tellers. The stereotypes displayed in the jokes (stupidity as the most notorious one, but also excessive fondness of alcoholic drinks, hypersexuality, or stinginess) are entrenched in the minds of people and become a way of delineating borders between "us" and "them." We can see these patterns clearly in the Polish and Estonian jokes about their mutual others: Russians and Germans, where the Poles or Estonians respectively are depicted as the ones outwitting their stronger neighbors (about ethnic jokes in both countries, see Laineste & Brzozowska, 2011; Brzozowska, 2012a, 2012b; Krikmann, 2012).

Only a century or two ago physical travel took a lot of time; the same was true about any kind of long-distance communication, e.g., postal services. Ideas of faraway places and the habits of their inhabitants were fragmentary and often inadequate, based on the few and far between letters or stories from the hinterlands, and left much room for imagination. The journey to these places seemed long and troublesome. Even close places could be perceived as very far away, e.g., in an Estonian archival recording from Jüri parish one local reminisces that "the distance between Rae and Lagedi [which on foot is ca. 12 kms—authors' note] was as long as nowadays the distance to Russia—it was very far away, and nobody knew in fact precisely where this Rae is at all" (Viikberg, 2015, p. 33). Such vernacular perceptions depend of course also on the landscape as well—localities that are separated by a swamp, for example, were less likely to have contacts with the outside world than those connected by a proper road or a waterway. Weeks of travelling to the open steppes of Russia—or to the border of Poland, as we will see in the examples presented in this paper—thus became a synonym or symbol for an immeasurable distance. The statement comparing the distance between two villages 12 kms apart to a journey to Russia gives a glimpse of what geographical distances meant for people who sang the songs or told/wrote the stories we will address in the paper. It will also define the places where they (who are essentially different from us) live. Fantasies about their food, clothing, and behavior added spice and excitement to the stories (and jokes) told and songs sung about the limits or borders of the imaginable and inhabitable world.

As we traverse into an era dominated by globalization and technological advancements, these borders have become less about fixed points on a map, less about fixed stereotypes, and more about fluid, subjective experiences that vary from individual to individual. Today, the notion of borders extends beyond the tangible lines that separate nations; it envelops the intangible realms of cultural interactions, transnational relationships, and digital communications. While geographical boundaries may seem to dissolve, only to be replaced by ephemeral constructs of identity that are continuously redefined through migration, in interactions taking place on social media, and general global interconnectedness, this oscillation does not erase the underlying tensions that persist at these borders. Conflicts emerge not only from traditional territorial disputes but also from the deeper psychological struggle to maintain a sense of belonging amidst growing diversity.

In focusing on specific cases like Poland and Estonia, we uncover how historical connections and traditional cultural narratives continue to influence perceptions of identity and belonging through time. The proximity to powerful historical neighbors (and, at times, also invaders), such as Germany and Russia, shapes local attitudes while underscoring a heightened sensitivity to identity threats from those perceived as "other." The historical lens provides context to current relationships but also reveals an enduring conflict of belonging that transcends mere political considerations.

Borders are important in the process of identification. It helps to understand who is "ours" and who is "foreign." Borders can be real, physical; they can also be imaginary. Folklore and literature express the imaginary borders. Folklore in fact is one of the main loci of pronouncing borders, even—or especially—when they are getting fuzzier, such as in the context of increased international contacts.

Historical Connections of Poland and Estonia with Russia and Germany

Poland and Estonia, countries located in Central and Northern Europe, respectively, do not currently have a shared border, but history has brought them close together and they have followed similar paths, especially with regard to their common neighbors Russia and Germany. Poland and Estonia have had a complex and interwoven history shaped by the political and military influences of these larger neighboring powers. In the early modern period, both nations found themselves caught in the geopolitical rivalry of that quickly developing area. During the 16th and 17th centuries, the Polish-Lithuanian Commonwealth, a powerful and multiethnic federation, was engaged in a series of wars with Russia, notably during the Polish-Muscovite Wars (1605–1618), and even reached (and included) southern Estonia under its reign. At this moment in the past, these two countries indeed shared a border, and the intercultural contacts were frequent, which left a mark in the common cultural narratives (songs, stories, and legends).

By the late 18th century, both Poland and Estonia saw their fates entwined with the expansion of Russian imperial power. Poland, in particular, faced successive partitions in 1772, 1793, and 1795, which resulted in the complete dissolution of the Polish-Lithuanian Commonwealth and its territories being divided between Russia, Austria, and Prussia. Estonia, meanwhile, was incorporated into the Russian Empire after the Great Northern War (1700–1721). In the 19th century, both nations experienced suppression of their national identities and cultures. The German influence on both regions also grew. German-speaking elites dominated in the Baltic countries, and the Prussian state played a central role in shaping Polish political developments.

The early 20th century marked a significant turning point for both countries. Following World War I, Poland regained independence in 1918, after more than a century of partitions, and Estonia declared its independence in 1918 as well, following the collapse of the Russian Empire. Both nations found themselves in a precarious geopolitical position, surrounded by the resurgent German Empire to the west and an increasingly aggressive Soviet Russia to the east. The interwar period saw attempts at cooperation, but both countries faced rising tensions from external threats, especially from Nazi Germany and the Soviet Union. Estonia was occupied by the Soviet Union in 1940, then by Nazi Germany from 1941 to 1944, and finally by the Soviet Union again until it regained independence in 1991. Similarly, Poland was devastated by both Nazi and Soviet occupations during World War II, only to find itself under Soviet influence after the war, though not as part of the Soviet Union.

In the post-Soviet era, both Poland and Estonia have integrated into European and transatlantic institutions, such as NATO and the European Union, marking a shift from their historical experiences of being caught between powerful neighboring states to now being part of a united Western bloc.

The Aim of the Study, Data Sources, and Methods

The aim of this paper is to illustrate the process of forming the perception of borderlands with examples from folklore and other texts of culture that tell stories about the imagined borderlands, real geographic locations with the role to demarcate national, ethnic, or other borders. The Polish data originates from the National Corpus of

Polish language[1] and the corpus of the 16th and 17th Century Polish language[2]. The main source of folk texts and songs is an electronic database based on Oskar Kolberg's vast collection of texts collected between the Middle Ages and the 19th Century[3]. 85 volumes of his works contain about 39,780 pages including several thousands of songs—some of them in different regional variants so it is why their exact number is questionable.[4] Keywords such as Estonian, Muscovite/ Russian, Prussian, Swab, and German were used to retrieve information from those sources.

Our Estonian part of the data for the study comes from *Eesti regilaulude andmebaas*[5], and for more contemporary data from two additional databases: *Eesti kõnekäändude ja fraseologismide andmebaas*[6] and *Eesti kaasaegsed anekdoodid*[7]. The song database includes songs collected by early folklore collectors and their correspondents like Jakob Hurt, MJ Eisen, and EÜS, dating to the end of 19th to the beginning of the 20th century. Some of the texts are undated but probably come from the same era. Keywords such as Estonian/Polish, as well as Russian and German were used to retrieve information from our sources. The songs make up the majority of the text base for this study on the Estonian side (359), while the search in Justkui (phraseology database) and Estonian contemporary jokes added another 36 and 560 texts respectively.

In a folkloristic and literary study focused on the borders of perception like this one, employing qualitative descriptive methods is crucial for capturing the nuanced narratives and cultural contexts embedded within the texts. These methods allow researchers to delve deep into the lived experiences that shape individuals' understandings of identity and belonging. We follow the works of Oring (2023) who employs qualitative descriptive methods to analyze folklore texts to explore identities, highlighting the fluidity of perception through detailed interpretations. We also rely on Ben-Amos and Weissberg (1999), who used qualitative close reading of texts to examine how folklore operates as a medium for negotiating cultural identity, particularly in borderland communities.

---

1. Narodowy Korpus Języka Polskiego, https://otwartezasoby.pl/narodowy-korpus-jezyka-polskiego/
2. Korpu tekstów VII-XVIII wieku, https://szukajwslownikach.uw.edu.pl/IMPACT_GT_1/
3. Instytut im. Oskara Kolberga, http://www.oskarkolberg.pl/pl-PL/Page/53
4. Institute of Oskar Kolberg is still preparing the next four volumes of his work; https://culture.pl/pl/artykul/pamietam-zem-mial-mamke-zuske-wiesniaczke-205-lat-kolberga.
5. *Estonian runosongs' database;* https://www.folklore.ee/regilaul/andmebaas/?
6. Database of Estonian sayings and phraseologisms; https://www.folklore.ee/justkui/andmebaas.php
7. Estonian contemporary jokes; https://www.folklore.ee/~liisi/02/

By engaging in close readings and thematic analyses, we can reveal how they reflect and perpetuate ideas about borders, both tangible and intangible. Moreover, qualitative approaches facilitate the exploration of how folklore and literature articulate the complexities of shifting identities in the face of globalization, inviting voices that may have been marginalized or overlooked in dominant discourses. Through this in-depth, descriptive analysis, we will illuminate the dynamics of perception and belonging, providing an understanding of how cultural narratives construct, negotiate, and ultimately transcend the borders that define human experience.

Analysis

Polish material shows a strong consciousness of geopolitical borders and is connected with historical fate and the fight for Polish state existence. Estonia is mentioned several times but most often as a part of the lost Polish-Lithuanian Commonwealth empire.

Stała się w Inflanciech szkoda, gdzie bracia naszy, Litwa i Polacy, przedtem bogacieli. Gdzie Estonia, gdzie teraz są starostowie narodów naszych w niej? Którą acz posłowie przysięgli oddać ją Koronie, ali teraz zdrajcom Inflanczykom miasto oddania Estoniej dano indigenatum regni za tego króla przeszłego, i tak Inflanczyk jest Polakiem i Litwinem. Zamki pobrawszy, poddali je zdradą nieprzyjacielom koronnem, które były krwią drogą dostane pod tyranem moskiewskim (https://korba.edu.pl/query_corpus/ sourse from the year 1607)

A loss hath befallen us in Livonia, where our brethren, the Lithuanians and the Poles, grew rich aforetime. Where is Estonia now? Wherein are the governors of our nations? Though their envoys swore an oath to render it unto the Crown, yet now the traitorous Livonians, instead of the surrender of Estonia, were granted the indigenatum regni under the late king. And so a Livonian is now a Pole and a Lithuanian. Having taken the castles, they have by treason delivered them to the enemies of the Crown, though they were won with precious blood from the Muscovite tyrant.

There are no songs about Estonians in the analyzed material but Russians (known at that time as *Moskale*, Muscovites) and Germans, Prussians, and Swabs are mentioned in multiple cases (22 and 12 and 12, 3 times respectively) in *Antologia pieśni polskich*[8]. The names of the representatives of different nations may be used in a single song side by side, as the following examples show. In the first song rich and powerful people are criticized for quarreling and thus allowing enemies—Germans and Muscovites—to steal the country's goods and cause misery for Polish citizens.

---

8. [*Anthology of Polish songs*] http://antologia.oskarkolberg.pl/

Znają mnie Niemcy, Moskale znają	Germans know me, Muscovites know me
Znają mnie Niemcy, Moskale znają, ja tu osiadły z dawności.	The Germans know me, the Muscovites know me, I have settled here for a long time.
Teraz wam bieda dla waszych złości, źli górę nad nami mają.	Now you are in trouble because of your anger, the evil ones have the upper hand over us.
Nasi panowie jeno się wadzą. O cóż? O wiatr, ten co wieje. Jak bronić skarbu Ojczyzny radzą, a skarb trzymają złodzieje.	Our gentlemen are just arguing. Oh well? O wind, the one that blows. They advise how to defend the treasure of the Fatherland, but the treasure is kept by thieves.

(http://antologia.oskarkolberg.pl/pl-PL/Home/Song?id=7430)

Germans, Muscovites, and Swabs characters are evoked in the rather offensive, humorous song that is ironically entitled "For the glory of Germans." Germans are mocked and called rags, dogs, and bloody pipe bowls. The last expression is a contemptuous way of referring to Germans as city dwellers. The especially unpleasant words are condensed and repeated in the chorus. The rhymes used in the song make it sound funny and catchy. Examples of rhymes are verses like *Na polskiej ziemi*cy, [on the Polish ground] [...] *Niemiec w szlaf*mycy [a German in a nightcap]. The regular form *ziemia*—"ground" or "country" is exchanged for its augmentative—*ziemica* just to be rhymed with *szlafmyca* [nightcap]. Interestingly the word *szlafmyca* is in Polish language a word adapted from German words: *Schlafmütze, Nachtmütze*. The word is evoking the stereotypical comic picture of a German sleeping in his nightcap.

Na chwałę Niemcom, rodaku kochany	For the glory of Germans, my beloved countryman
Na chwałę Niemcom, rodaku kochany, śpiewajmy sobie: Niemcy są gałgany, oj, juchy Niemcy, o juchy Szwaby, o juchy, psy, cybuchy. Dziś, gdzie się ruszysz na polskiej ziemicy, to wszędzie M[oskal], lub Niemiec w szlafmycy, [oj, juchy Niemcy, o juchy Szwaby, o juchy, psy, cybuchy].	For the glory of the Germans, my beloved countryman, let us sing to ourselves: Germans are rags, oh, Germans, oh, Swabs, oh, dogs, pipe bowls. Today, wherever you go in the Polish land, there is always a Muscovite, or a German in a nightcap, [oh, Germans, oh, Swabs, oh, dogs, pipe bowls].

(http://antologia.oskarkolberg.pl/pl-PL/Home/Song?id=7578)

The following song expresses a sense of nostalgia for a past marked by prosperity and national strength, juxtaposed with references to subsequent periods of oppression. It alludes to Russian persecution and the Prussian campaign of forced Germanization, known as the Kulturkampf, which sought to suppress the Polish language and undermine the cultural identity closely tied to Catholicism. Additionally, the lyrics reflect economic hardship attributed to Swabian fiscal policies, particularly the imposition of burdensome taxes that led to widespread impoverishment. Social exclusion is also emphasized, as access to respectable employment, particularly in administrative or prestigious sectors, was systematically reserved for Germans, marginalizing even the most loyal Polish citizens.

Gdzie się podział ów wiek złoty — Where has this golden age gone?

Gdzie się podział ów wiek złoty i te dawne czasy, gdy kontusze celowały i złociste pasy. Szpinka złota u koszuli, wąs w górę skręcony, karabela wedle boku i bucik czerwony.

Where has gone the golden age and the old times when there were robes and golden belts? A gold pin on his shirt, a mustache twisted upwards, a karabela at his side and a red shoe.

W takim stroju każdy Polak wszędzie zawsze chodził, w takim stroju Jan Sobieski Wiedeń oswobodził.

Every Pole always went everywhere in such clothes, and John Sobieski liberated Vienna in such clothes.

Od rozbioru naszej Polski wszystko jest inaczej, w Gdańsku Prusak, w Litwie Moskal, tu Niemiec dziwaczny. Prusak każe język łamać, Moskal daje baty, Szwab zaś nowe egzekutne rozseła mandaty.

Since the partition of our Poland, everything has been different, in Gdańsk it was a Prussian, in Lithuania it was a Muscovite, here it was a strange German. The Prussian tells you to break your tongue, the Muscovite gives you lashes, and the Swabian sends out new enforcement mandates.

[…]Jeśli jesteś Polak prawy, nie znajdziesz tu względu, gdyż już teraz samych Niemców biorą do urzędu.

[…]If you are a righteous Pole, you will not find any favor here, because now they are taking only Germans to office.

(http://antologia.oskarkolberg.pl/pl-PL/Home/Song?id=8666)

In the patriotic songs the battles with Russians are mentioned very explicitly also in the context of class inequalities and lack of support from the nobility for the struggle of peasants:

Hej, tam w karczmie za stołem	Hey, there at the inn behind the table
[…]Gdy na wojnę wołali, wiarę z naszych powiatów, myśmy bili Moskali, bez pomocy magnatów.	[...]When they called for war from our counties, we beat the Muscovites, without the help of magnates.

(http://antologia.oskarkolberg.pl/pl-PL/Home/Song?id=7494)

A recurring and symbolically significant motif in numerous Polish folk songs concerns the institution of marriage and its deep-rooted role within the sociopolitical fabric of the community. For Polish women, the act of choosing a marital partner extends beyond personal preference and enters the realm of political expression. Marriages to foreigners—particularly Russians or Germans—are portrayed not merely as undesirable, but as acts of national betrayal. Conversely, rejecting such unions, even to the point of self-sacrifice, is elevated as a patriotic ideal. This sentiment is powerfully illustrated in the folk song invoking the legendary figure of Wanda, who, according to myth, chose death in the Vistula River over marriage to a German suitor. The verses assert that the cities of Warsaw and Kraków flourish not for foreign powers but for Poles, reinforcing the exclusivity of national identity. The song explicitly encourages Polish women to seek spouses among their compatriots and to emulate Wanda's example, should they face the prospect of marrying an occupier. The refrain, "a Muscovite and a German are always foreigners," encapsulates the persistent delineation between national selfhood and external threat, illustrating how folk tradition encoded both gendered nationalism and resistance to cultural assimilation.

Świeci się Warszawa	Warsaw is shining
Świeci się Warszawa, świeci się i Kraków, nie dla was to Niemcy, tylko dla Polaków.	Warsaw is shining, Krakow is shining too, it's not for you Germans, but for Poles.
Wisło moja, Wisło, rzéko błękitnawa, kłania ci się Kraków, kłania i Warszawa.	My Vistula, Vistula, blueish river, Kraków bows to you, and Warsaw bows to you.
Bo się w tobie, Wisło, Wanda utopiła, by nie pójść za Niemca do wody wskoczyła.	Because Wisła, Wanda drowned herself in you and jumped into the water to avoid marrying a German.
I wy Polki, mężów rodaków szukajcie, jak was Niemiec zechce, do Wisły skakajcie.	And you Polish women, look for your countrymen, if the German wants you, jump into the Vistula.

Wande naśladujcie, Polaków całujcie;—bo Imitate Wanda, kiss Poles;—because
Moskal i Niemiec zawsze cudzoziemiec. a Muscovite and a German are always foreigners.

(http://antologia.oskarkolberg.pl/pl-PL/Home/Song?id=8468)

In another example, Polish women are encouraged to remember that Muscovites have been killed by their brothers but also shed Polish blood—so they should not be married and the memory and curse on the heads of the enemies should last and prevent pretty girls from even looking at oppressors even if their own folk is missing from the village due to the loss in battles and tragic fate of exile after them.

Ładna jak jagoda Pretty as a berry
[…] Ładna jak jagoda nasza Zosia młoda, wyszła na podwórze, patrzy do Podgórza. Na Podgórzu stali, powrócić nie chcieli krakowiacy śmieli, co bili Moskali. […] Our young Zosia, as pretty as a berry, went out into the yard and looked at Podgórze. They stood in Podgórze and the Krakow people who beat the Muscovites did not want to come back.

[…] […]
Niech im Bóg zapłaci za krew naszych braci, żeby przez wiek cały Polki to wiedziały. May God pay them for the blood of our brothers, so that Polish women will know this for centuries.

(http://antologia.oskarkolberg.pl/pl-PL/Home/Song?id=8651)

Polish girls are advised to look for spouses only among Polish boys also because they are considered good people who respect women, as opposed to cruel Russians who are merciless, and would be able to push someone from the bridge without hesitation about doing harm or even causing death.

Moście panny Warszawianki Misses from Warszawa
[..] [..]
Bo Polaki dobre ludzie panny obserwują, a Moskale stupajkowie jeszcze censurują. Żałości nie mają, z mostu na łeb spychają. Because Poles are good people, and respect girls, and Muscovites, policemen /idiots, censor you. They have no regrets, they push you over the edge so you fall down on your head from the bridge.

(http://antologia.oskarkolberg.pl/pl-PL/Home/Song?id=7583)

Generally, crossing borders of culture or the ones of state or region meant danger especially for females—boys who came from far away were not trustworthy, and when the naive girls married them, it could cost them their lives as the following rather sad and scary example shows:

Przyjechał Jasieńko	Jasieńko has arrived
Przyjechał Jasieńko z dalekiej krainy, namówił Kasieńkę do swojej rodziny.	Jasieńko came from a distant land and persuaded Kasieńko to join his family.
Kasia głupiusieńka, namówić się dała, swoje koniki wrone zakładać kazała.	Kasia, a silly girl, was persuaded to settle her black horses.
Oj, nabierzże, nabierz, srebra, złota dosyć, żeby koniki miały co za nami nosić.	Oh, take out, take out, enough silver and gold for the horses to have something to carry behind us.
[...]	[...]
Ujął ci ją, ujął, za te białe ręce i pozdejmał, pościągał złociste pierścieńce. Ujął ci ją, ujął, za te białe boki i wrzucił ją, wrzucił w ten Dunaj głęboki.	He took her, took her by those white hands and took them off, took off the golden rings. He took her from you, took her by those white sides and threw her, threw her into the deep Danube.
[...]	[...]
Już ci Kasiuleńce we dwa dzwony dzwonią, tego Jasia hultaja po granicach gonią.	There are already two bells ringing for Kasiuleńka, they are chasing this scoundrel around the borders.
Już ci Kasiuleńkę do grobu wstawiają, tego Jasia hultaja w drobny mak siekają.	They're already putting Kasiuleńka in the grave, and they're chopping up this scoundrel, Jaś.

http://antologia.oskarkolberg.pl/pl-PL/Home/Song?id=8665

It occurred that the fiancé was interested only in the rich girl's jewelry and other goods and was ready to take her from her family only to purposefully and mercilessly drown her in the water. She struggled for her life, and her clothes and long hair allowed her to stay on the board. The cruel *Jaś* (official version of *Jan*)—with great affection called by the tender double diminutive of his name—*Jasieńko*—cut them with the axe so she had no chances to stay alive. Also, the girl's name *Kasia* (already the diminutive from *Katarzyna*) is used in a double diminutive form *Kasieńka* to show great affection and pity on the miserable girl, who even when materially rich—and in possession of gold—was lacking luck in love, which cost her her life. The little consolation could be found in the fact that the thief and murderer was hunted along the borders, caught and punished with death by quartering.

Summing up Polish examples, one may notice that the songs were full of pain and rage and were mostly telling the sad story of Polish people losing their independence and being highly disappointed about it. The situation depicted in the songs shows double disadvantage for Polish women—they not only were part of the historical and political fate and suffered as people in an occupied country, they also mourn their lost children husbands, brothers, who gave their lives for patriotic reasons but also they were forbidden even to dream about finding fulfilment in love. Their own countrymen were missing or dead and the strangers even if young or prosperous were perceived as dangerous. Women falling in love with Russians or Germans not only risked their lives but also were condemned by their own people and perceived as treacherous and unpatriotic, so they found themselves at—literally and metaphorically—a dead-end.

We now present a similar analysis of the position and attitudes of Estonians with respect to Poland, Russia and Germany. In the case of relations with Poland, these can mostly be characterized by the phrase "Don't come through Poland," where Poland marks the end of journeys, or reaching the edge of vernacular perception. In all the contexts, the vast distance of Poland from Estonia is something that nearly always surfaces. Estonian folk songs often evoke distant lands and foreign territories, with Poland frequently appearing as a symbolic destination that marks the farthest reaches of the singer's world. In these songs, references to Poland serve as markers of geographical distance, cultural difference, and sometimes, even danger. Similarly to what we see in the Polish data when foreign means often not only danger but even death. It underlines Poland's status as the boundary of the singer's understanding and experience. Poland, in this context, is not merely a place but an abstract endpoint, representing the limits of the vernacular world. This distance is often reinforced through alliterative phrases that draw attention to the stark difference between Estonia and Poland, underscoring the foreignness of the latter, for example:

Kui sa saad kodu tulema	If you come home
Ära sina tule Poola kaudu	don't you come through Poland
Poolan palju poiste päida	There are plenty of boy's heads in Poland
Ära sina tule Narva kaudu	Don't you come through Narva
Narvan palju naiste päida	There are plenty of women's heads in Narva
Ära sina tule Rija kaudu	Don't you come through Riga
Rijan pailu ridtelida	There are plenty of knights in Riga

(H II 26, 271/2 [34] < Suure-Jaani khk.—J. Mein [1888])

One prominent theme in Estonian folk songs involving Poland is the notion of separation and loss. Often, the songs narrate the forced departure of people from their homes, with Poland symbolizing the furthest point to which they are taken. For example, the line "One was taken to Russia, the other to the Polish border" reflects the painful separation of individuals from their homeland, where Poland represents the outermost edge of exile. In another song, the "Sold Maiden," Poland is depicted as the distant land where young women are sent, possibly due to marriage or other societal obligations. These examples highlight how the geographical reference to Poland carries a sense of emotional distance, suggesting that the places where people are sent are far beyond the reach of normal life and community. "Normal" life implies also particular eating and drinking habits, that "they" might not adhere to:

Peä vineh vinelane	Boozy Russian
Peä purjo Poolakene	Tipsy Pole

(H, Jagomann 713/9 (50) < Räpina khk., Kõnnu k.—Jakob Jagomann < J. Jagomann [1880])

A no doubt alliteration-motivated contamination in phraseology is *lükkäp kui Poola pasunt* "pushing (or blowing) the Polish trumpet," meaning to blow one's nose accompanied with a loud sound.

In addition to the theme of forced migration, Polish references in Estonian songs are often used to convey ideas of danger or foreignness. The Polish border symbolizes a place fraught with peril. These songs imply that places like Poland, due to their distance and otherness, are dangerous or even deadly. This motif ties into broader folk traditions where faraway lands are viewed with suspicion, not just for their geographical remoteness but also for the cultural and social unfamiliarity they represent.

Despite the negative connotations associated with Poland in some Estonian folk songs, there are also more positive portrayals, especially in the context of marriage and relationships. In some songs, the idea of bringing a bride from the border of Poland is seen in a more favorable light, associating Polish women with beauty and refinement. These contrasting depictions—where Poland is both a place of separation and danger, as well as a site of potential romance—demonstrate the complexity of Poland's representation in Estonian folk culture:

Tooge naine Narvamaalta,	Bring a wife from Narva
Pruuti Poola piiri päältä.	A bride from the border of Poland
Narva naisõ' om ilusa',	Narva women are beautiful
Poola pruudi' peenik'ese'	Polish brides are *slim*

(H III 9, 827/8 (8) < Otepää khk., Ilmjärve v.—Gustaw Seen [1890])

The figure of Poland, therefore, emerges not only as a symbol of geographical and cultural distance but also as a multifaceted trope that captures a range of emotions and societal concerns in Estonian folklore. The imagery evokes emotional and cultural distance, reinforced by alliteration and vivid metaphors. Yet, this depiction is not entirely negative; in some songs, Poland is also seen as a source of beauty and refinement, especially in references to brides from its border. These contrasting themes highlight the ambivalent and multi-layered role of Poland in Estonian vernacular tradition. It is a symbol of loss and foreignness, and as a space of potential connection and admiration. All in all, the reference to Poland in songs and other genres of folklore has become to signify great distance, reinforced by alliterative use.

When it comes to Russia and Germany and the portrayal of Russians and Germans in the older layer of Estonian cultural narratives, these as well reveal feelings of conflict, fear, and cultural differentiation, though not all simultaneously.

Russia and Russians are often portrayed through the lens of foreign dominance, with Russia frequently symbolizing oppression, danger, and conflict. Many songs reflect historical experiences of Russian imperial rule, particularly during the periods when Estonia was part of the Russian Empire (from the early 18th century to 1918) and the Soviet Union (from 1940 to 1991). These portrayals often emphasize the threat of Russian soldiers, conscription, and the imposition of foreign rule. For example, songs depict Russian military officers as harsh and overbearing, and Russian soldiers are often associated with the brutality of war, suggesting the heavy toll of foreign occupations on the Estonian people. Additionally, Russians are sometimes portrayed as a symbol of danger, with songs narrating tales of Russian invasions. Russians might be even ridiculed in songs (like in jokes), for example:

Venelane, vennikene,	Russian, little fellow,
läks meie läbi õue,	Went through our yard,
sõi meie seasööma,	Ate up our pig's meal
lakkus meie lapse p...	Licked our baby's bottom

(ERA II 153, 346 [37] < Haljala khk)

However, this representation is not entirely negative, and some songs also reflect a sense of admiration or acknowledgment of Russia's power. For instance, Russian strength is sometimes mentioned in the context of the military might of the Tsarist army or the prowess of Russian warriors. Nevertheless, the overarching sentiment tends to focus on the suffering and loss caused by Russian domination, with Russian figures often appearing as oppressors or distant, unapproachable figures.

Germany, on the other hand, plays a somewhat different role in Estonian folklore, with Germans being depicted more frequently in relation to the landed nobility, the clergy (see Bender, 2024) and their cultural influences. German-speaking Baltic nobility had a long-standing presence in Estonia, and many songs, but also jokes and other texts reflect both the cultural superiority and exploitation of the Estonian peasants by the German aristocracy.

Mõisamees mõisamehe hobune	Landlord, landlord's horse
Mõisamees mõnesugune	What a landlord he is
Mõisamehe magu mädane	Landlord's stomach is rotten
Mõisamehe saabas sitane	Landlord's boot is shitty
Saksad söövad saiad soojad	Germans eat warm bread
Talupoeg sööb tammetõrud	But the peasant eats acorns

(H, Mapp 1047/50 [3])

Germans are often portrayed as distant and wealthy, holding power over the Estonian rural population, but also as figures of respect or admiration in certain contexts (see also Laineste et al., 2020). They speak broken Estonian and act in ridiculous ways (though the Estonians who want to be like them are described as even more ridiculous than the object of their imitation). The complex relationship between Estonians and the German nobility is often captured in the themes of feudal subjugation, with Germans appearing as authoritative but also sometimes as figures of pity or ridicule in folk narratives. The German character in Estonian folk songs can vary from the menacing invader to a more neutral or even sympathetic figure, depending on the historical and social context.

In the broader scope of Estonian folklore, the symbolic roles of Russia and Germany often reflect the shifting power dynamics in the region. While Russia is primarily viewed through the lens of oppression and external domination, Germany occupies a more ambivalent position, representing both a source of cultural and religious influence and a symbol of feudal oppression. The more direct and militaristic portrayals of Russia are balanced by the nuanced depictions of German figures, who are sometimes seen as oppressors, but also as cultural and economic figures integral to Estonian history. In cultural texts—especially jokes—where both Russia and Germany appear, they are often juxtaposed as symbols of conflicting political and military powers, in contrast to the oppressed, but clever and resourceful Estonians. Estonians are depicted as caught between the two forces, symbolizing the struggle for autonomy and the tension between these large empires. Polish and Estonian material displays similar tendencies here in the three nation jokes, where Estonian (or Pole, depending on who is the joke teller; see the two examples below) gets the upper hand in the depicted situation:

> *Estonian, Russian and German are imprisoned. One day they are promised that they will be pardoned, if they teach the donkey to say "ouch" and "no."*
> *The German goes to the donkey and demands: "Say ouch!" The donkey doesn't say anything, and the German has to stay in the prison.*
> *The Russian goes to the donkey and demands: "Say ouch!" The donkey doesn't say anything, and the German has to stay in the prison.*
> *The Estonian goes to the donkey and looks at the animal. He goes behind the donkey and hits him in the balls. The donkey screams: "Ouch!"*
> *The Estonian asks the donkey: "You want more?"*
> *"No!" replies the animal.*
> (Delfi naljad, https://www.folklore.ee/~liisi/02/, # 31626)

> *There was a competition in driving nails into a board using one's head. There were three competitors: a Pole, a Russian and a German. The German starts first: He hits one ... two ... three ... the nail has been driven in. The Pole is next: one ... two ... stuck. The last is the Russian: One ...—stuck! The results are announced: The German is second, the Pole is first and the Russian is disqualified for sticking the nail in the wrong end.* (https://www.dowcipy.ugu.pl/dowcipypolak3.html, last accessed on October 2, 2024)

Overall, the folklore reveals a complex relationship of Poles and Estonians with both Russia and Germany, shaped by centuries of political subjugation, military conflict, and cultural exchange. In the Estonian context, Russia is often portrayed as a distant, militaristic, and oppressive force, while Germany, though often associated with aristocratic control and feudalism, is portrayed in a more multifaceted manner, with both negative and positive aspects emerging in different contexts.

In the Polish context, Estonians are perceived as part of the bigger past, and both the Russians and Germans are pictured as enemies or in the best case, competitors. Russians and Germans are people men should fight against and women should avoid—no matter how attractive they are or what promises they make. The Polish people, at the same time, are criticized when represented by magnates or supported and pitied when pictured like folk, peasants, or soldiers. However, they are recommended as good husbands who know how to respect women.

Discussion and Conclusion

It is easy to notice in the Polish and Estonian songs, jokes, and other narratives that the cultural texts have constantly been preoccupied with formulating the relationship between "us" and "them." The analysis of the Estonian and Polish folk songs presented in this article highlights the rich interplay of historical memory, national identity, and the cultural dimensions of power dynamics in the Baltic region as reflected through vernacular song traditions across centuries. The temporal attribution of these songs cannot be confined to their dates of recording or publication, as their oral transmission and performance at communal events significantly predate the archival evidence available. These songs not only convey feelings of grief, rage, and disillusionment but also serve as a vivid lens through which the Estonian and Polish peoples have historically processed their experiences of foreign domination. This is consistent with the work of scholars such as Kristin Kuutma (1996), who examined the role of folklore in reflecting the nation's history and identity. In the following discussion, we will contextualize the key points, integrating relevant concepts from folkloristics and literary studies.

Polish folk songs, as described above, often focus on themes of loss, defeat, and the emotional toll of losing national independence, blaming their long-term enemies Russia and Germany. Polish folk songs serve as vehicles for national identity, especially in times of oppression, and they are marked by a recurring sense of sorrow over the loss of autonomy and hope for future liberation (Kordjak, 2016). The pain and rage found in these songs are indicative of a broader phenomenon in Eastern European folklore where music and narrative are tied to national struggles and resistance. Polish folk songs depict the rulers or the more powerful neighbors—oppressors—in a critical light. They contrast the native Poles not just with the oppressors but also with the aristocratic Polish elite who are portrayed as distant and indifferent to the plight of the common people.

Estonian folk songs emphasize the external threats posed by neighboring powers, particularly Russia and Germany, and see Poland as the faraway land positioned at the borders of the imagined world. Tiiu Jaago (2013) claims that the placenames in folklore form a fictional mind map of the tradition-bearer's world. The map, as if drawn by someone who doesn't have good measuring tools at hand, is not true to life. Instead, it places the more relevant places closer or more visible, and the less relevant ones further or forgets about them in general. Three main categories emerge: the close, the borderline and the faraway. The mention of place names—in this study, Poland, Russia, and Germany—is carried by the need to contextualise daily experiences geographically, but equally importantly to follow the logic of folk verse format, where every next locality expands on the previous one. The need to position the song in time and space is similar to the early folk jokes that also name a specific region that the main characters come from (Laineste, 2009). The next verses use the principles of harmony and alliteration. New imaginative synonyms replace the most important word in the verse (this is often a place name or a noun).

Hence, regular geographic imaging intermingles with the vernacular imaginary map. In the latter, place names have a generic meaning not really referring to the actual places as such. The alliterative contaminations in the Estonian data (*Poola piir, poola poiss, poola pull*) become something larger than the literal meaning and designate or symbolise a place that might be dangerous, where there might be war or battles, but also where women are pretty and kind and life is easier than at home. Such cumulative geographical positioning dispels concreteness and geographical exactness and brings in the symbolic dimension: that of dangerous, faraway, strange places. This is where the neighbors crucial to the formation of national identity have been situated in folk narratives in both Poland and Estonia, though over time their presence has been felt very strongly, and the representatives of these countries were not really very far away but governing the locals' daily life. Still, imagining them coming from somewhere, because of politics or any other reasons, is necessary for the locals, and the more alien the newcomers are, the farther away the country is imagined to be. This aligns with the historical experiences of Estonians and Poles under foreign rule, be it under Russia or Germany (or any other countries not studied in this article).

The Russian presence in these songs often evokes fear and anger, symbolizing a larger narrative of subjugation and suffering. The view of Russians as untrustworthy and belligerent is reflective of the broader trope in Eastern European folklore that associates foreign conquerors with both physical and moral danger. Rita Repšienė and Laima Anglickienė (2012) analyzed similar motifs in Baltic folk traditions in jokes, noting that "the optimistic view of reality has been altered into a pessimistic and destructive one, forbearing ridicule has turned into severe offence, strangeness into stupidity, funny situations into futile misunderstanding" (p. 9). However, the relationship between Estonians and the German nobility is more nuanced. While the Germans are often portrayed as wealthy, authoritative figures, their relationship with the Estonian peasantry is marked by both resentment and grudging respect. This complex portrayal is well documented by Bender (2024). However, their image as objects of ridicule for speaking broken Estonian reflects the paradoxical way in which the Estonian folklore (e.g., sayings and jokes) blends respect with mockery, capturing the tensions between the oppressed and their rulers.

Ultimately, the analyzed folk narratives from Poland and Estonia demonstrate how folklore can act as a form of cultural resistance, a means of preserving national identity, and ultimately a way of positioning "us" in contrast to closer and more distant "them." As "they" become a globalized category, the issues of identity and belonging do not differ much from what we see in century old narratives. Folk songs function as sites of memory and sites of power (Guillorel et al., 2018), where collective experiences of trauma, oppression, and resistance are encoded and transmitted across generations.

The Polish and Estonian folk traditions, as described, show how folk narratives create a collective understanding of past suffering and resistance. Sometimes, folk narratives make use of humor and ridicule when referring to the belligerent others.

Databases

Baran, A. (Comp.) Eesti kõnekäändude ja fraseologismide andmebaas [Database of Estonian sayings and phraseologisms]. Estonian Literary Museum. https://www.folklore.ee/justkui/andmebaas.php

Instytut im. Oskara Kolberga, Antologia pieśni polskich, http://antologia.oskarkolberg.pl/pl-PL/ [Oskar Kolberg's Institute, Anthology of Polish songs]

Korpus GT projektu IMPACT (wersja 2-w.), 1570–1756, https://szukajwslownikach.uw.edu.pl/IMPACT_GT_1/ [Corpus of texts from 16th and 17th Century]

Korpus tekstów XVI–XVIII w. Korpus GT projektu IMPACT (wersja 1-w.), 1570–1756

Laineste, L. (n.d.) Eesti kaasaegsed anekdoodid [Estonian contemporary jokes]. Estonian Literary Museum. https://www.folklore.ee/~liisi/02/

Narodowy Korpus Języka Polskiego [The National Corpus of Polish Language]. https://otwartezasoby.pl/narodowy-korpus-jezyka-polskiego/

Sarv, M. (Comp.). (n.d.). Regilaulude andmebaas [Estonian runosongs' database]. Estonian Literary Museum. https://www.folklore.ee/regilaul/andmebaas/https://www.folklore.ee/regilaul/andmebaas/?

References

Ben-Amos, D., & Weissberg, L. (Eds.). (1999). *Cultural memory and the construction of identity*. Wayne State University Press.

Bender, R. (2024). Baltisaksa huumor ja pastorianekdoodid. *Keel ja kirjandus* [Language and literature], *11*, 971–999. https://doi.org/10.54013/kk803a1.

Brzozowska, D. (2012a). Ethnic jokes. In D. Brzozowska & W. Chłopicki (Eds.), *Polish humour: Humour and culture* (pp. 451–474). Tertium Society for the Promotion of Language Studies.

Brzozowska, D. (2012b). Three characters in Polish jokes. In L. Laineste, D. Brzozowska, & W. Chłopicki (Eds.), *Estonia and Poland: Creativity and tradition in cultural communication* (pp. 21–32). EKM Teaduskirjastus.

Cohen, G. (2022). *Belonging: The science of creating connection and bridging divides*. W. W. Norton & Company.

Davies, C. (1990). *Ethnic humor around the world: A comparative analysis*. Indiana University Press.

Davies, C. (2002). *Jokes and their relation to society*. University of Chicago Press.

Davies, C. (2011). *Jokes and targets*. Indiana University Press.

Guillorel, É., Hopkin, D., & Pooley, W. G. (Eds.). (2018). *Rhythms of revolt: European traditions and memories of social conflict in oral culture*. Routledge

Jaago, T. (2013). Linnateema vanemas rahvalaulus [The topic of towns in old folk songs]. *Keel ja Kirjandus*, *7*, 490–506.

Kordjak, J. (Ed.). (2016) Poland—A Country of Folklore? Zachęta—National Gallery of Art. https://zacheta.art.pl/public/upload/mediateka/pdf/6078393ce74ab.pdf

Krikmann, A. (2012). Estonian three nation jokes. In L. Laineste, D. Brzozowska, & W. Chłopicki (Eds.), *Estonia and Poland: Creativity and tradition in cultural communication* (7–20). EKM Teaduskirjastus.

Kuutma, K. (1996). Cultural identity, nationalism and changes in singing traditions. *Folklore, 2*, 124–141. https://www.folklore.ee/folklore/vol2/pdf/ident.pdf

Laineste, L. (2009). Post-socialist jokelore: Preliminary findings and further research suggestions. *Acta Ethnographica Hungarica, 54*(1), 31–45.

Laineste, L., & Brzozowska, D. (2011). Eastern European three-nation jokes: A beta database. In Alicja Witalisz (Ed.), *Across borders IV: Migration in culture, language and literature* (pp. 115–127). PWN.

Laineste, L., Fiadotava, A., & Jonuks, T. (2020). When the moral mentors lapse: A comparative study of Estonian and Belarusian clergy jokes. *Folklore, 131*(3), 292–309. https://doi.org/10.1080/0015587X.2019.1708075

Oinas, F. (1979). Naabrid ja naaberrahvad kõnekäändude kõverpeeglis [Neighbors and neighboring nations in the distorted mirror of sayings]. *Tulimuld, 13*(1), 61–70.

Ong, W. (1982). *Orality and literacy: The technologizing of the word*. Methuen.

Oring, E. (2023). *The consolations of humor and other folklore essays*. University Press of Colorado.

Remmel, M. (2003). Viru mees viljapulli, Harju mees aganapulli. Piirkondlike suhete kajastumisest eesti rahvapärimuses [Viru man is a grain bull, Harju man is a chaff bull. Regional relations in Enstonian folklore]. *Mäetagused, 21*, 141–192.

Repšienė, R., & Anglickienė, L. (2012). Identity and stereotypes: Humor manifestations. *Folklore, 50*, 9–28. https://www.folklore.ee/folklore/vol50/identity.pdf

Saarlo, L. (2001). Regilaulude vormelid: kvantiteet ja kvaliteet [Runo song formulas: quantity and quality]. In T. Jaago & M. Sarv (Eds.), *Regilaul—Keel, muusika, poeetika [Runo songs—Language, music, poetics]* (pp. 271–297). Eesti Kirjandusmuuseum. http://www.folklore.ee/era/nt/PF7/7Saarlo.htm

Sarv, M. (2000). Regilaul kui poeetiline süsteem [Runo song as a poetic system]. Paar sammukest XVII. Eesti Kirjandusmuuseumi aastaraamat [A couple of steps XVII. Estonian Literary Museum yearbook]. J. Oras, E.-H. Västrik (Toim). Eesti Kirjandusmuuseum.

Valk, Ü. (1998). *Allilma isand: Kuradi ilmumiskujud eesti rahvausus [Underworld master: The devil in Estonian folk belief]*. Eesti Rahva Muuseum.

Viikberg, J. (2004). Murdenaabrist nimepidi [Calling the dialect neighbor by the name]. *Oma Keel [Own language], 1*, 45–52.

Viikberg, J. (2015). Vandiraiujad, ubamulgid, mehkad ja setud—ühed eestlased kõik [Beam cutters, bean mulks, mehkas and setus—All Estonians]. *Oma Keel [Own language], 1*, 32–36.

CHAPTER THREE | **RAFAEL VÉLEZ NÚÑEZ AND GIORDANO DURANTE**

(Un)Bordering Gibraltarian Literary Culture
Identity and Recognition

Abstract

This paper explores the burgeoning, yet at times contested, literary culture and production of Gibraltar, a British Overseas Territory with a complex postcolonial identity. Despite its rich history and unique socio-political context, Gibraltarian literature faces skepticism regarding its existence and value, often dismissed as parochial or lacking in quality. This analysis challenges these dismissals by highlighting the growing body of work produced by Gibraltarian writers, including novelists like M. G. Sanchez, poets like Rebecca Calderon, and playwrights like Julian Felice. The paper argues that Gibraltarian literature, while still developing, exhibits characteristics of a minor literature, as defined by Deleuze and Guattari, where individual voices contribute to a collective, often politically charged, utterance. It examines the reasons behind the denial of this literature, including elitism, cultural cringe, and misconceptions about self-publishing and thematic diversity. Furthermore, it showcases the increasing international academic interest in Gibraltarian writing, evidenced by scholarly publications, conference presentations, and literary awards. Ultimately, the paper asserts that Gibraltarian literature exists and is a vital expression of the territory's evolving identity, defying simplistic definitions and challenging entrenched prejudices. It underscores the importance of recognizing and critically engaging with this literature, not as a mere extension of British or Spanish literature, but as a distinct and valuable contribution to the global literary landscape.

Keywords: Gibraltar, local literature, "cultural cringe", British, Spanish

Gibraltar is one of 14 existing British Overseas Territories. Although they all have their own constitutions and governments, and do not form part of the United Kingdom, they share a historical link with it and are part of its sovereign territory. The United Nations includes Gibraltar on the list of "Non-Self-Governing Territories awaiting decolonization."[1] This colonial vestige, and its geographical location on the Iberian Peninsula, bordering Spain, has been shaping its history and politics since 1713, when Gibraltar was ceded to the United Kingdom by the Treaty of Utrecht and Spain started an, as yet, unsuccessful claim to sovereignty over the territory. In the 20th century, a tumultuous period in Spanish history, this claim ceased to be a rhetorical artifice, and it reached a sad milestone in 1969, when the dictator Francisco Franco enacted Spain's old claim and restricted movement between Gibraltar and Spain, closing completely the border and severing all communication links. The border with Spain was partially reopened in 1982 and fully reopened in 1985 as a condition of Spain's accession to the European Community.[2]

As David Alvarez (2001) states "one of the most marked effects of the closed border on the collective life of the Gibraltarians was the increasingly brittle and embattled tone it lent to their politics and to their cultural identity" (p. 5). Since then, Gibraltar has undergone a continuous process of self-determination and has tried to find an identity which reflects the complexity of its current situation.[3] The former minister of culture, Bernard Linares also reflected on this topic in an unpublished lecture from 1999:

> Genuine identity as a people is existentially realised not by reference to past monuments and memorials, historical relics, proclaimed shibboleths or loud-hailed slogans, but by (...) a living witness and a commitment to values and disciplines worthy of recognition in the global family of mankind. That, I would like to believe, is the philosophical, moral, and socio-political definition of a "people" who can lay claim to a genuine "cultural identity" and uniqueness. (Alvarez, 2000, p. 13)

Gibraltarian culture should be a determining and fundamental element in the construction of identity, which should not be based exclusively on nationalist rhetoric with a strong political profile. Nationalism, understood as a sentimental attachment to a certain territory, determines identities; and its construction is not monolithic. The

---

1. Gibraltar has been on the United Nations list of Non-Self-Governing Territories since 1946, following the transmission of information by the United Kingdom of Great Britain and Northern Ireland under Article 73 e of the Charter of the United Nations.
2. Some scholars have studied this episode in Gibraltar's recent history from different perspectives. Cf. Gold, Jackson, Canessa, or Sanchez Mantero.
3. At the time of writing this paper, the UK and Spain have reached a "historic" deal on Gibraltar's post-Brexit future, resolving the long-standing dispute. This agreement will ease the flow of people and goods across the border by introducing dual passport checks at Gibraltar's airport and eliminating land border checks. The deal preserves British sovereignty over Gibraltar, including the operational autonomy of UK military facilities.

space that is considered a country, a nation, is made up of multiple components, such as language[4], history, geography, and culture. All of them are determining factors in the way they define unique characteristics that make us different from other places, spaces or nations. Twenty-first century Gibraltar is witnessing an interesting process of self-definition and associated with it, there is an emerging literary culture that reflects (on) this transformation. Because of the number of writers and the space to which their production is attached to, Gibraltarian literature is now included among an important group of world minor literatures. Many of them are the products and consequences of postcolonialism and, likewise, the literature of Gibraltar, even if the territory still has a different political status, also shares and shows postcolonial traits and intersectionality.

The following pages will try to define and contextualize Gibraltarian literature which, even if it is mostly written in English, is not yet included in the canon of contemporary world English literatures. It is somewhat ironic, and a clear contradiction to what it was considered before, that a country which is in search of its identity is apparently little concerned with the native culture of Gibraltar; and a clear example of this is its literary production. Roger Chartier's (1996) idea of the order of the book[5] will help us understand some of the conditions and systems that regulate the production, dissemination, and appropriation of Gibraltarian literary texts; that is, how this literary production is subject to external conditions that define and determine it. The first section describes the corpus of contemporary Gibraltarian literature and its undeniable existence, despite some local skepticism. After this, the discussion focuses on the slippery realm of literary quality and it tries to refute several common criticisms, such as the idea that Gibraltarian writing is not "good enough" or that it is too parochial, by citing specific examples of published authors and their works, as well as the growing international and academic interest in their writing. Ultimately, the text posits that the denial of Gibraltar literature stems from a mix of academic prejudice, cultural cringe, and elitism rather than from a lack of literary merit.

---

4. Llanito, the language spoken in Gibraltar, apart from English and Spanish, is one of the most salient linguistic characteristics of Gibraltarian identity. The language(s) of Gibraltar have been the subject of numerous research in the last few years. To understand the impact of Llanito on Gibraltarian identity see Chevasco (2021).

5. Roger Chartier's "order of the book" theory argues that the meaning of a text is not solely determined by its words, but also by the material form and social context in which it is produced, circulated, and read. This theory, which is central to the field of book history, emphasizes the dynamic relationship between authors, publishers, and readers across different historical periods.

Literary Existence

In November 2021, *The Chronicle*, Gibraltar's main newspaper and one of the oldest in Europe, published an article signed by Priya Gulraj which offered a preview of upcoming events at the following month's Literature Week. The article mentioned that participants at one event would be discussing, among other things, "if Gibraltar literature exists" (Gulraj, 2006) and this caused a number of local authors to react with a mixture of disbelief and disappointment. The question seemed an academic mask for a deeper set of prejudices, because posing it sounded as a polite substitute for denying the quality of Gibraltar writing and for not considering it appropriate to label it as "literature." Simply put, to ask whether Gibraltar literature exists is to ask whether there are people with a significant connection to Gibraltar who are producing works of artistic merit intended to be taken seriously.

A good example of this is the writer M. G. Sanchez whose novels are set in Gibraltar and explore the raw experience of being Gibraltarian with all its confusions and paradoxes. His latest works, *The Fetishist* and *Marlboro Man*, shine a coruscating light on topics like Gibraltar's interest in the military and empire or less celebratory historical events such as smuggling in the 1990's. Jackie Anderson's works include "Fish Salters," a poem as finely wrought as anything published by the major poetry presses in the UK. The plays of Julian Felice, some of which have touched on episodes in Gibraltar's past (the IRA shootings in *Flavius*) and others which have received performances in the US and London and earned numerous prizes in successive Gibraltar Drama Festivals; the short stories and poems of Humbert Hernandez, which recreate the spirit of Gibraltar's forgotten patio life in his multivolume *Historias de Gibraltar* series; the memoirs, stories, and award-winning poems of Rebecca Calderon, that display complete mastery of form and tone; the popular *Exiliado Blogs* of Jonathan Pizarro, limpidly written reflections—often nostalgic—which examine Gibraltar from the perspective of the author's current life abroad. Poetry is a well-represented genre in Gibraltarian literature: the tender verses of Gabriel Moreno, a troubadour of the London night; the poems of David Alvarez, rendered in his pioneering "Zhanito" script, the haiku-like poetry of Marisa Salazar, tied to impressions of the seas that surround the Rock; the nostalgic and sensorial lines of Giordano Durante; the energetic poetry of Jonathan Teuma or Trino Cruz's poetical reflections on the intricate metaphorical depths of the strait. All these writers have a connection to Gibraltar, all of them are today producing work intended to be taken seriously, whether this intention is, in fact, satisfied. They are the embodiment of Gibraltar literature—living, working, writing, and breathing proof, in all their variety, energy, and originality—that the deniers are woefully wrong.

Although not all writers, in Gibraltar and abroad, are successful in securing the attention of literary critics and academics, the global interest in Gibraltar literature is growing; more than 20 articles have appeared in international scholarly journals on Sanchez's work, and over the past few years he has been invited to speak about his Gibraltarian novels at universities across Europe. Jonathan Pizarro appeared at an event at the Milton Keynes Lit Fest in October 2021, alongside the Iranian writer Golnoosh Nour, the event description setting out that both authors "explore cultural conflict and misunderstanding, not least as both writers speak with LGBT voices."[6] His fiction has also been published in several international literary magazines and journals and has secured him a place on the shortlist for the Aurora Prize for Writing.

In 2015, Rebecca Calderon's poem "Sunday" was shortlisted in the poetry section for the Bridport Prize and, in 2018, Julian Felice delivered a talk at Borderline VI: "Performing Across the Frontiers of Fear," a conference organized by the Drama Research Group and the Centre for Interdisciplinary Research in Dance at De Montfort University in Leicester. Felice used the opportunity to speak about his fascinating play, *Utrecht*, which also received a rehearsed reading.

Another example was an online symposium featuring seven Gibraltar writers which took place in October 2020. Titled "The Shadow of the Rock: Literature in Gibraltar," the half-day event was organized by two US-based academics: Professor Edwige Tamalet Talbayev (Tulane University) and Professor Robert Newcomb (UC Davis).

One of the participants was the Gibraltarian academic and poet David Alvarez, professor at the Department of English Language and Literature at Grand Valley State University, a perceptive critic and appreciator of local literature, who has said that Sanchez's work "manage[s] to capture the quiddity of the Rock's hybrid society and the complexity of its natural and cultural ecologies with [...] much psychological insight and writerly verve."[7]

Once again, this is local writing attracting and rewarding an academic gaze yet to manifest itself in public on the Rock itself.

The publication of the *Anthology of Contemporary Gibraltar Poets* in 2019 was also further collective evidence of what Humbert Hernandez called a "burgeoning" local literature. Not only does a worthwhile anthology require the existence of poets who are writing poetry worthy of inclusion; the bringing together of these disparate voices is itself an exercise, however small, in the creation of a canon, especially in a place with no firm literary traditions. Newcomb, who wrote one of the forewords in the anthology, said the collection showcased "the depth and nuance with which they [Gibraltar poets] use poetic language to describe experiences both ridiculous and sublime in their shared home in the shadow of the Rock" (Alvarez et al., 2019, p. 133). The second

---

6. https://www.destinationmiltonkeynes.co.uk/events/milton-keynes-lit-fest-presents-exiles-on-main-street-jonathan-pizarro-and-golnoosh-nur/
7. This commentary appears in the back cover of Sanchez (2019), *Border Control*.

foreword, by the Spanish journalist and writer Juan José Tellez, appreciatively noted the great variety of styles and outlooks within its 80 pages.

Postcolonial approaches to Gibraltar texts are also proving fruitful as are perspectives which focus on the unique linguistic diversity of the Rock.

More recently, and as proof of a growing interest in this literature, scholars have focused their attention on the works of Gibraltarian authors: a new special volume in the *Journal of Iberian Studies* edited by Newcomb (2025); a chapter in the groundbreaking study *Postcolonial Stylistics* by Esterino Adami (2025) and even a specific seminar on Gibraltarian literature led by professor Ina Habermann, who has also published on the topic, at the University of Basel.

Taking this short survey as a starting point, it could be affirmed that there is Gibraltar literature in the same sense as there is Gibraltar art. Of course, this comes with caveats: Gibraltar literature, such as it exists, is still in an early stage of development. There are, comparatively, just a handful of people producing work of artistic merit. Some of it is uneven. Some of it would benefit from the sharp editorial eye of a major publishing house. Some of it could even benefit from deeper contact with more established, larger literary traditions, but it remains a literature.

To earn the label "literature" does not imply to assume equivalence in scope and quality with other world literatures. What is needed is similarity in aims, in seriousness and openness to critical scrutiny. It would be very surprising indeed if Gibraltar did not have its own literature—it has, after all, its own artists like the late Mario Finlayson, Christian Hook and Alan Perez; it would be one of the only developed places in the world where writing of a certain aesthetic merit is not produced and shared and discussed and recognized by the establishment as such.

The denial of the existence of Gibraltar literature would be surprising and extremely puzzling to all those academics whose interest has been provoked by works emerging from the writers listed above.

Defying Definitions

A working definition, especially of the term literature as applied to any country or period, is a complex achievement and completely out of the scope of this paper. But, at times, concepts are paradoxically defined by what they are not, or what they lack. And this seems to be the case with Gibraltar literature. Out of academia, this production has been subject to a biased scrutiny with a priori expectations that do not favor its tumultuous existence but rather label it in the light of unfounded prejudice.

Ill-informed narratives about the quality of Gibraltar literary production abound. Because labeling some works as "literature" implies to elevate them to a certain standard; "real" or "true" literature must be good enough to earn that label, and local literature just does not make it. Therefore, there is no Gibraltar literature; it simply is not good enough to deserve the same term which is applied to the works of Yeats and Milton, for example.

One problem with this view is that it confuses the existence question (whether literature *exists*) with the value question (whether the literature that does exist *is of any value*) but these are separate matters. Building value or rank into a definition of "literature" gets things the wrong way around: the most plausible picture of the practice of evaluation is that first something is identified as art and then it is evaluated.

However, even if it were true that the term "literature" has this exalted sense, then it should be assumed that many works of Gibraltar literature are of sufficient quality to deserve the label. And this is not the authors' opinion, but rather that of knowledgeable experts who have no personal connection to the Rock and its writers like the academic and former Booker Prize judge Alastair Niven (2019) who chose Sanchez's novel *Jonathan Gallardo* as his book choice for 2015 in his article "Celebrating an Abundance," a piece which also mentions Felice's plays.

Another point which has been offered as a reason why Gibraltar literature is of an inferior quality is that most of it is self-published. Self-publishing is meant to indicate that the works in question are not good enough to merit the attention of a major publisher. So, the argument would run, Gibraltar literature is largely driven by works which are self-published (with all its negative connotations of vanity publishing) and this is a sure sign of their low quality: these works would not be of a sufficient standard to be published by consecrated publishing houses.

The trouble with this line of thinking is that it assumes that the only reason why many Gibraltar writers fail to get their books published (but see Moreno and Felice for counterexamples) is because their works are lacking in value. This argument ignores the unusual and unique position of Gibraltar writers, a combination of factors that militate against securing a publishing deal in an already highly competitive market. Many Gibraltar writers are physically and culturally isolated from the UK mainland. This makes it much harder to attend events and establish connections with other writers and agents at festivals and poetry readings, for example. It would require plenty of time off, and funds, for the typical Gibraltar writer (most of whom have full-time jobs) to spend a significant amount of time in the UK making the right connections. Sending unsolicited manuscripts, without a previous record of publication in the right literary journals, is often a waste of time and energy and that is without considering the numerous obstacles that Gibraltar writers might face from an establishment apparently wedded to its own entrenched prejudices of what Gibraltar and its culture stand for.

In this respect, Gibraltar writers are not helped by the vulgar depictions of the Rock in the popular *Britain in the Sun* series or the periodic tabloid interest shown in Gibraltar at moments of political crisis where it is reduced to a mere hunk of rock, draped in a Union Jack, a fortress and fish-and-chip-munching colony, a land without its own people and, certainly, a land without decent writers.

As a further point, to argue that Gibraltar writing is substandard because it is self-published is to commit a variation of the genetic fallacy. It is to say, in other words, that a work's origin or history determines its current value whereas one ought to examine a work *on its own terms*, regardless of its origin.

A third possible reason why the existence of Gibraltar literature might be denied is that it does not possess a unifying or common theme. The idea here would be that local writing is too disparate to be brought under a neat classification so there is no "movement" or "school" to be identified, just a ragbag of individuals ploughing their own furrows. It is odd that this argument should be accorded with any weight given the fact that there is little evidence of unifying or shared themes in any other literature across the globe. Insisting on thematic or stylistic unity is also a fallacy, the fallacy of essentialism; the habit of always searching for the essential nature of some phenomenon and holding the belief that if one term is applied to numerous objects, these objects must share an essence.

One other poorly argued reason why one might devalue local literature is the imputation that such writing is too tied down to local themes and concerns; that it is too parochial to compare to literature from elsewhere. In other words, local writers suffer from tunnel vision; they are too focused on Gibraltar as a setting for their works and they need to look beyond Gibraltar and expand their creative horizons.

As an example, Sanchez has been unfairly accused of being fixated on Gibraltar's postcolonial nature in his novels. In a recent interview conducted by Humbert Hernandez, and published at the end of *The Fetishist*, Hernandez raises this very point:

> HH. Is it true that you once had somebody high up in the Gibraltarian establishment advise you to stop focusing so much on Gibraltar?

> MGS: Yes, it's true. I was told that I shouldn't be so "Gibraltar-fixated" and that I should stop dwelling on things which happened in the past. (Sanchez, 2021, p. 276)

Once again, this approach betrays a stunning ignorance of literature and literary history; an ignorance of both how writing works and how authors mine their immediately accessible memories and impressions for insights of greater, interpersonal significance. Some of Sanchez's novels are about feeling alienated in a former colony still in thrall to a colonial mindset, but that is an endlessly fascinating aspect of living a sensitive and thoughtful life in Gibraltar; Jonathan Pizarro's blogs look back at the Gibraltar of his youth but they remain poetically written evocations of this sepia-tinted past; their writing is so appealing precisely because it is about local themes.

In this respect, Gibraltar writers are only doing what writers elsewhere have been doing for centuries. After all the work of Thomas Hardy is not deprecated for being "limited" to rural life in Wessex, nor is Philip Roth criticized for his "obsession" with Newark, characterized as the hometown he never really left. Similarly, Andrew Motion has confessed that he fundamentally writes the same poem repeatedly. Why should these authors be able to focus their energies on a handful of places and themes, but local authors be urged to "look beyond" the Rock? The only reason seems to be an inveterate prejudice lurking in the background of many of these judgments.

Writers work with what they know: their immediate surroundings, their pasts. This is the raw material they hew and fashion into stories and verses of lasting significance and resonance. Gibraltar, a life lived in Gibraltar, a Gibraltarian outlook, are all perfectly valid catalysts for literary inspiration in just the same way that family histories and hometowns have served writers as diverse as Joyce, Updike, and Angelou.

Finally, another spurious reason why a focus on Gibraltar themes is sometimes spurned is when these themes are deemed insalubrious or otherwise damaging to some prudish national self-image. Anything which mentions smuggling, thuggery, or prostitution, anything that paints the Rock in a less than flattering light is in bad taste and fit for the flames.[8]

Established Literature

Less savory aspects behind the denial and denigration of local literature are to be considered. These are the deeper currents both in society and at the individual level, currents that have nothing to do with conceptual errors and everything to do with elitism, snobbery and gatekeeping. An elitist mindset, scanning the local literary scene from a position of assumed superiority, will naturally latch onto the honorific sense of "literature."

Raising the question of the existence of Gibraltar literature, then, implies many things: it is provocative, perhaps partly rhetorical and contrary. But rather than being part of an honest, open-minded inquiry, not afraid to raise controversial or uncomfortable questions, it smacks instead of contrariness for its own sake and a sign of intellectual poverty where the simple posing of the question is a substitute for the tough task of serious, rigorous thinking backed up by reasons and arguments. In the end, it demonstrates a complete absence of the generosity and charity that should characterize academic discussion.

This is not to say that local literature is immune to criticism. Writers, readers, and critics have a duty to discuss these works and critically assess them. They should not be protected from harsh, justified criticism because of the size of the community or its closely-knit nature. A dud work is a dud work whether it is written in Gibraltar or

---

8. For one reaction in this vein, see Anthony Lombard's outrage directed at Sanchez's *Diary of a Victorian Colonial and Other Tales*, and the numerous replies. Cf. https://www.mgsanchez.net/readersresponsetodiaryofavc

Bloomsbury. Gibraltarian authors must be prepared to be judged by the highest standards if they want Gibraltar literature to be taken seriously. It does not help that this critical attitude is largely absent within the establishment where a well-intentioned egalitarian urge has erased all sense of merit and rank; and even with the local press lacking any discrimination when covering book launches and publishing book reviews.

Another factor behind the denial of local literature is the phenomenon of "cultural cringe," a term coined by the Australian author A. A. Phillips (2006). This manifests itself in the view that one's own culture is inferior to the cultures of other, often imperially dominant, nations. The possible explanation for a dismissive attitude toward local literature, in a society that experiences cultural cringe, is the unthinking assumption that anything "local" is automatically inferior when compared to the works of UK writers, for example.

These are just some hints at the reasons why one might feel compelled to doubt if Gibraltar literature exists despite overwhelming evidence to the contrary. They are complex and operate at societal and individual levels, but they can be overcome with patient correction and rebuttal.

Gibraltar literature is not a literature which has yet to be born. It is still undergoing development in fits and starts but the signs are promising so far as it takes ever more confident steps. Again, this is not the self-flattering opinion of the writers themselves; this is the shared assumption of foreign academics working independently.

Minor literatures, according to Deleuze and Guattari, have three main characteristics: the deterritorialization of the language, the connection of the individual and the political and the collective arrangement of utterance (Deleuze & Guattari, 1983, p. 18). The latter implies that everything has a collective value. That is, "because talents do not abound in a minor literature, the conditions are not given for an individuated utterance which would be that of some 'master' and could be separated from collective utterance" (Deleuze & Guattari, 1983, p. 17). In this way, the limited availability of extraordinary writers paradoxically allows for a literary landscape void of masters. A writer's individual voice becomes a communal and unavoidably political act, regardless of opposing views. In a context where national consciousness is often dormant or disintegrating, literature assumes the role of a charged, collective, and even revolutionary expression. Even when writers exist on the margins, their work has the power to articulate a potential community, shaping new forms of consciousness and sensibility. Literature acts as a catalyst for future revolutionary change, not through ideological doctrine, but by providing a necessary collective voice. Literature is fundamentally a public matter: "the affair of the people" (Deleuze & Guattari, 1983, p. 17).

This Deleuzian rationale, enhancing the potential "revolutionary" effects on the community of individual writers, proves a suitable background to understand Gibraltar literature in relation to its role in the political and cultural scenario of the Rock.

Whatever opposing views or voices might vilify a particular literary production, the individual writers will, even unknowingly, create a collective utterance that transcends skepticism and disagreement. That seems to be the reason why literary voices are difficult to silence; and Gibraltarian literary voices, in particular, are being heard and are receiving scholarly attention, regardless of a seeming lack of necessary attention from local institutions.

Finally, and in order to individualize the collectivity of Gibraltarian contemporary voices, their brief biographical notices will be provided in the appendix.

References

Adami, E. (2025). *Postcolonial stylistics*. Routledge.

Alvarez, D. (2000). Colonial relic: Gibraltar in the age of decolonization. *Grand Valley Review*, 21(1), 4–26.

Alvarez, D. (2001). Nation-making in Gibraltar: From fortress colony to finance centre. *Canadian Review of Studies in Nationalism*, 29(1–2), 9–25.

Alvarez, F., et al. (Eds). (2019). *An anthology of contemporary Gibraltar poets*. IWAP.

Canessa, A. (Ed.). (2019). *Bordering on Britishness: National identity in Gibraltar from the Spanish Civil War to Brexit*. Palgrave.

Chartier, R. (1994). *The order of books. Readers, authors, and libraries in Europe between the 14th and 18th centuries*. Stanford University Press.

Chevasco, D. (2021). Notes on "Contemporary bilingualism, Llanito and language policy in Gibraltar: A study" with a present-day view of linguistic challenges. *Cuadernos de Gibraltar–Gibraltar Reports*, 4, 1–8.

del Valle Gálvez, A., & González García, I. (Eds.). (2004). *Gibraltar, 300 años*. Servicio de Publicaciones Universidad de Cádiz.

Deleuze, G., Guattari, F., & Brinkley, R. (1983). What is a minor literature? *Mississippi Review*, 11(3), 13–33.

Gold, P. (2005). *Gibraltar: British or Spanish?*. Routledge.

Gulraj, P. (2021, November 16). Gibraltarian literature pondered. *The Gibraltar Chronicle*. https://www.chronicle.gi/gibraltarian-literature-pondered/

Jackson, W.G.F. (1990). *The Rock of the Gibraltarians: A history of Gibraltar*. Gibraltar Books Ltd.

Newcomb, R. P. (2019). "Foreword". In F. Alvarez et al. (Eds.), *An anthology of contemporary Gibraltar poets*. IWAP.

Newcomb, R. P. (Ed.). (2025). Strategies for writing Gibraltar into the world. *International Journal of Iberian Studies*, 38(1), 3–23

Niven, A. (2019). Celebrating an abundance, 1984–2019: Thirty-five literary highlights from Aotearoa to Zimbabwe. *Wasafiri*, 34(4), 133–138.

Phillips, A. A. (2006). *On the cultural cringe*. Melbourne University Press.

Sanchez, M. G. (2019). *Border control and other autobiographical pieces*. The Dabuti Collective.

Sanchez, M. G. (2021). *The Fetishist*. The Dabuti Collective.

Sánchez Mantero, R. (2010). Desde el otro lado de la verja (los gibraltareños y el bloqueo de Gibraltar en 1969). *Historia Contemporánea*, 41, 373–390.

Appendix
Alphabetical List of Contemporary Gibraltarian Writers

David Álvarez
David Álvarez teaches contemporary comparative world literature at Grand Valley State University in Grand Rapids, Michigan. Gibraltar born and bred, for the past 34 years he has lived abroad, first in the UK and then in the US.

Jackie Anderson
Jackie Anderson is a writer with over three decades of experience. She began as a copy writer, contributing articles to various publications such as *My Weekly*, local newspapers, and magazines. She is also a poet, whose works have appeared in several anthologies in Gibraltar and the UK. In 2022, she coauthored her first nonfiction book, *Myth, Monster, Murderer*, with her daughter, Ciara Wild. Jackie has received awards for her poetry and short stories and is now working on her latest poetry anthology.

Rebecca Calderon
Rebecca Calderon is a writer, poet and political campaigner. Her interest in social history led her to write *The Civil Garrison* (2004). The play was adapted into the collaborative work Llévame Donde Nací and staged in 2015. Rebecca won the Gibraltar Poetry Prize in 2014, 2017, 2020, and 2022 and the Short Story Prize in 2014 and 2015. She was shortlisted for the prestigious international Bridport Prize for Poetry in 2015.

Trino Cruz
Trino Cruz is a bilingual writer and translator whose work is profoundly shaped by his upbringing in the Strait region of Gibraltar, Morocco, and Spain. This has given him a unique perspective on the Mediterranean as a vibrant crossroads of cultures. Cruz's writing is a call to break down cultural barriers and promote exchange and collaboration between communities. He believes it is essential to build on our shared common ground to prevent division. He is actively involved in regional cultural initiatives and serves on the editorial boards of literary journals like *SureS* and *Banipal*—revista de literatura árabe moderna. He has published several poetry collections, including *Rihla* and *Mediodía del Cantor*, and has translated Arabic and French poetry into Spanish, notably *Adoniada* by Adonis. His work has been featured in international journals, such as *Banipal*, and he has performed his poetry at festivals in Spain, Morocco, and South America. His latest project, the Strait Rhapsody Project, involves collaborative live performances with other artists.

Giordano Durante
Giordano Durante is a Gibraltarian poet. He has released three collections: *West* (2017), *Machotes* (2020) and *Nostalgia Elsewhere* (2022). In 2025, he has released a book of poetic letters together with Gabriel Moreno titled *The Crooked Timber*.

Julian Felice
Julian Felice is Gibraltar's first ever internationally published playwright. His plays have been performed in the UK and in the US, including over thirty productions in the States. Julian's work was mentioned in a review of Gibraltarian literature in the 100th edition of *Wasafiri Magazine*.

Humbert Hernandez
Humbert Hernandez took up writing when he retired from teaching in 2002. Writing mainly in Spanish, he has published two memoirs, two poetry anthologies, and five collections of short stories. His latest book is the novel *Luciano*.

Gabriel Moreno
Gabriel Moreno graduated in philosophy and Hispanic studies at the University of Hull and later obtained a doctorate in Hispanic literature at the University of Barcelona. His published works in Spanish include *Londres y el susurro de las amapolas* (2007), *Cartas a Miranda* (2008), and *Identidad y Deseo* (2010); his works in English include *The Hollow Tortoise* (2012), *Nights in Mesogeois* (2013), *The Moon and the Sparrow* (2015), *The Passer-by* (2019), and *Heart Mortally Wounded by Six Strings* (2023), *The Crooked Timber* (with Giordano Durante, 2025), and *Nights in the Belly of Bohemia* (2025).

Jonathan Pizarro
Jonathan Pizarro is a Gibraltarian writer and teacher. His short fiction has been featured in *Popshot*, *Litro*, and *Queerlings* amongst others. He has been shortlisted for both the 2021 Aurora Prize and the 2022 Commonwealth Prize. His short story "Nobody's Sons," an extract from his forthcoming debut novel, was published in *Queer Life Queer Love 2* by Muswell Press and featured as one of Easyjet's "15 Summer Reads of 2023." His stories deal with desire, memory, the Mediterranean, language, borders, and the aftermath of empire.

Marisa Salazar
Marisa is a retired social worker and a licensed Gibraltar tour guide. She has a master's degree in social work from the University of Bristol, England. She worked as the head of social services for children and families in Gibraltar until she retired. She then decided to fill the gap in her early education by learning about the rich and diverse history of Gibraltar and its people, which became her passion. She is also interested in the creative arts, languages, and learning. She has published four poems, including "Calentita Haiku " (2017), in *Calentita Press*, 9, and "Mosquito, frontier, and afloat" in the *Anthology of Contemporary Gibraltar Poets* (2019).

Mark Sanchez
Mark Sanchez is a Gibraltarian writer based in the UK. He has written various novels with a Gibraltarian theme. Since 2001, he has published the following books: *Rock*

of Empire (2001), *Rock Black: Ten Gibraltarian Stories* (2006), *Writing the Rock of Gibraltar: An Anthology of Literary Texts, 1720–1890* (2006), *The Prostitutes of Serruya's Lane and Other Hidden Histories* (2007), *Diary of a Victorian Colonial and Other Tales* (2008), *Georgian and Victorian Gibraltar: Incredible Eyewitness Accounts* (2012), *The Escape Artist* (2013), *Solitude House* (2015), *Jonathan Gallardo* (2015), *Past: A Memoir* (2016), *Bombay Journal* (2018), *Crossed Lines* (2019), *Border Control and Other Autobiographical Pieces* (2019), *Gooseman* (2020), *The Fetishist* (2021), *Marlboro Man* (2022). His personal website can be found at www.mgsanchez.net/.

Jonathan Teuma

Jonathan Teuma, a.k.a Teu & Yanito, is an English professor, slammer, poet, and MC. He has participated in slams and jams of all shapes and sizes, hosting the 2nd National Poetry Slam final in Jaén (2012) and making special guest appearances at the 4th and 8th National Slam finals in Mallorca (2014) and Valencia (2018), respectively. He also won the International Comedy Slam at the Festival de Poesía y Prosa Humorosa de Ávila (2019). Known as Yanito, he currently MCs the monthly Poetry Slam in Madrid and has recently been presenting his book of poems *¡A-SLAM-BABA- LUBA, A-SLAM-BAM-BU!* in slams and other literary events in Gibraltar, Spain, and the UK.

SECTION TWO

Analyses of Messages Entailing Conflict Views

CHAPTER FOUR | LINDA KEAN AND TODD FRALEY

#MoreThanAnAthlete

The Building of Community in a Divided Neighborhood

Abstract

Athletes have a history of speaking truth to power through activism. This study is specifically interested in those athletes that used their celebrity as a platform to speak out in the wake of the George Floyd murder in 2020. In 2018, news correspondent Laura Ingraham told LeBron James to "shut up and dribble" when he spoke out regarding police brutality in America. In response, James claimed he was "More than an athlete" and with that, a hashtag was born. In reviewing images associated with tweets using the "More Than an Athlete" hashtag (#MTAA) the month after Floyd's death, we considered the use of social media by athletes participating in activism. This study revealed images that associated the current athlete activism with that of the athletes who spoke out during the 1960s Civil Rights Movement while increasing the breadth of those athletes that are willing to articulate their grievances and concerns regarding social justice utilizing slogans and images associated with the larger social justice movement. Ultimately, these images appear to have the potential to refocus the narrative about what it means to be Black, whose voice matters, and undoing the dismissal of the lived experience of Black people in America.

Keywords: #MTAA, athletes and activism, George Floyd, hashtags, media images, social media, Twitter/X

Background

Sport as a platform for social activism is not new, and just as Black athletes were central to the Civil Rights Movement of the 1960s, today the efforts of Colin Kaepernick, Lebron James, and others have supported and expanded the Black Lives Matter movement and led to increased awareness of social justice issues among athletes and inspired an increase in athlete activism. These efforts can be seen as the continuation of the heritage, an ongoing fight for racial equality that links the present struggle to a powerful legacy of resistance by athletes (Williams, 2022). In 1968, Tommie Smith and John Carlos raised their fists in protest on the Olympic medal stand and one year earlier, the "Ali Summit" united prominent Black athletes in support of Muhammad Ali's refusal to be drafted. Both instances were bold actions that were emblematic of the era's broader activist momentum (Wiggins, 2000). Other sports icons of the time—Bill Russell, Jim Brown, Arthur Ashe, Billie Jean King, and many others—also leveraged their fame for social change. Now, after decades of political silence, athletes are once again making bold statements, engaging in symbolic protests, and using their platforms to express opinions about who they truly are (Schmidt, 2018). As they do, they align with social justice movements and reinforce a sense of community among athletes and supporters (Cooper & Rodriguez, 2019; Fraley & Kean, 2024; Trimbur, 2019). These communities in turn contribute to important conversations regarding inequality and injustice and demonstrate to others that these cultural icons are "more than an athlete" (Kean & Fraley, 2024).

Athlete activism is a complex space because players are often expected to entertain and perform, not to challenge or dispute the world in which they live (Bryant, 2018). Behind this expectation lies the pervasive truth that the white majority still dictates what can be discussed (Bryant, 2018). White athletes, like white individuals in the US, tend to have more latitude in their ability to criticize or speak up without retribution. Mainstream media, complicit in this dynamic, patrols discussions relevant to Black athletes and creates an atmosphere where protest is framed as an affront to the military, to patriotism, and by extension, to American values themselves (Bryant, 2018). Amid this tension, "the heritage", a term often used in discussions of Black athletes using their position to speak out on issues related to race, social injustice and politics, creates a sense of brotherhood, connecting players (and others) across racial and cultural lines, (Bryant, 2018) and even time. Due to their prominent social status, athletes do often find themselves serving as active agents in social movements (Galily, 2019). Yet at times isolated and understandably hesitant, athletes still seek clarity about their roles in the search for equality. Michael Jordan was reluctant to engage in social or political issues during his career due to a fear of alienation (Bryant, 2018). This hesitancy stems from the reality that activism often invites fierce backlash. When athletes engage in political discourse or support social justice causes, they are met with intense criticism, which seeks to isolate them and label them as ungrateful or deviant (Kaufman, 2008). In 2018, when TV personality Laura Ingraham infamously told LeBron James to "shut up and dribble," she was underscoring the prevailing sentiment that athletes should keep their opinions to themselves (Galily, 2019). Similarly, Donald Trump encouraged the NFL to fire players who refused to stand for the national anthem (Thomas, 2020). This is not something that white athletes encounter when they speak up about politics and other issues outside of sports.

Social Media as a Tool for Social Change

Despite this pressure, many athletes are still raising their voices on controversial topics and now are utilizing social media to do so on their terms and timelines. Social media offers the ability to generate and share unfiltered content directly with global audiences. For athletes, they no longer must wait "until the TV cameras are focused on them to advocate for social and political issues" (Schmittel & Sanderson, 2015, p. 333). Following the tragic death of Trayvon Martin, sports activism saw an energized rebirth as Twitter, now known as X, was deemed a "viable mechanism for African American and other minority athletes to engage in activism and initiate important conversations about social justice issues" (Schmittel & Sanderson, 2015, p. 332). Simply put, social media creates connections that allow athletes to become part of larger networks, acquire knowledge, and resist (Yan et al., 2018, p. 412).

A particularly popular tool for X activism, is the hashtag (Gross, 2018). Through social media, users can disseminate information widely and quickly, and the hashtag symbol (#) allows for marking and indexing conversations (Bonilla & Rosa, 2015). The hashtag "allows users who are territorially displaced to feel like they are united across both space and time" (Bonilla and Rosa, 2015, p. 7). "In the last several years, numerous racialized hashtags—or *Blacktags*—have sprouted up in response to current events affecting the Black community" (Gross, 2018). They may be used to demonstrate "racial solidarity (i.e., #IAmTrayvon), critique racist bias (i.e., #OscarsSoWhite), or connect with larger a larger activist movement (i.e., #BlackLivesMatter)" (Gross, 2018, p. 423). Fraley and Kean (2024) demonstrated how the hashtag #MoreThanAnAthlete (#MTAA) emerged as a phrase and has grown into a movement. While the use of hashtags serves as an amplifier (Gross, 2018), creating awareness and potentially leading to action around an issue, this specific hashtag, #MTAA, and its message have given people a way to express themselves on and off the field of play and show that they are more than what the world says they should be. What started as a simple statement has emerged into a thriving movement. Seeing sport as a powerful site for activism, this research hopes to show how increased access to Black voices and perspectives, and images allows athletes to connect with others and share their truths. This process also makes visible realities and experiences not otherwise readily seen or articulated. Ultimately, "in a world where microaggressions of all kinds are very real, the virtual support shown in one's community through sharing images of goodwill and support can in fact make a difference" (Vie, 2014, p. 8).

Citizen journalists utilizing X allow typically marginalized voices a platform to reach wider audiences. X's power can be to elevate previously unknown stories into the national spotlight. X also serves as a place of communication, rapid information dissemination, and knowledge circulation. Black Twitter has become a space for "connecting networks, highlighting #hashtags, and popularizing the #BlackLivesMatter movement" (Hawkins, 2023, p. 2). (Black Twitter, now X, refers to the community of posts, authors, topics that focus on the Black experience and is not a separate platform). In addition, Black X allows individuals to "collectively organize, offer support, and increase visibility online for Black people and issues that matter to them," (Auxier, 2020, p. 1). "BLM-centered hashtags like #SayHerName, #HandsUpDontShoot,

#IfTheyGunMeDown, and #BlackLivesMatter circulated through X and often appeared as trending topics" (Hawkins, 2023, p.3). According to data from X, until 2019, #Ferguson was the single most-used hashtag in the platform's history, while #BlackLivesMatter was third (Bonilla & Rosa, 2015). Hashtags also "increase unity and draw attention to inequality, and erasure of important issues like police brutality" (Hawkins, 2023, p. 3). Some have questioned the usefulness of hashtag activism, (Hooge et al., 2015) but others (Vie, 2014) think the awareness digital activism creates can lead to action and potentially social change.

Imagery as a Tool for Social Change

Hand in hand with the hashtag, the images that accompany a tweet can have a powerful impact. Altogether, these component parts tell a story and provide a platform to those who might typically be marginalized. As Gallagher and Zagacki (2007) noted, photography may function to force the consumer "to look at subjects they have otherwise chosen to ignore" (p. 116). In addition, images were successful in transforming people's hearts and minds about race because they functioned rhetorically to "evoke common humanity" and "challenge the established images of blacks" (Gallagher & Zagacki, 2007, p. 113). This occurs as images disregard established caricatures, recognize the other, and connect political concepts to individual lives (Gallagher & Zagacki, 2007). Gross (2018) explains that photographs serve as mechanisms for addressing misrepresentation or objectification. For example, individuals have used imagery strategically through "respectable" presentation of Civil Rights leaders (Gross, 2018). Photographs of Black family life in the 1960s captured by Gordon Parks, revealed to white Americans the reality of segregation and racial discrimination (Google Arts & Culture, n.d.) and broadcast images seen on the nightly news have been credited with helping to impact white attitudes regarding the Civil Rights Movement as viewers witnessed the violence of dogs and firehoses turned on peaceful protesters (The Paley Center for Media, n.d.). Today, X images highlight how photographic images can be a tool for resistance, reframing, reconnecting, and reestablishing humanity (Gross, 2018). Research of major media outlets' X feeds following the shooting of Michael Brown, found a separation between police and protestors creating a racial and social divide for the consumer (Cowart et al., 2016).

The research presented here connects the examination of social media and the power of imagery and focuses on themes of social injustice and police brutality, along with how athletes use their voices as points of resistance and protest in the wake of the George Floyd murder. We demonstrate how, following the tragic murder of George Floyd, athlete activists took to X to demonstrate that they are more than athletes, connect with the larger activist community, and demand equality and justice. In this process, images were used intentionally, strategically, and powerfully, to share missing and misrepresented perspectives, challenge misguided/misleading but widely consumed prevailing narratives and highlight lived experiences of the marginalized. This engagement by high-profile college and professional athletes also moved the conversation to a larger community who may typically be less connected to the concerns of the marginalized, underrepresented, and silenced.

Methods

This study reviewed a collection of images associated with 401 original tweets using #MTAA in the one-month period following George Floyd's murder—May 25, 2020, to June 25, 2020—that contained social justice themes. Initially, the researchers utilized Tweetbinder to generate a cache of all tweets using #MTAA in the one-month period following George Floyd's murder. In total, 2,332 tweets used the hashtag in that period with 726 tweets being original tweets (not retweets). In parsing these 726 original tweets, the researchers selected only those tweets with a social justice message. The determination was made by two independent researchers/coders following typical quantitative methodology for content analyses. Initially training was done by the coders who reviewed the same 20 tweets. The coders discussed all disagreements and then coded an additional 20 tweets. Intercoder reliability of more than 90% was achieved. The sample included 726 original tweets/quote tweets that included the hashtag #MTAA from May 25, 2020, through June 25, 2020. However, only 631 were accessible at the time of analysis. Those unavailable had broken links or discontinued accounts. Of the 631 coded tweets, 401 (64%) had a theme that was relevant to social justice. The rest of this analysis focuses on the images associated with those 401 tweets that were relevant to social justice and were accessible at the time of analysis.

Semiotic visual analysis was used to examine the visual elements of the images associated with the tweets to determine the meanings that might be conveyed to viewers. Researchers considered the signs associated with the images which could include the individuals, materials, colors, language, and arrangement of items or elements within a given photograph. These signs can provide context and meaning to the viewer of the images. After reviewing these signs, the researchers analyzed the overall relationship between the multiple signs found in the images to draw conclusions about the overall connotations or meanings conveyed through exposure to the images. Four dominant themes materialized from this process which have been labeled Historical Perspectives, Solidarity/Challenging the prevailing narrative, "I Can't Breathe," and Widening the Circle.

Results

Historical Perspective

Numerous images tied the reaction to the murder of George Floyd at the hands of a Minneapolis police officer to larger conversations about social justice and police brutality. Athletes used social media to connect this important conversation and to remind people of the long history of athlete activism. The Ali Summit (also known as the Cleveland Summit) resurfaced during this time with images of the athletes attending the Ali press conference appearing multiple times. The Ali Summit refers to a meeting on June 4, 1967, at which 11 Black Athletes and one Black politician met to show support of Muhammed Ali's refusal to enter the draft for the Vietnam War. Participants included Kareem Abdul-Jabbar, Muhammad Ali, Walter Beach, Jim Brown, Willie Davis, Curits McClinton, Bobby Mitchell, Bill Russell, Jim Shorter, Carl Stokes, Sidney Williams, and John Wooten. A press conference held after the summit generated iconic images of the group[1] showing all 12 Black men in suits and ties sitting or standing around a press desk. Another image focused on historical context also included basketball legend Abdul-Jabbar. A contemporary image of NBA stars Lebron James, Carmelo Anthony, Chris Paul, and Dwayne Wade taking the stage at the ESPYs in July 2016, urging others to take a stand and fight for social justice. The image of these four contemporary athletes seemed to harken back to the Ali summit and show the historical connection to the heritage of athlete activism and confronting social justice issues. Images of Tommie Smith and John Carlos appeared quite frequently, as well as pictures of Colin Kaepernick and references to the Tulsa Race Massacre that occurred in 1921. By establishing a direct line between the work of those who came before them with the work current athletes are doing now, these images create a sense of community while also asserting the athletes' right to share their voices and ensure that others are not silenced.

One stark example of the connective tissue between past and present is the image of the raised fist. The raised fist as associated with resistance and protest has its history in the early 20th century where it was adopted by those in the labor movement to illustrate resistance. It has since been used by many groups to illustrate power and resistance. In the 1960, the Black Power movement embraced this action, and the raised fist has been utilized to protest racism and assert Black power. In 1968, the world saw this imagery on the international athletic stage when two US Olympic athletes raised their fists while on the podium in Mexico City (BBC, 2023). Tommie Smith and John Carlos, who received gold and bronze medals respectively in track and field, used this gesture to represent Black pride and unity during a time of heightened civil unrest in the US. As a result of this protest, the two athletes were suspended from the US team, had to leave the Olympic games, and faced threats to their lives and careers (BBC, 2023). In the images reviewed in this research, this gesture of the raised fist was again used by athletes as a symbol of protest. In a collage of images of college basketball player Natasha Cloud, she is seen marching with others wearing a Black Lives Matter shirt in which the words are embossed in white over a red and black image of a raised

---

1. https://en.wikipedia.org/wiki/Cleveland_Summit

fist. Cloud is also seen standing with marchers with her fist raised. When members of the Austin Packers Boys Basketball team participated in a protest and march, several young people were photographed with raised fists. In an image of the Elite girls' youth basketball team, a large group of marchers are standing with fists raised and "I can't breathe" t-shirts. The image of the raised fist in these contemporary images connects the message to a long-standing tradition of using the raised fist as one of power and resistance that has been used by activists, including athletes, in their efforts to bring to light the circumstances suffered by disenfranchised or marginalized individuals. By connecting to these earlier movements and images, the individuals in these images give strength to the raised fist as a symbol of ongoing protest.

Solidarity/Challenging the Dominant Narrative

The notion that athletes should remain quiet on social issues and stay focused on their roles as entertainers is one that continues to circulate widely in society. But challenges to this perspective are becoming more frequent. As has been discussed previously, Fox News anchor Laura Ingraham told LeBron James to shut up and dribble after he discussed numerous topics during a 2018 interview. After the murder of George Floyd, a white NFL quarterback made comments questioning teammates who took a knee during the national anthem. When this player received backlash, Laura Ingraham defended his right to share his perspective. This seemingly double standard ignited a tremendous response on social media. Some of the most common images found related to the Ingraham/LeBron conflict included everything from screen shots of Ingraham during a segment called Jocks on Politics to artist renditions of James landing on Ingraham during a dunk shot on the basketball court. In addition, other images highlighted support for athletes sharing their voices and reminded us of how influential these voices can be.

"I Can't Breathe"

Until very recently, chokeholds, or conscious and unconscious neck restraints, have been common practice among police departments in the US to incapacitate individuals (St. Fleur, 2020). In fact, even in municipalities where the restraint had been banned, some officers have been found to be still using this type of physical restraint. The utilization of this restraint practice has led to the death of many individuals in police custody with the most well know victims being Eric Garner who died in the custody of New York Police in 2017 and George Floyd who died in Minneapolis in 2020 when he was pinned to the ground for 9 minutes and 29 seconds by an officer there. When being held in a chokehold restraint, Eric Garner repeatedly gasped, "I can't breathe" (Balsamo, 2020). After his death, "I can't breathe" became a rallying cry taken up by activists protesting police brutality. In vocalizing their concern over these unnecessary deaths, Lebron James and other NBA players joined the outcry and took to the basketball courts on December 8, 2014, with the phrase "I can't breathe" emblazoned on the front of their warmup shirts.

When George Floyd was held down by Minneapolis police officer Derek Chauvin, Floyd repeatedly pleaded with the police officer restraining him, saying, "I am about to die" and "I can't breathe." Sadly, Floyd ultimately died via suffocation due to this restraint, and "I can't breathe" emerged again as an expressive slogan for those condemning police brutality. In this review of the images associated with #MTAA tweets in our research, we repeatedly noted that marchers carried signs, wore shirts, and held banners reading, "I can't breathe," indicating that this phrase had maintained its importance in the protest lexicon associated with police brutality. One of the more poignant sets of images showed more than 100 marchers with a girls' youth basketball team protesting police brutality who all wore identical black shirts with the words "I can't breathe" inscribed on the front in white letters. The group included the basketball players themselves and other youth and adults. The large group, many of whom wore surgical masks, were participating in a march/rally protesting police brutality and the death of George Floyd. Because the death of George Floyd and the protests that followed took place during the height of the COVID-19 pandemic, marchers were often photographed wearing masks to protect themselves and others from the spread of COVID-19. Masks most often seen in the images in this study were the blue and white papery surgical masks which became ubiquitous during the pandemic. Marchers also wore improvised masks, using bandanas, pieces of cloth, and other face coverings in addition to the more common medical masks. The mask provides an interesting visual statement considering the essential nature of breathing. Just as Eric Garner and George Floyd were robbed of life because they could not breathe, COVID-19 also kills those it infects by making it impossible to breathe. During the public response to Floyd's death, marchers took to the streets to protest police brutality but did so wearing masks to avoid the deadly disease COVID-19. However, many marchers used their masks to connect to and amplify Floyd's death by embellishing their masks with the words, "I can't breathe." In multiple images, marchers used markers to write these words on their masks or had it professionally printed on cloth masks. Thus, the wearing of masks both was both purposeful and a way to magnify the brutality of Floyd's death and bring to stark relief the importance of breathing to each of our lives. Masks emblazoned with "I can't breathe," reassert the message of the importance of breathing in our lives and the damage that can come when that essential physical act is obstructed.

Widening the Circle

As has been mentioned in this paper, athletes have been involved in activism for decades. One focus of this research into the images associated with #MTAA is the solidarity that athletes have shown in connecting with the larger community in the aftermath of the George Floyd murder. In utilizing the hashtag #MTAA, athletes are connecting themselves with the community outside of their world of athletics and focusing on the current social justice landscape. In addition to professional athletes like Lebron James standing up for social justice, the images in this study show a diversity of those engaging with #MTAA. A wider swath of athletes is becoming engaged and getting involved. Female athletes, those of different races, and individuals involved in college and youth sports have begun to speak up whereas in the past we have seen much of the activism come from Olympic or professional athletes and males. The inclusion of female, racially diverse, and collegiate athletes expands the conversation and creates a sense of confidence and safety for those whose voices have not always been valued.

Female athletes have demanded they be taken seriously as athletes for years, and now they are reminding us that they too are more than an athlete. Women in college and professional sports have become vocal in their support of social justice issues and the fight against police brutality. Members of the WNBA Minnesota Lynx posted photos of themselves in black t-shirts with the words Change Starts With Us, Justice and Accountability emblazoned on the front. Lexi Brown, from the Lynx, spoke out in a press conference saying, "If you don't see something wrong with our country right now, then you are part of the problem." This quote was posted on X along with her photo from that press conference. Zoe Christensen from the Bemidji State University's women's track and field team posted a link to a news story from the Lakeland PBS news which included a photo of Christensen's participation in a march with the words, "God has provided me with this platform, and I will continue to speak up". Natasha Cloud participated in marches wearing a Black Lives Matter shirt. Her image was captured and shared repeatedly on X during the time period of this study as part of other people's original posts in addition to her own. Female athletes were very visible in this community and shared images of themselves standing in solidarity with one another, but also with the larger community. Tennis professional Naomi Osaka (a woman of Haitian and Japanese descent) reminded people why all voices matter and why she was going to use her platform to "facilitate change." Another female collegiate basketball player posted a picture of herself on the basketball court next to a picture of herself with a Black Lives Matter sign on the steps of a courthouse. Her caption read "if you don't support me with this [referencing the protest] ... then don't support me with that [basketball] ... Simple." Similarly, a professional basketball player posted a picture of herself in a More Than An Athlete shirt next to her thoughts on what it means to be Black in America today. In addition to women as individual athletes becoming more visible in this protest, college teams have come out to vocally support social justice activism. Mississippi State Softball posted a computer drawn image of a huddle of players with their hands in the circle, one as a raised fist, with the caption "We Are Stronger Together." Not only are these teams and individuals posting these images, but they are being picked up and shared by others. These images and comments tell the story of individuals who see themselves as part of the solution and part of a powerful history of athletes using their voices for good. These images also include multiple racial backgrounds indicating that the circle is widening beyond a single gender or race in allowing voices to be heard. While female voices are often overlooked in history, these athletes made certain they were heard and that their participation was important.

Men's college sports also showed solidarity with their community on the topic of police brutality. The Missouri Tigers football team joined a school wide march on June 4 to protest the murder of George Floyd. Seth Towns, Harvard graduate and men's basketball player posted images of himself in his graduation cap along with images of his arrest during a rally protesting the murder of George Floyd. Clemson football player, Cornell Powell posted an image of himself and teammate marching. Powell wore an "I can't breathe" masks with others who held signs with a raised fist depicted or wore Black Lives Matters shirts.

Discussion

As this research has shown, in the days after the murder of George Floyd, athletes as individuals were seeking community, striving for equality and justice, and valuing the lived experiences of others. Utilizing powerful images presented through social media, they told stories of solidarity, connected to past social justice movements, and made way for even more voices. These were tough times, but people were responding to the challenge and creating spaces to come together, lean on one another, and share their perspectives. In the midst of this simultaneous disruption, conflict, and turmoil, we saw courage, growth, and understanding gaining a foothold. Black lives did matter. And athletes were seen as more than athletes. Once hesitant or dismissed voices were now not only part of the conversation, but the ones driving it. Change was occurring. Calls for diversity, equity, and inclusion garnered responses. X and hashtags had the power to reduce the distance between individuals and create and support social movements, and individuals sought and found communities of like-minded people.

We recognize that this research was limited in scope in that it focused only on the images posted at one specific point in time, one social media platform, and one hashtag. While we believe that this narrow focus was necessary to address the issue of importance to this research, future investigations should look at other platforms such as Instagram and TikTok that are garnering larger and more diverse audiences. We would also recommend investigating other social justice topics and related hashtags to determine how athletes are continuing to use social media to raise their voices.

This research began by reviewing the messages that were prevalent on social media in the summer of 2020 the month after the murder of George Floyd and at the height of the global COVID-19 pandemic. As discussed, in response to these protests, a large number of people, many of those in decision making positions, felt the impact of these messages and began working for change. In opposition to the negative backlash felt by Colin Kaepernick when he took a knee, these athletes were being heard and were able to affect real change. However, at the time of this writing, we are experiencing a very different rhetoric on topics related to social justice. We are witnessing change once again. The current landscape under President Donald Trump is one that stifles voices regarding social justice issues and terms like diversity, equity, and inclusion are under attack. It is hard to say how athletes and other individuals will respond to the next incident of police brutality or attack on civil liberties.

References

Auxier, B. (2020, December 14). *Social media continue to be important political outlets for Black Americans*. Pew Research Center. https://www.pewresearch.org/fact-tank/2020/12/11/social-media-continue-to-be-important-political-outlets-for-black-americans/

Balsamo, M. (2020, June 8). Was officer's knee on George Floyd's neck authorized? *AP News*. https://apnews.com/article/was-officer-knee-on-george-floyd-neck-authorized-639cab5a670173ea9cc311db4386abf2

BBC. (2023, October 11). In history: How Tommie Smith and John Carlos's protest at the 1968 Mexico City Olympics shook the world. *BBC Culture*. https://www.bbc.com/culture/article/20231011-in-history-how-tommie-smith-and-john-carloss-protest-at-the-1968-mexico-city-olympics-shook-the-world

Bonilla, Y., and Rosa, J. (2015). #Ferguson: Digital protest, Hashtag ethnography, and the racial politics of social media in the United States. *American Ethnologist*, 42(1), 4–17. https://doi.org/10.1111/amet.12112

Bryant, H. (2018). *The Heritage: Black athletes, a divided America, and the politics of patriotism*. Beacon Press.

Cooper, J., Macaulay, C., and Rodriguez, S. (2019). Race and resistance: A typology of African American sport activism. *International Review for the Sociology of Sport*, 54(2), 151–181.

Cowart, H. S., Saunders, L. M., & Blackstone, G. E. (2016). Picture a protest: Analyzing media images tweeted from Ferguson. *Social Media + Society*, 2(4). https://doi.org/10.1177/2056305116674029

Fraley, T. and Kean, L. (2024). Twittersphere, sports, and the creation of an (activist) community: Morethananathlete. In G. Abeza & J. Sanderson (Eds.), *Social media in sport: Evidence-based perspectives* (pp. 48–67). Routledge.

Freelon D., McIlwain C. D., & Clark M. D. (2016). Beyond the hashtags: #Ferguson, #Blacklivesmatter, and the online struggle for offline justice. *SSRN Electronic Journal*. https://doi.org/10.2139/ssrn.2747066

Galily, Y. (2019). "Shut up and dribble!"? Athletes' activism in the age of Twittersphere: The case of LeBron James. *Technology in Society*, 58, 1–4.

Gallagher, V. J., & Zagacki, K. S. (2007). Visibility and rhetoric: Epiphanies and transformations in the *Life* photographs of the Selma Marches of 1965. *Rhetoric Society Quarterly*, 37(2), 113–135. https://doi.org/10.1080/02773940601016056

Google Arts & Culture. (n.d.). VgURPkiyouv-Lw. https://artsandculture.google.com/story/VgURPkiyouv-Lw

Gross, N. (2017). #IfTheyGunnedMeDown: The double consciousness of Black youth in response to oppressive media. *Souls, 19*(4), 416–437. https://doi.org/10.1080/10999949.2018.1441587

Hawkins, D. S. (2023). "When you search a #hashtag, it feels like you're searching for death:" Black Twitter and communication about police brutality within the Black community. *Social Media + Society, 9*(2). https://doi.org/10.1177/20563051231179705

Hooge, M., Marien S., & Oser, J. (2015, February 28). "Hashtag activism" is not the solution to democratic inequality. Democratic Audit blog. http://www.democraticaudit.com/2015/02/28/hashtag-activism-is-not-the-solution-to-democratic-inequality/

Kaufman, P. (2008). Boos, bans, and other backlash: The consequences of being an activist athlete. *Humanity & Society, 32*, 215–237.

Schmidt, S. (2018). Sport reporting in an era of activism: Examining the intersection of sport media and social activism. *International Journal of Sport Communication, 11*, 2–17.

Schmittel, A., & Sanderson, J. (2015). Talking about Trayvon in 140 characters: Exploring NFL players' tweets about the George Zimmerman verdict. *Journal of Sport and Social Issues, 39*(4), 332–345.

St. Fleur, N. (2020, June 16). How decades of bans on police chokeholds have fallen short. *NPR*. https://www.npr.org/2020/06/16/877527974/how-decades-of-bans-on-police-chokeholds-have-fallen-short

Thomas, M. (2020, June 22). George Floyd's tragic death may forever change the sports landscape. *Sportscasting.com*. https://www.sportscasting.com/george-floyds-tragic-death-may-forever-change-the-sports-landscape/

Trimbur, L. (2019). Taking a knee, making a stand: Social justice, Trump America, and the politics of sport. *Quest, 71*(2), 252–265

Vie S. (2014). In defense of "slacktivism": The Human Rights Campaign Facebook logo as digital activism. *First Monday, 19*(4), 1–15.

Wiggins, DK. (2000). Critical events affecting racism in athletics. In D. Brooks & R. (Eds.), *Racism in college athletics: The African American athlete's experience* (2nd ed., pp. 16–36). Fitness Information Technology.

Williams, A. L. (2022). The heritage strikes back: Athlete activism, Black Lives Matter, and the iconic fifth wave of activism in the (W)NBA bubble. *Cultural Studies-Critical Methodologies, 22*(3), 266–275.

Yan, G., Pegoraro, A., & Watanbe, N. (2018). Student-athletes' Organizations of activism at the University of Missouri: Resource mobilization on Twitter, *Journal of Sport Management, 32*, 24–37.

CHAPTER FIVE | OLGA O'TOOLE

Unraveling Conflicting Attitudes Toward Rape

Victimization in Discourse and the Fine Line Between a Good and Bad Victim

Abstract

Victimology studies have pointed to several factors that might be viewed as contributing to the reasons for which a person might be raped, including precipitation, lifestyle, and deviant place (Hannon, 2004). In assessing the level of victim-blaming that takes place in public discourses (i.e., blame attribution theories (Grubb & Turner, 2012), rape victims are appraised either negatively or positively depending on the circumstances surrounding the assault. This includes the events accompanying the rape, the relationship or lack thereof with the alleged rapist, and the perceived lifestyle of the victim. This conflict of differing attitudes toward rape victims forms so-called borders between victim-supporting discourses and victim-blaming ones. As one site in which conflicting ideas of what makes an acceptable rape victim are comments sections in online media, the analysis investigates digital comments taken from American news media texts about rape written between 2015 and 2023. Three types of rape are analyzed for the linguistic representations of attitudes to rape victims in cases of stranger rape (including violent rapes committed by more than one offender), acquaintance rape, and rape in which the perpetrator is a well-known (i.e., famous) figure. In particular, the stance of online users toward victims is analyzed where indirect appraisement of actors in rape is concerned, including metaphorical representations of actors, as well as expressions of modality and negation. This analysis demonstrates that more direct, negative evaluation is expressed toward victims of acquaintance rape and rape in which the offender is a well-known or famous individual.

Keywords: rape victim-blaming, discursive evaluation, critical discourse analysis

Introduction

The evaluation of rape as a crime and the actors involved in rape is a subject that has received attention from sociologists, psychologists, and linguists alike (Ehrlich, 2001).

This paper's focus is seated in critical discourse analysis (CDA); however, it does not forego the importance of sociological aspects of researching a phenomenon like rape and rape victim-blaming. The "borders" investigated in this paper are those that exist in defining a victim of rape and the attitudes socially presented on their subject, i.e., what makes the difference between a good and bad victim.

The literature on victimization has highlighted that the circumstances of rape might lead to the occurrence of the crime, but that this, in turn, contributes to the social attitudes held about the rape victim. Nils Christie's (1986) seminal paper presenting a theoretical framework to outline the ideal victim posits that in the eyes of the public, an ideal victim possesses six basic characteristics, namely 1) weakness, 2) blamelessness, 3) nobility, as in they were carrying out a noble task at the time of their victimization, 4) being harmed by an evil force or actor, as well as 5) the forces in question. Christie's (1986) work refers to instances of rape that occur under varying circumstances. In his description, the treatment of rape victims presents itself as very circumstantial—i.e., if a young woman, who is a virgin, is raped after committing a noble act or something heroic, she is likely to be viewed as an ideal victim. Conversely, a woman who has been raped by her spouse does not possess traits that would make her blameless—after all, as sometimes the logic might go, she chose to marry this individual. Although Christie's (1986) paper has been criticized for its lack of empirical grounds, it brought to light the role of the perception of victims in social attitudes.

Similar observations of social attitudes can be made about publicized online discourses about rape, which tend to fall in line with the harmful stereotypes that classify rape victims as either good or bad actors along with the circumstances of rape. It has been argued that discourse in rape trial and sexual assault proceedings contribute to the revictimization of rape victims, as well as legitimizing "normative views of female and male sexuality" within situations of heterosexual sexual interaction (Sauntson, 2020, p. 117; Ehrlich, 2007), discourses of comments online do the same. Therefore, this analysis integrates criminalization and sociological theories of victimization with discourse analysis to understand how institutionalized discourse can legitimize victim-blaming by embedding such victimology frameworks into public consciousness. Of course, although the comments analyzed in this paper refer to rape cases in which the victims were female, it should be noted that not all rape victims are women.

Social Information Processing Theory and Discourse Analysis

One way of viewing the role of discourse in constructing social perception, in our case that of the actors[1] present in rape crimes, is through the lens of internet

---

1. I use the term actors here, as it is suitable when discussing people and the roles they play in society and how they are built in discourse (Touraine, 2000; van Leeuwen, 2013).

communication—i.e., communication that does not necessarily take place face-to-face. *Social Information Processing Theory*, developed by Joseph Walther (1992), explains how interpersonal communication can develop through computer-mediated communication (CMC) despite the prevalent absence of nonverbal cues. The theory posits that information can be exchanged without verbal cues, albeit at a slower rate, because humans naturally seek affiliation through communication, even in online contexts and spaces. This theory can be seen as interacting with theories on how collective discourses emerge, looking specifically at how verbal adaptation is used to convey emotion and how relationships are developed using in-group and out-group language, including constructions of ideological squaring, where a dichotomy between in-groups and out-groups is made very clear in discourse and discursive exchange (Van Dijk, 2011).

This theory is intrinsically tied to discourse, as discourse analysis can then be used to investigate and examine patterns in language use to identify stance and evaluation. Such an approach helps to look at how the framing of the victim and perpetrator (either negative or positive) comes about through social information processing theory (SIPT) but also provides insight into how individuals adapt impression management on the subject, and relational communication strategies within the constraints of CMC. As a result, the analysis can be deepened by the capacity of discourse analysis or critical discourse analysis to deconstruct the linguistic and discursive patterns that underlie these processes. The interdisciplinary integration of SIPT and DA may yield unique insights into the (oftentimes social) formation of attitudes, cultural norms, and resistance related to sexual assault.

Victimology Studies

As a distinct subdiscipline of criminology studies, victimology studies have pointed to several factors that might be viewed as contributing to the reasons for which a person might be raped, including *precipitation, lifestyle*, and *deviant place* (Hannon, 2004). Although these theories do not seek to blame victims of crimes for being victimized, they can be theoretically viewed, in part, as informing opinions about victims, not only the criminal justice system. In assessing the level of victim-blaming that takes place in public discourses (i.e., blame attribution theories (Grubb & Turner, 2012)), rape victims are evaluated either negatively or with a degree of sympathy in conjunction with the circumstances of the rape. This includes the circumstances of rape, the relationship with the alleged rapist, and the perceived lifestyle of the victim, adhering, as such, to social ideologies. It is for this reason that theories gleaned from victimology studies are used here as interacting mechanisms that contribute to the social attitudes toward victims—located in public discourse.

This paper draws from that idea, as the analysis pertains to the discursive construction of actors and events in comments written by anonymous internet users.

Such an examination of discourse aims to demonstrate that the negative and positive evaluation of actors and events in rape are expressed through indirect and direct evaluation by internet users who write comments in the online space that accompanies articles about rape (Mills & Grainger, 2016). This emerges from the overarching social context of revictimization and secondary victimization of victims in both American and Polish cultures, contributing to what can be referred to as discursive secondary victimization. The reason I highlight the implications that such discourse has for the victim of rape is the fact that modern scholasticism about rape has made a concerted effort to combat the problem of victim-blaming as a rising social phenomenon.

Additionally, Grant and Woodhams (2007) have extensively studied rape from a forensic linguistic perspective and conclude that rape is a social"—or, rather, antisocial—activity that can be divided into various "phases" (p. 3). These phases have been distinguished as the opening, raping, and escape in some of the literature (Holmström & Burgess, 1979), and initiation/approach/acquisition for the initial stage, offence/maintenance for the rape stage, and closure for the final stage, making for a description that goes beyond simply stranger rape situations (Dale et al., 1997; Davies, 1992). According to Grant and Woodhams (2007), the fact that rape as an activity possesses these stages provides evidence for its status as a social activity (pp. 3–4).

Several typologies of rape have been delineated in the literature and have been placed into the following types: blitz attacks, surprise attacks, and con attacks (Grant & Woodhams 2007, p. 3), as well as the better known distinction between *stranger rape* ("where victim and perpetrator are completely unknown to each other," *acquaintance rape* (in which "the victim and the perpetrator know each other, but have not had a sexual relationship," and *contact rape* "when the victim and the perpetrator have interacted in a romantic way or been in a situation that could evolve into a sexual relationship" (Friis-Rødel et al., 2021, pp. 102–103)). The rape typology relevant to this work is the more simplified one (and also more prevalently used), and includes acquaintance rape—including rape by a famous or well-known figure—and stranger rape as more general categories has made it easier to classify the rape type according to the information given in the articles under which the comments are located.

Victim Precipitation, Perceived Lifestyle, and Deviant Place

This paper takes as its core point of departure the criminological theories that describe and categorize victims, making victim-blaming seem circumstantial in informing victim-blaming or supporting discourse, including rape precipitation, lifestyle, and deviant place. These particular theories have been chosen as they are viewed as adequately describing and reflecting stereotypical beliefs about the circumstances in which rape might occur.

For one, victim precipitation, which is considered controversial, even in criminology (Petherick, 2017), has been defined as taking into account the characteristics or traits of a victim as provoking or initiating the crime. The notion is understood in victimology studies as circumstances that lead a person to be victimized in the first place, including factors such as race, ethnicity, and gender or gender identity (Petherick & Sinnamon, 2013). Lifestyle theory, on the other hand, suggests that people might become victims of a crime because of the choices they make, as well as their lifestyle (Turanovic, 2018). This can be understood as a reflection of one common rape myth, namely that a woman with a history of promiscuity cannot be raped (Iconis, 2008). Finally, deviant place theory posits that the place the crime occurred, or where a victim goes, plays a role in a person's victimization.

It is important to bear in mind that victimology studies uses these theories in a slightly different way, however, they can be seen as informing social choices to apply such theories to sexual crimes, which remain complex and intrinsically tied to gendered constructs and the reproduction of harmful stereotypes.

Rape Victimization

In investigating attitudes toward rape and sexual assault and any tendencies to engage in victim-blaming, it is crucial to acknowledge the impact of cognitive biases as well as their sources should be investigated. One of the key notions tied to acts of expressing negative perceptions of victims of rape (in this case, female victims) is what Williams (1984) called *secondary victimization*—the process by which a victim of the primary experience of rape "can be further victimized by negative and judgmental reactions following the rape incident, which may prompt feelings of guilt or shame *on the part of the victims*" (p. 67) regarding their role in the crime. Secondary victimization usually takes place at the hands of law enforcement (Patterson, 2011), but has also been described as coming about as a result of negative judgement expressed by third parties challenging the victim's honesty, morality, and soundness of mind. As such, this phenomenon can be investigated in particular from a critical discourse analysis perspective by looking at digital comments underneath articles about rape.

Secondary victimization is also intrinsically tied to theories that takes social biases surrounding rape into account, including *attribution theory*, which can be applied when investigating the placement of blame on rape victims by others. The theory posits that women who are the victim of rape are oftentimes judged by others as being responsible for what happened to them (Grubb & Turner, 2012). Attribution theory "relates to the way that individuals allocate or attribute responsibility to individual actors within a scenario" (Grubb & Turner, 2012, 444). The research on the subject of victim-blaming has demonstrated that such acts of attributing blame or sympathizing with a victim in a crime are influenced by various cognitive and motivational biases, resulting in an interpretation of the event that tends to be less factual. It is believed that attribution-making is impacted by cultural and personal differences (Maddux & Yuki, 2006).

Although acquaintance rape has been found to generate higher levels of blame attribution (Personn et al., 2018), the question of where victim-blaming occurs is of general importance to this work as is considering all types of rape to investigate the way that victim-blaming takes place in the American and Polish cultural contexts on a discursive basis. Blame attribution in the case of rape has been linked predominantly with aggressively sexist attitudes (Personn et al., 2018).

In general, attribution theory has provided researchers with a basis to investigate the way that victims of a crime are socially perceived, in this case, the victims of rape, and will be used as a guiding theoretical basis for the critical linguistic investigation of victim-blaming as it forms the cusp of where the boundaries of evaluative discursive behaviors meet.

Accounting for Rape Myths

Similarly to the reproduction of victimization theories in public discourse, rape myths are also accounted for in public opinion of the role that a victim plays in sexual crime. It has been found that in some cultures, people believe that rape is a justifiable act that is a natural consequence of provocative behavior and innate masculine sexual desire. This essentialist claim that rape is a natural human action (re)produces a variety of *rape myths*, which "are generalized and false beliefs about sexual assault that trivialize a sexual assault or suggest that a sexual assault did not occur" (Franiuk et al., 2008, p. 288). Some existing rape myths, as listed by Burt (1980, p. 217), which still apply today include "only bad girls get raped," "any healthy woman can resist a rapist if she really wants to," "women ask to be raped," "they 'cry rape' when they've been jilted or have something to cover up," "rape is about sex," and that "rapists are self-starved or insane."

It becomes clear that common rape myths can be informed by the victimology theories investigated, as they oftentimes refer to the same or similar circumstances surrounding rape. This includes the discursive dissection of where a victim was at the time of the crime, what they looked like, as well as what kind of lifestyle they represent.

Hypotheses and Research Questions

For the presented paper, the following two hypotheses were set forth for the qualitative linguistic analysis of blame attribution in digital comments and its relationship with victimization as a reflection of social attitudes among internet users. I have departed from the first hypothesis, reflected in O'Toole (2022), narrowing the analysis down to types of rape that might impinge on social attitudes. Hypothesis 2 has been emphasized in italics, as it specifies the aims of the paper to focus on the typology of rape and how the expression of evaluation in the form of negative or positive appraisal in discourse—here viewed as a dependent variable—depends on the circumstances of the crime.

H1. The negative evaluation of actors and events in rape is expressed through both indirect and direct discursive strategies by internet users who publish comments accompanying online articles about rape.

H2. Certain rape cases are accompanied by more victim-blaming comments, i.e., the nature of the rape case—and the circumstances—has an impact on how the victim is perceived (directly/indirectly) and language negatively framing a victim can be found in comments where the victim is seen as the following:

a) Being easily targetable (i.e., a young woman who is drunk or underdressed?)
b) Having a lifestyle that is socially deemed immoral in a way
c) Having been in the wrong place at the wrong time"

The present analysis aims to answer the following research questions:

RQ1. Is victimization reflected in the digital comments found underneath articles about stranger rape, acquaintance rape, and rape in which the offender is a well-known or famous figure?

RQ2. Is the evaluation of victims indirect or direct in the discourse of digital comments, and in what cases?

Thus, taking as the basis for this particular approach to the material victimization theories of precipitation, lifestyle and deviant place, I set them against the backdrop of rape myths analyzed in the work for my PhD dissertation (O'Toole, 2022).

Materials and Methods

The present project presents an extension on the materials gathered for a larger PhD project that was built on a specialized corpus of digital comments in the Polish language, as well as in American English (O'Toole, 2022). The examination presented in this paper is based in qualitative critical linguistic analysis that takes from Charmaz's (2004) grounded theory and content analysis methods used to investigate recurring patterns in digital comments about rape victims, offenders, and rape itself in American English comments located underneath American published articles about rape (i.e., constituting their adjacent, physical context). The digital comments in question were uploaded to the CAQDAS software MaxQDA (Yu, 2006; Verbi, 2024) and coded for sociological—those related to victimization and rape myths—and linguistic categories.

The aforementioned theories, blame attribution theory, and criminological theories of victim precipitation, perceived lifestyle, and deviant place are here viewed as informing attitudes expressed about and/or toward the person harmed in the crime. As such, sociological investigation combined with linguistic investigation provides a holistic view on rape victim blaming—the sociological theory aiding in the provision of evidence for different types of victim-blaming, and the linguistic strategies giving systematic insight of how attitudes are linguistically manifest. By looking at the evaluation of the rape victim—including victim-blaming and victim-supporting comments—and the circumstances surrounding the rape from a critical discourse analysis (CDA) standpoint, here seated within grounded theory, the examination of online discourse allows to see how the type of rape is relevant to the evaluation of the victim, whether positive or negative.

Bringing evaluation in discourse under a critical lens, namely the discourse of digital comments written by anonymous internet users, can demonstrate that evaluative language, as a context-dependent linguistic phenomenon, is amenable to investigation within the scope of the study of a social phenomenon and the action that surrounds it. This also follows the assumption that evaluation arises as an outward expression of attitudes or beliefs regarding that subject.

Linguistic or discursive evaluation is a subject integral to critical discourse studies that examines social attitudes and their impinging influence on ideological constructs embedded in social thought. The evaluative language studied in this paper is broken down into the positive and negative evaluation of the rape victim in a sexual crime, which is related to and reflective of the attribution of blame to the victim or both the victim and the perpetrator. This, in my view, is an important contributor to secondary victimization overall.

The material investigated was a small, specialized corpus made up of 326 comments accompanying articles on rape (some articles included images or visual representations of the victims or perpetrators, however the multimodal aspect has not been analyzed in this work) written in a ten-year period (between 2014 and 2024)[2]—made up of 712 sentences and 19,946 words—on the subject of the three types of rape enumerated earlier, i.e., acquaintance rape, rape by a famous person, and stranger rape.

---

2. A specialized corpus is one that is made up of selected texts, usually for the purpose of researching the discourse of particular genres—in this case, on a specific subject (Flowerdew, 2013). A period of ten years was chosen, by which to select the data, so that the data would reflect a decade of material and not less than that. I considered such a period to be more representative of trends in discourse, and the fact that comments were rather scarce under articles motivated me to collect the data for the specialized corpus over a longer period. I chose to include anonymous comments only from underneath articles about rape due to the ethical questionability of using textual comment data from sites like Facebook.

A brief breakdown of the rape types has been given below, accounting for the number of comments in the categories to provide a broader picture of the corpus that was examined. The comments enumerated in the examples are followed by the year the comments were written as well as what rape type they represent. It should also be noted that the choice to conduct a qualitative analysis on the material was partially motivated by the inconsistencies in the number of comments for each category. Comments pertaining to three types of rape cases were analyzed in the discourse, including 192 comments about acquaintance rape cases, 102 comments on stranger rape, and 32 comments regarding a rape committed by a famous person.

Digital comments are a genre of discourse prevalent on social media sites, as well as on news reporting websites where readers can write comments (i.e., express opinions) on a given subject. They typically range from about 11 to around 400 words, constituting relatively short pieces of text and have been described by Shchipitsina (2015, p. 532) as "short utterances of [online] users about [a] source text." The description of the register, as found in Biber and Egbert (2018) posits that such comments can be characterized by, but are not limited to, present tense verbs, first-person pronouns, mental verbs, contractions, abbreviations, activity verbs, discourse particles, and modals of possibility (pp. 15–17).

The study presents an analysis of English language comments on the subject of rape, taken from articles either about acquaintance rape, stranger rape or rape in which the perpetrator was well known. The comments were divided into those supporting the actors (the victim or offender) and those criticizing (or blaming the actors), then evaluated for their directness and indirectness.

Critical Discourse Analysis

Critical discourse analysis (CDA) can be interpreted as occurring at the intersection of sociology and linguistics as its main aim is to show how power relations are mediated through discourse in spoken or written text (Krzyżanowski, 2016). As a framework, CDA analyzes the ways that power and ideology manifest in discourse and can range from textual analysis to multimodal analysis as a way of investigating how other semiotic sources interact with text to reproduce ideologies. CDA has been viewed as the core for conducting discursive analyses of gender and power (Sauntson, 2020), thus making it a relevant analysis type by which to investigate rape culture in discursive settings. CDA and the aforementioned grounded theory (GT) can be seen as complementary, as both can allow for the inductive discovery and unpacking of categories in discourse data. The categories that emerge in the discourse can be critically interpreted for underlying power structures and ideologies within varying social contexts. Additionally, the iterative cycles of data collection in grounded theory, as well as the further analysis of them, enable researchers to refine their understanding of discourse practices as they uncover how language operates in social power relations. This iterative process neatly aligns with CDA's detailed attention to context and the dynamic nature of discourse.

Hence, when exploring social issues and the language that brings about the effects of discursive constructs, CDA nicely integrates the two, as it views language as a form of social practice, and social behaviors and expressions can be more deeply comprehended through critical inquiry. As such, it is a framework that provides relevant methods of analyzing stance, evaluation and discourse.

Evaluation Types

The discursive investigation of the negative or positive appraisal of a subject and/or any actors involved has been referred to as *evaluation in discourse* (Hunston & Sinclair, 2000; Hunston, 2011). This is also related to the notion of *stance*, which is comparable to an attitude on a subject. Evaluation can be either implicit or explicit, denoting stances that are expressed directly or indirectly. Explicit evaluation refers to the direct expression of a stance on a subject. Implicit evaluation, however, is not always obvious where the meaning behind a text—in this case, comments online—can be inferred, hence underlying implications must be read from the context. It should be made clear at this point that a greater number of comments in the corpus showed victim-blaming attitudes.

As such, implicit evaluation is the type of appraisement that requires processes of deduction from the surrounding context, as well as from the shared knowledge of both writer and reader of a text (i.e., epistemological context). Indirect evaluation has been investigated from linguistic features, including a) questions, b) negation, c) indirect reference to rape myths, d) conditional structures, e) verb choice, f) nominal reference, g) metaphor.

All of the above were considered in looking at how indirect victim-blaming or victim-supporting is accounted for in the digital comments about rape and rape victims.

Explicit evaluation, on the other hand, is more recognizable than implicit evaluation and is indicated more directly, such as by the following criteria, which were investigated in the analysis presented. This included instances of negative name-calling, the presence of direct sentences reflecting victim-blaming attitudes, direct sentences reflecting victim-supporting comments, and overt support for the victim.

Because the category of direct victim-blaming was less populated than indirect blame attribution, I have chosen to present the qualitative analysis of that category first.

Direct Victim-Blaming and Name-Calling

Direct victim-blaming was found in comments about acquaintance rape cases and cases in which a well-known person was the offender or alleged offender. The explicit evaluation of social actors and events is easier to recognize than implicit evaluation, because it can provide sentences that may be understood directly or cultural references that are so heavily ingrained in the social conscience that their meaning undoubtedly occurs at the surface level. The following examples are taken from comments referring to cases in which acquaintance rape occurred.

1. She admitted she offered sexual favors for booze.... **She is equally to blame** in this case. (2014, acquaintance rape)

Direct victim-blaming occurs when a direct statement (cf. example 1) of blame is expressed, making for the most obvious example. Other examples include name-calling of the victim and referring to the rape myth that woman who claim to have been raped might be promiscuous.

2. Looks like if all is true **she whored herself out** for her job. (2019, rape by a famous figure)
3. **She's a call girl** plain and simple. (2019, rape by a famous figure)

The fact that such comments did not occur in the corpus as often as those representing indirect victim-blaming is indicative of the tendency to discuss taboo subjects implicitly (Rosewarne, 2013). This includes subjects that are related to human sexuality, including sexual assault (Allan & Burridge, 2006, p. 145).

Indirect Victim-Blaming in the Corpus

The discursive strategies used by internet users writing comments are rarely directly evaluative. The evaluation is, conversely, often found within the structure of a comment and plausible upon looking at the illocution or conveyed meaning behind the "utterance." The examples below demonstrate the way indirect negative evaluation can follow from the context of a victim knowing the person who allegedly raped her.

4. He was married **and she knew it**. 2) He invites her to his room for a second visit **and she goes. Did she think** they were going to play Scrabble? 3) She says she hated "it" but tells him she liked it. (2019, rape by a famous person)
5. In this case, though I confess I can't help thinking **this would not have happened if the young woman had not allowed herself to get falling-down drunk**. (2017, acquaintance rape).

Example 4 presents a rhetorical conditional question, which in turn calls into question the testimony given by a victim. The fact that her recollection of the rape is doubted also calls her claim that she was raped into question. Other comments either suggested that the victim might be lying or that she might have misremembered a consensual encounter.

6. If she didn't remember anything how did it turn into her worst day? (2015, acquaintance rape).

The above examples have been provided to show that evaluative discourse about rape can take on indirect forms. The knowledge of victimization, as well as of rape myths aid in the interpretation of the comments.

At the Intersection of Evaluation, Precipitation, Lifestyle, and Deviant Place

The original analysis considers comments that are found on news websites, which were posted under articles that dealt with or described cases of stranger rape, acquaintance rape, or rape in which the offender was a well-known person. The analysis, however, has been extended by looking at the typology of rape as having an influence on the stances expressed in the comments—be they victim-blaming or victim-supporting. This was not an aspect considered in the original work.

Also relevant to the analysis is the question of rape myths, which overlap with the victimization theories described at the beginning of this chapter. The following rape myths were found to be most prevalent in the dataset about victims of acquaintance rape and rape by a famous or well-known individual. Some more prevalent rape myths included the belief that if a woman is drunk, it is her fault that she was raped, that there is a tendency for women to lie about being raped, and that victims want attention or fame and therefore claim that they were raped.

Other, less frequently occurring rape myths included that if the victim had consented to one thing, such as going on a date or going to someone's house, that meant automatically agreeing to have sexual intercourse, and that revealing clothing can lead to a woman being raped.

This adherence to rape myths is reflective of victimology theories such as precipitation and lifestyle as well as of a tendency for internet users who comment on such articles to follow the beliefs that lie behind such oftentimes harmful stereotypes. In the following sections I have broken down each victimization theory to see which comments containing attitudes reflect the theories that have been analyzed from a qualitative linguistic perspective.

Evaluation and Precipitation

Since victim precipitation posits that certain characteristics or behaviors of a victim of a crime may trigger a criminal act, I have considered traits that are either appearance-related or personality-based for this part of the analysis. One can note that a focus in comments on the victim's appearance tends toward holding views about precipitation in relation to a person's style of dress or level of attractiveness. This is visible in examples 7 and 8, where the age and attire of the victims is highlighted.

7. How old does the girl look? Maybe he didn't know she was 14. At 13, I looked like I was 16. The way they dress now, is a shame and no one can tell their age. There was a news article on a man whipping his 13-year-old daughter while the Mother looked on and was calling her names. The girl had been gone for 3 days. I couldn't see her face, but her body looked like she could have been 20. (2014, acquaintance rape)
8. Why aren't parents telling their daughters they should be able to get drunk and sashay down a dark alley in a miniskirt, or hang out in a parking garage, and not expect anyone to touch them? (2017, acquaintance rape)

Comments reflecting precipitation were only found with reference to a victim's appearance. The majority of negatively evaluative comments pointed to the fact that a person's lifestyle choices played a role in the assault. Precipitation can be said to go hand in hand with rape myths that consider a woman's appearance or behavior in a given situation to be the reason for the crime.

Evaluation and Lifestyle

Lifestyle theory, on the other hand, explains victimization through the lens of individual choices and behaviors that increase exposure to risk. Here, a person's daily routines, habits, and social associations can make them more vulnerable to crime, which is why associations of rape with alcohol can be viewed as a lifestyle choice, rather than a personality trait. Of course, this can be seen on the level of what a sentence might signify, such as in example 9, where rape is expressed as being a natural consequence of getting alcohol for free.

9. She **herself** admits to **bribing him with sexual favors for booze**!! (2016, acquaintance rape)
10. There just doesn't sound like there is enough evidence—sounds like **she was buzzed a bit when she was picked up** and probably went overboard at the kids house and then blacked out at some point. We have all done things while drunk that we don't remember—at her age reaching the limit doesn't take much. Lesson here—young teenage girls need to **think twice before getting drunk and partying** with older high school boys—it will lead to bad things—some consensual, some not (2016, acquaintance rape)

The following examples also place alcohol consumption among teens and young women as a possible cause for rape, thus directly linking to certain types of behavior to sexual assault.

11. There is no doubt that this fellow did rape this woman. That said, it's just amazing to me that the "victim" takes no responsibility for making herself vulnerable—**by getting falling-down-blacked-out-drunk**. It's all the guy's

fault for taking advantage of her, and if it hadn't happened, she'd have had no remorse for her own behavior. Girls, where are your mothers? Weren't you taught not to put yourself in any situations where your virtue might be questioned (2016, stranger rape)

12. In a college environment, **a woman can get drunk, have sex then regret it and call it rape. It's fairly common for women to drink and have regret sex** then it is for that same woman to be raped. I have more worry toward men because they are at more danger of having their lives ruined by a woman falsely accusing them of rape because a rape victim can heal and recover but a false accusation is more common in colleges and can have affects that can last decades. (2014, acquaintance rape)

13. I have to say that **if two adults are drunk, there is no violence or threat, there has been no rape.** Both parties engaged in sexual relations they might not have if either were sober. It is not helpful, in my opinion, to pretend like this sort of thing is the same as having sex by threat or violence. This false equivalence has caused more harm than good for all parties concerned. (2014, acquaintance rape)

The comments about alcohol consumption and the denial of a rape's occurrence reinforce the harmful myth that a person's intoxication reflects bad conduct and therefore places them at fault for a crime (Huntington et al., 2022). This harmful assumption upholds the idea that a woman should always be on guard in order to avoid the omnipresent possible threat of sexual assault.

Evaluation and Deviant Place

Deviant place theory focuses on the spatial and environmental context of victimization and can be seen as asserting that individuals are more likely to be victimized when they spend time in places that are characterized by social disorganization, high crime rates, and deviant behaviors. It differs from precipitation and lifestyle as it specifically focuses on the physical localization of the victim in conjunction with the crime. This is not a notion that can be ignored in the analysis of rape victim-blaming. The comments about acquaintance rape demonstrate that universal beliefs about campus drinking and going to a person's house after a date are examples of behavior that contribute to a woman's being raped.

14. I put my hand **in a shark tank** and got bit. It's all the sharks fault. (2015, acquaintance rape)

15. Not excusing the players (they should be prosecuted to the limit of the law) but haven't these young women found out that **drinking till you pass out at a frat party isn't a good idea?** (2015, acquaintance rape)

16. But **if you (repeatedly) jump into a lion's den, you're going to get mauled** (2019, rape by a famous figure)

The above examples point to the victim's decision to be present in a place where they might be raped or in the company of a person who might rape them. These examples are presented in the form of sarcastic or ironic remarks, rhetorical questions and conditional constructions that suggest an alternative to the situation and that it might have yielded an outcome other than rape, indirectly pointing to the choices of the victim and how it possibly led to her rape.

Evaluation and Acquaintance Rape or Rape by a Famous Offender

One aspect that has been found to highlight the varying attitudes toward rape victims was the type of rape. Contrarily to the question of lifestyle in which the role of alcohol consumption was linked to the rape, remaining in touch with one's rapist was something to which attention was brought, as in the following examples.

17. **You can't speak well of your rapist** after the "rape" and think anyone will believe your story 10 years later. (2020, rape by a famous figure)
18. Well, there is a difference between having your actual job on the line and "**wanting that big break into show business.**" (2020, rape by a famous figure)
19. Look, I have no idea what behavior is normal after a person is raped. I can attest somewhat to the human sense of preservation. **There is absolutely NO reason to initiate an email, phone call, text to the rapist, praising him**. PERIOD! Yeah, maybe if you ran into that person again (while trying your best to avoid him) and you felt that you needed to put on a good face and smile because you're in fear, maybe I can believe that. But willingly contacting the person again for any reason is suspect. NONE of us were there so all we have to go on is the behavior of the person and these women are not credible to me (in the way that I as a woman would react to a rapist. I don't care about my job that much...and I'm pretty poor). (2020, rape by a famous figure)

Having a past sexual relationship with the offender is indirectly given as a reason to call the rape into question, thus constructing the victim as a liar and even a predator herself. This kind of discursive construction further pushes the rape victim into a position of fault as it plays on stereotypes that if a woman regrets having sex with a man, there is a chance she will claim that she has been raped (Lichty & Gowen, pp. 5543).

20. That woman has low self esteem **to have relations with him again after** that? I think she thought he'd promote her career. When he didn't she let the axe fall. So **she's somewhat of a predator herself**, if that were the case. Everyone quit having extra-marital affairs. Don't get married if you're prone to being a cheat. (2015, rape by a famous figure)

The victim's relationship with the offender, especially in cases where the raped woman was perceived as having received favors from the rapist, links the questionable nature of the relationship with the questionable status of the sexual crime.

Evaluation and the Case of Stranger Rape

More victim-supporting discourse was found under comments that regarded stranger rape. This is seen as a contrast to the mixed comments about acquaintance rape and rape in which the offender was a well-known person. This takes the form of negative lexical reference to the offender and highly negative evaluative language with reference to the crime.

21. This **makes my blood boil** and the law does nothing to a) prevent this d isgusting abuse b) give a proper sentence to the perpetrators and those that condone it. Really hope this young woman gets support but again due to cutbacks this is also limited (2024, stranger rape).
22. My gosh, **not even safe** to walk our OWN streets. (2023, stranger rape)
23. This is **terrible** on all levels (2023, stranger rape)
24. **we should guard** our women
25. This creatures have **predatory instincts** (2023, stranger rape)
26. We **shouldn't let them come near** our homes (2024, stranger rape)

The fact that such comments are only found under articles where a stranger—i.e., a classic or by-the-book—rape occurred speaks volumes to further understanding how discourse manages the placement of victims on the sliding scale between good and bad victim. In the case of acquaintance rape and rape by a famous individual, comments tended to be either indirectly or directly blaming of the victim.

Discussion

The analysis has attempted to prove that by unpacking discourse on sexual crime, one can take note of emergent patterns that reflect stereotypical beliefs about rape. Such stereotypes are reflective of rape myths which are related to both sexual and gendered ideologies, commonly-held beliefs about the role of the victim in a sexual crime, including whether the circumstances of the rape are in some way related to the surrounding circumstances. Because this analysis discusses rape, the investigation of the presence of rape myths in anonymized digital comments demonstrated a tendency for victims of stranger rape to be more sympathetically viewed that those victim of acquaintance rape or rape committed by a famous person. This may be due to the fact that, among other erroneous beliefs, the conviction that knowing a perpetrator should make a potential victim more aware of the surrounding environment, circumstances, or even how they should be monitoring their behavior and therefore should be aware of the possible consequences of supposed improper behavior for that setting.

Therefore, if a victim has been described as being raped in circumstances where nothing might be viewed as tarnishing their reputation, the discourse about their subject might present them in a more positive light and express attitudes and appraisal in favor of the victim. Conversely, if the victim's appearance or behavior, lifestyle choice, or even the place of the rape match up with harmful rape myths that work against the victim, she could be discursively constructed as being more to blame. The idea of the so-called good and bad victim, a dichotomy that should be borne in mind when considering beliefs about the role of the victim in perceptions, is persistent in lay discourse about rape and the actors involved in rape. A "good victim" might be seen as one who fits the description of being naïve, innocent, and completely unrelated to the offender in any way, therefore making the victim of a stranger rape what many might view as a good or better victim. A "bad victim," however, might be someone who has been raped by an acquaintance or has done something to place themselves in the situation, as a number of the comments analyzed have shown that there exists an unspoken expectation of others to be aware of what rape myths might reflect bad victim behavior and place a possible victim into the so-called clutches of the rapist.

The presented study of course has its limitations, namely that the current dataset presents discourse that is negatively evaluative of the victim for the most part and, as such, these small online communities underneath articles on rape might be more biased toward blaming victims. This might result from the fact that they are anonymous and therefore may be more open to being critical and insensitive toward the suffering of the victim and their adverse experience.

Conclusions

By combining victimology and CDA, one can see how language does not simply reflect social biases but actively constructs them. An inadvertent discursive classification of a rape victim into a good and bad victim can be seen to reflect the original victimization attitudes posed by Nils Christie (1986).

Digital comments are largely reflective of evaluative attitudes not only toward the perpetrator of a sexual crime, but also toward the rape victim, contributing to a more global secondary victimization. This is carried out through the publishing of comments that reflect victimization and rape myths in the discourse, as well as overt instances of blame and support of the victim.

Because secondary victimization can make a victim feel bad or guilty about having been raped, such accounts of anonymized discourse may also be viewed as violating victims of rape in the same way. And victims who were raped in situations in which she could be seen as precipitating the crime were more negatively and more strongly evaluated than those who were not. This expression is linked to the nature of the crime, where victims who knew the offender or were raped by a well-known or famous person were more negatively and more strongly evaluated by internet users.

As such, online discourses, the discourse category to which digital comments belong, are demonstrative of a genre that introduces space for users to spread ideologies about women and their role in sexual crime that work against any system attempting to help them in their victimization. This includes the perpetuation of harmful rape myths, which can occur when authors of such comments directly or indirectly refer to a myth as justification for rape or reason that a sexual crime has occurred in conjunction with beliefs that align with rape myths.

To recognize that attitudes toward and beliefs about rape that give rise to secondary victimization or revictimization of the person harmed do not only belong to the institutional settings that deal with it (e.g., the police as an institution or the legal system), and that they are also intimated within various settings, including those that are readily available and made interactive to the public, is a crucial factor in making visible the prevalence of the problem of victim-blaming in American discourse. The reproduction of the stereotypical beliefs surrounding the idea that a victim is in some part, if not fully, to blame for being raped presents itself quite evidently in various discursive settings.

References

Allan, K., & Burridge, K. (2006). *Forbidden words: Taboo and the censoring of language*. Cambridge University Press.

Biber, D., & Egbert, J. (2018). *Register variation online*. Cambridge University Press.

Burt, M. R. (1980). Cultural myths and supports for rape. *Journal of Personality and Social Psychology*, 38(2), 217–220.

Christie, N. (1986). The ideal victim. In E. A. Fattah (Ed.), *From crime policy to victim policy: Reorienting the justice system*, pp. 17–30. Palgrave Macmillan.

Ehrlich, S. (2001). *Representing rape: Language and sexual consent*. Routledge.

Ehrlich, S. (2007). Normative discourses and representations of coerced sex. In J. Cotterill (Ed.), *The language of sexual crime* (pp. 126–138). Palgrave Macmillan UK.

Flowerdew, L. (2013). Corpus-based discourse analysis. In M. Handford & J. P. Gee (Eds.), *The Routledge handbook of discourse analysis* (pp. 174–188). Routledge.

Franiuk, R., Seefelt, J. L., & Vandello, J. A. (2008). Prevalence of rape myths in headlines and their effects on attitudes toward rape. *Sex Roles*, 58, 790–801.

Friis-Rødel, A. M., Leth, P. M., & Astrup, B. S. (2021). Stranger rape; distinctions between the typical rape type and other types of rape. A study based on data from Center for Victims of Sexual Assault. *Journal of Forensic and Legal Medicine*, 80, 102159. https:// doi.org/10.1016 /j.jflm.2021.10215

Grant, T., Woodhams, J. (2007). Rape as social activity: An application of investigative linguistics. In J. Cotterill (Ed.), *The language of sexual crime* (pp. 1–15). Palgrave Macmillan UK.

Hannon, L. (2004). Race, victim precipitated homicide, and the subculture of violence thesis. *The Social Science Journal*, 41(1), 115–121.

Hunston, S. (2011). *Corpus approaches to evaluation: Phraseology and evaluative language*. Routledge.

Hunston, S., & Sinclair, J. (2000). Towards a local grammar of evaluation. In S. Hunston & G. Thompson (Eds.), *Evaluation in text: Authorial stance and the construction of discourse* (pp. 74–101). Oxford University Press.

Huntington, C., Berkowitz, A. D., & Orchowski L.M. (2022). False accusations of sexual assault: Prevalence, misperceptions, and implications for prevention work with men and boys. In L. M. Orchowski & A. D. Berkowitz (Eds.), *Engaging boys and men in sexual assault prevention: Theory, research, and practice*. Academic Press.

Iconis, R. (2008). Rape myth acceptance in college students: A literature review. *Contemporary Issues in Education Research*, 1(2), 47–52. https://doi.org/10.19030/cier.v1i2.1201

Krzyżanowski, M. (2016). Recontextualisation of neoliberalism and the increasingly conceptual nature of discourse: Challenges for critical discourse studies. *Discourse & Society*, 27(3), 308–321.

Lichty, L. F., & Gowen, L. K. (2021). Youth response to rape: Rape myths and social support. *Journal of Interpersonal Violence*, 36(11–12), 5530–5557.

Maddux, W. W., & Yuki, M. (2006). The "ripple effect": Cultural differences in perceptions of the consequences of events. *Personality and Social Psychology Bulletin*, 32(5), 669–683.

MAXQDA. Software for qualitative data analysis, 1989–2024, VERBI Software. Consult. Sozialforschung GmbH, Berlin, Germany.

Mills, S., & Grainger, K. (2016). *Directness and indirectness across cultures*. Springer.

O'Toole, O. (2022) *CMC as a reflection and a source of social ideologies: A critical discourse analysis of rape victim blaming in Polish and American internet communication* [Doctoral dissertation]. Jagiellonian University, JU Repository.

Pesta, R. (2011). Provocation and the point of no return: An analysis of victim-precipitated homicide. Youngstown State University, USA, 1–67

Petherick, W. A., & Sinnamon, G.C.B. (2013). Motivations: Victim and offender perspectives. In W. A. Petherick (Ed.), *Profiling and serial crime: Theoretical and practical issues* (3rd ed., pp. 393–430). Anderson Publishing.

Petherick, W. (2017). Victim precipitation: Why we need to expand upon the theory. *Forensic Research & Criminology International Journal*, 5(2), 262–264.

Sauntson, H. (2020). *Researching language gender and sexuality: A student guide*. Routledge.

Shchipitsina, L. Y. (2015). "Genre status of an online comment." *Vestnik Bashkirskogo Universiteta*, 20(2), 528–532.

Touraine, A. (2000). A method for studying social actors. *Journal of world-systems research*, 900–918.

Turanovic, J. (2018). Toward a life course theory of victimization. In S. H. Decker & K. A. Wright (Eds.), *Criminology and public policy: Putting theory to work* (2nd ed.). Temple University Press.

Van Dijk, T. A. (2011). Discourse and ideology. *Discourse Studies: A Multidisciplinary Introduction*, 2, 379–407.

Van Leeuwen, T. (2013). The representation of social actors. In C. R. Caldas-Coulthard & M. Coulthard (Eds.), *Texts and practices* (pp. 32–70). Routledge.

Walther, J. (2016). Social information processing theory (CMC). In C. R. Berger & M. E. Roloff (Eds.), *The international encyclopedia of interpersonal communication* (1st ed., pp. 1–14). John Wiley & Sons.

Williams, J. E. (1984). Secondary victimization: Confronting public attitudes about rape. *Victimology*, 9(1), 66–81.

Yu, G. (2006). winMAX and MAXQDA Workshop (half day). *School of Language, Linguistics and Area Studies, University of West England*. University of West England, [online].

CHAPTER SIX | CHARLES MEADOWS AND
CARRIE MEADOWS

Voices of Outrage and Support

Understanding Public Reaction to the Larry Nassar Sentencing

Abstract

This study analyzed 8,969 tweets following Larry Nassar's sentencing using a mixed-method approach that combined semantic network analysis and content analysis. The semantic network analysis revealed four major themes based on the interconnections among key concepts: (1) accountability of organizations and individuals, (2) sentencing of Nassar, (3) criticism of Nassar, and (4) support for victims. In addition, the content analysis identified a clear gendered pattern about sexual harassment: women were more likely to discuss victims, whereas men tend to focus on facts and accountability. By uncovering distinct public sentiments and rhetorical patterns surrounding the Larry Nassar sentencing, the findings offered an alternative lens to understand how the public constructed meaning from a major crisis and how individual attributes can play a role in this process. These findings underscored the importance of understanding how the public engage with crisis events on social media. By recognizing the meanings embedded in public discourse and the rhetorical cues that emerge in real time, organizations can more effectively align their crisis communication strategies with public sentiment.

Keywords: Semantic network analysis, social media discourse, gender differences, crisis communication, public sentiment

Literature Review

January 24, 2018, marked the end of one of the most publicized sexual abuse scandals in the United States. It was the day that Judge Rosemarie Aquilina sentenced Larry Nassar to 40 to 175 years in prison on 10 counts of first-degree sexual assault and three counts of felony sexual misconduct. The sentencing followed an intensive investigation about the sexual abuse scandal of Larry Nassar, a former Michigan State University (hereafter MSU) employee and a USA Gymnastics' team physician. As the biggest sex abuse scandal in sports history, this case garnered widespread publicity

(Graham, 2017). Over 300 victims were involved in the investigation and all the organizations involved, MSU, the National Collegiate Athletic Association (hereafter NCAA), USA Gymnastics, and even the U.S. Olympic Committee were accused of violating multiple policies and safety practices designed to protect young women athletes from predators.

The scandal received extensive coverage from media, significantly raising public awareness about the issue of sexual abuse among female athletes. As the events of the Larry Nassar case unfolded, the public witnessed a series of outcomes. For example, beyond the firing and resignation of key personnel in the organizations mentioned above, the Karolyi Ranch, formerly the national training center for the USA Gymnastics was closed. The U.S. Center for SafeSport launched in 2017 to investigate and address child abuse in sports.

The public engaged in widespread conversation on X (formerly Twitter) about the scandal. The magnitude of the crisis was clear as several key actors were mentioned throughout the trial and afterwards. For example, on January 24, 2018, Larry Nassar was the 11th trending keyword on X, and Judge Aquilina's name was trending in the 38th place. Simone Biles, a 2016 Olympic gold medalist, was a trending topic the following day, when she announced that she was a survivor of Nassar's abuse. The series of trending keywords demonstrates that this crisis not only garnered public sentiment on social media but presented a sustained dialogue regarding the events that were unfolding. Therefore, it is of the utmost importance to understand how the public was perceiving and making meaning of the events that were taking place. One means of exploring this question can be found in semantic netwok analysis.

Semantic Network Analyses of Social Media Content

Semantic network analysis (hereafter SNA) has been implemented in communication research as a means of demonstrating the relationships among concepts. Relationships can be revealed by showing the network structure of human communication as clusters and even the relationships among actors and different frames (Shin, 2020). Calabrese et al. (2019) stated that "semantic network analysis can highlight the most salient information in a body of text through developing networks that are representative of meaning" (p. 956). This ability to understand meaning is important to researchers as a large proportion of the population utilizes mediated communication platforms that have an inherent underlying network structure, such as social media. Although several SNA approaches exist, most utilize a combination of word frequencies and co-occurrences, generating a network map and possible clusters/frames from the data (David et al., 2014).

A growing body of research has employed SNA to explore how individuals interact on social media during public events, including the strategies used in the BP Oil Crisis (Schultz et al., 2012), celebrity news coverage (Murphy, 2010), and foreign diplomacy (Yang et al., 2012). For instance, Cho et al. (2021) analyzed the United Airlines' passenger removal crisis on X, focusing on how ethnicity-related words appeared in English and Chinese tweets. Their findings revealed that compared to English tweets, Chinese-language tweets were more likely to invoke ethnic focused discussions regarding the crisis. Similarly, Mizoroki and Kim (2021) used SNA to examine how users discussed sexual abuse allegations made by two women against their powerful superiors in Japan and South Korea. They found that the discourse about sexual abuse was highly politicized, with political scandal narratives overshadowing the core issue of the rape allegations. More recently, Dai et al. (2024) analyzed tweets containing the hashtag #TexasAbortionBan, finding that the dominant themes centered on women's access to abortion services and their autonomy over reproductive decisions.

Although the X users who commented on the Nassar sentencing are unlikely to know each other, and they may have various life experiences or backgrounds, when they post (and repost) about Nassar's sentencing, they exchange symbols and their underlying meanings. Communication has a great impact on the rhetorical development of the event as it helps construct a reality within a virtual shared community. A shared community is defined as "an audience that comes together around similar interests and concerns and often reshares information they comment and post on" (Perreault & Perreault, 2019). Therefore, X users who contribute to the rhetoric community collectively create a narrative to an online event (Hossain et al, 2019).

In sum, prior research has demonstrated the utility of SNA in analyzing public discourse across a range of events, highlighting how meaning is negotiated within social media communities. In the context of the Larry Nassar case, applying SNA to X conversations can provide critical insight into how the public collectively constructed narratives around justice, gender, and institutional accountability. As such, the approach offers a powerful lens through which to understand the symbolic and rhetorical dimensions of social media communication during crises. Therefore, the following research questions are asked:

RQ1: What were the words that had the most direct links to other words in the Tweets through a SNA?
RQ2: What themes existed in the Tweets about the Larry Nassar sentencing?

Gendered Narration in the Context of Sexual Harassment

The literature on gender attitudes toward sexual harassment provides valuable insights into how men and women might differ in their responses to Nassar's sentencing. Research has shown that men and women perceive sexual harassment differently (Richardson & Taylor, 2009). Specifically, women tend to discuss sexual harassment from the perspective of the victim more than men (Dougherty, 2001). Furthermore, women tended to recognize a broader range of behaviors as sexual harassment (Berryman-Fink & Riley, 1997; Dunn & Cody, 2000; Rotundo et al.,

2001). In addition, men were less likely to endorse a severe punishment for the perpetrator of sexual harassment than women (Nodeland & Craig, 2021). Dougherty (2001) suggested gender differences in perceptions of sexual harassment can be explained through the Standpoint framework. According to this framework, men often focus on fears of false accusations, while women are more concerned with physical harm.

Prior studies have shed light on the gender difference of perceptions of sexual harassment. For example, Mizoroki and Kim (2021) found that compared to their female counterparts, males' conversation about the sexual harassment on social media was "all about politics" (p. 146). Several studies found that women were less tolerant of sexual harassment than men (e.g., Bitton & Shaul, 2013; Russell & Trigg, 2004). More recently, Lam and Mesch (2025) found that women perceived offline and online sexual harassments as more serious, more harmful, and less moral. The literature led us to wonder whether men and women would have different responses when discussing Nassar's sentencing event on X. Thus, we pose the following research question:

RQ3: Are there differences between men and women in the themes present in Tweets about the Nassar sentencing?

Method

Sampling

Tweets for this analysis were collected from January 24 to January 28, 2018. This time frame was selected because Larry Nassar was sentenced by Judge Rosemarie Aquilina on January 24, 2018. The keyword "Nassar" was selected to capture any mention of the event. The final sample contained 8,969 Tweets. Only English-language Tweets were included.

The genders of the individuals who posted the tweets were manually coded using a coding scheme. For the purpose of this study, gender was categorized as male, female, or other. Two coders who were authors of the paper assessed users' profile pages by carefully examining both the profile descriptions and profile pictures. For example, a user who described themselves as "a wife, a mom, and a coffee lover," was coded as female. A user's gender was coded as "other" when (1) gender could not be inferred from the profile description or profile picture, or (2) the user identified with a gender outside the male/female binary. We used 10% of the user profiles as a training corpus. The intercoder reliability reached .80 after training. Then the two coders split the user profiles and coded the entire data set.

Semantic Network Analysis

In the first stage of the SNA, the raw Tweets were downloaded from a X archive service, Sifter, and pre-processed in R to produce an organized data set. Pre-processing steps included the lowercasing of Tweets, removal of hyperlinks, punctuation, emojis,

Table 1. Caption text here including any relevant permission information.

The 20 Most Frequent Words and Degree

Words	Frequency	Degree
Nassar	3381	581
judge	1201	489
MSU	951	489
woman	859	517
year	853	482
sentence	834	478
prison	680	418
175	561	391
sexual	527	475
victim	494	485
abuse	484	451
deserve	470	402
fuck	465	341
girl	438	447
man	426	410
need	417	425
hope	409	392
people	395	445
hell	354	321
good	353	354

hashtags, and non-ASCII characters. Contractions were replaced and stop words (content free words) such as articles and conjunctions were also replaced. Stemming was applied to each Tweet to replace plurals and word variations with their singular form.

After preprocessing, we generated a word frequency list using R. The words whose frequencies were greater than the mean frequency (mean = 13.90) were included to produce a co-occurrence matrix. Co-occurrence was defined as two words appearing in the same Tweet. Visualization of the networks was created using Gephi, a software program for the analysis and visualization of social networks (Bastian et al., 2009). We conducted modularity analyses in Gephi to identify word clusters. Each word cluster indicated a theme with closely linked words. Each node represented a word, and each link represented a co-occurrence relationship within a Tweet. The size of each node indicated its degree centrality. Line thickness represented co-occurrence frequency. Only words with degree centrality larger than the mean were included in network (mean = 126.58). This way we can insure readability of the network. Each color represented a theme.

Results

RQ1 examined which words had the highest number of direct connections to other words within the semantic network. The top ten frequently mentioned words were

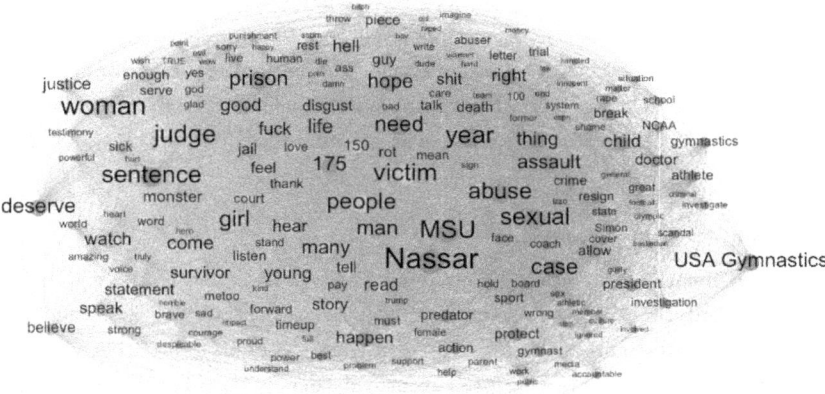

Fig 1. Caption text here including any relevant permission information.

Nassar (n = 3,381), *judge* (n = 1,201), *MSU* (n = 951), *woman* (n = 859), *year* (n = 853), *sentence* (n = 834), *prison* (n = 680), *175* (n = 561), *sexual* (n = 527), and *victim* (n = 494). Table 1 shows the top 20 words that had most direct links to other words in the network.

RQ2 investigated what themes existed in the Tweets. Four themes emerged from analyzing the interconnections among symbols: (1) accountability of organizations and individuals, (2) sentencing of Nassar, (3) criticism of Nassar, and (4) support for victims. Figure 1 shows the semantic network of Nassar's sentencing. The label size reflected the degree centrality of each word in the network. Below is a more detailed analysis of each theme.

Theme of Accountability of Organizations and Individuals

This theme came in response from the X discussions revolving around the cover-ups and apathetic responses from the organizations and individuals, specifically in their actions and relationships to Larry Nassar. Often, the organizations involved were directly mentioned alongside Larry Nassar (i.e., MSU and Nassar or USA Gymnastics and Nassar). Words such as *allow, happen, sexual, assault, abuse, scandal, cover, protect, resign, investigation, shame, accountable, involved, ignore* frequently appeared in this theme, often in conjunction with named organizations and individuals such as *Simon, president, Izzo, board, member, MSU, USA Gymnastics,* and the *NCAA*. These terms reflected a strong public focus on institutional responsibility and systemic failure. Examples include: "The NCAA shows bold leadership! (20 years after the first reported abuse)" (Blanchard, 2018); "As it should. The culture of covering up sexual assault goes much deeper than the Nassar case and reaches all corners of the university" (Mac, 2018); and "Now USA Gymnastics and Michigan State need to be fully investigated and punished" (Beetner, 2018).

This set of words also indicate what corrective actions the public want the blamed personal to take (e.g., *resign*). An example Tweet was: "As a parent of a young woman who drove change at colleges on sexual assault—I applaud the courage of the young women who spoke out vs. Larry Nassar; the system that allowed this to continue for so long. USAG and organized sports—you are on notice. The world is watching" (Ilse, 2018).

Theme of Nassar's Sentencing

In this theme, the law and legal consequences are used to address Larry Nassar's behaviors and crimes. The words such as *sentence, 175, year, prison, sign, death,* and *warrant* alluded to the public's sharing of the consequences of his crimes. The words—*sentence, 175, year, prison*—were used to provide details regarding the judgement of Nassar. This theme focused on the basic fact of the sentencing of Larry Nassar. Specially, the length of sentence, 175 years, was frequently shared by individuals as both novel and debatable points. The tweet: "Larry Nassar has been sentenced to 175 years in prison and I've never been happier, rot in prison, then in hell. No words can describe how disgusting of a human being he is! So happy justice has been served, bless all the victims you have a world of support" (Stefff, 2018), is an example of how these keywords are employed to share Nassar being sentenced to 175 years in prison. Another example was "#BREAKING: Larry Nassar sentenced to 175 years in prison" (Bryant, 2018).

Theme of Criticism of Nassar

This theme was characterized by the emotional venting in response to Nassar's sentencing. Many people expressed their feelings toward Larry Nassar and his legal punishment. Emotional venting took the form of words such as *rot, hell, piece, shit, deserve, fuck, jail, man, life, disgust, sick, scrum, evil, ass, die, bad,* and *guy*. These words could be viewed as expressions of outrage at the unfolding events during the sentencing. Examples included: "What a disgusting human being how can they get away for so long & hurt so many children" (Palestine, 2018); "What a sick monster. Give him the death penalty" (McDonalds, 2018); "Rot in jail but still not enough for this monster" (Buis, 2018); and "Holy shit this letter that Nassar wrote are you kidding me? His 'apologies' ring completely hollow as the judge is reading excerpts. Audible gasps and laughter from those present, particularly his claims that he was manipulated. This is unbelievable" (Koenig, 2018).

Theme of Support for Victims

This theme was composed by a set of feminine-related and emotional words such as *woman, victim, girl, young, survivor, power, 150, many, come, forward, tell, female, help, strong, speak, love, stand, voice, amazing, truly, love, hear, hero, heart,* and *thank*. In this theme, the *women, victims, girls,* and *survivors* became the center of the discourse on X.

The public expressed sympathy for the females who were abused and appreciated those who chose to speak up. This theme captured the need of individuals to offer emotional support to the victims involved in the situation. Example tweets included: "Thank goodness! May our prayers and strength go out to the family and friends of these victims and survivors. Now time for USA Gymnastics and US Olympic Committee to step up" (Kirschke, 2018), and "My heart goes out to all the families affected by what Larry Nassar did to those girls. Its sickening" (AP, 2018).

RQ3 investigated whether there were any differences between males and females on the themes in the Tweets about the Nassar sentencing. Overall, males (n = 4,320, 47.6%) tweeted slightly more than females (n = 3,998, 44%) on the theme of Nassar's sentencing. To examine the differences between gender and how their posts fell into different themes, we ran a series of Chi-square tests, and all tests showed significant results. For the theme of support for victims, females (n = 2,970, 74.3%) were significantly more likely to post about this theme than males (n = 2,783, 64.4%). $\chi^2(1, N = 8,318) = 94.76, p < .001$. Males (n = 1,329, 30.8%) were significantly more likely to post about the theme of Nassar's sentencing than females (n = 1,044, 26.1%), $\chi^2(1, N = 8,318) = 22.03, p < .001$. For the theme of criticism of Nassar, males (n = 3,429, 79.4%) were significantly more likely to post about this theme than females (n = 3,014, 75.4%), $\chi^2(1, N = 8,318) = 18.91, p < .001$. Males (n = 2,995, 69.3%) were significantly more likely than females to post about the theme of accountability of organizations and individuals (n = 2,502, 62.6%), $\chi^2(1, N = 8,318) = 42.18, p < .001$.

Discussion and Conclusions

Semantic network analysis is a valuable tool to assist identifying key public sentiment. Through computer-assisted methods, we can efficiently analyze large volumes of tweets. More importantly, this approach enables flexible coding of words and themes that emerge from tweets, rather than code the content with more qualitative approaches. This objective tool allows new and unexpected themes to emerge.

X facilitates the creations of shared communities by enabling users to connect despite typical barriers to online communication. By examining the individual themes, a classical hero and villain theme emerged as Bormann noted often occurs among small groups who dramatize events (Bormann, 1972). The hero portion of the rhetorical vision can be seen in two elements. The first hero, Judge Rosemarie Aquilina, emerged from the themes of *Nassar's Sentencing* and *Support for Victims*. In the *Nassar's Sentencing* theme, Judge Rosemarie Aquilina presided over the prosecution of Larry Nassar and sentenced him. The fact that a female judge both presided and sentenced a man, Larry Nassar, in this sexual abuse scandal strongly resonated among individuals. The *Nassar's Sentencing* theme places the hero directly in the middle of the story as she is credited with sentencing Nassar. There is even a scene in the court room of Judge Rosemarie Aquilina dramatically tearing a letter Nassar wrote to the court regarding the accusations again him. In the *Support for Victims* theme, the hero can be seen as offering justice for the victims. There are many examples of Tweets crediting the judge for giving the victims hope by her actions and even a role model for women. For example, one news anchor tweets: "Judge took time w/sentencing reading back a letter Nassar wrote 2 months after accepting the plea deal where he blamed victims and said they were lying. Says it played a large role in her sentencing. Mocked his words, making people laugh in courtroom" (Ubaka, 2018). The second hero found in the themes is that of the victim. This hero emerged from the *Support for Victims* theme recognized above. In many Tweets, the public highlighted the strength and persistence of the victims involved in the scandal. Individuals shared positive comments regarding the victims and recognized their heroic actions.

The villains of the tweets can be found among the individuals and organizations involved in this crisis that had direct or indirect actions in the scandal. Individual villains were identified as Larry Nassar and the MSU president. Organizational villains included MSU and USA Gymnastics USA Gymnastics. These villains were identified from the *Accountability of Organizations and Individuals* and *Nassar's Sentencing* themes in the analysis. It is clear from examining the valences and keywords in the SNA that the public viewed both Nassar and the organizations involved as villains. In the United States, child molesters and other criminals are consistently identified as evil by society, given the established moral and ethical Western traditions.

During the Nassar sentencing, the public mainly used X for information seeking (manifested by the *Accountability of Organizations and Individuals* theme) and emotional venting (manifested by the *Criticism of Nassar* and *Support for Victims* themes). Based on a centrality analysis, the majority of the top ten words in the analysis were news related. The public focused on the facts associated with the sentencing, (i.e., information related to who, what, when, how, and why). The analysis indicated that the public were logically thinking about the next steps for protecting athletes and how the organizations involved should respond, such as requesting leadership changes. The public also reshared facts based on popular news stories. Predominately negative emotions were expressed about Nassar and the organizations that sheltered him during his acts of sexual abuse.

Sentencing of Larry Nassar is only one aspect of the public discourse. The public also use X to demand accountability from involved institutions. Although the crisis originated with an individual, public scrutiny and accountability ultimately extended to the organizations that were held responsible for their lack of oversight and protections for young athletes. For instance, within the *Accountability of Organizations and Individuals* theme, it is evident that the public outrage extended beyond Nassar to include institutions like USA Gymnastics and MSU. Tweets referencing MSU frequently included keywords such as *Nassar, sexual, assault, abuse, president, resign, need, victim,* and *sentence*. Similarly, tweets about USA Gymnastics often included terms like *Nassar, doctor, sexual,* and *abuse*. X users indicated that key personnel *need to resign* because they *allowed the sexual abuses* to happen. The co-occurrence of these words suggests that the public attribute responsibility not only to Nassar, but also to the institutions that enabled his actions through negligence or inaction. The public discourse surrounding the Nassar sentencing demonstrates a broader demand for systemic change and institutional accountability. Rather than limiting blame to individual actors, X users actively call for organizational reform and preventative measures to ensure the protection of young athletes moving forward. This shift in responsibility from the individual to the institutional level underscores the critical role of organizational communication and crisis response strategies in regaining public trust. These emergent themes offer valuable insight into public sentiment during a sexual abuse crisis and serve as critical input for shaping organizational response strategies.

The findings reveal a significant gender difference in how users engage with themes related to sexual harassment on social media. Females are more likely to center their discourse around the victims, offering emotional support and empathy, while males tend to focus on factual element of the news, expressing criticism toward Larry Nassar and the organizations that enable his actions. The findings suggest that gender influences not only the emotional tone but also the framing and focus of public discourse surrounding sexual abuses. Understanding the differences has important implications for developing more effective communication strategies and victim advocacy campaigns.

To conclude, this study uncovers important and distinct public sentiment and rhetorical pattern surrounding the Larry Nassar sentencing through the lens of SNA. By analyzing a large volume of tweets, this study identified central themes and key actors in the collective construction of meaning within an online rhetorical community. X serves as a platform not only for information sharing and emotional venting, but also a venue for online rhetorical community building and advocating for organizational accountability. In addition, the study identifies a clear gendered pattern about sexual harassment: women were more likely to discuss victims, whereas men tend to focus on facts and accountability. The gender distinctions have critical implications for crisis communication strategies, suggesting that organizations must be attentive to the various ways that different demographics of the public respond to crisis cases. By understanding how the public use social media to navigate a crisis and create meaning, organizations can better respond to public sentiment and implement meaningful strategies during and after a crisis.

References

AP [@Ashelypotter007]. (2018, January 24). *My heart goes out to all the families affected by what Larry Nassar did to those girls. It's sickening* [Tweet]. X. https://x.com/Ashleypotter007/status/956224212989022208

Bastian, M., Heymann, S., & Jacomy, M. (2009). Gephi: An open source software for exploring and manipulating networks. *Proceedings of the International AAAI Conference on Web and Social Media*, 3(1), 361–362. https://doi.org/10.1609/icwsm.v3i1.13937

Beetner, G. [@gkbeetner]. (2018, January 24). *Now USA Gymnastics and Michigan State need to be fully investigated and punished* [Tweet]. X. https://x.com/gkbeetner/status/956222751693529088

Berryman-Fink, C., & Riley, K. V. (1997). The effect of sex and feminist orientation on perceptions in sexually harassing communication. *Women's Studies in Communication*, 20(1), 25–44. https://doi.org/10.1080/07491409.1997.10162399

Bitton, M., & Shaul, D. B. (2013). Perceptions and attitudes to sexual harassment: An examination of sex differences and the sex composition of the harasser-target dyad. *Journal of Applied Social Psychology*, 43(10), 2136–2145. https://doi.org/10.1111/jasp.12166

Blancard, G. [@Blanch344]. (2018, January 24). *The NCAA shows bold leadership! (20years after the first reported abuse)* [Tweet]. X. https://x.com/Blanch344/status/955994896397107200

Bormann, E. G. (1972). Fantasy and rhetorical vision: The rhetorical criticism of social reality.

Bryant, C. [@CourtneyDBryant]. (2018, January 23). *#BREAKING: Larry Nassar sentenced to 175 years in prison* [Tweet]. X. https://x.com/CourtneyDBryant/status/956219486759260160

Buis, N. P. [@buisnick] (2018, January 24). *Rot in jail but still not enough for this monster* [Tweet]. X. https://x.com/buisnick/status/956219526206672899 *Quarterly Journal of Speech*, 58(4), 396–407.

Calabrese, C., Ding, J., Millam, B., & Barnett, G. A. (2019). The uproar over gene-edited babies: A semantic network analysis of CRISPR on X. *Environnemental Communication*, 14(7), 954–970. https://doi.org/10.1080/17524032.2019.1699135

Cho, M., Xiong, Y., & Boatwright, B. (2021). Through the lens of ethnicity: Semantic network and thematic analyses of United Airlines' dragging crisis. *Public Relations Review*, 47(1). https://doi.org/10.1016/j.pubrev.2020.102006.

Dai, Z., Jiang, W., & McNickle, C. (2024). Social network analysis and semantic analysis of #TexasAbortionBan on Twitter. *Sexuality Research and Social Policy*, 21, 591–597. https://doi.org/10.1007/s13178-023-00848-6

David, C. C., Legara, E. F. T., Atun, J. M. L., & Monterola, C. P. (2014). News frames of the population issue in the Philippines. *International Journal of Communication*, 8, 21. https://doi.org/1932–8036/20140005

Dougherty, D. (2001). Sexual harassment as [dys]functional process: A feminist standpoint Analysis. *Journal of Applied Communication Research*, 29(4), 372–402. https://doi.org/10.1080/00909880128116

Dunn, D., & Cody, M. J. (2000). Account credibility and public image: Excuses, justifications, denials, and sexual harassment. *Communication Monographs*, 67(4), 372–391. https://doi.org/10.1080/03637750009376518

Graham, B. (2017, December 16). Why don't we care about the biggest sex abuse scandal in sports history? *The Guardian*. https://www.theguardian.com/sport/2017/dec/16/gymnastics-larry-nassar-sexual-abuse

Hossain, M., Islam, M.T., Momin, M.A., Nahar, S., & Alam, M. S. (2019). Understanding communication of sustainability reporting: Application of Symbolic Convergence Theory (SCT). *Journal of Business Ethics,160*, 563–586. https://doi.org/10.1007/s10551-018-3874-6

Ilse [@ilsebacchus]. (2018, January 24). *As a parent of a young woman who drove change at colleges on sexual assault—I applaud the courage of* [Tweet]. X. https://x.com/ilsebacchus/status/956355014007562240

Kirschke, J. F. [@JanKirschke]. (2018, January 24). *Thank goodness! May our prayers and strength go out to the family and friends of these victims and survivors. Now* [Tweet]. X. https://x.com/JanKirschke/status/956223955139833861

Koenig, S. [@sara_koenig]. (2018, January 24). *Holy shit this letter that Nassar wrote are you kidding me? His apologies ring completely hollow as the judge is reading* [Tweet]. X. https://x.com/sara_koenig/status/956215285098434560

Mac [@MvcPlvce]. (2018, January 24). *As it should. The culture of covering up sexual assault goes much deeper than the* [Tweet]. X. https://x.com/MvcPlvce/status/956212735083208704

McDonalds, J. [@Tyus_jones_fan]. (2018, January 24). *What a sick monster. Give him the death penalty.* [Tweet]. X. https://x.com/Tyus_jones_fan/status/956213715178749954

Mizoroki, S., & Kim, B. (2021). Sexual assaults blindsided by politics on Twitter. In E. Segev (ed), *Semantic network analysis in social sciences*, pp. 136–158. Routledge. https://doi.org/10.4324/9781003120100

Murphy, P. (2010). The intractability of reputation: Media coverage as a complex system in the case of Martha Stewart. *Journal of Public Relations Research*, 22(2), 209–237. https://doi.org/10.1080/10627261003601648

Nodeland, B., & Craig, J. (2021). Perceptions of legal and extralegal punishments for sexual harassment in the 'MeToo' era. *Deviant Behavior*, 42, 850–861. 10.1080/01639625.2019.1702615

Palestine, F. [@ladydi10350]. (2018, January 24). *What a disgusting human being how can then get away for so long & hurt so* [Tweet]. X. https://x.com/ladydi10350/status/956212470665891842

Perreault, M. F., & Perreault, G. (2019). Symbolic convergence in the 2015 Duggar scandal crisis communication. *Journal of Media and Religion*, 18(3), 85–97. https://doi.org/10.1080/15348423.2019.1678945

Richardson, B. K., & Taylor, J. (2009). Sexual harassment at the intersection of race and gender: A theoretical model of the sexual harassment experiences of women of color. *Western Journal of Communication*, 73(3), 248–272. https://doi.org/10.1080/10570310903082065

Rotundo, M, Nguyen, D. H., & Sackett, P.R. (2001) A meta-analytic review of gender differences in perceptions of sexual harassment. *Journal of Applied Psychology*, 86(5), 914–922. doi: 10.1037/0021-9010.86.5.914.

Russell, B. L., & Trigg, K. Y. (2004). Tolerance of sexual harassment: An examination of gender differences, ambivalent sexism, social dominance, and gender roles. *Sex Roles: A Journal of Research*, 50(7–8), 565–573. https://doi.org/10.1023/B:SERS.0000023075.32252.fd

Schultz, F., Kleinnijenhuis, J., Oegema, D., Utz, S., & Van Atteveldt, W. (2012). Strategic framing in the BP crisis: A semantic network analysis of associative frames. *Public Relations Review*, 38(1), 97–107. https://doi.org/10.1016/j.pubrev.2011.08.003

Shin, Y. (2020). What can tripartite semantic network analysis do for media framing research? *Communication & Society*, 33(1), 121–137. https://doi.org/10.15581/003.33.35280

Stefff [@stefanikalab]. (2018, January 24). *Larry Nassar has been sentenced to 175 years in prison and I've never been happier, rot in prison, then in* [Tweet]. X. https://x.com/stefanikalab/status/956349475395694592

Ubaka, A. [@AmakaUbakaTV]. (2018, January 24). *Judge took time w/sentencing reading back a letter Nassar wrote 2 months after accepting the plea deal where he blamed* [Tweet]. X. https://x.com/AmakaUbakaTV/status/956226207179264001

Yang, A., Klyueva, A., & Taylor, M. (2012). A relational approach to public diplomacy in a multipolar world: Building public relations theory by analyzing the US-Russia-China relationship. *Public Relations Review, 38*(5), 652–664. https://doi.org/10.1016/j.pubrev.2012.07.005

SECTION THREE

Examination of Messages in Russia

CHAPTER SEVEN | DAIKI HORIGUCHI

Russophobia Frame and Dysphemism in Russian Sports Discourse During Wartime

Abstract

The paper analyzes the Russophobia frame and dysphemisms in Russian sports discourse during wartime. Sports discourse, like political discourse, has an inherently adversarial nature, particularly in the context of state-sponsored Russian sports. In Russian sports media, the Russophobia frame was used to condemn alleged discriminatory measures against Russia before 2022, especially with regard to doping issues. However, since Russia's suspension from major international competitions, the Russophobia frame has been reinforced, as evidenced by the increased use of derivatives with *rusofob*, "Russophobe," in leading Russian sports media. Russian athletes, coaches, sports officials, and politicians criticize the international sports community, employing the Russophobia frame to stigmatize their targets while portraying Russia as a victim. In those instances, dysphemisms—nouns or nominal phrases that harshly degrade their referents—are frequently used. The targets of these dysphemisms include international sports organizations and their measures against Russia, competitions without Russian athletes, as well as foreign sports figures perceived as "anti-Russian." Apart from commonly used offensive words, dysphemisms are based on references to illness, sexual acts, historical atrocities, animalization, betrayal, doping violations, and physical appearance. Textually, dysphemisms used by sporting figures often appear in article headlines to attract readers' attention. Journalists also employ dysphemisms in periphrasis, repeatedly referring to the same target throughout a text to reinforce negative perceptions among readers. Overall, Russian sports discourse reflects an antagonistic nature marked by emotional intensity and hostility.

Keywords: Russia, sports discourse, war, Russophobia, dysphemism

Russian Sports Discourse

Sport, as one of the key social phenomena in the modern world, has attracted attention in linguistics and discourse analysis. The terminology used to describe how individuals engage in talking about sport varies, including terms such as "sports discourse" (Schirato, 2013), the Russian equivalent "sportivnyj diskurs" (Zil'bert, 2001a, 2001b), "discourse of sport" or "language in sport" (Caldwell et al., 2017, p. 2). Sports discourse broadly encompasses both sports-proper communication, which covers interactions between athletes and coaches during training and competitions, as well as live commentary, and sports-themed media discourse, which comprises commentary, sports news, and online communication among fans. In the latter case, sports discourse is closely related to media discourse. Moreover, sports discourse intersects with political and war discourses, sharing an agonistic nature (Zil'bert, 2001b, p. 105) and cognitive concepts such as rivalry, battle, rules, strategy and tactics, and victory and defeat (Šejgal, 2000, p. 45). Sport is often closely linked to politics, giving rise to politicized sports discourse in which political content dominates, and the sporting aspect becomes secondary (Novikov, 2015, p. 212), or sports-related political discourse.

Elite sports, in which athletes compete at the international level representing their country, are deeply intertwined with national identity and state ideology, often serving as a tool of state propaganda. This is particularly evident in Russia, where the government financially supports elite sports since the Soviet era (Vladimirova, 2020). Russia utilizes sports as a means to cultivate a positive national image and reinforce the idea of a strong state (Kijamova, 2018), a goal effectively pursued through state-controlled media. For example, Match TV, one of Russia's most popular sports channels, is owned by Gazprom-Media, a subsidiary of Gazprom, the state-owned energy corporation.

Today, two major issues have fueled conflict between Russia and the West: doping and exclusion from global sports. The state-organized doping scheme in Russia for the 2014 Olympic Games in Sochi led to serious confrontation between Russia and Western countries, forcing Russia to adopt a defensive and justificatory position (Korneeva, 2017, p. 273). Following Russia's full-scale invasion of Ukraine in 2022, Russian athletes have faced bans from major international competitions, most notably the Olympic games, making this exclusion a prominent wartime topic in Russian sports discourse. In contrast to Ukrainian sports discourse, where athletes actively discuss the war's impact on their sporting careers and national identity (Horiguchi, 2024), the Russo-Ukrainian war, despite being the underlying cause of the challenges faced by Russian sport today, remains a less explicit theme in Russian sports discourse.

Russian sports discourse prominently reflects the state's antagonistic political rhetoric. The dichotomy of *us/them* persists, positioning Russia in direct opposition to the West. Russia's isolation from both the West and global sports is perfectly mirrored in its narrative, which asserts that the country's presence and strength are indispensable for the proper functioning of global systems, thereby justifying its international significance. This belief is echoed in official rhetoric, as illustrated by the following statements:

(…) *bez suverennoj, sil'noj Rossii nikakoj pročnyi, stabilnyi miroporjadok nevozmožen.*
(…) without a sovereign and strong Russia, no durable and stable world order is possible.
—Vladimir Putin, Russian president (Putin, 2024)

(…) *bez Rossii razvitie mirovogo sporta nevozmožno.*
(…) without Russia, development of global sports is impossible.
—Oleg Matycin, Russian sports minister (Matycin, 2023)

As demonstrated in these statements, the messianic narrative propagated by Russian officials in both political and sports discourse, is reinforced within contemporary domestic academia. For instance, it is argued that "the decision to 'cancel' Russia, anti-Russian sentiments, and hatred toward everything Russian pose a serious long-term threat to global sports, which could ultimately destroy the entire international sports movement" (Čebar' & Nazarov, 2023, pp. 478–479). The exclusion of Russian athletes from international competitions is framed by Russian scholars as part of a broader phenomenon of cancel culture (Artamonova & Rustamova, 2023, p. 125), equating sports with other national attributes such as culture. The narrative of cancelling Russian culture has been strategically employed by the Kremlin both domestically and internationally as a propaganda tool, fostering a sense of self-victimization while simultaneously diverting attention from domestic censorship and the repression of dissenting voices (Romashko, 2024, pp. 3,11). This self-victimizing rhetoric is also evident in Russian sports discourse, particularly through the Russophobia frame, which is explored in the next section.

Despite Russia's absence from global sports, contemporary Russian sports discourse remains rich with topics that warrant multimodal linguistic analysis. This study conducts a lexical analysis of Russian sports discourse during wartime, focusing on the Russophobia frame and dysphemisms used by Russian sports figures, politicians, and journalists. These dysphemisms target perceived "enemies," such as international sports organizations, foreign sports figures, and domestic athletes accused of "betraying" the country. The empirical data consists of written texts published mostly after 2022 in Russian sports media, sourced from the Russian media database Integrum (www.integrumworld.com), which enables keyword searches over specific time periods across multiple Russian sports media outlets. Additionally, social media accounts of selected Russian athletes were examined. This research primarily employs qualitative analysis and does not aim to extend beyond its defined scope.

Russophobia Frame in Russian Sports Discourse

Historically, the term *rusofobija*, "Russophobia," dates back to the 19th century in Russian and Western political discourses. Its initial concept emerged in two contexts:

domestically, it was used to accuse critics of the tsarist regime inside the Russian Empire (Darczewska & Żochowski, 2015, pp. 9–10), while internationally, it referred to the perception of a Russian threat prevalent in Western Europe (McNally, 1958).

Since 2014, the notion of Russophobia has been increasingly employed by the Russian government in the context of the Russo-Ukrainian war (Darczewska & Żochowski, 2015, p. 16; Robinson, 2019, p. 64; Fortuin, 2022, p. 330). This usage can be described as the Russophobia frame (Zelenkauskaitė, 2022, p. 192), the Russophobia narrative (Ventsel et al., pp. 31–32; Hoyle et al., 2024) or as part of a broader "Nazi-genocide-Russophobia" frame (Fortuin, 2022). In this framework, the term is decontextualized from its historical meanings and is typically used, from a Russian perspective, to describe alleged negative or discriminatory attitudes toward Russia, Russians, and Russian culture in Western countries. The Russophobia rhetoric allows Russia "to position itself as a moral victim despised by the West and its allies" and "nip in the bud the accusations by the opponent perceived as malevolent and destructive, and to attribute to the enemies precisely those condemnable qualities that the latter use to characterize Russia" (Ventsel et al., 2021, p. 32). At the same time, Russia does not acknowledge that this narrative serves its own strategic goals. Instead, it perceives Russophobia as a concept imposed by Western political agendas, against which it must actively defend itself (Sizov, 2015, p. 254).

Although the term lacks a unified definition, the Russian government introduced it in 2024 at the legislative level. Vladimir Putin signed a decree approving the updated "Strategy for Combating Extremism in the Russian Federation," in which the notion of Russophobia, alongside xenophobia, is defined as a form of extremism. The decree defines Russophobia as "an unfriendly, biased, and hostile attitude toward Russian citizens, the Russian language and culture, Russia's traditions and history, manifested, among other things, in aggressive sentiments and actions of political forces and their individual representatives, as well as in discriminatory actions of the authorities of unfriendly states against Russia" (Decree of the President of the Russian Federation, 2024). Given the term's extensive prior use and its inherently vague definition, it remains unclear how its legal codification will impact political discourse. Nevertheless, due to its broad scope, any criticism of Russia can potentially be labeled as Russophobia in official Russian discourse.

The Russophobia frame has been present in Russian sports media before the outbreak of the full-scale war. Its use intensified as tensions between Russia and the West deepened. In 2015, the World Anti-Doping Agency accused Russia of state-sponsored doping, leading international sports organizations to impose full or partial bans on Russian athletes from international competitions. Although these sanctions were based on institutional procedures, they were widely perceived within the mainstream Russian sports discourse as politically motivated attacks driven by alleged hostility toward Russia and Russians. This perspective is reinforced by a recurring argument in Russian sports discourse: "our rivals want to defeat us in everything, but in some sports, realizing that they cannot win, they resort to "low and petty" means to eliminate stronger opponents in the battle for medals" (Zmeev, 2017, p. 93).

The Russophobia frame, which constructs a self-victimization narrative, is not limited to doping-related issues but is also invoked when Russia contests official competition results deemed unfavorable. A notable example occurred during the Tokyo Olympics, in the individual all-around rhythmic gymnastics competition on August 7, 2021. Russian gymnast Dina Averina won the silver medal, while Israel's Linoy Ashram secured gold despite making a mistake in her ribbon routine. Following this outcome, Maria Zaharova, the official representative of the Russian Ministry of Foreign Affairs, expressed her outrage over the judging in her Telegram account, stating that "the scoundrels who started a Russophobic war against sports could not allow this victory" (Jampol'skaja, 2021). This reaction aligned with the overall tone of Russian sports media, further reinforcing the Russophobia frame.

The Russophobia frame has been actively employed in Russian media to criticize sanctions against Russia, particularly during wartime, as the country remains banned from major international competitions and isolated from global sports due to its full-scale invasion of Ukraine. According to data from the Russian media database Integrum, the frequency of the words derived from the element *rusofob-* 'Russophobe' across 6,457 sources of the Russian media nearly doubled in the period from February 24, 2022, to February 23, 2024 (132,402 texts), compared to the period from February 24, 2020, to February 23, 2022 (78,826 texts). This trend extends to sports media. In eight popular Russian sports websites (RIA Novosti Sport, RIA Novosti Sporta, Sovetskij sport, sport.ru, sportbox.ru, Sport-Ekspress, Chempionat, and Match TV), the usage of *rusofob-*derivatives has increased fivefold during the same two-year period (from 245 to 1,253 texts), reflecting the growing prominence of the Russophobia frame in Russian sports discourse.

Derivatives containing the element *rusofob-* "Russophobe" include various words such as *rusofob/rusofobka* "Russophobe" (in masculine and feminine forms): *rusofobija* "Russophobia"; *rusofobstvo* "Russophobia"; adjective *rusofobskij* "Russophobic"; verb *rusofobstvovat'* "behave in a Russophobic manner"; compound nouns *rusofob-otmorozok* "scumbag Russophobe," *hokkeist-rusofob* "Russophobic hockey player." The semantics of the words *rusofobija* "Russophobia" and *rusofob/rusofobka* "Russophobe" alone are not sufficient to stigmatize their referents. Therefore, their negative connotations are intensified by adjectives such as *žutkij* "creepy"; *jaryj* "ardent"; *ogoltelyj* "reckless"; *neprikrytyj* "blatant"; *ot''javlennyj* "notorious"; *bessovestnyj* "shameless," as evidenced by their frequent co-occurrence with *rusofob-*derivatives in the Integrum database.

During wartime, these terms have been extensively used to describe foreign sports officials who decided to ban Russia from international competitions due to the war and doping violations, as well as individual foreign athletes and coaches who publicly support these bans. Russian athletes, coaches, sports officials, politicians, and journalists employ these terms to stigmatize their targets and portray their actions as ungrounded and discriminatory, reinforcing Russia's self-victimization narrative.

Sport propitan sil'neishej rusofobiej.
Sport is imbued with the strongest Russophobia.
—Sergej Borodavko, biathlon coach (Borodavko, 2022)

Rusofobija USADA ne znaet granic.
USADA's Russophobia knows no bounds.
—Irina Alekseeva, UFC fighter (Počežircev, 2024)

V IBU sobralis' ot"javlennye rusofoby, somnitel'no, čto nas vernut na meždunarodnye starty.
The IBU is full of the most notorious Russophobes, so it's doubtful that we will be allowed back into international competitions.
—Dmitrii Vasil'ev, president of Russian Biathlon Federation (Levkovich, 2024)

Diskvalifikacija Valievoj—vopijuščij slučaj neprikrytoj rusofobiej.
Valieva's disqualification is an egregious case of blatant Russophobia.
—Tatiana Moskal'kova, politician (Moskal'kova, 2024)

The expression *Nas b'jut, my krepčaem* "They hit us, we get stronger," sporadically used by athletes, coaches, and officials to react to the sanctions can also be interpreted within the Russophobia frame. Here, we clearly observe the binary opposition of *us/them*, which is frequently employed as a rhetorical tool for speech manipulation. Russia is portrayed as a resilient victim, capable of overcoming adversity.

Nas b'jut, my krepčaem.
They hit us, we get stronger.
—Tat'jana Pokrovskaja, artistic swimming coach (Pokrovskaja, 2024)

Čem bol'še nas b'jut, my krepčaem.
The more they hit us, the stronger we get.
—Nikolaj Valuev, former boxer (Neradovskaja, 2022)

Nas davjat sankcijami, no my stanem ešče sil'nee.
They are crushing us with sanctions, but we will become even stronger.
—Denis Lebedev, former boxer (Puškarev, 2024)

The image of victimhood is reinforced through verbs such as *unizit'* "humiliate"; *pritesnjat'* "oppress"; *prinizit'* "belittle." Additionally, figurative verbs such as *ubivat'* "kill"; *uničtožat'* "destroy"; *razrušit'* "destroy"; *uščemljat'* "pinch"; *razdavit'* "crush"; *zažat'* "squeeze"; *zadušit'* "strangle"; and *pohoronit'* "bury" depict Russia and Russian sports as victims in the sporting context.

> *Oni unizili rossijskij sport i hotjat postavit' na koleni.*
> They [IOC] have humiliated Russian sport and want to bring it to its knees.
> —Valentina Rodionenko, artistic gymnastics coach (Astahov, 2024)

While the Russophobia frame helps construct Russia as a victim and serves as a tool of self-defence against the West, current Russian sports discourse exhibits offensive verbal aggression toward the West through dysphemisms, which are discussed in the next section.

Dysphemism

Dysphemism is defined as "an expression with connotations that are offensive either about the denotatum or to the audience, or both," and is used when "talking about one's opponents, things one wishes to show disapproval of, and things one wishes to be seen to downgrade" (Allan & Burridge, 1991, p. 26). Dysphemism represents the hyperbolization of negative attitudes toward a target and often contrasts with euphemism, which mitigates impact through less harsh language, and neutral words and expressions. This linguistic triad frequently appears in politically sensitive and socially tabooed themes, such as death: the neutral verb *umeret'* "die" and its euphemism *ujti iz žizni* "pass away" (lit. go away from life), and dysphemism *sdohnut'* "croak."

However, dysphemisms can be understood more broadly beyond this triad. Some scholars adopt a wider definition, suggesting that any linguistic unit can be pragmatically dysphemistic when used with negative connotations in a given context. Dysphemisms can be identified based on formal criteria, such as indefinite pronouns, which may mark speaker's distanced attitude to the object (Sładkiewicz, 2023, p.139), or derivationally modified words, including diminutives and augmentatives, which may convey dysphemistic semantics in many languages. They can also be identified based on lexical criteria, such as colloquial, expressive, and stylistically marked lexical units (Kameneva & Rybkina, 2021, pp. 511–512). Although dysphemisms are most commonly found among nouns, a broader understanding of the concept encompasses all parts of speech, including adjectives, verbs, and adverbs.

A dysphemistic effect can also be achieved through metalinguistic operations, such as the intentional omission of certain linguistic elements, for example, honorific title. When the International Olympic Committee president, Thomas Bach suggested that Russian athletes who distance themselves from the regime might be allowed to compete internationally (Bonarrigo & Dallera, 2022), his statement provoked strong reactions from Russian politicians and sports figures. Aleksandra Packevič, a former artistic swimmer, expressed her reluctance to use the honorific title *gospodin* "Mr." to refer to Bach:

> *Včerašnee vystuplenie gospodina Baha, hotia gospodinom u menja lično jazyk ne povoračivaetsja ego nazyvat', vyzvalo vo mne burju èmocij.*
> Yesterday's statement by Mr. Bach, although I personally can no longer bring myself to call him "Mr.," stirred up a storm of emotions in me. (Packevič, 2022)

This metalinguistic refusal to use an honorific title can indeed be interpreted as dysphemistic.

To narrow the scope of our analysis, this research focuses only on lexical units used in a directly referential manner to denote the target. Consequently, the examples include only nouns and nominal phrases. For instance, in a Russian sports media article, a journalist persistently derogates a Polish tennis player, who, according to the journalist, was leniently penalized for a doping violation and favored by judges in a match:

> *Ni styda ni sovesti. Pol'skuju mošennicu taščat k titulu Australian Open.*
> No shame, no conscience. The Polish fraudster is being dragged to the title at the Australian Open. (headline) (Gal'cov, 2025)

The journalist's disapproval of her continued participation is conveyed through the first phrase *Ni styda ni sovesti* "No shame, no conscience" and the verb *taščat* "they drag" in the headline. However, in this analysis, we consider only the noun *mošennica* "fraudster" as a dysphemism which directly refers to the target.

In current Russian sports discourse, dysphemisms are directed at international sports organizations, primarily the International Olympic Committee, its president Thomas Bach, as well as events held without Russia's participation. They are also used against foreign athletes and coaches perceived as "anti-Russian" or as violating the interests of Russian sports, with the aim of downplaying the significance of global sports in Russia's absence. Additionally, dysphemisms are applied to Russian athletes who have chosen to change citizenship and represent other countries, especially after 2022, when the international sports community imposed bans on Russian sports.

In political discourse, dysphemism serves to manipulate public perception and shape evaluations of political events, figures and organizations, contributing to the construction of an enemy image. This function is also evident in Russian sports discourse. From a textual point of view, two key points—headlines and periphrasis—should be noted.

Dysphemisms frequently appear in headlines at the top of an article. Regardless of whether they originate from statements made by sports figures and subsequently cited by journalists, or they are coined by journalists themselves, they are often used in headlines. Compared to other lexical units, dysphemisms are particularly effective at capturing readers' attention, as they are perceived as striking and provocative enough to be featured in headlines. At the same time, they may influence audience perception and contribute to the dissemination of a negative image of the downgraded target. The following two examples illustrate how an original utterance is cited in a headline, where a journalist emphasizes the speaker's use of a dysphemism to label the target.

Pozdnjakov nazval ograničenija MOK «sportivnym genocidom» rossijan.
  'Pozdnyakov called the IPC restrictions a "sports genocide" of Russians.' (headline)
—Stanislav Pozdnjakov, president of the Russian Olympic Committee (Sport RBC, 2023)

'On rab Ameriki': Tihonov žestko prošelsja po glave MOK Tomasu Bahu.
  "He is a slave to America": Tihonov harshly criticized IOC President Thomas Bach. headline,
—Aleksandr Tihonov, former biathlete (Tihonov, 2022)

Journalists mark dysphemisms through various metalinguistic means: verbs such as *nazvat'* "call" or *ščitat'* "regard" marking the act of naming, quotation marks, and adverbs to exhibit the speaker's emotional intensity.

Another textual function of dysphemisms is periphrasis, or circumlocution, in which a writer avoids repeating the same denotation and instead refers to it using various lexical means. For example, at the beginning of an article, a journalist uses four periphrastic expressions to downgrade the 2024 Olympic Games Paris: *doping advertisement, doping competition, Steroid Games, a place to advertize doping*. They reflect criticism of the event, where foreign athletes allegedly involved in doping violations were allowed to compete, while also emphasizing the perceived lower competitive level of the Games due to the exclusion of Russian and Belarussian athletes.

Olimpiady v Pariže prevratjat v reklamu dopinga. Sportsmeny b'jut trevogu. Desjatki sportsmenov gotovy vystupit' na sorevnovanijah dlja dopingistov. Letnjaja Olimpiada vo Francii uže postradala iz-za otsutstvija polnocennoj konkurencii—bez Rossii i Belorussii Igry nel'zja nazyvat' polnocennymi. No pomimo togo, est' i reputacionnye riski. Stalo izvestno, čto v Pariž poedut sportsmeny, kotorye planirujut učastvovat' v tak nazyvaemyh "Igrah na steroidah". Olimpiada prevratit'sja v mesto reklamy dopinga!

The Olympics in Paris will be turned into a doping advertisement. Athletes sound the alarm. (headline) Dozens of participants in the 2024 Games are ready to compete in doping competitions. The Summer Olympics in France have already suffered from a lack of full competition—without Russia and Belarus, the Games cannot be considered complete. But beyond that, there are other reputational risks.

It has become known that athletes planning to participate in the so-called "Steroid Games" will be heading to Paris. The Olympics will turn into a place to advertise doping!' (Železnov, 2024).

There are commonly used offensive words that are considered dysphemisms *per se*, such as *idiot* "idiot"; *negodjaj* "scoundrel"; *merzavec* "scoundrel"; *izgoj* "outcast"; *govno* "shit"; *pridurok* "fool"; *mraz'* "scum"; *durak* "fool"; and *bestoloch'* "dimwit." Additionally, some dysphemisms fall into the semantic category of subordination, including *rab* "slave"; *podkablučnik* "whipped man"; *podstilka* "doormat"; and *zombi* "zombi." These dysphemisms are directed at foreign sports figures either individually, when used in singular form, or collectively, when used in plural form.

There are also contextual dysphemisms, that is, words that acquire a dysphemistic function through context, particularly via metaphor. In the following example, a World Championship without Russian figure skaters is deemed valueless:

Rossijskie figuristy byli by brillijantovym ožerel'em na čempionate mira, a bez nih èto deševaja bižuterija.

Russian figure skaters would be a diamond necklace at the World Championship, and without them, it's just cheap jewelry. [headline]
—Aleksej Železnjakov, figure skating choreographer
(Železnjakov, 2024)

The identification of one dysphemism within a particular semantic category suggests the presence of other dysphemistic expressions in the same category. This justifies a category-based, semantic-pragmatic approach, where categories are treated as productive areas for further data collection and the potential clustering of dysphemisms within specific conceptual domains is explored. As part of the methodology, a thorough examination of the texts was conducted, with careful attention paid to identifying potential dysphemisms in context. In addition, targeted keyword searches were carried out based on meaning-related categories, using terms that are semantically associated with each category. This twofold approach—close reading combined with category-driven keyword exploration—enabled the identification and classification of dysphemistic words that might not be evident through formal or structural criteria alone.

One prominent category includes dysphemisms related to illness. This semantic field often serves as a source of dysphemisms (Rezanova 2008, p. 278): *rakovaja opuhol'* "cancerous tumor"; *rasstrojstvo* "disorder"; *zaraza* "infection"; *epidemija* "epidemic"; *šizofrenija* "schizophrenia"; and *samye bol'nye ljudi na planete Zemlja* "the sickest people on the planet Earth," among others.

Pozdravljaju olimpijskuju sem'ju s tem, čto oni vyrezali ètu rakovuju ohupol' v vide Tomasa Baha.

Congratulations to the Olympic family for cutting out this cancerous tumor in the form of Thomas Bach.
—Umar Kremlev, president of International Boxing Association (Kremlev, 2024b)

Ja ne dumaju, čto umestno reagirovat' na takie èmocional'nye i obsessivno-kompul'sivnye rasstrojstva, pričinu kotoryh čašče vsego možno najti v trudah Frejda.
I don't think it's appropriate to react to such emotional and obsessive-compulsive disorders, the causes of which can most often be found in Freud's works.
—Filipp Švetskij, former doctor for Russian figure skating national team (Gončarov, 2023)

Russophobia is perceived as a disease, as exemplified with adjectives such as *hroničeskij rusofob* "chronical Russophobe," *kliničeskij rusofob* "clinical Russophobe."

Some dysphemisms fall into a semantic category related to sexual acts, as seen in *prostitutka* "prostitute"; *impotencija* "impotence"; *sodomit* "sodomite"; and *sodomija* "sodomy."

Kremlev nazval MOK političeskimi prostitutkami posle isključenija IBA.
Kremlev called the IOC political prostitutes after excluding IBA. [headline]
—Umar Kremlev, president of International Boxing Association (Antonov, 2024)

Irina Rodnina, Olympic champion and politician, uses a dysphemism to criticize the IOC for the decision to deny accreditation to journalists from RIA Novosti Sport for the 2024 Olympics in Paris. The inserted phrase "excuse me" indicates her awareness of the taboo nature of the dysphemism.

Oni že nam tol'ko rasskazyvajut pro svoju demokratiju, a tak u nih suščestvuet absoljut-nejšaja, izvinite, gruppovuha. Ili, inymi slovami, krugovaja poruka.
They only tell us about their democracy, but in reality, they have an absolute, excuse me, gang bang. Or, in other words, a mutual cover-up.
—Irina Rodnina, former figure skater and politician (Rodnina, 2024)

Sex-based dysphemisms also appear in discussions about the opening ceremony of the 2024 Olympic Games in Paris, which featured drag queens. This was viewed as conflicting with Russia's so-called "traditional values."

Olimpijskie igry 2024—èto prjamaja sodomija i uničtoženie tradicionnyh cennostej vo vsem mire.
The 2024 Olympic Games are outright sodomy and the destruction of traditional values worldwide.
—Umar Kremlev, president of the International Boxing Association (Savinova 2024)

Dysphemisms arise from historical atrocities that evoke negative reactions in specific cultures. Terms such as *nacisty* "Nazis," *fašisty* "fascists," and *genocid* "genocide," which are widely circulated in Russian official narrative against Ukraine (Fortuin, 2022), are also extended into Russian sports discourse and used against perceived enemies in international sports community.

> *Opjat' že, dumaju, èto vse èto ne sportsmeny, a politika ih strany i NOK. Real'no vedut sebja kak nacisty.*
> Again, I think this is not about the athletes but rather the politics of their country and the NOC. They really behave like Nazis.
> —Ol'ga Zajceva, former biathlete (Guščina, 2024)

> *A MOK v svoju očered' vedet sebja slovno fašisty, ustrajvaja genocid sportsmenov po nacionalnomu priznaku i prinimaja političeskie rešenija.*
> And the IOC, in turn, behaves like fascists, committing genocide against athletes based on nationality and making politicized decisions.
> —Umar Kremlev, president of the International Boxing Association (Konov-ml, 2024)

Some dysphemisms are based on animalization to humiliate the target, such as *barany* "sheep"; *kliacha* "nag"; *ameba* "amoeba"; *amorfnaja meduza* "amorphous jellyfish"; and *ručnaja obez'janka* "pet monkey."

> *A te, kto ego podderživajut, nastojaščie barabany, u kotoryh otsutstvujut čelovecheskie cennosti.*
> And those who support him [Thomas Bach] are real sheep who lack human values.
> —Umar Kremlev, president of the International Boxing Association, 2024 (Kremlev, 2024a)

> *Olimpiada i ee ideja v zapadnom ispolnenii—to staraja kljača, kotoruju davno pora pristrelit'.*
> The Olympics and its idea in the Western execution are like an old nag that should have been put down long ago. [headline]
> —Tina Kandelaki, deputy general director of Gazprom Media Holding (Kandelaki, 2024)

Dysphemisms are related to betrayal. Russian athletes who changed their citizenship to other countries are described using past active participles that remind their "unpatriotic" behavior: *sbežavšij ot Rossii* "who fled Russia'"; *otkazavšijsja ot Rossii* "who rejected Russia"; *otrekšijsja ot Rossii* "who renounced Russia"; *brosivšij Rossiju* "who threw away Russia"; *pokinuvšij Rossiju* "who left Russia." Athletes are referred to as *predatel'/predatel'nica* "betrayer," *perebežčik* "turncoat," and their actions are framed as *predatel'stvo* "betrayal" and *pobeg* "escape."

> *Sbežavšie iz Rossii čempiony moljatja o pasportah SŠA. Predateli gotovy na vse.*
> Champions who fled Russia are praying for US passports. Traitors are ready for anything. [headline] (Nikitina, 2024)

> *Tem bolee peremanivanie rossijskih zvezd v moment, kogda im prosto zapreščeno vystupat' na krupnejših turnirah—grjaznaja igra i proizvol. Pora otvetit' na otkrovennoe vorovstvo kadrov.*
> All the more, poaching Russian stars at a time when they are simply banned from competing in major tournaments is dirty play and arbitrariness. It's time to respond to the blatant theft of talent. (Kovalenko, 2023)

From a Russian perspective, little attention is given to positive doping tests among Western athletes, with their use of performance-enhancing substances perceived as justified by medical exemptions (Zmeev, 2017, p. 91). Consequently, foreign athletes who are permitted to use substances under medical exemptions are marked as targets: *legalizovannye dopingisty* "legalized doping athletes"; *otkrytaja dopingistka* "open doping girl"; *norvežskij dopingist* "Norwegian doping athlete"; *francuskaja dopingistka* "French doping girl"; *amerikanskaja dopingistka* "American doping girl"; and *hodjačaja reklama tabletok* "walking ad for pills."

Journalists do not hesitate to attack foreign athletes who negatively commented on Russian athletes, by using adjectives related to their physical appearance: *krupnaja* "big" or *tjaželaja* "heavy" in order to disparage their figures, although these terms may be seen as euphemistic alternatives to *tolstaja* "fat."

> *Bonus za rusofobiju. Medlennuju i krupnuju figuristku tjanut k zolotu čempionata mira.*
> Bonus for Russophobia. A slow and large figure skater is pulled to the gold medal of the World championship. [headline] (Gal'cov, 2024)

Dysphemisms are often employed by certain sports figures, such as the president of the International Boxing Association, Umar Kremlev, who provides rich material for the dysphemisms presented in this paper. This suggests that dysphemization may be indicative of an individual's linguistic behavior. Indeed, such a personalistic approach has been adopted in researches on Vladimir Putin (Kameneva & Rabkina, 2021, pp. 510–512), and Dmitrij Medvedev (Sładkiewicz, 2023, p.139). Dysphemisms are also characteristic of tabloid media platforms. For example, in the sports media outlet Sportbox.ru, journalists deliberately use harsh comments from sports figures as headlines, and persistently employ dysphemisms themselves to express irony or disdain toward their targets.

Without addressing the ethical aspect of dysphemization by Russian sports figures and journalists, linguistic aggression in the form of dysphemisms in Russian sports discourse symbolizes its adversarial nature and resentment toward the international sports community.

Conclusions

Wartime conditions politicize Russian sports discourse and have strengthened Russia's antagonistic stance in this domain. Contemporary Russian sports discourse exhibits both defensive aggression, articulated through the Russophobia frame—which serves to self-victimize and construct enemies—and offensive aggression in the form of dysphemisms targeting perceived adversaries.

As this is our first attempt at analyzing Russian sports discourse, this paper opens avenues for further research. A more thorough comparison between Russian sports discourse and other forms of discourse, such as political discourses, would contribute to a deeper theoretical understanding. The Russophobia frame is not the only narrative device employed in Russia's official rhetoric. Further analysis is needed to explore its parallels with other frames employed in Russian wartime discourse, such as the Nazism frame and the cancel culture frame. In terms of the timing, war-driven topics in Russian sports discourse overlap with global discussions on transgender athletes. Given Russia's increasing emphasis on so-called "traditional values," a comparative discourse analysis across different national contexts would be particularly illuminating.

Discourse may vary depending on the discipline, including factors such as media coverage, the competitiveness of Russian athletes, the degree of commercialization, and the prominence of individual sports figures. For example, in disciplines where Russian athletes have traditionally dominated—such as figure skating, rhythmic gymnastics, artistic swimming, and biathlon—sporting figures are more dependent on state support and may express greater frustration over international bans and thus exhibit resentment to global sports community. In contrast, sports where Russia has not consistently succeeded on the global stage—or where commercial viability within the country provides a degree of independence such as soccer—may display different discursive patterns.

References

Allan, K., & Burridge, K. (1991). *Euphemism & dysphemism: language used as shield and weapon.* Oxford University Press.

Artamonova, U. Z., & Rustamova, L. R. (2023). "Otmena" Rossii: posledstvija dlja kultur'noj diplomatii. *Mirovaja èkonomika i meždunarodnye otnošenija, 67*(4), 123–131.

Bonarrigo, G., & Dallera, D. (2022, September 22). Thomas Bach: «I Giochi per la pace. Facciamo gareggiare i russi contro la guerra». *Corriere della Sera.* https://www.corriere.it/sport/22_settembre_30/intervista-thomas-bach-giochi-avranno-missione-pace-128976c4-402c-11ed-815f-9b7904035c1c.shtml

Caldwell, D., Walsh J., Vine, E. W., & Jureidini, J. (2017). Discourse, linguistics, sport and the academy. In D. Caldwell, J. Walsh, E. W. Vine, & J. Jureidini (Eds.), *The discourse of sport. Analysis from social linguistics* (pp. 1–12). Routledge.

Čebar' E. V., & Nazarov, V. L. (2023). Vlijanie antirossijskih sankcij kollektivnogo Zapada na rossijskij sport. *Fizičeskaja kul'tura, sport i molodežnaja politika v uslovijah global'nyh vyzovov,* 473–480.

Darczewska, J., & Żochowski, P. (2015). Russophobia in the Kremlin's strategy. A weapon of mass destruction. *Point of View, 56,* 5–28.

Decree of the President of the Russian Federation. (2024). http://publication.pravo.gov.ru/document/0001202412280115

Fortuin, E. (2022). Ukraine commits genocide on Russians: The term "genocide" in Russian propaganda. *Russian Linguistics, 46,* 313–347. https://doi.org/10.1007/s11185-022-09258-5

Horiguchi, D. (2024). Language issues in Ukrainian sports Media during the wartime. *Półrocznik Językoznawczy Tertium, 9*(1), 130–155. https://doi.org/10.7592/Tertium.2024.9.1.284

Hoyle, A., Powell, T., Doosje, B., van den Berg, H., & Wagnsson, C. (2024). Weapons of mass division: *Sputnik Latvia*'s Russophobia narratives and testing the rejection-identification model in Russian speakers in Latvia. *Political Psychology, 45,* 753–772. https://doi.org/10.1111/pops.12964

Kameneva, V. A., & Rabkina N. V. (2021). Disfemizacija političeskogo diskursa glavy gosudarstva. *Aktual'nye problemy gumanitarnyh nauk, 676,* 509–513.

Kijamova, K. È. (2018). Političeskij diskurs v sportivnyh SMI Rossii i Velikobritanii. *Vek informacii* (online media) *2*(1-2). https://doi.org/10.33941/age-info.com21(2)2018007

Korneeva, V. A. (2017). Aktualizacija sportivnogo diskursa «mjagkoj sily» v uslovijah èskalacii političeskogo naprjaženija. *Diskurs-Pi, 3–4*(28–29), 269–275. https://doi.org/10.17506/dipi.2017.2829.34.269275

McNally, R. T. (1958). The Origins of Russophobia in France: 1812–1830. *The American Slavic and East European Review, 17*(2), 173–189.

Novikov, N. V. (2015). Politizacija frankojazyčnyh sportivnyh SMI. Vlast' političeskogo diskursa. *Političeskaja lingvistika, 2*(52), 206–213.

Rezanova, A. N. (2008). Klassifikacija disfemizmov po leksiko-semantičeskim razrjadam. *Izvestija Rosijskogo gosudarstvennogo pedagogičeskogo universiteta im. A. I. Gercena, 27*(61), 277–280.

Robinson, N. (2019). "Russophobia" in official Russian political discourse. *De Europa, 2*(2), 61–77. https://hdl.handle.net/10344/8429

Romashko, T. (2024). Who is actually cancelling Russian culture and art? Conference paper, *Compendium of Cultural Policies and Trends,* 1–13. https://www.culturalpolicies.net/wp-content/uploads/2024/05/Romashko_Compendium-2024.pdf

Schirato, T. (2013). *Sports Discourse.* Bloomsbury.

Šejgal, E. I. (2002). *Semiotika političeskogo diskursa* [Doctoral dissertation]. Volgograd State Pedagogical University.

Sizov, S. G. (2015). Rusfobija kak raznovidnost' političeskogo i kul'turnogo ėkstrematizma (Ukraina i Rossija). *Vestnik Omskogo universiteta. Serija "Pravo,"* 2(43), 254–257.

Sładkiewicz, Ż. (2023). Rola dysfemizmow w kreowaniu obrazu rzeczywistości wojennej: pragmalingwistyczna analiza rosyjskiego dyskursu medialnego na temat wojny w Ukrainie. *Studia Rossica Gedanensia, 10,* 133–148. https://doi.org/10.26881/srg.2023.10.09

Ventsel, A., Hansson, S., Madisson, M.-L., & Sazonov, V. (2021). Discourse of fear in strategic narratives: The case of Russia's Zapad war games. *Media, War & Conflict, 14* (1), 21–39.

Vladimirova, A. (2020). *Sport as a part of the state propaganda system in Russia.* Reuters Institute Fellowship Paper. University of Oxford. https://reutersinstitute.politics.ox.ac.uk/sites/default/files/2020-05/Sportspropaganda.Final-%20Alexandra%20Vladimirova.docx%20%281%29.pdf

Zelenkauskaitė, A. (2022). *Creating chaos online: Disinformation and subverted post-publics.* University of Michigan Press. https://doi.org/10.3998/mpub.12237294

Zil'bert, A. B. (2001a). Sportivnyj diskurs: bazovye ponjatija i kategorii; issledovatel'skie zadači. *Jazyk, soznanie, kommunikacija, 17,* 45–55.

Zil'bert, A. B. (2001b). Sportivnyj diskurs: točki peresečenija s drugimi diskursami (problemy intertekstual'nosti). *Jazyk, soznanie, kommunikacija, 19,* 103–112.

Zmeev, N. D. (2017). Pojavlenie rusofobii v sporte. *Molodež' v menjajuščemsja v mire: vyzovy sovremennosti. Materialy VIII Vserossijskoj naučno-praktičeskoj konferencii molodyh učenyh, 2,* 90–93.

Sources of Illustrative Materials

Andrijanov, A. (2024, December 21). Fetisov: «Gašek—bol'noj čelovek na golovu. Šajba emu po golove popadala na neskol'ko raz». *Match TV.* https://matchtv.ru/hockey/matchtvnews_NI2149379_Fetisov_Gashek__bolnoj_chelovek_na_golovu_Shajba_jemu_po_golove_popadala_neskolko_raz

Antonov, M. (2024, July 23). Kremlev nazval MOK političeskimi prostitutkami posle rešenija isključit IBA iz spiska priznannyh federacij. *Sport-Express.* https://www.sport-express.ru/olympics/summer/news/kremlev-nazval-mok-politicheskimi-prostitutkami-posle-resheniya-isklyuchit-iba-iz-spiska-priznannyh-federaciy-2235846/

Astahov, S. (2024, March 18). Trener sbornoj RF po sportivnoj gimnastike: «Što važnee, gibnuščie za rodinu muždiny ili potencial'naja medal' na Olimpiade?». *Match TV.* https://matchtv.ru/olimpijskije_igry/matchtvnews_NI2031202_Trener_sbornoj_RF_po_sportivnoj_gimnastike_Chto_vazhneje_gibnushhije_za_rodinu_muzhchiny_ili_potencialnaja_medal_na_Olimpiade

Borodavko, S. (2022, November 8). Ves' sport propitan sil'nejšej rusofobiej, ščitaet Borodavko. *RIA Novosti Sport.* https://rsport.ria.ru/20221108/borodavko-1829936878.html

Gal'cov, K. (2024, March 21). Bonus za rusofobiju. Medlennuju i krupnuju figuristku tjanut k zolotu čempionata mira. *Sportbox.ru.* https://news.sportbox.ru/Vidy_sporta/Figurnoe_katanie/spbnews_NI2032488_Bonus_za_rusofobiju_Medlennuju_i_krupnuju_figuristku_tanut_k_zolotu_chempionata_mira

Gal'cov, K. (2025, January 22). Ni styda ni sovesti. Pol'skuju mošennicu taščat k titulu Australian Open. *Sportbox.ru.* https://news.sportbox.ru/Vidy_sporta/Tennis/WTA/spbnews_NI2159748_Ni_styda_ni_sovesti_Polskuju_moshennicu_tashhat_k_titulu_na_Australian_Open

Goncharov, M. (2023, September 28). Vrač Švetskij: «U Djuamel' obsessivno-kompulsivnoe rasstrojstvo, pricinu kotorogo možno najti v trudah Frejda». *Match TV*. https://matchtv.ru/figure-skating/matchtvnews_NI1954612_Vrach_Shvetskij_U_Duamel_obsessivnokompulsivnoje_rasstrojstvo_prichinu_kotorogo_mozhno_najti_v_trudah_Frejda

Guščina, N. (2024, July 19). Zajceva: «U NOK Ukrainy nacistskie sklonnosti. Oni ne sohranjajut principy olimpijskoj hartii». *Match TV*. https://matchtv.ru/olimpijskije_igry/matchtvnews_NI2082349_Zajceva_U_NOK_Ukrainy_nacistskije_sklonnosti_Oni_ne_sohranajut_principy_Olimpijskoj_khartii

Jampoľskaja, Ju. (2021, August 7). Zaharova nazvala rusofobskoj vojnoj sudejstvo Averiny na Olimpiade. *Lenta.ru*. https://lenta.ru/news/2021/08/07/warr/

Kandelaki, T. (2024, August 12). Kandelaki: «Olimpiada i ee ideja v zapadnom ispolnenii—èto staraja kljača, kotoruju davno pora pristrelit'». *Match TV*. https://matchtv.ru/olimpijskije_igry/matchtvnews_NI2092661_Kandelaki_Olimpiada_i_jeje_ideja_v_zapadnom_ispolnenii__eto_staraja_klacha_kotoruju_davno_pora_pristrelit

Konov-ml, V. (2024, July 23). «MOK vedet sebja slovno fašisty, èto političeskie prostitutki, kotorye bojatsja sobstvennoj teni»—glava IBA Kremlev. *Match TV*. https://matchtv.ru/boxing/matchtvnews_NI2083913_MOK_vedet_seba_slovno_fashisty_eto_politicheskije_prostitutki_kotoryje_bojatsa_sobstvennoj_teni__glava_IBA_Kremlev

Kovalenko, E. (2023, December 26). Žestkij otvet Rossii na proizvol v figurnom katanii. Sami naprosilis'! *Sportbox.ru*. https://news.sportbox.ru/Vidy_sporta/Figurnoe_katanie/spbnews_NI1999199_Zhostkij_otvet_Rossii_na_proizvol_v_figurnom_katanii_Sami_naprosilis

Kremlev, U. (2024a, July 31) Glava IBA Umar Kremlev nazval baranami teh, kto podderživaet Tomasa Baha. *Sportbox.ru*. https://news.sportbox.ru/olympics/spbnews_NI2087419_Glava_IBA_Umar_Kremlev_nazval_baranami_teh_kto_podderzhivajet_Tomasa_Baha

Kremlev, U. (2024b, August 14). «Pozdravljaju olimpijskuju semju tem, čto oni vyrezali ètu rakovuju opuhol v vide Tomasa Baha»—glava IBA Kremlev. *Match TV*. https://matchtv.ru/olimpijskije_igry/matchtvnews_NI2092557_Pozdravljaju_olimpijskuju_semju_s_tem_chto_oni_vyrezali_etu_rakovuju_opuhol_v_vide_Tomasa_Baha__glava_IBA_Kremlev

Levkovič, P. (2024, December 15). «V IBU sobralis' ot"javlennye rusofoby, somniteľno, čto nas vernut na meždunarodnye starty»—Vasiľev. *Match TV*. https://matchtv.ru/biathlon/matchtvnews_NI2147073_V_IBU_sobralis_otjavlennyje_rusofoby_somnitelno_chto_nas_vernut_na_mezhdunarodnyje_starty__Vasiljev

Matycin, O. (2023, October 19). Matycin zajavil, čto Rossii ne sleduet razryvať svjazi s mirovym sportom. *TASS*. https://tass.ru/sport/19061179

Moskaľkova, T. (2024, January 31). Moskaľkova nazvala diskvalifikaciju Valievoj neprikrytoj rusofobiej. *RIA Novosti Sport*. https://rsport.ria.ru/20240131/valieva-1924512638.html

Neradovskaja. S. (2022, February 3). Vdvojne cenno: Valuev vyskazalsja o pobedah atletov, lišennyh flaga i gimna RF. *Pravda.ru*. https://www.pravda.ru/news/sport/1680079-olimpiada/

Nikitina, M. (2024, January 12). Sbežavšie iz Rossii čempiony moljatja o pasportah SŠA. Predateli gotovy na vse. *Sportbox.ru*. https://news.sportbox.ru/Vidy_sporta/fehtovanie/spbnews_NI2003641_Sbezhavshije_iz_Rossii_chempiony_molatsa_o_pasportah_SShA_Predateli_gotovy_na_vso

Packevič, A. (2022, October 1). *Telegram.* https://web.telegram.org/k/#@vashasashasynchro

Počežircev, S. (2024, July 20). «Rusofobija ne znaet granic». Rossijskuju zvezdu UFC žestko podstavili s dopingom. *Sportbox.ru.* https://news.sportbox.ru/Vidy_sporta/edinoborstva/spbnews_NI2082559_Rusofobija_ne_znajet_granic_Rossijskuju_zvezdu_UFC_zhestko_podstavili_s_dopingom

Pokrovskaja, T. (2024, March 31). Pokrovskaja otvetila mèru Idal'go: «My ne v Pariž sobiralis', a na Olimpijskie igry». *Sport-Ekspress.* https://www.sport-express.ru/olympics/paris2024/news/pokrovskaya-otreagirovala-na-slova-mera-parizha-v-adres-rossiyskih-sportsmenov-2195769/

Pozdnjakov, S. (2023, October 6). *Pozdnjakov nazval ograničenija MOK «sportivnym genocidom» rossijan.* https://sportrbc.ru/news/651ff92a9a79471fb2a649b5

Puškarev, V. (2024, July 23). «Nas davjat sankcijami, no my stanem, ešče sil'nee»—Lebedev o rešenii MOK isključit' IBA. *Match TV.* https://matchtv.ru/boxing/matchtvnews_NI2083895_Nas_davat_sankcijami_no_my_stanem_jeshhe_silneje__Lebedev_o_reshenii_MOK_iskluchit_IBA

Putin, V. (2024, February 29). Bez sil'noj Rossii pročnyj miroporjadok nevozmožen, zajavil Putin. *RIA Novosti.* https://ria.ru/20240229/putin-1930187955.html

Rodnina, I. (2024, July 22). «Tam absoljutnejšaja gruppovuha». Rodnina ob"jasnila otkaz rossijskim žurnalistam v rabote na Olimpiade. *Match TV.* https://matchtv.ru/olimpijskije_igry/matchtvnews_NI2083547_Tam_absolutnejshaja_gruppovuha_Rodnina_objasnila_otkaz_rossijskim_zhurnalistam_v_rabote_na_Olimpiade

Savinova, A. (2024, July 31). Kremlev nazval Olimpiadu v Pariže prjamoj sodomiej: «Otvetstvennym javljaetsja Bah». *Sport-Ekspress.* https://www.sport-express.ru/olympics/summer/news/kremlev-nazval-olimpiadu-v-parizhe-pryamoy-sodomiey-otvetstvennym-yavlyaetsya-bah-2238822/

Tihonov, A. (2022, May 4). "On rab Ameriki": Tihonov žestko prošelsja po glave MOK Tomasu Bahu. *RIA Novosti Sport.* https://rsport.ria.ru/20220504/bakh-1786757543.html

Železnjakov, A. (2024, March 25). «Rossijskie figuristy byli by brilliantovym ožerel'em na čempionate mira, a bez nih èto deševaja bižuterija»—Železnjakov. *Match TV.* https://matchtv.ru/figure-skating/matchtvnews_NI2033791_Rossijskije_figuristy_byli_by_brilliantovym_ozhereljem_na_chempionate_mira_a_bez_nih_eto_deshevaja_bizhuterija__Zheleznakov

Železnov, A. (2024, May 8). Olimpiadu v Pariže prevratjat v reklamu dopinga. Sportsmeny b'jut trevogu. *Sportbox.ru.* https://news.sportbox.ru/olympics/spbnews_NI2054000_Olimpiadu_v_Parizhe_prevratat_v_reklamu_dopinga_Sportsmeny_bjut_trevogu

Acknowledgements

This research was supported by Kyoto University Foundation.

CHAPTER EIGHT | **ELENA KURANT**

A War Between Generations

The Generational Boundary in Contemporary Russian Drama

Abstract

The conflict between generations has traditionally been an existential problem for Russian culture and literature, attracting considerable literary research in the process. The gap in intergenerational continuity, combined with the destruction of the generational transmission of values, reflects the cultural, political, and social shifts in society at the most dramatic points of its growth. The crux of this issue can be found in the current situation where the values of the older generation have become outdated, and its legacy is not only rejected on an ideological level but also in terms of external forms (clothing, language, appearance). On the other hand, the Putin-led gerontocratic regime has specifically targeted the values of the new generation, forcing young and educated individuals to leave the country. Using selected dramaturgical texts by contemporary authors such as Asya Voloshina, Lyubov Strizhak, and Alexey Zhitkovsky the article analyzes how the conflict between generations escalated during the 2010s–2020s, a period which can be delineated as a kind of transitional border zone. It will also examine how the war in Ukraine is becoming the final boundary separating the current generation of children from that of their parents. The new generation, dissociated and lost, is trying to cope with generational trauma while bearing the weight of collective guilt and shame.

Keywords: generation conflict, antiwar Russian drama, generational trauma, Russian drama in exile

The problem of generations has long been a central, existential concern in Russian culture and literature—and a persistent focus of scholarly inquiry. The breakdown of intergenerational continuity and the recurring rift between *parents and children* often mirror dramatic political, cultural, and social upheavals. Questions of self-identification, belonging, and personal formation bring generational conflict to the forefront of reflections on the *hero of our time*.¹ Soviet and post-Soviet culture produced several ideologically charged generational labels—such as the *Sixtiers* (*shestidesyatniki*), the *Generation of Stagnation* (*pokoleniye zastoia*), and the *Lost Generation* (*potieriyannoye pokoleniye*). These terms do not reflect age per se, but broader sociopolitical transitions and disillusionments.²

In the Russia of today, amid accelerating change and ideological fractures, we are witnessing another wave of generational rupture. Established values are being contested, habitual norms violently dismantled, and fundamental questions of meaning and direction reopened. The problem of generations has once again become one of the most urgent and traumatic concerns in Russian society. On one hand, the values of the older generation are increasingly rejected—not only ideologically but in their outward forms (clothing, language, appearance); on the other hand, the gerontocratic regime led by Vladimir Putin has aggressively suppressed the emerging worldview of younger Russians. It is this younger, educated generation—often forced into exile—that has become both a target of repression and the bearer of an alternative future.

Professor Aleksander Etkind (2023) describes the Russo-Ukrainian War as "a war between generations: an Oedipus conflict of enormous scale" (p. 104). He argues that

> The political regime that launched the war in Ukraine was as gerontocratic as in the last years of the Soviet Union. [...] Putin, aged seventy, could easily be the forty-four-year-old Zelensky's father, and the same was true of almost every Russian member of cabinet in comparison to their Ukrainian counterparts. (p. 103)

According to Etkind, the conditions for the war emerged from generational conflicts within Russia and Ukraine—particularly between septuagenarian boomers entrenched in power and the younger generations demanding change. In this sense, the war can not only be seen as a geopolitical conflict but also as a symbolic generational war—a backlash against modernity, cultural pluralism, and progressive values. The longstanding generational separation and mutual alienation, deeply rooted in Soviet history and perpetuated throughout the post-Soviet period, only intensified in the 2020s. This article examines generational conflict in contemporary Russian-language drama by analyzing a selection of plays that represent the experiences of young Russians across different stages of growth and political consciousness. Drawing on Yuri Lotman's concept of the *semiosphere*—the culturally coded space in which

---

1. The concept of the *hero of our time* (after the title of Mikhail Lermontov's novel [1840]) describes a collective image of the young generation of the historical period in question.
2. The idea of a political generation refers to Karl Manheim's theory of a generation as a "group that is distinctive in any number of respects by virtue of having experienced a specific set of social, economic, technological, and/or political circumstances as a formative period in their lives" (Stoker, 2014).

communication and identity are formed—we investigate how dramatic texts reflect and shape generational boundaries in Russia during the post-Soviet and Putin eras.

The focus of our attention is the generation of people born between the late 1980s and the early 2000s, whose political socialization took place during the period of authoritarian consolidation in the 2000s–2010s. This cohort is often referred to as the *Putin generation*—as they grew up under Putin—implying ideological loyalty; however, it cannot be assessed unambiguously. In Mikita Kuchinski's (2025) article *Generation P* it is argued that, unlike older generations who largely internalized Soviet and post-Soviet authoritarian norms, young Russians—especially those born after 2000—tend to be more digitally literate, oriented toward global cultural codes, and likely to experience internal conflict between their personal values and the state's ideology. Viewing this generation as monolithic seems both implausible and impossible: some are apolitical, others socially engaged; some oppose the Kremlin, while others support it. For instance, a report by the Friedrich Ebert Foundation (Gudkov et al., 2019) emphasizes that young Russians are increasingly rejecting the state's moralizing and violent discourse, even if they remain politically passive. One can only assume that their initial political inertia, extreme individualism, and nonconformism have ultimately made them more resilient to the aggressive propaganda of militarized Putinism and more irreconcilable in their conflict with the older generation.

Informed by this sociopolitical context, the article analyses four plays: *Sneakers* (*Kedy*, 2012) by Lyubov Strizhak; *To Plant a Tree* (*Posadit' derevo*, 2015) by Aleksey Zhitkowski; and Mama (2016) and Crime (2022) by Esther Bol (Asya Voloshina). Lyubov Strizhak is a playwright who has worked with various progressive and independent theaters such as Theatre.doc, Praktika Theatre, Gogol Center (which was closed down by the authorities in 2022), the Meyerhold Centre and others. She was the winner of Texture Theatre and Film International Festival in 2012. Alexey Zhitkovsky is a playwright, screenwriter, director, and winner of many theater awards and festivals (The Culmination Award for Contemporary Drama, Eurasian Drama Competition, the Lubimovka Independent Playwriting Festival and others). In 2022, he was charged with extremism because of his anti-war statements on social media. Asya Voloshina is one of the most prominent modern authors in Russia, as well as the winner of many prestigious literary and theater awards. Her plays have reached audiences in Russia, Poland, France, Lithuania, Latvia, Estonia, the Czech Republic, and Uruguay. After leaving Russia in 2022, she changed her name to Esther Bol.

The texts by the aforementioned authors collectively offer a portrait of the younger generation at different stages of development: adolescence, early adulthood, and post-invasion political crisis. Thus, we can trace the evolution of generational self-perception in response to shifting historical and ideological conditions. The selection of plays is deliberate: each dramatizes a moment of socialization, rupture, or dissent, mapping the formation of generational identity within the ideological contours of

Putin's Russia. The earliest of these texts—*Sneakers*—engages with the 2000s, when the so-called "sovereign democracy" model began to dominate state discourse. Later works, such as *Crime*, dramatize the existential and ethical crisis triggered by the 2022 invasion of Ukraine, representing a clear break with inherited worldviews and generational expectations. The theoretical lens of Yuri Lotman's (1990) semiosphere provides a useful framework for analyzing how these texts negotiate between official culture and counter-discourses. In Lotman's terms, generational identity can be understood as a semiospheric boundary: a contested zone where meaning is produced, resisted, and redefined. These boundaries are not only visible in ideological terms but also in embodied and linguistic differences, as seen in the generational clashes between parents and children. By combining sociological data, political commentary, and cultural theory, this article aims to demonstrate how contemporary Russian drama participates in the negotiation of generational boundaries and contributes to the broader semiospheric struggle over meaning, memory, and dissent.

This pattern creates a boundary between generations as a "frontier between one's own good and harmonious culture and its bad, chaotic or even dangerous counter-cultures" (Nöth, 2015), separating *the Self* from *the Other*. As Lotman (1990) claims:

> Whether we have in mind language, politics, or culture, the mechanism is the same: one part of the semiosphere (as a rule one which is part of its nuclear structure) in the process of self-description creates its own grammar [...]. Then it strives to extend these norms over the whole semiosphere. (p. 128)

Generational rupture not only leads to political and ideological alienation but also to psychological trauma—especially among the youth. The loss of a shared moral basis and the erosion of familial bonds render the family unable to perform its traditional role as the existential anchor of identity. In such a vacuum, young individuals experience trauma not as a singular event but as a chronic condition of life under systemic disconnection and suppression. As Van der Kolk and Van der Hart (1991) suggest, trauma disrupts meaning-making, identity coherence, and one's relation to time and memory—all of which are central themes in contemporary Russian drama.

Taken together, these dynamics converge in what may be called a broader crisis of identity—a theme central to contemporary Russian drama and one that manifests itself in both generational and personal registers:

> Crisis of identity has become the content of an entire epoch, when one hierarchical system has been overlapped by a multitude of new and also competing social hierarchies, [...], modern man cannot accept as natural any of the places he occupies in the world and in society. (Bolotyan & Lavlinsky, 2010)

Gradually moving away from the acute social problems, the authors of modern texts for theater remain in the semantic area of searching for identity, feeling loneliness, and experiencing a sense of desolation.

The family issue is considered precisely in terms of trauma in the works of contemporary playwrights. The Other as the object and subject of violence, the painful dependence on the Other, which is necessary in the process of self-identification, have become the dominant generational themes in contemporary dramatic texts. The family is traditionally perceived as a guarantor of identity formation, as it forms the existential foundation for discovering the meaning of one's own existence (Starovotov, 2018). When the family is no longer a source of moral support, when family bonds are broken, when there is "the existential vacuum of the family system," the individual must assert themselves by means of opposites:

> through pain, through his own emptiness, through resistance and the inner conflict of acceptance, through the awareness of the loss of existential supports in the family and the need to rebuild it. (Starovotov, 2018)

In the play *To Plant a Tree* the main characters are family members: Father and Son. The list of characters specifies that Father is in his 40s, originally from the USSR, while Son is a software student in his 20s. Their origins are thus marked by a significant historical and political shift between the Soviet past and the post-Soviet present. Father brings his son out of town, to a field, to accomplish "the duty of every man": "to plant a tree, to build a house, to raise a son. That's what every man must manage."[3] The play starts as a parable, one which invites the audience to search for symbolic meaning and allegory: "the action takes place in an open field. The time of action is summer. The grass is green, birds are singing, bugs are buzzling" (Zhitkovsky, 2015). It is likely due to the parable-like nature of the play that the characters have no names or physical descriptions—they are symbolic figures embodying certain typical traits.

Father offers Son something akin to an initiation rite. Planting a tree is an accomplishment of his male role, as a family tree seems to be Father's attempt to incorporate Son into some traditional formula of generic continuity: "Shame on the one, who hasn't planted. To plant a tree… it was considered sacred!" (Zhitkovsky, 2015).

Planting a tree symbolizes life, growth, and the cycle of creation and birth. It represents the desire to "put down roots," connect with nature, and achieve a form of immortality through lasting legacy:

> Your children, my son […], will come, chew off a piece, thank you. And then perhaps they will remember me. Our grandfather and father—they will say—planted this apple tree, and now we eat the apples. I may be gone, but the apples… The apples will stay! (Zhitkovsky, 2015)

Son does not share Father's enthusiasm; he does not understand the meaning of the tradition. For him, all the talk about men, family, and honor are just "cheap thrills," and his Father is clearly a liar and a traitor: "What can you even teach me? To lie? To spit

---

3. Unless otherwise indicated, all translations from the original texts are by the author.

on the family. I'm sick of it." Each of them represents their own ideology: for Father the new generation has no roots, has nothing to give, it is not prepared for life: "Since they admitted someone like you to college, what will become of us?" (Zhitkovsky, 2015). For Son, Father's generation is duplicitous, meaningless, not worthy of respect: "All you men are shit. Mill operators, turners, officers, engineers, football players— you all lie. You lie all your lives!" (Zhitkovsky, 2015).

The way of following traditions turned out to be false: planting a tree is impossible, firstly, because the seedling Father bought at the market is a cheap Chinese plastic fake. Father, who had thus far acted as an expert, had been unable to distinguish it from a real one:

> My boy, I grew up in the Soviet Union, if I didn't know that, I wouldn't have been accepted into Pioneers, I wouldn't have been accepted anywhere… I would have been killed! We didn't graduate from college, son, but we knew everything, just everything! We knew what the capital of Honduras was, and all the parts of the body inside, and how to build a rocket. We knew everything, we could do everything! (Zhitkovsky, 2015)

Secondly, the field where Father takes Son also turns out to be a fake: the two security guards charged with protecting it inform the "gardeners" that it is an exclusive private golf course where international competitions are held. The traditional values that Father tries to rely on as guidelines fail. Closeness to nature and the return to one's roots turn out to be impossible, because even nature itself is revealed to be fake—a false construct within a traditional ideology. It is impossible to put down roots and achieve a lasting connection to the world—even the hope of gaining wisdom or transcendence, symbolized by the fruits of the Tree of Knowledge, which in this case takes the form of the apple tree, is out of reach. Instead of cherubs in the Garden of Eden, we see the security service with holstered guns at their waists. The conflict is settled in a somewhat superficial manner when, with their lives in danger, it is Son who negotiates with the guards. In the final scene, which takes something of a comic turn, everybody is reconciled, and the plastic tree is planted, with Son proclaimed a hero by one security guard: "Your son will be a big man" (Zhitkovsky, 2015). Also, as far as we keep in mind the parable character of the play, it can be assumed that the author is bringing the generations together in the face of real danger, when all fake beliefs lose their relevance, and it is the younger generation who is able to adapt to the new situation and find a solution. In *To Plant a Tree*, the ecological metaphor of growth and rootedness becomes a counterpoint to the experience of rupture. The older generation is embedded in narratives of duty and sacrifice, while the younger seeks care and emotional presence. The symbolic act of planting—which could imply continuity—instead becomes a moment of melancholy: a gesture toward a future that may never come. Here, the semiosphere is still imagined as reparable, but its fragmentation is profound and political.

Sneakers, a well-known and somewhat iconic play, is a portrait of the young generation. We can define its genre as a road story where hardly anything happens. The main character, 26-year-old Grisha, is a loafer who has just lost his job. As he goes to the store to buy himself a new pair of sneakers he meets his friends, musicians Misha and Sasha, they go to a house party at Katya's, Sasha's girlfriend, then go clubbing. The next morning, Grisha goes to an orphanage with a group of volunteers led by Cristina, his former boss's daughter, after which he gets into a scuffle with Cristina's father in his apartment, finally crashing his bike into a police van filled with people detained by OMON during the March of Those Who Disagree on Mayhakovsky Square in Moscow. The sneakers, which Grisha never manages to buy, not only become an obsession, but also a kind of azimuth in this chaotic disorderly journey of the main character who remains mostly in an altered state of consciousness, and apparently the only reason motivating his actions.

The author defines its genre as "a play-poem. Aka epopee" (Strizhak, 2011). An epopee, or an epic novel as a genre in which a heroic personality is presented in the background of history, "embodies the fate of peoples, the historical process itself":

> epopee is characterized by a broad, multifaced even comprehensive worldview including historical events, and the pictures of everyday life, and multi-voiced human chorus and deep reflections on the fate of the world, and intimate experiences of the individual. (Timofeev & Vengrov, 1963)

Thus, taking the author's definition of the genre into account, we can interpret the text as an attempt to portray the generation of the 1990s with its disorderly, aimless, everyday life, its lostness and unwillingness to follow the path of the parents. Each of "the heroes" of this modern epopee has a monologue revealing their fear of *adult life*, a lack of motivation and goals, inner emptiness, desolation, insecurity, loneliness, and the pain of misunderstanding:

> Sometimes I think I have nothing to add to this world not because there is everything already there, but because I am empty," "No one should ever know how scary it is for me to make a decision." (Strizhak, 2011)

Critics (Minaev, 2012) have repeatedly drawn parallels between the characters of the play *Sneakers* and the heroes of the Soviet films of the Thaw period, i.e., *Walking the Streets of Moscow* (1963) by Georgy Danelia, *I Am Twenty* (1965) by Marlen Khutsiev. Indeed, the manner in which the characters act can be traced in the seemingly carefree behaviour of the young people in both, but there is also a huge difference: these modern times do not truly require new heroes, and the younger generation themselves are all too aware of it.

Their aloofness, their deep feeling of loneliness in the crowd, their unwillingness to take responsibility and fear make them a lost, superfluous generation:

We are a generation of fear. I'm afraid of the future. Looking at our parents I see what it will look like, and I don't want it that way [...]. I am too delicate to lose, too coarse to keep. (Strizhak, 2011)

The adults in the play are something of a discrete, closed group and any dialogue with them is impossible. The essence of their relationships with the children is their stern voice, use of coercion, and denial of subjectivity. There is nothing in common between the two generations, neither real contact nor any attempts to be closer to each other. So, behind the cynicism, rebellion and escapism of the new *Oblomovs*,[4] there is confusion and a pessimistic worldview: "this is a war, I just don't see the enemy" the main character says (Strizhak, 2011).

The ending of the play is a bitter one: Grisha crashes his bicycle into a police van after witnessing the police beating Misha, who was filming the brutal detention of women at the March of Dissenters on his phone. Grisha is not driven to the march by a clearly expressed ideology or firm stance; he ends up there by chance. Yet his impulsive and singular act becomes the play's extreme expression of dissent. The *lost* generation becomes the *doomed* generation because both its inaction and action prove ineffective.

Grisha demands personal freedom—in his room and in life—but constantly clashes with institutions imposing rules and roles: his mother, his boss, Misha, and his pregnant girlfriend. He is caught between them, forever the child denied the chance to *be himself*. Yet he doesn't know who he is or how to handle freedom, except by smoking, yelling, running away, and—accidentally—speaking the truth. Grisha is a generational Everyman: neither a fighter nor submissive, trapped inside a storm he cannot name. This sharp contrast between *childish* and *adult* modes renders adulthood both shameful and necessary. Grisha's rejection of fatherhood marks not just a personal conflict but a cultural crisis of male subjectivity.

Grisha's generation cannot transcend their inner space—they are symbolically unable to master the language of family, parenthood, and responsibility. Their coordinates remain post-ironic, joking, and playing. Grisha's political gesture at the play's end—crashing his bike into a police van detaining protesters—is an impulsive act of protest. It embodies the frustration of a young man caught between a desire for freedom and oppressive institutional structures. This gesture is neither a strategic political manifesto nor naïve bravado but a raw, emotional refusal to accept the status quo.

As a representative of the *Putin generation*, Grisha epitomizes a youth which is shaped by authoritarianism, surveillance, and limited freedoms. This generation is

---

4. Ilya Ilyich Oblomov is the main character of the novel *Oblomov* by Ivan Goncharov, published in 1859. He is often used as a symbol of generosity and idealism combined with apathy, stagnation, and the inability to act—ultimately paralyzed by his own detachment from reality.

marked by internal conflict: craving freedom but unsure how to assert agency, blending passivity and protest, alienation and self-assertion. His act of defiance reflects the contradictions of a generation raised under a regime that suppresses civic engagement but cannot fully extinguish the urge to resist.

The next two texts in which the generational topic is a relevant issue were written by Asya Voloshina. The play *Mama* (2016) was performed on the Small Stage of Sankt Petersburg State Academic Lensovet Theatre in the form of performative reading by Yuri Butusov, a renowned director and former artistic director of Lensovet, as well as the chief staging director at the E. Vakhtangov Theatre (2018–2022), who has directed performances not only in Russia but also in Poland, Korea, Norway, Bulgaria, Lithuania, and Denmark.[5]

The play is written in a documentary style—specifically in the mockumentary genre—and takes the form of a monologue-letter by Olya, a 28-year-old woman, interwoven with fragments from letters written by her mother, Nastya. Nastya died of cancer at the age of 28, and before she died, she had been writing letters to her daughter for half a year. Olya received the letters from her mother on each birthday from 7 to 28. The traumatic experience of her mother's absence and the world seen through the prism of this absence overlap with the process of Olya's growing up and the episodes of her adolescence.

For the daughter, the dead mother becomes the very unreachable, inaccessible Other from Levinas's philosophy,[6] the Other whom she seeks to cognize sometimes by denying, sometimes by comparing with herself, trying to feel from the letters what exactly her mother felt, who she was, how she would behave in different situations.

The pain and resentment that little Olya feels upon receiving the first letter from her mother on her seventh birthday are expressed by painting over her mother's picture (the first letter is a pencil drawing of a girl and a woman holding hands):

> I've painted it with anger. Because it seemed to me: that's obvious that something is extremely wrong here. You shouldn't smile stupidly like that from ear to ear to the girl, or mom should be painted over. Otherwise, it doesn't make sense [...]. There also was an inscription Olya and Nastya. I also did it. Painted it over. Because if that

---

5. After Russia's full-scale military invasion of Ukraine in 2022, Yury Butusov left the country and has continued his artistic career in Europe.
6. The Other is a crucial concept in Levinas's philosophy. The encounter with the Other changes everything: it occurs when we recognize the Other as a unique human being. The Other calls us out of our self-centered existence. The desire to understand and respond to the Other is endless, but it can never be fully satisfied, because the Other always remains partly unknowable—mysterious, uncontrollable, and undefined.

mum is coloured, she is alive. And my mum is dead. So it's not me and her, but some other mum. Not Nastya. Such a childish protest all that means. (Voloshina, 2016)

The letters of her mother become a burden that cannot be dropped, they make her re-experience the trauma of being abandoned again and again. They intensify the presence of absence, establishing the surrounding world as incomplete, one in which something is irrevocably lost and which makes any self-realization impossible. Just like the boar's skull in the Ramsey children's room in *To the Lighthouse* by Virginia Woolf, the mother's letters remind Olya every year that death is always there nearby, and that loneliness is absolute. They embody the impossibility of getting closer to the mother and, at the same time, the inability to separate from her. The understanding, experience and ultimate acceptance of loneliness, doom and orphanhood is presented in the play as a painful process of self-exposure of the human being in their pain and suffering, in all the intimate details of their existence. The culmination of this process is the decision of the main character not to have children, a rejection of being a link in the predetermined biological chain of mother-daughter-granddaughter, a refusal to accept the succession of generations as her inevitable fate. The space of the play is saturated with asymmetrical generational codes of memory and trauma. Olya and her mother, Nastya, exist in distinct semiotic universes with nonoverlapping temporal and experiential coordinates. The mother's letters form for Olya a closed system of signs, feelings, and maternal narratives that she attempts to decipher from the outside. As Olya matures, her attempts to understand her mother's words not only become a personal confrontation with trauma but also an act of intergenerational translation, where meanings, values, and subjectivities no longer align. Each reading of a birthday letter becomes a repeated crossing of the border of this maternal semiosphere. Rather than integrating Olya into a coherent generational continuity, the letters intensify her liminal position—they emphasize the gap rather than bridge it. Nastya's worldview, emotions, and expectations remain fundamentally opaque, and Olya gradually comes to recognize the impossibility of a full semiotic translation between generations. Her ultimate decision not to become a mother is not merely personal, but symbolic; it marks a refusal to enter a generational scheme governed by repetition rather than renewal. By means of this gesture, Olya chooses to remain at the boundary—resisting absorption into continuity that would erase the uniqueness of her traumatic experience.

Asya Voloshina, as "one of the most politically outspoken Russian playwrights" (Meerzon, 2023), is known for her anti-war position: all the royalties coming from the staging of her texts proceed to support the Armed Forces of Ukraine. Due to her strong pro-Ukrainian position, performances of *Mama* scheduled in Moscow Centre for Dramaturgy and Directing were cancelled in April 2023 and her name has disappeared from all theater programs in Russia.

In the autofiction text *Crime* (2022), which is probably one of the most direct and tense anti-war dramaturgical statements, it comes to the definitive separation, the generation gap, i.e. belonging to a particular generation becomes a political attribute and determines one's political identification. The protagonist does not have any name, it is just a general "You" at the beginning of the message in this "screen prose," as the author defines the text. She is in love with a Ukrainian sculptor who has left for the front and, as it later transpires, has died. She is in correspondence with her friends, acquaintances from Russia who support the Putin regime, with Ukrainians who appreciate her position, and with those who despise her. She makes a harsh anti-war post on Facebook and reads the news on Russian and Ukrainian websites, reads about Bucha, Mariupol, Irpen, about the killing of civilians, about the atrocities of the Russian occupiers on the territory of Ukraine, revealing her pain, fear, shame, and guilt in a stream of consciousness.

Mutual understanding and dialogue with the older generation are shown as largely impossible, with only rare exceptions. This generational rupture is illustrated through a range of examples—from a personal break with a pro-Putin grandmother, who accuses her granddaughter of hatred and betrayal before cutting off all contact, to broader cultural metaphors. One such metaphor is the image of the old country as a place "where an old man infected people with old age," culminating in the figure of a "rapacious, bloodthirsty old-timer, Papa Yaga, whose phobias and obsessions are currently being documented by psychiatrists all over the world" (Bol, 2022).[7]

Russia is associated with images of sickness and old age, infirmity and backwardness: "Medieval ice age," "senility," "disgusting old age." This war has drawn a definitive line between generations—between parents and grandparents who, in many cases, have turned away from their children and grandchildren:

> [...] at some point at the start of the war Ukraine declared that the mothers of Russian soldiers could go retrieve their captured sons and take them home [...]. Apparently, no one showed up [...] In the First Chechen War all over the front line you could find quiet, anguished women from Russia whom the Chechens would leave alone. They would wander along the foxholes and forests digging through the rubble. They were looking for the dead. Upon finding yet another corpse, they would inspect it thoroughly. Without flinching they would peel open the scorched uniform and pull the dog tag off the rotting flesh. They were looking for their sons. There was a very large number of them and over time they became an ordinary part of the war. Whereas these mothers didn't even go. (Bol, 2022)

---

7. Translated by Ricardo Marin Vidal.

Age and generational experience are no longer synonymous with wisdom and understanding—instead, they are portrayed as examples of senile decay and backwardness. One rare exception is the heroine's mother, who meets her outside the detention centre with a one-way ticket to Istanbul in hand, tearfully pleading that she not end up in prison. This rare exception—the supportive mother—is not presented in the text as a sign of systemic change or hope, but rather as a minor, accidental disruption within a system portrayed as fully governed by ideology. "There are no more shades of grey," says the heroine (Bol, 2022). The loneliness seen in the play *Mama* becomes total, and the break from the roots is imminent and it is obviously not a single, individual, but a generational phenomenon. The vast majority of the young generation in *Crime* experiences this break by changing their names, their country, cutting off relations with their relatives, feeling fear, shame and desolation, trying to answer the question of "how to redeem an unredeemable guilt" (Meerzon & Voloshina/Bol, 2022). *Crime* expresses the generational rupture as an open form of dissent. The young protagonist's refusal to comply, and the state's reaction—framing this refusal as betrayal—demonstrate how protest acquires an age-related dimension. The authorities seek to expel the younger generation from the realm of legitimacy, portraying it as a threat and a deviation from the norm. Yet from a moral and ethical perspective, it is the youth who carry clarity and integrity. The play shows how vitality and renewal emerge from those marginalized by the system, while the centre itself becomes rigid and aggressive.

The world is falling apart, breaking interpersonal ties under the pressure of ideology and propaganda—that is the reality of *Crime* and other dramatic texts whose authors address the theme of generational conflict as a political and existential subject. Thus, in different drama texts of the 2010s and 2020s, we are not merely witness to an irreconcilable conflict but rather a complete rupture between generations, one accelerated by both sides. As Aleksander Etkind said, citing the Russian-British sociologist Mikhail Anipkin,

> Anipkin compared the Russian political life of the pre-war period to a theater: Born in the 1950s, the boomers occupied the stages and performed their endless play. In the wings were the millennials born in the 1980s, helplessly waiting for their turn on stage. Uninterested, generation X—the lost people born in the 1970s—drank at the bar. The youngest from the most recent generation whistled in protest, but the *babushka* ushers kicked them out. (Etkind, p. 104)

The party-administrative, patriarchal, corrupt, vertical structure not only destroys hundreds of thousands of human lives on the territory of Ukraine but also systematically oppresses, eliminates, and persecutes representatives of the younger generation, labeling them as "foreign agents" and "extremists", seeking to retain power at any cost. Between the systemic conformists, representatives of the older generation, and the generation of young people not loyal to the regime and opposed to the war, a gap has formed, exacerbating the dysfunctionality of family relationships, and rupturing the process of transgenerational transmission. Sharp differences in the perception of the situation and the world, in envisioning the future, have become elements of a destructive tension between generations. As Mikhail Anipkin (2022) claims, there is an ongoing generational cold war—more specifically, a war waged by Putin's generation against younger generations. In this context, the regime's obsessive persecution of Alexey Navalny serves as a symbol of the struggle of Putin's generation against the older segment of their children's cohort.

Using Lotman's concept of cultural semiotics in relation to sociopolitical processes, one can imagine the space of interaction between generations, their languages (linguistic and cultural codes), their values, their communication systems, and cultural coordinates as a semiosphere, that is, a certain heterogeneous space characterized by multilingualism, multicodedness, and both verbal and nonverbal manifestations. It will also be characterized by intralingual translation as an element of intergenerational discourse, of nonlinearity. Lotman (1990) wrote that the semiosphere is divided into a center and periphery. In the case of traditional intergenerational discourse, a temporal intergenerational shift occurs, where the younger generation gradually moves to the center, while the older generation is pushed to the periphery. However, both in contemporary Russian society and in the plays discussed in this paper, we can observe a disruption of this dynamic: the older generation often retains a central symbolic and ideological authority, while the younger generation remains marginalized or is actively excluded from the cultural core. The older generation has retained a dominant, central position in shaping cultural and ideological narratives. This imbalance has intensified the process of othering—the younger generation is clearly marked as "different" or "deviant," often portrayed as disloyal, naive, or dangerous in contrast to the so-called wisdom and patriotism of the elders. Moreover, the notion of dissent has increasingly begun to acquire age-related characteristics, and the boundary between the generations—age-related, verbal, and nonverbal—has been supplemented by ideological, political, and physical boundaries (due to the high percentage of emigration among representatives of the younger generation). Thus, the discourse of the older generation is established as dominant, while the actions of the younger generation are viewed as subversive and oppositional.

This intergenerational conflict which resulted from contradictions in cognitive structures, particularly differing attitudes toward dominant ideological concepts ("morality," "power," "freedom"), has definitively solidified the boundary between generations as a division between "us" and "them." This boundary not only manifests itself metaphysically and ideologically but also physically, reinforcing the notion that in modern Russia, the theme of generations is not just a conflict discourse, but a conflict-generating discourse with its own conflict-generating factors—both verbal and nonverbal.

The dramatic texts discussed in this article reveal how generational ruptures are expressed both thematically and structurally. In *Sneakers*, generational estrangement is conveyed through fragmented language, symbolic objects, and spatial detachment, highlighting the break between the younger generation and any sense of cultural or familial continuity. *Mama* explores the loss of maternal transmission and the emotional burden of orphanhood, portraying grief and the search for selfhood through the daughter's internal monologue. In *To Plant a Tree*, the idea of continuity and care is exposed as a simulation: the ecological project loses its authentic meaning, becoming a tool of submission in which care is replaced by imitation and values are hollowed out. *Crime* presents dissent as a generational stance: the protagonist's moral clarity and refusal to comply underscore the younger generation's drive to preserve its ethical autonomy under pressure. In all these plays, communication between generations is broken or impossible, reflecting not only a crisis of shared codes but also a deeper transformation of ethical and emotional worlds shaped by political and symbolic trauma. These plays visualize the semiosphere not as a continuum but a battlefield, one where communication collapses and the center resists its own temporal displacement.

The urgent and painful reflection on reality in anti-war theater texts, which is now only possible outside Russia, may mark the emergence of a new "lost generation" in Russian dramaturgy: a dissociative cohort, struggling to process generational trauma while bearing the burden of collective guilt and shame.

References

Anipkin, M. (2021, February). К чему приведет холодная война поколения Путина с поколением перестройки [What will the cold war between Putin's generation and the perestroika generation lead to?]. *The Insider*. https://www.academia.edu/57785228/К_чему_приведет_холодная_война_поколения_Путина_с_поколением_перестройки

Bol, E. [Voloshina, A.]. (2022). *Crime* (R. Marin-Vidal, Trans.). Critical Stages. https://www.critical-stages.org/26/crime-alwaysarmukraine/

Bolotyan, I., & Lavlinsky, S. (2010). Новая драма: опыт типологии [New drama: A typological approach]. *Вестник РГГУ. Серия: Литературоведение. Языкознание. Культурология [Vestnik RGGU. Series: Literary Studies, Linguistics, Cultural Studies, 2*(45)].

Etkind, A. (2023). *Russia against modernity*. Polity Press

Gudkov, L., Zorkaya, N., Kochergina, E., Pipiya, K., & Ryseva, A. (2019). *Russia's "Generation Z": Attitudes and values* [Report]. Friedrich-Ebert Stiftung. https://library.fes.de/pdf-files/bueros/moskau/16134.pdf

Kolesnikov, A. (2023, February 20). As war rages, Russian society has assumed the fetal position. *Carnegie Politika*.

https://carnegieendowment.org/russia-eurasia/politika/2023/01/as-war-rages-russian-society-has-assumed-the-fetal-position?lang=en

Kuchinski, M. (2025, January 3). *Generation P: What we know about the Russians who came of age under Vladimir Putin*. Meduza. https://meduza.io/en/feature/2025/01/03/generation-p

Lotman, Y. M. (1990). *Universe of the mind: A semiotic theory of culture* (A. Shukman, Trans.). Indiana University Press.

Meerzon, Y. (2023). Playing a tyrant—Rethinking an autocrat in Asya Voloshina's *Antigona: Redukciia*. *Theatralia, 1*, 29–54. https://doi.org/10.5817/TY2023-1-3

Meerzon, Y., & Voloshina, A./ Bol, E. (2022). On the rightlessness for compassion or how to redeem an unredeemable guilt. *Dialogue. Critical Stages/Scènes Critiques, 26*. https://www.critical-stages.org/26/on-the-rightlessness-for-compassion-or-how-to-redeem-an-unredeemable-guilt/

Minaev, B. (2012). *Udobnye "Kedy"* [Comfortable "Sneakers"]. *Октябрь [Oktyabr'], 11*, 190–192.

Nöth, W. (2015). The topography of Yuri Lotman's semiosphere. *International Journal of Cultural Studies, 18*(1), 11–26. https://doi.org/10.1177/1367877914528114

Starovotov, A. V. (2018). *Sem'ya kak ekzistentsial'naya sistema* [The family as an existential system]. *Ekzistentsial'naya traditsiya: Filosofiya, psikhologiya, psikhoterapiya [Existential Tradition: Philosophy, Psychology, Psychotherapy], 1–2*(31–32), 183–209. https://syg.ma/@starovoytov/siemia-kak-ekzistientsialnaia-sistiema-chast-1

Stoker, L. (2014). Reflections on the study of generations in politics. *The Forum, 12*(3), 377–396. https://doi.org/10.1515/for-2014-5012

Strizhak, L. (2011). *Kedy: P'yesa v 4 ch.* [Sneakers: A play in 4 acts]. https://theater-rovesnik.ru/kedy/

Timofeev, L. I., & Vengrov, N. (1963). *Kratkij slovar' literaturovedcheskih terminov* [An abridged dictionary of literary terms]. Uchpedgiz.

Tyczko, K. (2023). A co to jest Rosja—teraz już nie wiem: Ewolucja światopoczucia w *Crime* Asi Wołoszyny wobec innych jej sztuk [What is Russia—now I don't know: The evolution of the worldview in Asya Voloshina's *Crime* in relation to her other plays]. *Rusycystyczne Studia Literaturoznawcze [Russian Studies in Literary Theory], 33*(2), 1–39. https://doi.org/10.31261/RSL.2023.33.02

Van der Kolk, B. A., & Van der Hart, O. (1991). The intrusive past: The flexibility of memory and the engraving of trauma. *American Imago, 48*(4), 425–454.

Voloshina, A. (2016). *Mama*. Lyubimovka Festival. https://www.lubimovka.art/bol

Zhitkovsky, A. (2015). *Posadit' derevo* [Plant a tree]. Teatral'naya biblioteka Sergeya Trofimova [Sergey Trofimov's Theatre Library]. https://theatre-library.ru/authors/zh/zhitkovskiy_aleksey

CHAPTER NINE | OREST SEMOTIUK

Intertextuality vs. Transtextuality
Political Cartoons on the Russian-Ukrainian War

Abstract

This paper explores the critical role of political cartoons in the contemporary discourse on the Russian-Ukrainian War, emphasizing their unique capacity to address issues through humor and satire. Cartoonists create nuanced commentaries that resonate within a broader socio-political context by utilizing intertextuality, visual analogies, and cultural memory. The concepts of intertextuality, as articulated by Roland Barthes and Julia Kristeva, and transtextuality, suggested by Gerard Genette, are examined as a framework for understanding how multimodal texts are interconnected, influencing each other, and enriching meaning. The distinction between monomodal and multimodal cartoons further highlights the various methods through which artists communicate ideas, with multimodal works combining visual and verbal elements for deeper engagement. This study explores political cartoons through the lens of three key parameters: goals, frame of reference, and means. These parameters align with the core elements of political satire, including target, focus, social acceptability, and presentation. The paper argues that visual analogies serve as vital tools in cartoons, sparking interest and reflection by drawing connections between depicted scenarios and broader political and societal issues. By examining these dynamics, this study underscores the significance of political cartoons as instruments of critique that invite audiences to engage with pressing topics of our time.

Keywords: political cartoon, political satire, intertextuality, transtextuality, Russian-Ukrainian war, visual analogy, cultural memory

Introduction

Since the dawn of time, cartoonists have used humor and satire to address social, political, and religious issues. Driven by a strong moral perspective, they critique and expose perceived injustices. Their comedic frame helps distance them from feelings of anger, allowing for nuanced expression.

The significance of cartoons in contemporary political and media discourse is profoundly rooted in their ability to deliver precise and compelling messages. By employing conceptual imagery, artists can distill the essence of complex social phenomena, articulating their viewpoints and the broader societal attitudes toward the events or figures they depict. This clarity transforms cartoons into potent instruments of critique and commentary, effectively bridging the gap between intricate issues and public understanding. Through their visually engaging representations, cartoons ignite critical dialogue, prompting audiences to reflect deeply on the pressing topics of our time.

Situated at the crossroads of journalism and art, cartoonists blend sharp insights with a diverse range of multimodal resources, such as imagery and text. This combination enables them to create messages ranging from overtly clear to subtly ambiguous. The interplay of apparent and latent meanings forms the essence of cartooning, producing intricate, multilayered texts that invite thoughtful engagement and dialogue about contemporary issues. As an integral element of contemporary culture, political cartoons feed on the cultural heritage of past eras, using literary, artistic, cinematic, and religious works as a source.

Intertextuality, Visual Analogies, and Cultural Memory

The term *intertextuality* was introduced by Roland Barthes and Julia Kristeva (Barthes, 1977; Kristeva, 1980). Both scholars contend that all texts are interconnected. This concept arose within the poststructuralist framework and refers to the continuous exchange and relationship-building between texts. Poststructuralism offers a compelling framework for examining narratives, highlighting the dynamic nature of intertextuality. This concept illustrates that texts do not exist in isolation but are intricately interconnected, influencing and redefining one another. Poststructuralism offers a perspective that focuses on the narrative itself. It suggests "that meaning is not transferred directly from writer to reader but is mediated through writer and reader by other texts" (Kristeva, 1980, p. 21). Interpreting a text through intertextuality involves recognizing it as a tapestry of interconnected texts, ideas, and contexts.

Later publications define intertextuality as extending a story across multiple texts. (Caselli, 2005; Bazerman, 2004; Freeman, 2016). Intertextuality positions a text as an individual piece that can be appreciated independently and as part of a broader literary framework, much like a strand incorporated into a larger tapestry. As a result, a text can be perceived as an independent work or a component within a network of connections. The interpretative influence of the intertextuality stems from its ability to enrich and shape the meanings and reception of texts. By drawing on other texts, intertextuality allows for layered and nuanced interpretations, creating connections and associations that enhance the depth and complexity of the work. The objectives behind the use of intertextuality were encapsulated by Bazerman as employed in texts for (a) utilizing authoritative sources; (b) depicting social dramas; (c) providing background, support, and contrast; (d) drawing on shared beliefs and ideas, and (e); ultimately evoking specific social worlds (Bazerman, 2004, p. 86).

This perspective was subsequently extended beyond fictional works to various forms of multimodal texts, including comic books, graphic novels (Lewandowski, 2020), and political cartoons (Adeeb, 2024; Weydan & Howard, 2021; Pinar-Sanz, 2020; Chu, 2020). These publications suggest terminological innovations or adaptations of existing concepts. The concept of *intervisuality* (visual intertextuality) incorporates iconic images or symbols associated with certain politicians or historical events (Adeeb, 2024). Charles S. Peirce's concept of *hypoiconicity* applies to political cartoons, as they uniquely combine iconicity features: direct resemblance, diagrammatic schematization, and metaphoric displacement (Chu, 2020). Accordingly, cartoon viewers can reconstruct direct resemblance relations with actual, historical persons and situations from their metaphoric distortion provided in the cartoon and retrace the cartoonist's schematized, diagrammatic reasoning to arrive at the cartoon's satirical message.

Based on their structure, political cartoons can be divided into *monomodal* and *multimodal*. Monomodal cartoons rely solely on visual elements to convey humor and meaning without using verbal elements. In contrast, multimodal cartoons combine visual elements with accompanying verbal text to deliver a cohesive and integrated message (Agüero Guerra, 2016). The first category exclusively relies on its pictorial components to convey humor and intentions, with no real inclusion of the verbal mode. In contrast, the multimodal ones employ a blend of visual elements and accompanying verbal texts to deliver a cohesive and integrated message. Cartoonists often apply various rhetorical devices (such as metaphors, allusions, hyperbole, parody, etc.) to colorize vague issues that need clarification. The metaphor-rich nature of editorial cartoons makes them a fertile ground for metaphorical expression. Accordingly, metaphors assume a central role as a defining characteristic within political cartoons (Schilperoord et al., 2009).

According to the systemic-functional approach to multimodality, each modus is organized as a network of interacting options, from which the sign maker chooses the most optimal ones to express a specific meaning in a particular context (van Leeuwen, 2004). Taking this approach into account, intertextuality enhances the significance of any artwork, irrespective of its form, and effectively situates it within a broader cultural and sociopolitical context. (Lewandowski, 2020). This additional meaning of intertextuality is supported by two related concepts: *visual analogies* and *cultural memory* (Burack,1994; Werner, 2004).

Visual analogies form the core of cartoons, giving life to thoughts and feelings. The purpose of an analogy is not merely to express a viewpoint but also to engage interest and provoke thought. Meanings emerge as each viewer draws connections between the depicted scene and the broader issue. By linking two elements and suggesting a similarity, a metaphor inherently carries ambiguity, as it emphasizes specific meanings while obscuring others, thus allowing for various implications and interpretations (Burack, 1994).

Visual analogies can be drawn from various sources that resonate with readers: (1) everyday situations and ordinary objects, which most people can easily relate to; (2) contemporary popular culture, including movies and TV shows; and (3) historical events, notable figures, and classic literary and art works, which may be less recognized but provide valuable context. These sources help connect complex ideas to readers' experiences. (Werner, 2004).

Cultural memory refers to the background knowledge one uses when interpreting the everyday world. Political cartoons are part of this world as long as viewers share their areas of understanding. According to Werner (2024), this understanding is influenced by various factors.

The *first consideration* is the contextual knowledge of the subject that the cartoonist addresses, which may pertain to a pressing social issue or a specific news event. *Secondly*, understanding the mechanisms by which the cartoon operates is essential, encompassing its visual language of signs, including images, symbols, captions, and quotations, as well as the conventions that shape expectations regarding the meaning of these signs. The usage of rhetorical devices, or in other words, humorous techniques, plays a critical role in communicating satire, irony, and ridicule. *Thirdly*, references to historical events, notable figures, or previous cultural texts—such as poems, novels, famous quotations, or works of art—will be effective only if the reader possesses the requisite knowledge to comprehend the presented analogies. Political cartoons are distinct from comics, political/commercial ads, and photojournalism due to their unique understanding of broader discourse (Werner, 2024).

A political cartoon is a form of persuasive communication that relies on symbols. At the same time, the cartoonist must consider the cultural, political, and literary knowledge of the audience, along with their value system, to ensure the cartoon is understandable. In other words, intertextuality works effectively only if readers can tap into the shared memory bank that facilitates communication. In reality, this collective memory often excludes individuals within a diverse society. This exclusion creates a small group of people who can connect easily, while others outside the group struggle because they lack the same cultural knowledge. This difference often arises from varied backgrounds in terms of generations, ethnic culture, or social class compared to the cartoonist. Consequently, the result is a cartoon that "often functions as a sort of inside joke between the cartoonist and the readers" who get the veiled reference (DeSousa & Medhurst, 1982, p. 49).

Transtextuality and Humorous Techniques

The concept of transtextuality, as introduced by G. Genette, is defined as the "textual transcendence of the text" (Genette, 1992, pp. 83–84) concerning its implicit or explicit relationships with other texts. We concur with Genette's assertion that the term *transtextuality* encompasses a broader range of meanings than intertextuality. There are five aspects of transtextuality: architextuality, metatextuality, paratextuality, intertextuality, and hyper/hypotextuality.

Let us consider how these aspects can be applied to political cartoons. If we consider political cartoons as a genre of humorous discourse, we can assume that their functions overlap with those of humorous discourse. These functions are as follows: *identificational, ideological, communicative, cognitive-emotive, constructive* (shaping the world view, and *epistemological* (visual testimony). This compilation reflects an interdisciplinary perspective on political cartoons, acknowledging their multifaceted nature. Political cartoons employ various humorous techniques to engage the audience's sense of humor. These techniques are typically intertwined, resulting in a humorous effect. They include *association, transposition, transformation, contradiction, exaggeration, parody, punning, disguise, narration,* and *appropriation* (Roukes, 1997).

Architextuality positions a text within a system known as the "architecture of genres," emphasizing the reproducibility of the same structural model across various texts. In the case of political cartoons, which are considered multimodal texts, architextuality is evident in their dual role: they function not only as a genre of humorous discourse (alongside memes and comics) but also as mediums for political discourse. Despite their sociocultural specificity, political cartoons generally share common structural components: (a) message (the central idea the cartoonist aims to communicate, such as a critique, opinion, or commentary on a specific event, issue, or person); (b) context (the historical, social, or political background that aids in understanding the cartoons' meaning); (c) rhetorical devices (techniques employed to persuade or influence the audience).

Metatextuality refers to a text's critical and evaluative stance toward other texts or reality. This concept is inherently present in political cartoons, as this medium's critical perspective on reality is a key characteristic. Political cartoons serve as visual commentaries on other media and political discourse texts.

On the other hand, *paratextuality* examines the relationship between a text and its accompanying elements, highlighting the development of themes or ideas. Most cartoons include verbal elements, such as captions, speech bubbles, or inserts, which interact with nonverbal elements to create a humorous effect and to enhance the visual elements.

Intertextuality and *hyper-/hypotextuality* refer to the relationships between texts. This interaction can occur in both explicit and implicit ways. *Explicit intertextuality* in cartoons is evident when a character's phrase or caption quotes a specific statement from another text. On the other hand, *implicit intertextuality* is expressed through humorous techniques such as association, disguise, transformation, and contradiction, which utilize allusions, metaphors, and allegories.

Hypotextuality and *hypertextuality* describe the relationship between two texts, where one serves as the original text (hypotext), and the other(hypertext) modifies this original and places it in a new context. In political cartoons, these hypo-/hypertextual connections are represented by humorous techniques: transposition, parody, and appropriation. The *technique of transposition* "transfers" characters to a new, uncommon context (time, place). *The parody technique* uses imitation and alludes to certain customs, ways of behaving, and artifacts. *The technique of appropriation* is a "quote" from a famous literary or artistic work adapted to the current situation. This technique uses the principle of alienation. This principle means that political cartoonists regard the situation and comment on it, taking a distance and using Aesopian language to convey a concealed meaning to the audience.

Corpus and Methodology

The data set consists of 12 political cartoons. It is a fragment of the corpus containing 3,785 political cartoons and 2,840 memes from 65 countries in North and South America, Asia, Australia, Africa, and Europe (including Ukraine and Russia as conflict parties), which are part of the research project "Laughter During the War: Russian Aggression in Ukraine in Political Cartoons and Memes."

The following parameters can describe political cartoons as a humorous genre: (a) *goals*, (b) *frame of reference*, and (c) *means*. These parameters correspond with elements of political satire: *target, focus, social acceptability*, and *presentation* (Paletz, 1990). The *goal/target* means the politician and/or institution depicted in the cartoon, the *frame of reference (focus)* describes the particular aspect of the political reality/activity, and the *means (setting)* refers to verbal/nonverbal elements, metaphors, and symbols used in cartoons. These interrelated parameters serve as a methodological framework for this study, supported by the multimodal discourse analysis (MDA).

Analysis

The research material represents the following source domains: *photography* (2), *art and street art* (2), *film and animation* (2), *religion* (3), and *literature* (2). These domains are parts of broader sources of visual analogies, described by Werner (2004), namely, to: (a) contemporary popular culture, and (b) historical events, notable figures, and classic literary and art works. Some of the hypotexts are well known, allowing the audience to decode the hypertexts easily, but some visual analogies require additional cognitive effort.

Photography

Cartoons by Ukrainian artist Volodymyr Kazanevsky (Figure 2.1) and Russian cartoonist Alexandr Troitsky (Figure 2.2) have similar settings and different focuses. The

Fig 1. Joe Rosenthal.tif

hypotext is the picture *Raising the Flag on Iwo Jima* by AP photographer Joe Rosenthal (Figure 1). It is an American symbol of heroism and sacrifice. Figure 2.1 (monomodal cartoon) recontextualizes that symbol into Ukrainian defense effort against Russian aggression (appropriation). Blue and yellow dominate the flag—these are the national colors of Ukraine. Red arrows metaphorically pierce and distort the blue-yellow unity, symbolizing Russian military intrusion. The cartoon's *setting* anchors the cartoon in the context of the Russian-Ukrainian War. The flag becomes not just a symbol of victory, but a battleground for values and sovereignty *(focus/frame of reference)*. Figure 2.2 (monomodal cartoon) has the same hypotext (appropriation) but carries a radically different ideological message. The flag is the Ukrainian national flag, but it is tattered, symbolizing degradation and victimhood. The soldiers have US-American flags on their uniforms, indicating that these are not Ukrainians, but Americans raising Ukraine's flag. The tattered flag and American uniforms shift the symbolism significantly. Where Rosenthal's photo originally conveyed heroism, this hypertext implies mockery: the triumph is not earned by Ukraine but is propped up artificially by the US. The cartoon's *setting* discloses its *target/goal*: Ukraine as a vassal state in a broader geopolitical power play. The cartoon critiques the perceived US hegemony and Ukraine's lack of sovereignty *(focus/ frame of reference)*, conveying the message: Ukraine's defense is driven or even orchestrated by the United States. The cartoon is a semiotic counterpoint, turning a symbol of independence into one of dependence and manipulation. Both cartoons are examples of implicit intertextuality.

Fig 2. Volodymyr Kazanevsky (Ukraine)

Art and Street Art

Art and street art (murals) are the most popular sources for modern political cartoons. Figure 3.1 is a lithograph cartoon, *The dream of the inventor of the needle-gun on All Saints' Day* (1866), by French artist Honoré Daumier (1808–1879). It comments on the Prussian army's victory over Austria in the Seven Weeks War, capturing the artist's concerns about the destructive capabilities of modern warfare. Figure 3.2 is a multimodal cartoon by Rainer Hachfeld (Germany). It has a caption *Actualités* (latest news) and depicts Russian President Vladimir Putin *(goal/target)*. The cartoon's *setting* combines verbal and nonverbal elements (in terms of *paratextuality*) and addresses Putin's guilt in fomenting a war that led to mass casualties *(frame of reference/focus)*. The cartoonist uses the technique of transposition. It "transfers" Putin to a battlefield from 1866 using the visual analogy with a historical event (the Austro-Prussian War).

The social context of Figure 4.1 is the Bucha massacre (the mass murder of Ukrainian civilians by the Russian Armed Forces during the fight for and occupation of the city of Bucha in April 2022). The multimodal cartoon by another German cartoonist, AGO (Figure 4.1), shows a mural that depicts Putin *(goal/target)* and Death kissing, with the ruined city in the background. These visual elements are supported by a verbal element (broken street sign with the "Bucha" insert. The *setting* of the hypertext combines the techniques of appropriation and transposition. The source of visual analogy is contemporary popular culture. The cartoonist alludes to the graffiti painting by Dmitri Vrubel from 1990 on the Berlin Wall (Figure 4.2), and puts this graffiti into a new context, fitting it to the course of the Russian-Ukrainian War. The hypotext depicts Leonid Brezhnev and Erich Honecker in a socialist fraternal kiss, reproducing a photograph taken in 1979 during the 30th anniversary celebration of the

146 | DIFFICULT NEIGHBORHOODS

Fig 3. Alexandr Troitsky (Russia)

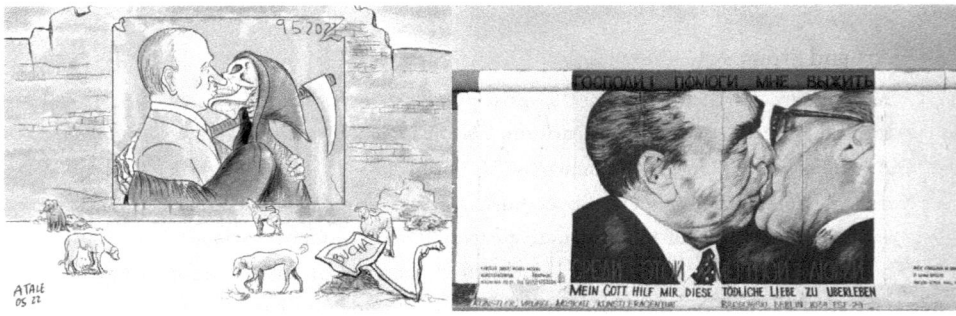

Fig 4. Honoré Daumier (France)

foundation of the German Democratic Republic. The mural has a caption: *My God, Help Me to Survive This Deadly Love.* The element of the caption (*"Deadly Love"*) in the hypotext interacts with another verbal element of hypertext (*"Bucha"* insert) and with the nonverbal element (*"fraternal"* kiss" of Putin and Death). This interaction *(paratextuality)* is supported by the technique of transposition (it "moves" Putin to Bucha) and activates the metaphor Putin Is A Brother Of Death, making him responsible for the casualties in Bucha *(focus/frame of reference)*. Figures 4.1 and 4.2 illustrate implicit intertextuality.

Cinematography

Animated cartoons and films (contemporary popular culture) serve as hypotexts for political cartoons. (Figures 5.1 and 5.2). Figure 5.1's *social context* is the visit of Xi Jinping, general secretary of the Chinese Communist Party and Chinese president, to Russia in March 2023. The work by Ukrainian cartoonist Andriy Petrenko (mul-

Fig 5. Rainer Hachfeld (Germany)

timodal cartoon) is a visual analogy to *Winnie the Pooh and the Honey Tree* (1966), an American animated short film based on the book by A. A. Milne. The Piglet has a face of Putin *(goal/target)*, and the Pooh is wearing a red shirt with the golden stars (allusion to the Chinese national flag). Additional element—the honey pot with inscription *Russia* activates the metaphor RUSSIA=HONEY POT. Along with the images of small Piglet (Putin) and big Pooh (Xi Jinping *(setting)*, this element reveals the *focus/frame of reference* of the hypertext—dependence of Putin's Russia on Xi Jinping's China and Putin's subservience. Figure 5.2 is a multimodal cartoon by the Greek cartoonist Dimitris Hantzopoulos (hypertext). The hypotext is the image from the Soviet silent film *Battleship Potemkin* (1925), directed by Sergei Eisenstein. It glorifies the 1905 mutiny aboard the Russian battleship Potemkin, depicting revolution against oppressive Tsarist forces. The cartoon's caption *(Battleship Putinmkin)* is slightly modified *(explicit intertextuality* via text and image). It references Russian President Vladimir Putin *(goal/target)*. The verbal element interacts with the image *(paratextuality)*, alluding to a famous scene: a woman is shot in the eye while wearing pince-nez glasses, symbolizing brutal repression. The cartoon's *setting* is stylized in a way that mimics Soviet propaganda, reinforcing the historical connection. It takes a Soviet symbol of revolutionary heroism and flips it to comment on contemporary authoritarianism in Putin's Russia (technique of *appropriation*) and to imply state violence under Putin's regime. The cartoonist critiques modern Russian political leadership by drawing parallels to the repressive regime depicted in Battleship Potemkin *(focus/frame of reference)*.

Religion and literature

Besides fine art, street art, and cinematography, other popular sources for political cartoons are Bible stories and literature. Cartoonists use a broad spectrum of religious plots to depict different events of the Russian-Ukrainian War (Figures 6–8).

Fig 6. AGO (Germany)

Fig 7. Dmitri Vrubel (Russia)

The monomodal cartoon by Ukrainian artist Olexiy Kustovsky (Figure 6) alludes to the painting *The Last Supper* by Leonardo da Vinci (1495–1498). The *setting* of hypertext compositionally echoes the hypotext. It mimics the hand gestures and placements of the apostles in da Vinci's original, reinforcing the parallel (technique of appropriation). Vladimir Putin *(goal/target)* replaces Jesus Christ at the center of the table (transposition). The setting of the cartoon is quite comprehensive and contains many details. Putin is wearing a military uniform and an armband with the

Fig 8. Andriy Petrenko (Ukraine)

letter Z (one of several symbols, including "V" and "O") painted on military vehicles involved in the Russian invasion of Ukraine. Jesus and the disciples are depicted as cinder blocks with human features. The table is cluttered with missiles, grenades, burning cinder blocks, and broken windows in the background. These symbols stand for devastation caused by Russian aggression against Ukraine. Mimicking *The Last Supper*, the cartoon suggests that Putin has perverted a symbol of peace and sacrifice into one of violence and destruction. By replacing Christ with Putin, the cartoonist communicates a message of moral and cultural inversion, where peace is replaced by violence, faith by fear, and divinity by dictatorial power *(focus/frame of reference)*. The cartoon is a direct condemnation of Russia's aggressive actions in Ukraine.

The work of Turkish cartoonist Ahmad Rahma (Figure 7) is based on visual analogies with Bible stories and Greek mythology. The hypertext (monomodal cartoon) comments on Ukraine's struggle for NATO membership in the face of Russian aggression *(social context)*. It shows President Zelensky *(target/goal)* carrying the cross with the Ukrainian flag in the background *(setting)*. The cross resembles the NATO emblem (a four-pointed compass rose). Its size and sharpness suggest it is both difficult to carry and potentially painful, even as it's being embraced. In addition, the hypertext's setting mirrors the Greek myth of Sisyphus, who was condemned to eternally push a boulder uphill—only to have it roll back down. These metaphors (WAY OF THE CROSS and Sisyphus reveal the *focus (frame of reference)* of the cartoon: Zelensky is a modern-day Sisyphus, endlessly and painfully striving for NATO's support or membership. His efforts walk the line between futility and heroic perseverance to achieve the goal, which is also an obstacle that may be strategically useful but slow-moving. This cartoon highlights the immense challenge Ukraine faces in gaining support from Western alliances like NATO. Figure 8 (multimodal cartoon) by Austrian cartoonist Marian Kamensky, alludes to the Christian nativity scene, where the birth of Jesus Christ is traditionally shown as a moment of hope, salvation, and peace. The setting is based on paratextuality and contradiction. The screaming baby, stamped with the Z symbol, is grotesquely aggressive and unnatural. It has Putin's face *(target/goal)* and is labeled "ANTICHRIST," suggesting a total inversion of sacred values. The Holy Family in the cartoon consists of Hitler, Stalin, and Putin (Ruscism as the ideological successor of Fascism and Stalinism). The Three Kings are Syrian dictator Bashar al-Assad, Chinese leader Xi Jinping, and Iranian Grand Ayatollah Ali Khamenei, bringing sacred gifts (opium, gunpowder, and poison) to the newborn Antichrist (implicit intertextuality). These authoritarian leaders are portrayed as empowering evil, reversing the traditional Christian symbolism of goodwill and peace. Additional symbols (a missile across the sky replacing the Star of Bethlehem, a solar eclipse, indifferent onlookers) convey the message: "The heavens no longer bless humanity—they now herald war." The cartoon's *setting* reveals its *focus (frame of reference)*: the rise of authoritarian alliances fostering global instability.

Literature is a crucial and dynamic source of inspiration for creating incisive political cartoons. Its rich narratives provide a compelling backdrop for satirical commentary, making complex ideas accessible and entertaining. Figure 9.1 and Figure 9.2 are visual "quotes" of William Shakespeare (1564-1616), the most quoted writer in the history of the English-speaking world, and Miguel de Cervantes (1547–1616), the most important figure in Spanish literature.

The setting of both cartoons is a combination of explicit and implicit intertextuality. Figure 9.1 is a work by Croatian cartoonist Dragan Kovasevic. The *setting* of the hypertext (monomodal cartoon) is visually rich. The figure is dressed in Elizabethan garb with a contemplative expression, wearing a necklace with the Z symbol. Its face resembles Putin *(goal/target)*. The figure is holding a skull (a symbol of death), overlaid with a map of Earth. This setting is a direct allusion to Hamlet's "To be or not to be" soliloquy, repurposed as a question for the world's future (technique of appropriation). The cartoon's setting discloses its *focus (frame of reference)*: the person contemplating the Earth's fate may be directly complicit in its destruction.

Figure 9.2 (monomodal cartoon by Italian artist Paolo Lombardi) has a simple setting and uses the technique of appropriation. A lone figure resembling Don Quixote

Fig 9. Dimitris Hantzopoulos (Greece)

stands with a lance against a tank marked with Z. Those images symbolize idealism, delusional heroism, and Russian destructive power. The cartoon's *setting* possibly creates a David vs. Goliath scenario where an idealistic figure confronts a modern, brutal war machine (*focus/frame of reference*). It can be interpreted in two ways: a) the futility of resistance against overwhelming force, and b) the glorification of the moral courage of Ukrainian defenders. The cartoon is possibly sympathetic to Ukraine, implying a critique of asymmetric warfare: one side with overwhelming firepower, the other with symbolic resistance and chivalry.

Conclusions

Political humor, as a relevant part of modern culture, impacts politics, especially in wartime. Political satire, as a narrower category within political humor, represents an efficient channel for political criticism, offering a reinterpretation of political reality.

As an interdiscursive phenomenon, the political cartoon is an object of study for many disciplines: political science, media studies, art history, linguistics, and culture studies. The interdisciplinarity of this humorous genre, which draws on classical and contemporary cultural heritage, makes it an interesting research object and a specific document of the era. In times of the dominance of visuality, political cartoons serve as discursive practices and visual testimony of armed conflicts. Despite their interdisciplinarity, political cartoons have standard parameters by which they can be described: (a) goals, (b) frame of reference, and (c) means. These parameters correspond with political satire's target, focus, social acceptability, and presentation (setting). The interrelated criteria served as analytical tools for this study, supported by multimodal discourse analysis (MDA). The multimodality, intertextuality, and transtextuality of political cartoons empower cartoonists to convey messages that range from strikingly clear to intriguingly ambiguous. The dynamic interplay of explicit and nuanced meanings on the one hand, and of verbal and nonverbal elements on the other (in terms of paratextuality), forms the foundation of cartooning, resulting in rich, multilayered works that provoke deep thought and spirited dialogue about pressing contemporary issues.

The intertextuality and transtextuality of political cartoons put them in a broader cultural and sociopolitical landscape. This understanding of intertextuality and transtextuality is reinforced by two interconnected concepts: visual analogies and cultural memory. As a crucial aspect of modern culture, political cartoons tap into the cultural legacies of past eras, drawing inspiration from literature, art, cinema, and religious narratives to create impactful visual commentary. This chapter established the research corpus of 12 political cartoons on the Russian-Ukrainian War from Ukraine, Russia, Germany, Croatia, Turkey, Greece, and Italy, of which 6 are monomodal and 6 multimodal.

The analysis shows that cartoonists use various source domains: photography, art and street art, film and animation, religion, and literature. The examples bridge classical works (Daumier, Da Vinci, Shakespeare, Cervantes) with contemporary geopolitical narratives, demonstrating how iconography is recontextualized to comment on modern armed conflicts. Some hypotexts are widely recognized, enabling the audience to decode the corresponding hypertexts effortlessly. However, certain visual analogies (Figures 5, 6, 9) demand deeper cognitive engagement, challenging viewers to explore and uncover more profound meanings. The setting of the cartoons was determined by their target, focus, and the political and cultural specifics of the countries represented by the cartoonists. This research illustrated: (a) how political cartoons repurpose iconic cultural texts to critique modern armed conflicts, and (b) how the interplay between familiar hypotexts and provocative hypertexts enables nuanced readings that span political satire, condemnation, and moral inquiry.

References

Adeeb, E.R. (2024). Visual intertextuality as a backbone of political cartooning: Homogenous and heterogeneous visual juxtaposition. *The Grove—Working Papers on English Studies, 31*, e8643. https://doi.org/10.17561/grove.v31.8643

Agüero Guerra, M. (2016). Beyond verbal incongruity: A genre-specific model for the interpretation of humour in political cartoons. In L. Ruiz-Gurillo (Ed.), *Metapragmatics of humour: Current research trends* (pp. 57–77). John Benjamins. https://doi.org/10.1075/ivitra.14.04gue

Barthes, R. (1977). *Image music text*. Fontana Press.

Bazerman, C. (2004). Intertextuality: How texts rely on other texts. In C. Bazerman & P. Prior (Eds.), *What writing does and how it does it: An introduction to analyzing texts and textual practices* (pp. 83–96). Lawrence Erlbaum Associates.

Burack, J. (1994). *Understanding and creating editorial cartoons: A resource guide*. Knowledge Unlimited.

Caselli, D. (2005). *Beckett's Dantes: Intertextuality in the fiction and criticism*. Manchester University Press. http://www.jstor.org/stable/j.ctt155j88d

Chu, Y. (2020). On the hypoiconic structure of cartoons. *Social Semiotics, 32*(2), 262–278. https://doi.org/10.1080/10350330.2020.1756587

DeSousa, M. A., & Medhurst, M. J. (1982). The editorial cartoon as visual rhetoric: Rethinking boss tweed. *Journal of Visual Verbal Languaging, 2*(2), 43–52. https://doi.org/10.1080/23796529.1982.11674355

Freeman, M. (2016). Intertexts, trantexts and paratexts: Following the yellow brick roads of fin-de-siecle children's fiction. *Kultura popularna, 1*, 4–15.

Genette, G. (1992). *The architext: An introduction*. University of California Press.

Kristeva, J. (1980). *Desire in language. A semiotic approach to literature and art* (L.S. Roudiez, Ed.). Columbia University Press.

Leeuwen van, T. (2004). *Introducing social semiotics: An introductory textbook*. Routledge.

Lewandowski, W. (2020). Intertextuality and the depiction of ideological conflicts. The case of V for vendetta. *The Copernicus Journal of Political Studies, 2*, 85–100. https://doi.org/10.12775/CJPS.2020.016

Paletz, D. (1990). Political humor and authority: From support to subversion. *International Political Science Review, 11*(4), 483–493.

Pinar-Sanz, M.J. (2020). Humour and intertextuality in Steve Bell's political cartoons. *The European Journal of Humour Research, 8*(3), 16–39. https://doi.org/10.7592/EJHR2020.8.3.Pinar-Sanz

Roukes, N. (1997). *Humour in art: Celebration of visual wit*. Davis Publications.

Schilperoord, J., Maes, A., & Ferdinandusse, H. (2009). Perceptual and conceptual visual rhetoric: The case of symmetric object alignment. *Metaphor and Symbol, 24*(3), 155–173. https://doi.org/10.1080/10926480903028110

Wejdan, A., Howard, M. (2021). Intertextuality: Allusion and parody in cartoons. In A.Wejdan & M.Howard (Eds.), *The multimodal rhetoric of humour in Saudi media cartoons* (pp. 44–70). De Gruyter Mouton. https://doi.org/10.1515/9781501509902-005

Werner, W. (2004). On political cartoons and social studies textbooks: Visual analogies, intertextuality, and cultural memory. *Canadian Social Studies, 38*(2), 1–10. https://files.eric.ed.gov/fulltext/ EJ1073912.pdf

Appendix

Picture Credits

Figure 1
https://www.sfgate.com/news/article/joe-rosenthal-1911-2006-photo-was-his-fame-2490706.php

Figure 2
https://cagle.com/cartoonist/vladimir-kazanevsky/2023/06/27/275929/counteroffensive-in-ukraine

Figure 3

Figure 4
https://www.meisterdrucke.pl/wydruki-artystyczne/Honor%C3%A9-Daumier/1245468/Marzenie-wynalazcy-pistoletu-ig%C5%82owego....html

Figure 5
https://www.cartoonstock.com/directory/l/lithograph_from_1866.asp

Figure 6
https://www.cartoonmovement.com/cartoon/putins-army-parade

Figure 7
https://commons.wikimedia.org/wiki/File:East_Side_Gallery_-_Dmitri_Vrubel_-_Le_baiser_(Berlin).jpg

Figure 8
https://www.cartoonmovement.com/cartoon/si-give-me-new-gun-because-old-one-completely-broken-pu

Figure 9
https://www.ekathimerini.com/opinion/cartoon/1180270/cartoon-by-dimitris-hantzopoulos-19-03-2022/

Figure 10
https://uainfo.org/blognews/1696837883-pidbirka-blogozhab-ta-fotoprikoliv-vid-uainfo-za-9-listopada.html

Figure 11
https://www.cartoonmovement.com/cartoon/salvation-1

Figure 12
https://www.toonpool.com/cartoons/UNFROHE%20WEIHNACHTEN_417275

Figure 13
https://ns-dubrava.hr/2024/01/08/godisnja-izlozba-karikatura-clanova-hrvatskog-drustva-karikaturista-u-galeriji-vladimir-filakovac/

Figure 14
https://de.toonpool.com/cartoons/Resistence_403669

SECTION FOUR

Conflicts in Classic and Modern Literature

CHAPTER TEN | **DOROTA RYGIEL**

From Victims to Survivors

The Impact of Migration on Women in Novels by Female Migrant Writers

Abstract

This paper contrasts the effects of international migration and difficult urban settings on immigrant women in Monica Ali's *Brick Lane* and Dana Parys-White's *Emigrantka z wyboru. Opowieść londyńska* [*The Emigrant by Choice. A London Story*]. Both writers examine the intricacies of the immigrant experience in challenging metropolitan environments, offering perspectives on issues of relocation, resilience, assimilation, and cultural identity. Nazneen and Ewa, the two main characters, come from different countries and were raised in different cultures. They appear to have relatively little in common when taking into account disparities in education, religious background, marital status, and perspectives on migration. However, in spite of these differences, their experiences of marginalization, cultural displacement, and economic hardship are comparable. They are further united by the contrast between their traditional ideals and the contemporary realities of their lives in London. This paper examines themes of identity conflicts, alienation, and the protagonists' pursuit of a brighter future in Britain. It also explores whether the problems associated with assimilation and difficult neighborhoods can positively affect the immigrant women who attempt to establish new lives in Britain.

Keywords: immigrant women's writing, migration from Poland to the UK, identity, transformation, assimilation

Gender has long been an overlooked factor in studies of migration, with early discussion mostly focused on men, their needs, expectations, and reasons for relocation. Women's international mobility received little scholarly attention and was often viewed through the lens of family reunification, with women perceived as passive participants rather than active agents (Morokvasic, 1983; Slany, 2008). Female migration was seldom voluntary and, as Engle (2004) notes, it was usually associated with "family reunification or depended on a male migrant" (p. 17). Women's dependence was mirrored in the phrases such as "migrant workers and their families," where the "migrant workers" always referred to men (Erel et al., 2003, p. 10). Female international movement resulted mainly from the family's needs and was occasionally women's independent choice. As Morocvasic (1983) puts it, women who left their home countries were "dependants, migrants' wives or mothers, unproductive, illiterate, isolated, secluded from the outside world and the bearers of many children," who either cared about their household or worked illegally, hardly ever in the waged labor market (p. 13). Despite comprising a significant part of host societies, women were largely regarded as "sociologically invisible" (Morocvasic, 1983, p.13).

From the mid-1970s onward, scholars began to change their approach, recognizing migration as a phenomenon that involved both genders. This could have been the result of a noticeable increase in female migration, especially from Ireland, Poland, and Uganda, as well as of the emergence of women's liberation movements in Britain that brought issues of gender inequality to light. Scholars understood that women were not a homogenous group travelling overseas to join their families. Rather, they migrated across borders for diverse reasons, and their experiences differed from the experiences of men. This change initiated discussions about the feminization of migration and brought attention to how it affected men and women individually (Christou & Kofman, 2022; Ryan & Webster, 2008; Slany, 2008). Aspects such as age, race, ethnicity, religion, cultural background, and economic class, which are the main elements of individual identity, have become increasingly integrated into migration studies, with gender as a significant factor (Crenshaw, 1991). Migrant lives, job opportunities, acculturation experiences, and levels of sexual discrimination in the workplace are all impacted by gender. Therefore, a gendered awareness of these dimensions is important to understand migration dynamics thoroughly.

The works of many female migrant authors, in which they often draw upon elements of their own lives, examine the complexities of gender and international movement. Among such novels are *Brick Lane* by Monica Ali and *Emigrantka z wyboru. Opowieść londyńska* [*The Emigrant by Choice. A London Story*] by Dana Parys-White, which portray the migrant experiences of two women and focus on the issues of identity and belonging.

Monica Ali was born in Bangladesh to an English mother and a Bangladeshi father. As a young girl, she moved to England, where she has lived ever since. She has been an acute observer of the life of Bangladeshi immigrants in London and draws on these observations as well as her personal experience as a person from a mixed-race family in her novel. Dana Parys-White was born in Poland but moved to Britain to learn English. She met her future husband there and eventually settled down in London. She worked as a journalist for a music magazine and hosted a popular radio show before she devoted herself fully to writing novels. Being actively involved in the life of the Polish diaspora in London, she reflected both her own and other migrants' experiences with language barriers, assimilation problems and cultural differences in *Emigrantka z wyboru*, which was shortlisted for a literary award in 2009.

This paper will attempt to compare the impact of displacement on the heroines of the two novels, who represent major diasporas in London and who emigrated to Britain from very different worlds: one from predominantly Catholic Poland and the other from Muslim-majority Bangladesh. Both countries have distinct cultural, historical, geographical, and political backgrounds. While *Brick Lane* emerges from a postcolonial context and *Emigrantka z wyboru* from a post-communist Eastern European one, both novels reflect different migrant experiences shaped by each country's unique past. The paper will also examine how varying motivations for migration (voluntary migration vs. necessity-driven displacement) influence the heroines' migrant life and perspectives.

Exploring the Determinants of Migration: Economic, Political, and Gender Factors

People have moved throughout history in pursuit of a better life, to flee violence or reunite with their loved ones. Significant challenges, including overcoming legal restrictions and prejudice based on their cultural background, race, or ethnicity have often stood in their way.

Before World War II, the percentage of South Asians who lived in Britain was very low but this number grew exponentially in the postwar years. Serious labor shortages emerged in Britain immediately after the war, primarily due to the mobilization of people into the armed forces (Zig, 1985). According to Mason (1995), an important reason for this deficiency problem was the reorganization of industry, which became large-scale and capital intensive. Britian filled these gaps partly by the recruitment of women, countryside and Irish workers. When the postwar economic boom began, this soon proved insufficient. A lot of native British employees moved to new posts, whereas the posts for semiskilled and unskilled ones remained unfilled. It was the time when workers coming from the former British colonies satisfied the demand for this kind of jobs in the British labor market.

High proportions of Indian subcontinent migrants moved to Britain in order to improve their economic situation and access more favorable working conditions than they had in their countries. The British labor market opened up in the late 1940s, allowing people of color to obtain jobs that had previously been unavailable to them. Those already settled in Britain, who worked as peddlers selling cheap items, began entering freely available fields of employment. Their countrymen soon followed, finding work in the north of England and London foundries, textile mills, engineering factories, and the service sector.

The first migration policy implemented after WWII, the 1948 British Nationality Act, was favorable and offered the early group of postwar migrants unrestricted access to the UK and legal employment. A lot of men left the Indian subcontinent at that time with the aim of working in Britain temporarily and returning home after saving some money. The subsequent years, however, brought a considerable change to migration patterns.

South Asians who emigrated from East Africa, particularly from Uganda in the 1970s, also made up a significant part of migrants in Britain. Many of them were descendants of laborers originally recruited by the British in the 19th century to build railways across the continent. Like migrants from the Indian subcontinent, they sought better economic opportunities after the end of World War II. Some of them voluntarily moved to Britain in search of better economic conditions, whereas others were forcibly expelled from Uganda as a result of the xenophobic policies of President Idi Amin, who wanted to remove foreigners from his country. The government's rhetoric of the early 1970s defined "true Ugandans" as Amin's black brothers and sisters, excluding South Asians from national identity (Muhammedi, 2022). Over 24,000 people of South Asian descent were forced to leave their homes in Uganda (Brown, 2006). They were distinct from those whose migration path lay outside Africa. Unlike those who travelled individually, Ugandan South Asians moved to Britan with their families and were usually much better educated. In contrast to their less educated or even illiterate counterparts who had come directly from the Indian subcontinent, statistics show that 77% of East African South Asian men and 57% of women spoke English, which enabled them to find more demanding and better-paid jobs (Brown, 2006).

Bangladeshis started to migrate to Britain in the 1970s in search of refuge and economic opportunities, when their nation was involved in the civil war. They primarily originated from the Sylhet District and established a large diaspora in the London borough of Tower Hamlets. They initially worked in factories, just like other South Asian immigrants, but as time went on, they started their own tiny businesses.

Following World War II, the South Asian diaspora in Britain increased immensely, reaching 4 million people by 2021, with over 640,000 having come from Bangladesh (Office for National Statistics, 2021). Despite sharp restrictions on the migration of women until the early 2000s, Bengali women began moving abroad during the 1980s. Early female migrants frequently travelled with their families, since they were not permitted to migrate alone until 2003, when the ban on migrant women over 35 years was lifted. By 2006, the age limit was lowered to 25, and eventually, restrictions were removed for all ages (Humera & Ambreen, 2017). Prior to the early 2000s, migration of unskilled or semiskilled women from Bangladesh was also limited. Consequently, the percentage of Bengali females was very low, i.e., only 1% of the entire migrant population at that time (Humera & Ambreen, 2017).

The number of Bengali women moving overseas steadily rose after the restrictions were lifted in 2003, reaching 4% by 2004. This proportion increased in the 2010s, averaging almost 19% of all migrant workers annually (Blanchet & Biswas, 2021). This increase was mainly caused by the need for unskilled female labor rather than the low demand for middle-class, well-educated women, who tended to stay at home instead of accepting low-skilled employment overseas. The majority of the unskilled Bengali women who came to Britain worked in catering, housekeeping, caring, and the textile sector (Islam, 2008).

The prewar migration from Poland to the UK resulted mainly from economic hardship and was regarded as a chance for stable income, safe work, and financial support for families left behind in Poland. Generally identified as the breadwinners, men migrated primarily to enhance their families' standards of living. Research by Slany and Ślusarczyk (2019) indicates that women during this period largely moved to join their male relatives: husbands, fathers, or brothers. As a result, their role in the process and input in the economies of host countries is often underestimated in statistical reports. This is unjust, as both men and women were equally affected by relocation, which often forced them to abandon their old way of life and adopt new patterns of behavior Początek formularza and Dół formularza(Slany & Ślusarczyk, 2019).

Immediately after World War II, forced migration became prevalent due to the new borders, which made Poland nearly ethnically homogenous. During the communist era, cross-border movement was officially prohibited. The process of Sovietization led to political terror, poverty and chaos. The Polish borders were closed, as the authorities regarded the communist system as the most appropriate and therefore prohibited free movement (Kupiszewski, 2018). In addition, restrictive visa and passport controls discouraged foreign travel. Poland was fully integrated into the Soviet sphere, and as Churchill (1946) described it, an iron curtain had descended across Europe. Men often left the country illegally, as remaining in Poland usually brought significant dangers to the opponents of the regime. The authorities gradually issued permits for short overseas excursions, but they always set strict time limits. Many people took advantage of this to move abroad and settle there permanently, with minimum chances of going back home. In cases where some of them overstayed illegally, their families lost the opportunity to join them. During this period, men primarily migrated to Western Europe or the United States due to economic crises within their families or because they were seen as a threat by the communist government that frequently suppressed any opposition. Meanwhile, women travelled to Western Europe to contribute to the family income by taking seasonal jobs. As in the prewar period, family, friends or acquaintances often encouraged would-be migrants to leave their homeland, offering hope for a brighter future in a prosperous country and providing assistance with the search for employment or housing (Slany & Ślusarczyk, 2019). However, extensive censorship led to the underreporting of both male and female mobility.

The turning point in the history of Polish international movement was the accession to the European Union in 2004, which resulted in a significant emigration flow of both men and women. Many Poles were compelled to leave for financial reasons, hoping for economic opportunities and a more comfortable life in Western countries, primarily to Britain, Germany, Holland, and Ireland. Over 100,000 of them are believed to have relocated to Britain soon after Poland joined the European Union in 2004. This number grew exponentially in the years that followed, peaking over 1 million in 2017 (Clark, 2024). In the post-accession migrant wave, there was a growing proportion of well-educated individuals, for whom the migration determinants included not only economic opportunities but also prospects for personal development. In certain sectors, the number of Polish employees is comparable to that of native British nowadays; for example, 11% of them pursue academic careers or work in administrative roles (Garapich, 2019). The majority of Poles with lower levels of education work in manufacturing, construction, or the tourism industry, according to the Labour Force Survey (Garapich, 2019). However, the number of Poles leaving their homeland has declined since 2018, as more people decide to stay in Poland because of better job opportunities and the uncertainty brought about by Brexit (Główny Urząd Statystyczny, 2019).

Slany and Ślusarczyk (2019) state that women seldom migrated independently prior to the 2004 accession, but in the following years they began to consider their own expectations, needs, and plans when deciding to leave. Furthermore, they relied less on family contacts and networks than before. This change was a big challenge, as starting a new life abroad without friends or knowledge of the local language was risky. The post-accession female migrant thus contradicted the traditional Polish feminine ideal, which had conventionally been associated with domestic and mother-centered roles.

The majority of those Polish female migrants were initially driven by economic reasons, which led them to accept even low-paying jobs, as wages abroad were much higher than in Poland. As a result of the gendered characteristics of the labor market, which located women as better suited for care work than men, the majority of female migrants worked in the service sector. They helped bridge the UK's labor gap by allowing women in the host country to remain in the workforce without having to change their childcare and household responsibilities. According to some scholars, the growing need for domestic and care services in host countries was a major cause of the feminization of migration (Kordasiewicz, 2010). While this may have been the case at the time of Poland's accession to the European Union, current research shows that an increasing number of educated and skilled women are now migrating, sometimes even exceeding male migration (Grabowska-Lusińska & Okólski, 2008).

The causes of women's mobility go beyond economic needs and include limited employment opportunities, professional ambitions, and limited access to cheap housing in Poland (Okólski & Salt, 2014). Many women have also learnt to make independent decisions and to relocate not only out of curiosity but also in search of better opportunities for personal development. For others, migration has become a way of life and a means of social advancement (Cook et al., 2010). This viewpoint supports Morokvasic's argument that women's migration is, at times, a form of resistance and rebellion against the patriarchal order in their home countries (Morokvasic, 1983).

Given that many women began migrating with few social ties and minimal command of the host country's language, this shift in agency required a great deal of courage. Their migrant experience was often characterized by difficulties such as increased racial and religious discrimination, as well as challenges related to multilingualism and multiculturalism. Moreover, due to poor institutional support, many women ended up with insecure social and legal statuses or resorted to working illegally. Despite these hardships, women continued to migrate to Britain and eventually began to outnumber male migrants (Aziz, 2015).

The Dreams and Expectations: The Protagonists' Perspectives on Britain

Ewa, the protagonist of *Emigrantka z wyboru. Opowieść londyńska* by Dana Parys-White, is a born-and-bred Polish woman in her twenties who had worked in Poland for a few years before she decided to emigrate. Her impression that living and working in Poland was unviable because of low wages and limited opportunities for career progression was strengthened during this short period of her professional life. She feels the need for a significant change; therefore, she resigns from her unfulfilling job and moves to London. Disappointed by the constrained career prospects in Poland, she longs for greater financial stability and personal development in the UK. She states that she will not passively "wait for better times to come" (Parys-White, 2008, p. 17).[1]

Nazneen, the 18-year-old protagonist of Monica Ali's novel *Brick Lane*, was born into a poor family in a small village in Bangladesh. Unlike Ewa, she has no formal education and qualifications, as she has spent her entire life assisting her parents and managing household responsibilities. Consequently, an arranged marriage to Chanu, a Bengali man twice her age who has lived in London for the past 20 years, appears to be a favorable opportunity. She joins him, becoming one of the thousands of Bangladeshi

---

1. All quotations from D. Parys-White (2008) and K. Slany (2008) are my translations unless otherwise noted.

women who have migrated to London. While most other migrants are driven by economic hardship or hope for self-improvement, Nazneen's migration is not voluntary. Instead, she travels to Britain in obedience to her parents, who arranged the marriage.

Ewa regards Britain as a "promised land", where she can fulfil her ambitions and attain a higher standard of living than her peers in Poland. She is determined to overcome obstacles to get to Britain and disregards any discomfort along the way. She cannot afford airfare and instead embarks on a 30-hour journey on an overcrowded and uncomfortable bus to what she views as "the land of well-being and tolerance" (Parys-White, 2008, p. 22). Ewa is optimistic that London will offer her the opportunity to start a new life and to develop personally and professionally.

In contrast, Nazneen does not have any particular vision of England prior to her migration from Bangladesh. Her reason for leaving her home country is not economic or self-development driven but rather a demonstration of her obedience to her husband and parents. She is used to obeying traditional beliefs and taking life as it comes. As testified by her own words, her mother taught her passive endurance: "Just wait and see. That's all we can do. (…) Amma always wiped away her tears with those words" (Ali, 2003, p. 27). Nazneen's philosophy is shaped by this attitude of submission: "What could not be changed must be borne. And since nothing could be changed, everything had to be borne" (Ali, 2003, p. 4). Consequently, she dutifully accompanies her husband to London without having any specific expectations about her life there.

Behind the Dream: The Challenges of Life as an Immigrant

Ewa's initial love for London, which was fueled by its stunning architecture, rich greenery, and kind locals, soon fades. When she arrives in Britain, financial constraints force her to share a cheap room in a run-down neighborhood known for drug usage, violence, and homelessness. Additionally, her job chances do not meet her expectations. She obtains a low-paid job as a hotel maid for a Moroccan employer in spite of having a university degree. As she is restricted to positions typically ascribed to women, her degree is of no value in the labor market. Due to the harsh reality of migrant labor, she is forced to give up her career aspirations and accept any job that she is offered, even if it does not fit her qualifications. She humbly abandons her goals and "convert[s] [her] intellectual competence into the broom and shovel" (Parys-White, 2008, p. 96). Ewa admits that, when faced with the reality of life in London, her ambitions "disappeared like the first snow—rapidly" (Parys-White, 2008, p. 29), leaving her with a sense of shame. She hides her job from her friends because cleaning hotel rooms and making beds clashes with how she sees herself. She was raised to value education and equates menial labor with disgrace.

Ewa experiences exploitative working conditions, as do other migrant women employed in the domestic and hospitality sectors. Her boss is still unhappy with her performance and underpays her despite her hard work. Moreover, she has no proper protection and is susceptible to labor rights violations because she works illegally. She is part of what Kronenberg (2017) refers to as "the ghetto of domestic industry," where female migrant workers are predominantly employed in catering, cleaning and caregiving, as a result of ingrained gendered stereotypes (p. 136). Such women receive low pay, face institutionalized prejudice, and refrain from voicing complaints for fear of losing their jobs. Ewa's friend, who works in a hair salon, is subjected to similar exploitative working conditions, with the owner constantly increasing her workload, leaving her disillusioned and exhausted:

> She told me recently to wash her car but only after the hair salon's closing time. I had been waiting for an hour until she did her shopping, so I finished polishing her wheels at 9 p.m. And what did she do? She cut my wage rate because I had forgotten the bumpers, and there were some smudges remaining on the rear window (Parys-White, 2008, p. 52).

Ewa, like many other women, is afraid of being forced to seek new employment, therefore, she does not dare to speak out against her exploitation. Such women suffer in quiet accepting their fate because they feel helpless to oppose a labor market largely dominated by men.

Nazneen embodies this submissive role, obediently following her husband to Britain. When they move into their London home, she is initially impressed by its modern conveniences, a contrast to the living conditions in her Bengali home: "When she thought of Gouripur now, she thought about inconvenience. To do without a flush toilet, to give up on her two sinks (kitchen and bathroom), to light fire for the oven instead of just turning a knob (...)" (Ali, 2003, p. 51). Raised in a highly conservative family, Nazneen does not receive any formal education, as Bangladeshi traditional society expects women to focus on domestic responsibilities rather than educational or professional life. In this patriarchal system, men are primarily expected to work and support their families financially, which positions women economically reliant on them. Dominelli (2006) asserts that "[p]aid work (...) belongs to men. Unpaid work in the home is generally a woman's lot" (p. 160). Despite the psychological and physical price that domestic work has, it is frequently downgraded, which justifies women's subordination in the household.

In *Brick Lane*, both Nazneen and her husband uphold traditional gender roles, mirroring a patriarchal structure in which "women are made for the home" (Blanchet & Biswas, 2021, p. 18). The religious and cultural values that Nazneen adheres to delay her full independence and integration into the host society. Research by Benn and

Jawad (2003) reveals that "some Muslim women experience double oppression from the culture of their community as well as the culture of their religion: 'our parents' traditional attitudes ... their cultural values, their family honour, their stubbornness to let go of the traditions'" (p. 2). However, these limitations are not burdensome for Nazneen; rather, she is unaware of the natural independence that women are entitled to. Confined to her home, she gives her all to her husband's service and to raising her children. Her duties include everything from regular housework to personal care for Chanu, for example ear hair removal, nail care, and corn treatment. With time, the monotonous domestic responsibilities that lie with her further her sense of alienation because the only social connections she has are with a few Bangladeshi women in her neighborhood. At times, she feels overwhelmed by emotional detachment and yearns for human connection:

> What she missed most was people. Not any people in particular (apart, of course, from Hasina) but just people. If she put her ear to the wall she could hear sounds. The television on. Coughing. Sometimes the lavatory flushing. Someone upstairs scraping a chair. A shouting match below. Everyone in their boxes, counting their possessions. In all her eighteen years, she could scarcely remember a moment that she had spent alone. Until she married. And came to London to sit day after day in this large box with the furniture to dust, and the muffled sounds of private lives sealed away above, below, and around her. (Ali, 2003, p. 24)

Before, Nazneen used to find comfort in her faith, but after moving to London, even the teachings of the Quran fail to provide her with peace and strength. Nazneen "took the Qur'an. She looked for familiar passages, the words that she knew that would give comfort. In her panic, she could find none and the words on the page kept her out, hid their meaning and pushed her away" (Ali, 2003, p. 332).

Nazneen's sense of isolation is intensified by a deep fear of navigating London. Her unfamiliarity with the city and poor command of English make her feel insecure and vulnerable. The world outside appears unfriendly and even simple daily activities can be challenging. She says that "[t]o go across the street to the other side without being hit by a car [is] like stepping out during the monsoon and attempting to avoid raindrops" (Ali, 2003, p. 34). Her sense of safety is restricted to her home, which then becomes her only refuge.

The stereotypical placement of women in low-paid labor is highlighted by Oakley (2019), who states that this allows men to pursue higher-earning employment with more social and economic rewards. Chanu is an educated man with a degree from Dhaka University, who feels he is entitled to a more dignified position. However, he is unable to achieve the professional peak he wishes for because his qualifications are not valid in Britain. As a result, he becomes more paternalistic in his marriage, discouraging Nazneen from continuing her education or obtaining employment, and acting as her only connection to the outside world. He demonstrates his intellectual superiority and takes charge of their life in London. Raised with the values of sacrifice and patience, which are deeply rooted in traditional Bangladeshi femininity, Nazneen accepts her boring daily existence as an unavoidable part of her fate rather than a burden, reinforcing her dependence on him (Jahan, 1975).

Upholding Tradition: The Importance of Instilled Values in Immigrant Life

The main character in *Emigrantka z wyboru* is not a forced migrant but chooses to leave her homeland. Although she made her decision on her own, she still feels homesick while living in London. By joining a close-knit group of Polish migrant women, she protects her ties to her homeland and keeps a strong connection to her Polish identity. This community gives friendship, support and help anytime it is needed. For example, Ewa's Polish friends emotionally support Julia, whose father objects to her plan to marry an Egyptian man. Similarly, Jagoda's roommates sympathize with her and offer to assist her in finding another job when she struggles with the huge workload at the hair salon. For the Polish women living in London, this group is like a real family, compensating for the loss of their Polish relatives. Ewa acknowledges this relationship and asserts that her friends are "the surrogate family, but the best we could have here" (Parys-White, 2008, p. 89). The sense of belonging to this community comforts migrants and helps them cope with the difficulties of living abroad. Ewa states that it "gave a sense of security and suppressed the feeling of loneliness" (Parys-White, 2008, p. 69).

Ewa's integration into this group goes beyond social interactions and includes shared living arrangements and cultural activities. She rents a room from a Polish landlord or landlady and forms strong friendships with the other Polish female migrants living in the same house. They maintain their Polish identity and a sense of solidarity by attending frequent get-togethers and adhering to cultural and religious traditions. Homi Bhabha (2004) emphasizes the value of culture in ensuring survival in a foreign environment. This claim is especially relevant to the female characters in Parys-White's book, for whom celebrating Christmas and other religious festivals together helps to strengthen their national identity. For example, Ewa and her friends make traditional Polish dishes and observe customs such as going to a midnight service and singing Christmas carols. Although the women are separated from their homeland, these traditions maintain their cultural heritage and establish a spiritual bond with their Polish families.

Similarly, Nazneen in *Brick Lane* is determined to uphold Bengali traditions and feels nostalgia for home. However, as the years pass, she finds her memories of Bangladesh diminishing and gradually comes to accept that London is her home now:

"The village was leaving her. Sometimes a picture would come. Vivid; so strong she could smell it. More often, she tried to look and couldn't" (Ali, 2003, p. 156). Despite this change, Nazneen still follows the traditional gender roles that she was taught by her parents, even though they lead to gender inequality. Her reliance on her husband is deeply rooted in Bengali culture, where patriarchy is the dominant ideology: "[H]ighly patriarchal and gender discrimination is present at all levels of community. Women are reliant on men throughout the whole time of their lives. The range starts from father to husbands to sons" (Ferdaush & Rahman, 2011, p. 8).

By wearing the traditional sari, cooking Bengali dishes, and socializing with other women in Tower Hamlets, Nazneen actively preserves her cultural identity while living in London. But as a migrant, she often feels alone since she does not interact much with people outside of her community. She contemplates her isolation that overwhelmed her migration:

> In all her eighteen years, she could not remember a moment that she had spent alone. Until she married. And moved to London to sit day after day in this large box with the furniture to polish, and the muffled hum of private lives closed above, below and around her. (Ali, 2003, p. 11)

Her interactions with other Bangladeshi women in Tower Hamlets, who provide her with a sense of belonging and emotional support, is crucial to her adjustment. In addition, her involvement with this group allows her to preserve traditional values and reconstruct her own identity as she becomes more independent and wants to take control of her own life.

Awakening to a New Approach: The Protagonists' Transformation

Migration's transformative force causes considerable changes in both protagonists. Their future is determined by the expanded options and broader perspectives that result from being exposed to Western ideals and values of individual freedom.

Ewa wants to start over in Britain after growing up in communist Poland, where social inequality and political oppression were common. She would like to achieve professional success there and live in a society that she perceives as the "paradise with equal opportunities" (Parys-White, 2008, p. 19). Ewa sees Britain as the country that values equality for all people, regardless of gender, age, or ethnic background. However, she faces a contrast between her expectations and the actual experience of emigrant life in London. She is exploited by her employer, like a lot of other women who work in the hotel industry. Her frustration grows when she is forced to do more unpaid work and is still unable to make a formal complaint because she is an undocumented worker. She observes that "most of the human rights of the 20th century" are often violated by her Moroccan employer (Parys-White, 2008, p. 30). Despite her first image of Britain as a land of prosperity and fairness, she is subjected to systemic discrimination and exploitation of workers. These hardships, however, do not weaken her; on the contrary, she feels strong enough to resist the oppressions she and her colleagues face. In a brave act of defiance, Ewa rebels against her boss, calling it "personal revolution and independence announcement" (Parys-White, 2008, p. 26). She starts her fight against gender-based limitations by encouraging her colleagues to oppose discrimination in the workplace. She is no longer quiet and insecure but becomes a strong and independent woman who can stand up for other people.

The sour apples that Ewa eats symbolizes her strength and ability to overcome problems. They represent something unpleasant or difficult to accept, but, in the context of migrant life, they may signify some assimilation problems and disappointments that Ewa encounters. Her willingness to eat the sour apples, despite not liking them, reflects her transformation into a resilient woman, who is able to deal with the harsh realities of migrant life and will not be defeated by any hardships.

Ewa enrolls in an English course at London College, realizing that proficiency in the language will "boost her career prospects and ensure a better future," since professional progress requires higher qualifications and linguistic competence (Parys-White, 2008, pp. 52–53). This decision marks a great leap in social movement and self-sufficiency. Once limited by language barriers, she has now improved her ability to communicate effectively with local people. What is more, her English proficiency helps her to find a more fulfilling and better-paid job. Her decision to join the English course has an enormous impact on her entire life because she falls in love with the owner of the language school and marries him.

Nazneen's experience of migration and her interactions with other Bengali women, some of whom have already accepted elements of Western culture, have a considerable impact on her way to self-awareness and strength. Unlike Ewa, Nazneen comes to London with traditional expectations, having imbibed the belief that a woman's place is in the home. However, her attitude later changes as she sees other Bengali women who have achieved social integration and economic independence. Her awakening starts when she questions her previous acceptance of fate. She does not resign herself to her destiny when her little son becomes seriously ill and acts decisively by taking him to a doctor. His eventual death is a turning point, which propels her to take control of her own life. Her being able to communicate effectively with an Englishman is a seemingly insignificant but symbolic event: "It was very little. But it was something" (Ali, 2003, p. 39). This incident demonstrates her increased self-confidence and sets her on the path to independence.

Learning a language plays an important part in Nazneen's personal growth. As she improves her English fluency, her sense of agency increases, and she is able to interact more actively with her environment. She starts her own tailoring business and supports the family although her husband opposes it, driven by his patriarchal fears that a working wife will threaten his dominance. This action marks her transition from financial reliance to self-sufficiency and challenges the traditional gender roles that were imposed on her in Bangladesh. She eventually becomes a breadwinner, even financially helping her husband when he gets a low-paying job driving a taxi.

Additionally, Nazneen's involvement with the Bengal Tigers, a local activist group, makes her develop intellectually and psychologically. She listens to talks on social justice, racial prejudice, and political issues that concern Muslims globally. Her discussions with Karim, who is an influential member of the group, acquaint her with world crises, for example those happening in Bosnia, and help her understand how religion and politics interact: "She learned of her Muslim brothers and sisters. She learned how many they were, how dispersed, and how tormented. She discovered Bosnia" (Ali, 2003, p. 175). She also realizes that racial discrimination is a prevalent feature of London life rather than a far-off issue.

In one of the group's sessions, Nazneen takes part in a vote, which plays a significant role in her transformation. For the first time ever, she comes to understand the power of her own decisions in forming her own destiny: "By raising her hand, or by not raising it, she could change the outcome of events, of affairs of the world from which she had known nothing" (Ali, 2003, p. 175). Given her cultural background, which does not usually permit women to participate in decision making, this awareness is especially ironic. Through these events, Nazneen gradually redefines herself by accepting her new independence and leaving behind the limitations of her old life.

The love affair between Nazneen and Karim is another major turning point in pursuing independence and the redefinition of traditional gender roles. She is first impressed by his anti-racist views and the depth of his knowledge that he shares with her. Karim also occasionally asks for her opinion, which her husband has never done. It makes Nazneen feel appreciated and acknowledged. Despite having a great library, Chanu has never provided her with a book or expressed any interest in her intellectual growth: "Chanu had never given her anything to read" (Ali, 2003, p. 176). Moreover, he also reinforces Nazneen's subordination in the home by viewing her as only a "good worker" and confining her to domestic labor (Ali, 2003, p. 9).

Nazneen's romance with Karim serves as a spur for her personal development and boosts her self-esteem. She gains confidence in asserting her independence and dropping the old identity as a submissive wife. Al Mamun (2014) notes, "Nazneen views herself, not as mother and wife, but as a woman" (p. 516). She is able to question the conventional beliefs that her parents instilled in her because of her new sense of self. She was expected to be a dutiful wife and obedient daughter for the rest of her life, but her affair with Karim shows that she is a mature, independent woman who no longer blindly accepts her husband's rule. She finds strength to scold him when the situation calls for it and rejects Karim's romantic advances as well as Chanu's offer to go back to Bangladesh. Nazneen knows that she would like to keep her tailoring business growing and bring up her daughters on her own, free of the influence of men. Her transformation is demonstrated by her rejection of Chanu's patriarchal attitudes, which are indicated by his insistence that she comply with his rulings with the words "if you say so, husband" (Ali, 2003, p. 68). From a submissive personality, she transforms into a dominant, strong, and independent woman who adopts her own status in the host society.

Conclusions

Migration has a psychological and cultural impact on the lives of both characters. Ewa and Nazneen move from the settings that once provided them with a sense of security to the new world that is considerably different. Through migration, both protagonists are thrown into the unfamiliar society, where they encounter cultural values and principles that often clash with the norms inculcated in them by their parents. For Nazneen, who comes from a strictly patriarchal Bangladesh, this change is a cultural shock because Western values are rather dissimilar from the traditional society from which she is coming. Paradoxically, the host country, where she felt alienated and insecure in the beginning, becomes a space of liberation in terms of autonomy and the possibility of her personal growth. In contrast, Ewa, who comes from post-communist Poland, arrives in Britain with expectations of Western equality and professional opportunity, only to experience gender-based discrimination, especially in the labor market. For her, London proves to be more patriarchal than her home country. This contrast suggests that the idea of the "liberating" West is not universal. The experiences of female migrants are shaped not only by their host countries but also by the social frameworks of the countries they come from.

Migration increases both characters' self-confidence and enables them to make important decisions about their lives and families. Both Ewa and Nazneen redefine traditional gender roles and undergo significant self-transformation, evolving from individuals who were constrained by tradition into successful women who no longer feel insecure in Britain. While Nazneen finds the strength to develop her tailoring business and raise her two daughters on her own, Ewa marries an Englishman and starts a comfortable life in London. Displacement thus triggers their economic independence and personal development, greatly increasing their self-esteem. According to Slany (2008), "[m]igrations can radically change traditionally understood womanhood and traditional gender roles, rip an inflexible cultural corset, which previously connected them to their former home and country… [They] shatter temporarily or permanently usually accepted women's social structures and reconstruct them" (p. 9). Moreover, migration gives new prospects and leads to personal transformations, allowing both characters to take control of their lives. No longer submissive or bound by male rule, they move forward in the world, gaining higher qualifications and overcoming language barriers, both becoming fluent speakers of English.

Despite employing two different types of narration, both novels remain close to the realistic fiction and use simple and straightforward language with few poetic devices. Parys-White uses very little figurative language to represent Ewa's transformation into an independent woman who feels strong enough to overcome obstacles and support other women. One exception is a scene in which Ewa eats sour apples, which serve as a metaphor for the difficult migration experience she faces and later transforms into opportunities for professional growth and a successful life in London. In *Brick Lane*, Nazneen's awakening is symbolically represented by her attempt at ice-skating, instead of passively watching it on TV. She is able to "race on, on two legs" and maintain her composure on the ice (Ali, 2003, p. 369). Ice-skating is a metaphor for her newfound independence, which she attains by taking control of her life and making her way in cosmopolitan London.

References

Al Mamun, H. (2014, August). Brick Lane: Mirroring Nazneen's metamorphosis. *European Scientific Journal*, 509–517. https://eujournal.org/index.php/esj/article/view/4056/3895

Ali, M. (2003). *Brick Lane*. Scribner.

Aziz, K. (2015). Female migrants' work trajectories: Polish women in the UK labour market. *Central and Eastern European Migration Review*, 4(2), 87–105.

Benn, T., & Jawad, H. (2003). *Muslim women in the United Kingdom and beyond: Experiences and images*. Brill.

Bhabha, H. (2004). *The location of culture*. Routledge: Classics.

Blanchet, T., & Biswas, H. (2021). *Migration and gender in Bangladesh: An irregular landscape*. The International Labour Office.

Brown, J. (2006). *Global South Asians*. Cambridge University Press.

Crenshaw, K. (1991). Mapping the margins: Intersectionality, identity politics, and violence against women of color. *Stanford Law Review*, 43(6), 1241–1299 https://doi.org/10.2307/1229039

Christou, A., & Kofman, E. (2022). *Gender and migration*. Springer.

Churchill, W. (1946). 'Iron curtain' speech. The National Archives. https://www.nationalarchives.gov.uk/education/resources/cold-war-on-file/iron-curtain-speech/

Clark, D. (2024). *Number of Polish nationals resident in the United Kingdom from 2008 to 2021*. Statista. https://www.statista.com/statistics/1061639/polish-population-in-unitedkingdom/#statisticContainer

Cook, J., Dwyer, P., & Waite, L. (2010). The experiences of accession & migrants in England: Motivations, work and agency. *International Migration*, 49(2), 54–79.

Dominelli, L. (2006). *Women and community action*. Policy Press.

Engle, L. B. (2004). *The world in motion. Short essays on migration and gender*. International Organisation for Migration.

Erel, U., Morokvasic, M., & Shinozaki, K. (2003). Introduction: Bringing gender into migration. In M. Morokvasic, U. Erel, & K. Shinozaki (Eds.), *Crossing borders and shifting boundaries* (Vol. 1). Springer Fachmedien Wiesbaden GmbH.

Ferdaush, J., & Rahman, K. M. (2011). *Gender inequality in Bangladesh*. Unnayan Onneshan-The Innovators.

Garapich, M. P. (2019). Migracje z Polski do Wielkiej Brytanii: Geneza, stan dzisiejszy, wyzwania na przyszłość [Migrations from Poland to Great Britain: Origins, current state, challenges for the future]. *Studia BAS*, 4(60), 13–30. https://doi.org/10.31268/StudiaBAS.2019.28

Główny Urząd Statystyczny. (2019). *Informacja o rozmiarach i kierunkach czasowej emigracji z Polski w latach 2004–2018* [Information on the scale and directions of temporary emigration from Poland in the years 2004–2018]. https://stat.gov.pl/obszary-tematyczne/ludnosc/migracje-zagraniczne-ludnosci/informacja-o-rozmiarach-i-kierunkach-czasowej-emigracji-z-polski-w-latach-2004-2018,2,12.html

Grabowska-Lusińska, I., & Okólski, M. (2008). Migracja z Polski po 1 maja 2004 r.: Jej intensywność i kierunki geograficzne oraz alokacja migrantów na rynkach pracy krajów Unii Europejskiej [Migration from Poland after May 1, 2004: Intensity, geographic patterns, and the distribution of migrants in the labour markets of EU countries]. *CMR Working Papers*, 33(91). Centre of Migration Research. http://igsegp.amu.edu.pl/wp-content/uploads/2019/01/Raport-o-stanie-bada%C5%84-nad-migracjami-w-Polsce-po-1989-roku.pdf

Humera, S., & Ambreen, F. (2017). Factors influencing migration of female workers: A case of Bangladesh. *IZA Journal of Development and Migration*, 7(4), 1–15. https://doi.org/10.1186/s40176-0170090-6

Islam, N. (2008). *Gender analysis of migration from Bangladesh*. Bangladesh Bureau of Manpower, Employment and Training. https://old.bmet.gov.bd/BMET/resources/Static%20PDF%20and%20DOC/publication/Gender%20Analysis%20of%20Migration.pdf

Jahan, R. (1975). Women in Bangladesh. In R. Rohrlich-Leavitt (Ed.), *Women cross-culturally* (pp. 5–30). Mouton Publishers.

Kordasiewicz, A. (2010). Profesjonalizacja i personalizacja—strategie Polek pracujących w sektorze usług domowych w Neapolu [Professionalization and personalization: Strategies of Polish women working in the domestic services sector in Naples]. In M. Kindler & J. Napierała (Eds.), *Migracje kobiet: Przypadek Polski* (pp. 37–68). Wydawnictwo Naukowe Scholar.

Kronenberg, A. (2017). Migracje kobie—Między emancypacją a wyzyskiem [Women's migration: Between emancipation and exploitation]. *Studia Historica Gedanensia*, 8(2017), 125–140. https://doi.org/10.4467/23916001HG.17.007.9061

Kupiszewski, M. (in cooperation with M. Okólski) (2018). Demograficzne aspekty badań nad migracjami [Demographic aspects of migration studies]. In A. Horolets, M. Lesińska, & M. Okólski (Eds.), *Raport o stanie badan nad migracjami w Polsce po 1989 roku* (pp. 30–67). Komitet Badań nad Migracjami PAN.

Mason, D. (1995). *Race and ethnicity in modern Britain*. Oxford University Press.

Morokvasic, M. (1983). Women in migration: Beyond the reductionist outlook. In A. Phizacklea (Ed.), *One way ticket: Migration and female labour* (Vol. 18). Routledge Library Editions: Immigration and Migration.

Muhammedi, S. (2022). *Gifts from Amin*. University of Manitoba Press.

Oakley, A. (2019). *The sociology of housework*. Policy Press.
Office for National Statistics. (2021, November 25). *Ethnicity, national identity, and religion in the UK and non-UK born population*. https://www.ons.gov.uk/peoplepopulationandcommunity/culturalidentity/ethnicity
Okólski, M., & Salt, J. (2014). Polish emigration to the UK after 2004; Why did so many come? *Central and Eastern European Migration Review*, 3(2), 11–37. http://www.ceemr.uw.edu.pl/vol-3-no-2-december-2014/articles/polish-emigration-uk-after-2004-why-did-so-many-come
Parys-White, D. (2008). *Emigrantka z wyboru. Opowieść londyńska.* [*Emigrant by choice. A London story*]. Videograf II.
Ryan, L., & Webster, W. (2008). *Gendering migration: Masculinity, femininity, and ethnicity in post-war Britain*. Ashgate Publishing Limited.
Slany, K. (2008). Co to znaczy być migrantką? [What does it mean to be a female migrant?] In K. Slany (Ed.), *Migracje kobiet: Perspektywa wielowymiarowa* (pp. 7–30). Gender Studies ISUJ.
Slany, K., & Ślusarczyk, M. (2019). Mobilność międzynarodowa Polek na przestrzeniwieków: W odkrywaniu sprawstwa [International mobility of Polish women across the centuries: In the discovery of agency]. *Studia Migracyjne. Przegląd Polonijny*, 4(174), 7–26.
Zig, H. (1985, December). The New Commonwealth migrants 1945–1962. *History Today*, 35(12). https://www.historytoday.com/archive/new-commonwealth-migrants-1945-62

CHAPTER ELEVEN | MONIKA COGHEN

Kościuszko's Name in Byron's Poetry
Echoes of the News from Poland in *Don Juan* and
The Age of Bronze

Abstract

In Canto X of *Don Juan*, Juan travels through Poland, where, despite the country bearing "yokes of iron"(X 58.457), one might still find comfort in "Kosciusko's name, [which] / Might scatter fire through ice, like Hecla's flame" (X 59. 471–472). Thomas McLean suggests that these lines refer to the Constitutional Reform of May 3, 1791, as, according to Jerome McGann's notes to *Don Juan,* Juan crosses Poland in the year when the Diet approved the constitution. Kościuszko was the supporter of the reform and the leader of the doomed attempt to preserve Polish independence. In such a reading the eruption of the volcano might be seen as a reference to the Kościuszko's Uprising of 1794. Yet the lines on the power of Kościuszko's name have a much more positive resonance than allusions to the ill-fated struggle for freedom. They follow the narrator's reflections on Napoleon's disastrous Russian campaign, placing Kościuszko as a positive counterpart to the "god of clay." Thus, they may suggest that Kościuszko's ideals were alive in Poland at the time of writing Canto X in 1822. In this paper, I would like to argue that the references to Kościuszko and to Poland both in *Don Juan* and *The Age of Bronze* may, at least partly, reflect Byron's reading of *Galignani's Messenger*. The examination of news items from Poland in 1820–22 reveals a close correspondence between Byron's verses and the paper's entries on Poland, which reported on the enthusiasm of the Poles for the construction of the monument to Kościuszko in Kraków.

Keywords: Byron, Kościuszko, Napoleon, Poland, *Don Juan, The Age of Bronze*

While writing to Augusta from Cephalonia on October 12, 1823, Byron refers to Alexander Mavrocordatos, one of the leaders of the Greek War of Independence, as "the only *Washington* or *Kosciusko* kind of man amongst them" (*BLJ*[1] 11, p. 44), and

---

1. All quotations from Byron's letters and journals follow Leslie A. Marchand's *Byron's Letters and Journals*, 13 vols. (John Murray, 1973–94). Hereafter *BLJ*.

the same comparison recurs in the letter to Thomas Moore on December 27, 1823 (*BLJ* 11, p. 84). For Byron, George Washington, and Tadeusz Kościuszko (1746–1817) belonged to a select group of great freedom fighters, whose names reverberated with symbolic value.[2] Unlike the names of thousands of valiant men dead on battlefields, which ended up in the "Gazette" (*DJ*[3] VIII. 18. 138), the names of Washington and Kościuszko possessed agency and had the power to inspire the living. In *Don Juan* Washington is listed along with Leonidas as one of those whose "names will be / A watchword till the future shall be free" (*DJ* VIII. 5), and Kościuszko's name might "warm" travelers on their way across Poland (*DJ* X. 59. 469-472). Significantly, Byron thought of them when considering the practicalities of the fight for Greek independence. An earlier mention of Kościuszko in Byron's personal writings appears in the Ravenna Journal entry for January 30, 1821, where he alludes to the Carbonari's preparations for a revolution, in which he was deeply involved. He records a conversation with the Gambas about Kościuszko, when Count Ruggero de Gamba (the father of Teresa Guiccioli, Byron's Italian lover) told him that "he [had] seen the Polish officers in the Italian war burst into tears on hearing [Kościuszko's] name" (*BLJ* 8, p. 40). These officers must have served in the Legions, Polish military units formed in 1797–99 with the hope of restoring Polish sovereignty through the alliance with revolutionary France. Some of them might have fought in the 1794 Polish Uprising led by Kościuszko. Kościuszko was implicitly the highly desirable type of leader for any national revolution.

Nowadays Washington is easily recognizable as the first president of the United States, but beyond his native Poland, Kościuszko is known mostly to students of the long 18th century. At the time, he was celebrated as a champion of liberty both in America and in Europe.

A son of a landowner in the eastern part of the Polish-Lithuanian Commonwealth, Kościuszko was educated at a newly established military academy in Warsaw.[4] In years 1769–1774, he studied military engineering in Paris, where he became imbued with revolutionary ideas. He made his name, contributing to American victories as a military engineer and strategist during the Revolutionary War. As Michał Burczak (2014) points out, his supporters in Poland referred to him as "Washington's disciple," which

---

2. Roderick Beaton (2013) intimates in this comparison a suggestion that like Washington and Kościuszko, Mavrocordatos has the potential for becoming a leader of a modern nation. Mavrocordatos at this stage appears to Byron as a man "not only of talents but integrity"(p. 203).
3. All quotations from Byron's *Don Juan* are from J. Stabler & G. Hopps, Eds., (2024), *The Poems of Lord Byron—Don Juan: Volumes IV & V* (Longman Annotated English Poets). Routledge unless otherwise indicated. Hereafter *DJ*. The references are to cantos, stanzas, and lines; thus *DJ* VIII. 18. 138 refers to canto 8, stanza 18, line 138.
4. For an English-language biography of Kościuszko, see Storożyński (2010).

implied that "the Polish leader's republican values had been reinforced, if not molded, by George Washington and the American Revolution" (p. 28). That moniker must have been popular at the time: in an 1822 article in the *Edinburgh Review* he is referred to as "the scholar of Washington" (*Edinburgh Review*, 1822, p. 515).

On his return to Poland, which at the time was being partitioned amongst Russia, Prussia, and Austria, he became the commander-in-chief of the 1794 military attempt at preserving Polish national sovereignty. After some initial successes, the Polish forces were defeated, and Kościuszko was rumored to have been killed in the battle of Maciejowice. In fact, he was wounded and taken prisoner. The remnants of the insurgent forces gathered in Warsaw; General Suvorov's siege of Warsaw's suburb of Praga ended in the indiscriminate massacre of the city's population. The failure of the so-called Kościuszko Uprising marked the end of the Polish-Lithuanian Commonwealth in 1795. In Thomas Campbell's *Pleasures of Hope*, "Hope, for a season, bade the world farewell, / And Freedom shriek'd as KOSCIUSKO fell" (Campbell, 1800, p. 30). Yet Kościuszko did not die on the battlefield nor in prison as it was believed (McLean, 2012, p. 47), but was held prisoner in Saint Petersburg. After Catherine II's death in 1796, he was released by her successor, Tsar Paul I, and left for America, visiting Sweden and Britain on his way. He was greeted enthusiastically as a tragic champion of freedom in England (McLean, 2012, pp. 50–52). He spent two years in the States, trying to sort out his financial affairs, but in 1798 he returned to Europe, hoping that Polish independence might be regained with the support of revolutionary France, which at the time was at war with Austria and Prussia. He took part in the organizations of the Polish Legions, but he refused to become their military commander, insisting that he could only lead Polish military forces fighting on the geographical territory of the Polish Lithuanian Commonwealth.

For Byron, like for many of his contemporaries, Kościuszko was one of the heroes of the age, not surprisingly so, as his name had widely appeared in English publications of the period. Thomas McLean (2012) in his book *The Other East and Nineteenth-Century Literature* has thoroughly examined the representation of Kościuszko and the fate of Poland in the works of the British writers and the British press at the time. He has shown that while in the late 1790s Kościuszko was depicted in Britain as a "defeated hero" (McLean, 2012, p. 57), two decades later he appeared as "a model of individual liberalism" owing to Leigh Hunt's publications in *The Examiner*, which had formed the perception of Kościuszko for its readers including Byron (McLean, 2012, p. 89).[5]

In this paper I would like to focus further on Byron's references to Kościuszko and Poland, suggesting that Byron uses Kościuszko as a foil to Napoleon and that

---

5. MacLean (2012) also offers a reading of *Mazeppa*, in which he presents the poem as Byron's commentary on the fate of Poland, and sees in Mazeppa a Kościuszko figure (pp. 106–112).

his fascination with the sound of the Polish leader's name, very strongly echoing that of his contemporaries, was shaped not only by *The Examiner* but also by *Galignani's Messenger*, which might have directed the poet's attention to the events in Poland in the early 1820s.

In Byron's poetry, Kościuszko's name appears in Canto X of *Don Juan* and in *The Age of Bronze*, written in the autumn of 1822. On both occasions, he is mentioned in the context of Napoleon's expedition to Moscow, and both present Kościuszko in contrast to periphrastic references to Bonaparte, whose name is not directly mentioned. The *Don Juan* stanzas offer a compressed image of political and military conflicts in the Polish lands from the 1730s to the early 1820s. This geographical area is associated with enslavement and desolation and makes Byron reflect on the nature of fame and infamy.

Juan travels with little Leila:

> …through Poland and through Warsaw,
> Famous for mines of salt and yokes of iron;
> Through Courland also, which that famous farce saw
> That gave her dukes the graceless name of 'Biron';
> 'Tis the same landscape which the modern Mars saw
> Who marched to Moscow, led by Fame, the siren!
> To lose by one month's frost some twenty years
> Of conquest—and his Guard of Grenadiers.
>
> Let not this seem an anti-climax; 'Oh!
> My Guard! my Old Guard! exclaimed that god of clay;
> Think of the Thunderer's falling down below
> Carotid-artery-cutting Castlereagh!
> Alas! that glory should be chilled by snow!
> But should we wish to warm us on our way
> Through Poland, there is Kosciusko's name
> Might scatter fire through ice, like Hecla's flame. (*DJ* X. 58–59. 457–472)

Jerome McGann places Byron's reference to Kościuszko within the chronological frame of the poem's narrative. As Juan travels across Poland in 1791, Byron refers to the process of annexation of Polish territories by Russia and the Polish uprising led by Kościuszko in 1794 (Byron, 1992, p. 745). McLean (2012, p.106) elucidates the 1791 date even further, pointing out that 1791 was the year of the proclamation of the progressive Constitution of May 3 in Poland, which gave pretext for the Russian military intervention in the following year. While I find McGann's and McLean's readings persuasive, I think that Byron's allusion to Kościuszko is rooted in the present of 1822 when Byron wrote Canto X, the two stanzas offering a condensed history of the region from that perspective. Significantly, unlike the other names referred to in the passage in the past tense, "Kosciusko's name" resonates with the present through the use of the present tense. This use of tenses also stresses a contrast between the Birons of Courland, Napoleon, and Castlereagh, on the one hand, and Kościuszko, on the other.

Byron's association of Poland with salt mines is familiar from *Mazeppa*, where, in a note to line 157, he accounts for his comparison of the Count's wealth to a salt mine by explaining that Poland's wealth "consists greatly in the salt mines." But in *Don Juan* salt mines placed together with yokes of iron point not only to the natural resources of the country but also to its enslavement. The geographical location makes the poet think of the region's recent history—in particular, the story of the false Birons of Courland and Napoleon's Russian campaign of 1812. The two stanzas are partially structured around the opposition of two names—"the graceless name of 'Biron'" and "Kosciusko's name."

The Birons of Courland were of interest to Byron because of what he regarded as usurpation of his family name, which he makes apparent in his note to the poem:

> In the Empress Anne's time, Biren her favourite assumed the name and arms of the 'Birons' of France, which families are yet extant with that of England. There are still the daughters of Courland of that name; one of them I remember seeing in England in the blessed year of the Allies—(the Duchess of S.)—to whom the English Duchess of S———t presented me as a namesake. (Stabler & Hopps, 2024, p. 794)

In his letter to his half-sister, Augusta Leigh (June 18, 1814), he reports that the Duchess of Somerset "insisted on presenting me to a Princess *Biron* Duchess of Hohen— God knows—what—and another person to her two sisters—Birons too—but I flew off—& *would* not—saying I had enough of introductions for that night at least' (*BLJ* 4, p.128).

Byron would have known the story of the Courland Birons from Henry Tooke's *Life of Catharine II*, which he enumerates in his "List of Historical Writers Whose Works I Have Perused in Various Languages" (Moore, 1831, p. 34). Ernst Johann Bühren (1690–1772) or Biron (sometimes also spelled Biren) was the favorite of Tsaritsa Anna Ivanovna, the empress of Russia from 1730 to 1740; his notoriety led to the period of Anna's rule being referred to as the *Bironovhchina*, "the era of Biron" (Bitter, 2014, p.104). According to Tooke (1800), he was "born in Courland" in "a family of mean extraction" (vol. 1, p. 160 note). Tooke presents him as a social climber, who won the favor of Anna Ivanovna and became her secretary when, as the widow of Frederic William, duke of Courland, she resided in Mittau (nowadays Jelgava). In Tooke's account:

> On her being declared sovereign of Russia, Anne called Biren to Petersburg, and the secretary soon became duke of Courland, and first minister or rather despot of Russia. All now felt the dreadful effects of his extreme arrogance, his base intrigues,

and his horrid barbarity. The cruelties he exercised on the most illustrious persons of the country almost exceed belief: and Manstein conjectures, that during the ten years in which Biren's power continued, above twenty thousand persons were sent to Siberia, of whom scarcely five thousand were ever heard of more" (Tooke, 1800, vol. 1, pp. 160–161 note).

Biron's abuse of power allegedly took place in Russia as he did not reside in Courland (nowadays Latvia), which was a vassal state of the Polish Lithuanian Commonwealth at the time. Anna had used her influence to have Biron elected duke of Courland to strengthen Russian influence in the region. Michael Bitter (2014) has argued that Biron's infamous reputation may have been caused by the fact that he was a Baltic German and hence resented as a foreigner by the Russians (p. 104). Byron, however, must have been struck by the image of his namesake as a base, tyrannical social upstart, thus he writes of "the farce" of Bühren adopting the ancient, noble name of "Biron." Stabler and Hopps (2024, p. 776) suggest that Byron may have been familiar with the story of Biron published in *The Annual Register* for 1770 (1771), which describes the duke of Courland's abuses of his political opponents by having them sent on rides in closed wooden wagons to the remote parts of Russia. When one of them complained about his treatment on his return, the duke "did not fail of acting the farce of representing his grievance to the court of Russia" (as cited in Stabler & Hopps, 2024, p. 776). But for the reader of Tooke's *Life of Catharine II* "the farce" may have evoked wider associations; after all, Byron mentions not only Ernst Johann Biron but the dukes of Courland in the plural.

According to Tooke, on Anna Ivanovna's death, Biron became regent, but after twenty days he was arrested and banished to Siberia for twenty years (Tooke, 1800, vol. 3, p. 384). Catherine II released him from exile, after which he took residence in Courland, but he only ruled for a short time, resigning "the reign of government to his son Peter, already elected by the influence of Russia" (Tooke, 1800, vol. 3, pp. 384–85). Peter was "avaricious, litigious and greatly disliked;" he got into the conflict with his nobles by raising the prices of land lease and introducing "agronomical alterations." According to Tooke (1800), he "seemed by his imprudent conduct to urge his subjects to invite the russian [sic] yoke." (vol. 3, pp. 370–371). Eventually, the dissatisfaction with his rule and the clever maneuverings of Catherine II led to the Courish nobles formally asking for the withdrawal of Courland from Polish protection and placing it under the direct rule of Russia, which took place on March 18, 1795 (Tooke, 1800, vol. 3, p. 373). At this point, Tooke fails to mention the fact that at the time after the failure of the Kościuszko Uprising in 1794 Poland was being wiped off the map of Europe. Thus, if Byron read the story of Duke Peter Biron in the third volume of Tooke, he would associate the Birons of Courland with the complete subjection of that region of Europe to the Russian Empire.

Piqued at the existence of such unworthy namesakes, Byron gives the passage an ironic undertone through the seemingly awkward repetition of the words "which" and "famous" and the use of feminine rhymes iron/"Biron"/siren. "Famous" is used here in the double sense of "Celebrated in fame or public report" (*OED* 1a) and the obsolete sense of "notorious" (*OED*+3). "[T]he famous farce" (l. 459) is the farce of the appropriation of the ancient name and arms, the farce of the Tsaritsa and her lover, and the farce of the Russian Empire's expansionism. It also brings to mind the scandal surrounding Byron's separation from his wife. By referring to the name of "Biron" as "graceless" (l. 460) in the sense of "not in a state of grace, unregenerate; hence depraved, wicked, godly, impious" (*OED* 1a), he is alluding to his own scandalous reputation and possibly to that of his great-uncle "the Wicked Lord" though it is the Birons of Courtland who were truly "graceless." The parallel syntactic structure in lines 459 and 461 with the deliberate verbal repetition ("which that famous farce saw" / "which modern Mars saw") establishes an analogy between the fortunes of both the Courtland and the British "Birons" and the fate of Napoleon, compressed in the images from his Russian campaign and his final defeat at Waterloo.

The repetition of "My Guard! My Old Guard" brings forth the possible Polish associations to the reader. According to Byron's editors, this exclamation comes from the often quoted account of Napoleon's deliberations on whether or not to surrender after the Battle of Waterloo, when on the suggestion of Hugues Maret, his chief of staff, that their remaining troops should defend them, he complained, "Ah! my Old Guard! Will they defend themselves like thee?" (Booth, 1817, p. 158).[6] Napoleon's famous "Old Guard," apart from the ill-fated grenadiers (line 464), who synecdochically stand for the losses of the Grande Armée on its retreat from Moscow, included a well-known regiment of Polish Lancers, the Chevau Legers Polonais de la Garde Imperiale, who distinguished themselves during the Russian campaign and were known for their devotion to the emperor. An anecdote about a Polish officer, Colonel Pistowski who offered to accompany Napoleon to St. Helena (Booth, 1817, p. 168), had served Byron as a basis for a poem "From the French" (1816), which is the first-person declaration of blind love to the emperor.

In the Polish stanzas of *Don Juan,* Napoleon is ironically referred to as a godlike figure—"modern Mars" and Jove. Seduced by fame, he becomes exposed as a "god of clay," certainly a false god followed by the Poles. This echoes the criticism of the

---

6. Stabler & Hopps (2024, p. 777) are the first editors of *Don Juan* who track down Napoleon's exclamation to Booth, 1816. In the earlier editions of *Don Juan,* the apostrophe to the Old Guard was explained on the basis of Walter Scott's *Life of Napoleon* (1827), which Byron could not have known. The quotations in this paper follow Booth, 1817.

war in Canto VIII: "Call them Mars / Bellona, what you will—they mean but wars" (VIII. 1.7-8).

Nonetheless, Byron marks his well-known ambivalence toward Napoleon, lamenting the emperor's defeat by the Holy Alliance, condensed in the figure of Castlereagh. Robert Stewart, Viscount Castlereagh (1769–1822) was British foreign secretary and leader of the house in 1812–1822, playing a major part in organizing the coalition against Napoleon on the Continent, and thwarting political radicalism in Britain. Owing to a mental breakdown, possibly caused by sexual blackmail, he committed suicide by cutting his throat with a penknife on May 13, 1822. By the use of the mock Homeric epithet "Carotid-artery-cutting Castlereagh" (line 468), Byron questions his political success, especially as the ironic comment, "Alas! that glory should be chilled by snow!" (line 469), though directly referring to Napoleon's disastrous retreat from Moscow, syntactically refers both to Napoleon and Castlereagh.

The figure that appears in opposition to Napoleon, Biron, and Castlereagh is Kościuszko. The contrast between Castlereagh and Kościuszko is marked by the alliteration of the initial consonants of their names. For anybody knowledgeable about their political views, as Byron was, it is above all the opposition between the politician blamed for the Peterloo Massacre (1819) and the introduction of oppressive measures against the radicals in England, and the fierce champion of freedom and egalitarianism. While Napoleon and Castlereagh were defeated by "one month's frost" (line 463), Kościuszko's name still has a living potential: it "might scatter fire through ice, like Hecla's flame" (line 472).

As McLean (2012) has noticed, Byron follows Leigh Hunt's article in The *Examiner* and John Keats's sonnet "To Kosciusko" in its emphasis on the resonance of the strangely sounding foreign name (p. 105). The emphasis on the semiotic power of the name also brings to mind Byron's preoccupation with words as things:[7]

> But words are things, and a small drop of ink
> Falling like dew upon a thought produces
> That which makes thousands—perhaps millions think;
> 'Tis strange, the shortest letter which man uses
> Instead of speech may form a lasting link
> Of ages; to what straits old Time reduces
> Frail man, when paper—even a rag like this—
> Survives himself, his tomb, and all that's his.
> (*DJ* III. 88. 793–800)

---

7. *CHP* III 114, 4, *Don Juan* III 89 1, or *PoD* II 2., MF. On Byron's use of the phrase, see, for instance Gross (2001, pp. 123–124).

Byron takes for granted the contemporary resonance of the strange-sounding Polish name of Kościuszko with its repeated velar plosives and sibilant fricatives. Placing it against Biron/Byron, Castlereagh, and the unnamed but well-recognizable "god of clay," he assumes his audience's knowledge of the symbolic value of that name as that of a freedom fighter uncorrupted by fame and ambition.

McLean (2012) himself points to the symbolic status of Kościuszko in post-Waterloo Britain, which was exploited by Leigh Hunt and other writers to "advance their political agendas" (p. 89). When Kościuszko died in 1817, Leigh Hunt described him as

> the most unequivocally noble being that adored the age. He was also no dupe, either to the illegitimate or the legitimate. The Allied monarchs and their tools, none of whom, not even BONAPARTE, could make a tool of him, were a mere set of cheating boys in comparison, who made promises which he knew to despise, and who unfortunately succeeded but too well in regaining powers to which they had no right. (*The Examiner*, 1817, p. 711)

As McLean has shown, in 1814 Leigh Hunt briefly linked his hopes for the restoration of independent Poland after the exile of Napoleon to Elba with Kościuszko:

> the glorious patriot, KOSCIUSKO, has appeared on the scene again, and is mentioned in the Paris Papers as about to return to his native country with the Polish troops... We thought that he had been living in America, covered with wounds that disabled him from action.... The very mention of the name of KOSCIUSKO, after having been compelled to ring the changes so often upon the BONAPARTES and the FERDINANDS,—the mighty tyrants and the mean,—is like a new music, coming to us in a summer wind. (*The Examiner*, July 3, 1814, pp. 428–429, cited after McLean, 2012, p. 95)

Kościuszko, as a staunch republican, mistrusted Napoleon after Bonaparte had first declared himself consul, and then emperor, and he was also mindful of the fate of Polish troops sent to quell Toussaint l'Ouverture's uprising in Santo Domingo.[8] When asked by Napoleon for aid in the formation of Polish armed forces in 1806, he demanded Bonaparte's guarantee for the reconstruction of an independent Polish state with a British-like constitution, freedom for serfs and the territory of 1772, which Napoleon would not commit to, though a false address to the Poles in Kościuszko's name was issued by Joseph Fouché, Napoleon's Minister of the Police (Storozynski, 2010, p. 260). Likewise, when in 1814 Tsar Alexander I invited him to return to Poland

---

8. For the story of the Polish armed forces under Napoleon, see Chwalba, (2000, pp. 224–228); Davies (2005, pp. 216–224).

and help in the formation of the Kingdom of Poland, he refused to collaborate with the tsar, whose intentions he distrusted.

Byron's use of Kościuszko's name falls within the contemporary fascination with the figure of the Polish patriot, which may be linked to the news in *Galignani's Messenger* in the years 1820–22. As Jane Stabler (2002, p. 138) has shown, *Messenger* was for Byron one of the major sources of information on current affairs, from which he drew in *Don Juan*. On April 7, 1820, the *Messenger* informed of Kościuszko's bequeathing "a fund exceeding twenty thousand dollars [...] to be laid out on the purchase of young female slaves who are to be educated and emancipated" (no. 1604, April 7, 1820), a clear proof of Kościuszko's virtue and magnanimity.

Byron must have noticed two entries related to Poland and Kościuszko in *Galignani's Messenger* for Saturday, September 30, 1820 (no. 1752, p. 4), especially as they appeared on the same page as the editors' disclaimer about Byron's arrival in London for the trial of Queen Catherine. The first of these items was an account of the speech given by Tsar Alexander I at the opening of the Diet (Sejm) of the Kingdom of Poland on September 13; the second—the proclamation of the Senate of the Free City of Cracow announcing the construction of the monument to honor the memory of Kościuszko.

At the Congress of Vienna, the partitions of the Polish Lithuanian Commonwealth among Russia, Austria, and Prussia, which had taken place at the end of the 18th century, were essentially confirmed. Nonetheless, Poles were given vestiges of national independence in the form of the so-called Congress Kingdom of Poland under the Russian protectorate. Polish soldiers who had served in Napoleon's army were granted amnesty and Kościuszko was invited to return. Tsar Alexander agreed to a liberal constitution, which gave the Polish Diet considerable power of self-government, and placed the Russian tsar in the position of the King of Poland. Alexander's 1820 Warsaw speech is pervaded with rhetoric binding liberty to "good order." In view of revolutions spreading in Europe at the time, he warns that he is determined to "prescribe violent remedies which shall stifle in their growth the germs of revolution in the very moment, they make their appearance" (p. 4). Historians point to Alexander's address as one of the early signs marking the tightening of Russian control in Warsaw, and so would any liberal reader in 1820. In 1822 when Byron wrote Canto X, Alexander's threats were being fulfilled and on February 15, 1822, the *Messenger* reported on the introduction of "new very severe prohibitive measures" against secret societies including the free masons in Poland (no 2173). The hypocritical self-representation of Alexander I as a champion of liberty is exposed in *The Age of Bronze*: "How nobly gave he back the Poles their Diet, / Then told pugnacious Poland to be quiet!"(lines 446–447).[9]

---

9. All quotations from *The Age of Bronze* follow G.G.N. Byron (1993), *The Age of Bronze*. In J. J. McGann, Ed., *Lord Byron: The Complete Poetical Works*, Vol. 7.

In 1820, the news from Warsaw was followed by a note on the suppression of patriotic debating societies not in Poland but in Spain. But after these reports on autocratic threats against freedom, one comes across the announcement of the construction of an unusual monument to Kościuszko in Kraków, the former capital of Poland, which at the Congress of Vienna had been granted neutral status albeit under the control of Russia, Prussia, and Austria. Although usually not much attention was paid to the news from that part of Europe in *Galignani's Messenger*, the text of the proclamation of the Cracow Senate was printed in full, showing the depth of commitment of the Poles to "the last defender of the liberty of his country":

> Full of consideration of the hero who has been consigned to eternity, of the extent of the country, and of the importance of the object, the Senate wishes to give to its homage an expression, which in approaching to the sublime simplicity of the first days of our country, shall proclaim to posterity the duration of our sorrow and the height of our respect. Near the spot of our ancient fortress, the traveller is struck with the simplicity and sublimity of the colossal hills of Wander [sic] and Cracus. Forty generations have descended to the tomb, the magnificent edifices and venerable castles of our country have disappeared from the face of the earth; the monuments which the feeble hands of art had reared to so many great men have fallen to ruin; whilst the noble hills, raised by the exertions of our forefathers, brave, and will brave the mightiest efforts of time. Thus, then, it is that he who has so gloriously closed the high circle of the high deeds of our ancient Poland, should enjoy the same honours as the founders of the National Power. […] This monument will have no other ornament than the word "KOSCIUSKO." (September 30, 1820, p. 4)

What is striking about this passage is the Poles' desire to honor Kościuszko in an extraordinary way—not with a statue, but through the collective construction of a hill-like monument. Although the text states that Kościuszko is the hero with whom the history of Poland comes to an end, the expected durability of the monument suggests continued aspirations for freedom. The name "Kościuszko," whose significance any Pole should be able to recognize, is the sufficient ornament. The Kościuszko Mound was constructed in the years 1820–23, with the participation of inhabitants of Cracow and contributions from all the Polish lands.

I wonder if Byron may have read the proclamation in *Galignani's Messenger* as an expression of continuous enthusiasm for freedom, unextinguished by the frost and snow that Napoleon with his troops encountered on their retreat from Moscow, which for Poles put an end to the hopes for the re-establishment of an independent state. The power of Kościuszko's name is compared to "Hecla's flame." The volcanic image, often used to refer to revolutionary outbursts, had been used by Byron so often that in Canto XIII of *Don Juan*, he rejects it as "a tired metaphor" (36. 285). But here Byron may have been inspired by the conical shape of the Kościuszko Mound, which resembles a volcano. That certainly was the case of the Polish Romantics, who exploited the volcanic imagery in their representation of the Mound (for instance, in Edmund Wasilewski's lines written in the album at Kościuszko's grave, the mound is shown as a mountain with eternal fire burning at the top[10]), and who in turn may themselves been inspired by volcano imagery in Byron's works.[11]

It might seem that in *The Age of Bronze*, written in December 1822, just a couple of months after Canto X, Byron undermines the value of the volcanic power of Kościuszko's name: it is Moscow allegedly set on fire by its inhabitants to prevent it from providing shelter to Napoleon's army that is apostrophized as "Sublimest of Volcanos!" in comparison with which "quenchless Hecla's tame" (lines 179–180). But in both cases, the volcanic images appear in opposition to Napoleon. I think that Byron recognized that Kościuszko's ideals were not only nationalist, but above all liberal. He would also have known of Kościuszko's republican opposition to Napoleon. Instead of comparing Kościuszko's name to a volcanic flame, in *The Age of Bronze* he refers to it as "that sound that crashes in the tyrant's ear" (line 166).

Earlier in the poem when Byron writes of Napoleon's Russian expedition, he addresses those who dwell

> Where Kosciusko dwelt, remembering yet
> The unpaid amount of Catherine's bloody debt!
> Poland! o'er which the avenging angel past,
> But left thee as he found thee, still a waste;
> Forgetting all thy still enduring claim,
> Thy lotted people and extinguished name;
> Thy sigh for freedom, thy long-flowing tear,
> That sound that crashes in the tyrant's ear;
> Kosciusko! on—on—on—the thirst of war
> Gasps for the gore of serfs and of their Czar. (lines 159–168)

While Napoleon may have appeared as "the avenging angel" for "Catherine's bloody debt", i.e., the Russian invasion of Poland, and the bloody massacre in Warsaw in 1794, he bitterly disappointed the Poles who had linked their hopes for the restitution of the Polish state to him. The syntax of the apostrophe to Poland is ambiguous; the semi-colon after "extinguished name" makes one wonder if Napoleon forgot Poland's sighs and tears and the sound of Kościuszko's name, or whether it is the poet that

---

10. "Gdy świątyńkę czas zetrze,... górę tę ocali,/ Ażeby na niej gorzał ogień czysty,/Święty, niezmienny wśrod zaburzeń fali" [After time wipes away the shrine..., it will preserve this mountain/ So that a pure fire burns on it/ Sacred and unalternable amidst the disturbing waves, trans. by the author of the article], Edmund Wasilewski, "Z pamiętnika na mogile Tadeusza Kościuszki," *Poezje*, Ed. Emil Haecker (1925, p. 105).

11. On the use of volcano imagery in Byron's poetry, see Coghen (2015); Coghen (2020).

apostrophizes them. If the former, that places Napoleon in the position of a tyrant, which is confirmed by the depiction of his Russian expedition as driven by bloodthirst and defeated by the power of ordinary Russian people.

Whichever way one reads the passage, even though Poland is defeated, Kościuszko's name still resonates as a warning to autocrats and may have served as a warning to Napoleon that he was bound to encounter the people's resistance in Russia.

Kościuszko, who refused to command the Polish armed forces under Napoleon, offered an alternative model of an egalitarian leader whose name had acquired a status similar to those of Leonidas and Washington: "a watchword, till the future shall be free"(*DJ* VIII 5.40). In his Memoranda for January 28, 1821, the same day that he noted the conversation with the Gambas on Kościuszko, Byron wrote, "What is Poetry?— The feeling of a Former world and Future." And then he went on to meditate on Fear and Hope: "It is useless to say *where* the Present is, for most of us know; and as for the Past *what* predominates in memory? *Hope baffled*. Ergo, in all human affairs, it is Hope—Hope—Hope" (*BLJ* 8, p. 37).

Despite the baffled hope for Polish independence, Kościuszko's name appears in Byron's poetry as metonymy not only for the selfless fight for freedom but also for hope. With its "sound that crashes in the tyrant's ear," it may inspire hope and fear like a smoking volcano.

References

Art, X. (1822). [Review of the books:]1. *Denkwurdigkeiten Meiner Zeit*. Von C.W.V. Dohm. 5 vols. 8vo. Lemgo u. Hanover. 1814–1819. 2. *Histoire des Trois Démembremens de la Pologne*. Par M. FERRAND. 3 vols. 8vo. Paris, 1820. 3. *Memoires et Actes Authentiques relatifs aux Negociations qui ont précedées le Partage de la Pologne*. (Without the name of the author, or the place of publication.) 1 vol. 8vo. 1810. *The Edinburgh Review*, 74, 462–527.

Beaton, R. (2013). *Byron's war: Romantic rebellion, Greek revolution*. Cambridge University Press.

Bitter, M. (2014). Count Ernst Johann Bühren and the Russian Court of Anna Ioannovna. In C. Beem & M. Taylor (Eds.), *The man behind the queen: Male consorts in history*, pp. 103–123. Palgrave Macmillan US.

Booth, J. (1816). *The Battle of Waterloo: Containing the series of accounts publ. by authority ... in the Campaign of the Netherlands 1815, [&] additional particulars to the 9th and preceding editions ... containing also the names of the officers ...* Egerton.

Booth, J. (1817). *The Battle of Waterloo: Also of Ligny, and Quatre Bras, containing the series of accounts published by authority, British and foreign, with circumstantial details relative to the battles, from a variety of original and authentic sources, with connected official and private documents, forming an historical record by those who had the honour to share in the operations of the campaign of the Netherlands, 1815*. J. Booth.

Burczak, M. (2014). The creation of an enduring legend of the national hero: A comparison of Tadeusz Kościuszko and George Washington. *The Polish Review*, 59(3), 25–39. https://doi.org/10.5406/polishreview.59.3.0025

Byron, G.G. (1974). *Byron's letters and Journals* (L. Marchand, Ed., pp. 1–12). John Murray.

Byron, G.G. (1992). *The complete poetical works. 5: Don Juan* (J. J. McGann, Ed.; Repr. with corr., Vol. 5). Clarendon Press.

Byron, G.G. (1993). *The age of bronze.* (J. J. McGann, Ed.), *Lord Byron: The complete poetical Works* (Vol. 7). Oxford University Press [Oxford Scholarly Editions Online].

Campbell, T. (1800). *The pleasures of hope: With other poems.* J. Mundell.

Chwalba, A. (2000). *Historia Polski: 1795–1918.* Wydawnictwo Literackie.

Coghen, M. (2015). The Poet as a volcano: The case of Byron. *Studia Litteraria Universitatis Iagellonicae Cracoviensis, 2015, 10*(2), 79–90. https://ejournals.eu/czasopismo/studia-litteraria-uic/artykul/the-poet-as-a-volcano-the-case-of-byron

Coghen, M. (2020, June 19). *Kościuszko's Mound—European Romanticisms in association.* https://www.euromanticism.org/kosciuszkos-mound/

Davies, N. (2005). *God's playground: A history of Poland: Volume II: 1795 to the present.* Oxford University Press.

The Examiner. (1817, November 9), 711–712. https://www-1proquest-1com-1yp8ogaha0625.hps.bj.uj.edu.pl/historical-periodicals/untitled-item/docview/8738286/se-2?accountid=11664

Galignani's Messenger. (1820, April 7). Google Books.

Galignani's Messenger. (1820, September 30). Google Books.

Galignani's Messenger.(1822, February 15). Google Books.

Gross, J. D. (2001). *Byron: The erotic liberal.* Rowman & Littlefield.

McLean, T. (2012b). *The other east and nineteenth-century British literature.* Palgrave Macmillan UK. https://doi.org/10.1057/9780230355217

Moore, T. (1831). *Letters and journals of Lord Byron: With notices of his life, by T. Moore* (Harper's stereotype ed.) Galignani.

Stabler, J. (2002). *Byron, poetics and history.* Cambridge University Press.

Stabler, J., & Hopps, G. (Eds.). (2024). *The poems of Lord Byron—Don Juan: Volumes IV & V* (1st ed.). Routledge.

Storozynski, A. (2010). *The peasant prince: Thaddeus Kosciuszko and the age of revolution.* Thomas Dunne Books, St. Martin's Griffin.

Tooke, W. (1800). *The life of Catharine II, empress of Russia ...* 3 vols. A. Strahan.

Wasilewski, E. (1814–1846). (1925). *Poezje* (E. Haecker, Ed.). Krakowska Spółka Wydawnicza.

CHAPTER TWELVE | **MICHAŁ KOWALSKI AND AGNIESZKA ROMANOWSKA**

"What's in a Name?"

Shakespearean References in the Case Law of the European Court of Human Rights

Abstract

This chapter focuses on the role of a shared cultural heritage in resolving conflicts on international level as represented in the discourse of the judgements issued by the European Court of Human Rights. The efforts undertaken by European states to develop judicial mechanisms that would ensure effective protection of human rights are reflected in the European Convention on Human Rights which the Court interprets in its case law. It can be expected that such a judicial institution—gathering an international community of judges and dealing with cases that range from a variety of cultures—would be characterized by discourses which necessarily recall and refer to a repertoire of common cultural elements. The authors present in this chapter an overview of references to the works of William Shakespeare identified in the case law of the European Court of Human Rights, precisely in the separate opinions attached by individual judges to the judgements. The authors first situate the discussion in the wider context of the field known as law and literature and explain the function and specificity of the separate opinions. In the main body of the chapter, the references are analyzed against the background of the cases and in relation to the Shakespeare plays they come from with the aim of describing their nature and intended function and assessing their overall effect. The conclusions drawn from the analysis shed some light on the role of the common cultural heritage in the conflict resolution processes undertaken internationally.

Keywords: Shakespeare, European Court of Human Rights, law and literature

Our aim in this chapter[1] is to analyze Shakespearean references in the judgements issued by the European Court of Human Rights, an international human rights court

---

1. The content of this chapter originates from and is a considerable extension of the research presented in M. Kowalski (2024).

established to rule on applications alleging violations of the rights and freedoms set out in the European Convention on Human Rights. Adopted under the auspices of the Council of Europe, the Convention is an international instrument used by the European states that seek to find common grounds which would enable them to ensure fundamental human rights to individuals and shape mutual relations based on confidence and on effective mechanisms of conflict resolution. It can be expected that communication in such international judicial institutions as the ECtHR would be, on the one hand, characterized by discourses specific to particular member-states, but, on the other, that it would reveal a repertoire of common cultural elements, such as references to canonical works of world literature. Shakespearean references in the case law of the European Court of Human Rights identified in separate opinions attached by individual judges to the judgements delivered as a result of the proceedings belong to such a repertoire. In the discussion presented in this chapter the authors explain the reasons why international judges refer to Shakespeare's plays in their opinions, disclose some regularities that characterize these references, and examine the argumentative effectiveness of the judges' choices.

Law and Literature

The topic of literary references used in legal documents and pronouncements can be situated in the interdisciplinary field called law and literature. As explained by Richard Posner:

> Law and literature brings together two overlapping bodies of thought, the legal and the literary, that have much in common, including an emphasis on rhetoric. Many works of literature deal with law . . . . Law itself is formulated and announced in writings, such as statutes, the Constitution, and judicial opinions, that sometimes exhibit a density, complexity, and open-endedness comparable to what one finds in literary works. (2009, p. 1)

Research in this field is conducted from two complementary perspectives. The first, and more obvious one, deals with law in literature i.e., studying the depiction of law, lawyers, and legal issues as they are presented in literary texts. The second, law as literature, deals with studying legal texts with methods acquired from literary interpretation, analysis, and critique. The studies on law and literature encompass also areas such as legal norms regulating writing, freedom of artistic expression and copyright; literature as law, that is historical studies of literary text that were sources of law, like scriptures; and legal literature in which legal works, mainly belonging to philosophy of law, are studied as literary texts. Last, but for the purposes of our discussion definitely not least, they include literature in law, that is all kinds of literary references in legal texts, including pronouncements of legal institutions, especially courts.

Generally speaking, studies within literature in law focus on the contexts in which literature is quoted in legal texts, on the role literary references can play in legal argumentation, and, most importantly, on how "certain cultural codes, hidden in literature and, broader, in art help to understand and perceive more than what is overtly said"[2] (Kamień, 2024, pp. 110–111). This poses a question about the linguistic and cultural nature of such references, especially about the extent to which their terseness, recognizability, and associative potential enhance the force and effectiveness of judicial argumentation. It is natural that such references, reflecting the cultural background of those who make them, are shaped by a variety of cultural determinants. This diversity is especially interesting when we deal with international judicial institutions—"a melting pot of different national and legal cultures" (Gadbin-George, 2013, section 2, para. 6)—like the European Court of Human Rights which consists of 46 judges from all state-parties to the European Convention of Human Rights.[3]

The European Court of Human Rights and Its Case Law

The European Court of Human Rights (known also, because of its location, as the Strasbourg Court) was set up in 1959. It rules on individual or interstate applications alleging violations of human rights and freedoms set out in the European Convention on Human Rights and its additional protocols. The Convention, which was signed in 1950 and entered into force three years later, obliges the state-parties, being the member-states of the Council of Europe, to secure fundamental human rights, not only to their own nationals but also to everyone within their jurisdiction. The Court's judgments are binding on the states concerned and have led them to alter domestic legislation and administrative practice in a wide range of areas. The Court's case law makes the Convention a modern and powerful instrument for meeting new challenges in the area of human rights and consolidating the rule of law and democracy in Europe. The Convention guarantees in its Chapter 1 the right to life; the prohibition of torture; the prohibition of slavery and forced labor; the right to liberty and security; the right to fair trial; the no punishment without law principle; the right to respect for private and family life; the freedom of thought, conscience, and religion; the freedom of expression; the freedom of assembly and association; the right to marry; and the right to effective remedy and the prohibition of discrimination. Other rights and

---

2. Translated from Polish by the authors.
3. The Russian Federation was excluded from the Council of Europe in 2022 as the result of its aggression against Ukraine and, consequently, ceased to be a state-party to the ECHR. Two other European states that remain, for different reasons, outside this legal framework are Belarus and Kosovo.

freedoms are introduced by additional protocols to the ECHR to which the state-parties may adhere.

As the ECHR provisions are very laconic, it is the role of the Court to interpret them in its case law, that is, in fact, to decide on their meaning and, in this way, on the scope of state-parties' legal obligations under the Convention. That is why it is commonly referred to, also by the Court itself, as "a living instrument" (see note 14 below). The subtle borderline between the interpretation of an international agreement and the judicial law making (labeled as judicial activism) lies in the center of the legal debates on the role of the ECHR and the Court's legitimacy. As the Strasbourg Court combines the common law and the civil law legal traditions of the state-parties, while remaining an international court, it is a court of *de facto*, yet not *de jure*, precedent.

Thanks to the official database of the Court (HUDOC, i.e., Human Rights Documentation), which provides full access to its case law [4] from 1959 until 2018, 43 literary references were identified in the separate opinions attached to the Court's judgments. It has been calculated that in this period literary references were used by 19% percent of the Court's judges (Maroń, 2019, p. 67ff). The fact that literary references appear in separate opinions, rather than in the judgements, ensues from the very nature of international judicial institutions and is relevant for our examination of the Shakespearean references.

When the Chamber (consisting of 7 judges) or the Grand Chamber (consisting of 17 judges) of the Strasbourg Court is not able to reach a unanimous decision, separate opinions can be written by one or more judges who do not agree with the majority's final decision (a dissenting opinion), or who voted with the majority but do not share the approach taken in the reasoning, and wish to present a different kind of argumentation (a concurring opinion). Unlike the majority opinion reflected in the judgement, the annexed separate opinions are not legally binding. There are certain controversies surrounding separate opinions. On the one hand, when a separate opinion is made public, the fact that the court was not able to reach a unanimous decision is also revealed. Those who oppose the publication of separate opinions argue that it undermines the judgment and diminishes its value as a precedent. On the other hand, the proponents claim that the plurality of opinions supports the legitimacy of law and enables its development. As explained by Kovler, "[t]he concept of separate opinion in some international judicial organs is inspired by the common law system and is an expression of the openness of international adjudication, especially in the field of human rights" (2021, para.1). What is more, as argued by Ziemele, a former judge at the ECtHR:

> Separate opinions as a rule enter into a discussion with the judgment. One can even say that the first commentary on a judgment is a separate opinion. Generally, one can learn from separate opinions about where the possible future development of

---

4. https://hudoc.echr.coe.int [as of February 28, 2025].

the Court's case law might lie. Especially in matters of human rights law which are intrinsically linked with the evolution of society, interaction between majority and minority views is of great importance since it is likely to represent a snapshot of the state of European debate. (2017, p. 19)

Last but not least, separate opinions, as a rule, are less formalized than the collectively formulated judgement reasonings and, therefore, leave more freedom for individual expression, including style and rhetoric.

Shakespeare and Law

Among the canonical authors focused on by scholars who study legal issues present in works of literature, Shakespeare is one of the most frequently chosen. This can be rooted in the fact that:

> William Shakespeare in his function of man of letters has often put the law at the centre of his analysis or in the background of his plays. Some law cases are frequently emplotted within his dramatic narrations, either secretly lurking in metaphors or openly present in his so-called trial scenes. He clearly realized that the literary and juridical worlds had many elements in common that could foster the intertwining of the two fields, also by means of the use of legal terminology. (Carpi and Gaakeer, 2015, p. 2)

Owen Hood Phillips (1972) calculated that as many as two thirds of Shakespeare's plays include a trial scene, and some of these scenes belong to the most emotionally charged moments. Shakespeare's interest in law is most evident in *The Merchant of Venice* and *Measure for Measure*, but Desdemona's defense of Othello in act one, scene three, or Hemione's self-defense in *The Winter's Tale* are also very evident and frequently discussed examples, not to mention the legal issues connected with the right to rule depicted in the chronicles. It can be said without much overstatement that in many of his play-texts "Shakespeare staged legal dilemmas" (Carpi and Gaakeer, 2015, p. 3). While the ubiquity of legal terms in Shakespeare's plays and his fascination with the possibilities of law as a source of dramatic material have led some biographers to imagine Shakespeare had worked as a legal clerk during his lost years, the source of the playwright's long-life interest in legal matters seems to have more to do with the widespread interest in law during the Elizabethan and Jacobean periods. "Legal proceedings were popular both as a form of entertainment and as a way for the litigious English to assert their rights . . . People found attending the courts and watching judicial procedure a dramatic and diverting pastime" (Kornstein, 1994, p. 13). Lawyers and legal apprentices of the Inns of Court were an important component of theater audiences at that time and other playwrights from this period composed texts that are even more loaded with legal vocabulary than Shakespeare's (Keeton, 1967, pp. 24–42; Button, 2001, p. 252). It comes as no surprise, therefore, that

Shakespeare and law has grown into a separate filed of Shakespeare studies, as well as that of law and literature, as testified by a growing number of books and collected volumes (e.g., Keeton, 1967; Phillips, 1972; Meron, 1993; Kornstein, 1994; Ward, 1999; Sokol & Sokol, 2004; Zurcher, 2010; Watt, 2016; Raffield, 2017; Curran, 2017), as well as journal articles authored by historians, literary and theater scholars, law scholars, and practicing lawyers.[5]

While most of these publications deal with the presentation of law, lawyers, and legal problems in Shakespeare's epoch and his works, the issue of Shakespearean references in legal documents and pronouncements has gained much less scholarly attention. And this is so in spite of the fact that Shakespeare seems to have always been eagerly quoted by lawyers, especially in the common law countries. According to Jenkin Chan (2016), who about a "collective obsession" (n. p.), Shakespeare was first quoted by the US Supreme Court in 1893. In American courts alone, Shakespeare's plays have been quoted in more than eight hundred judicial opinions, from common divorce proceedings to murder cases. Gadbin-George (2013, para. 3) links the frequency of quoting Shakespeare in international European courts with the already emphasized multiculturality of these institutions.

In her article, which focuses on education of law students and advocates incorporation of literature into legal education, Gadbin-George refers to the case law of two European courts, the European Court of Justice (the EU Court of Justice, EUCJ) and the European Court of Human Rights. She claims that Shakespearean references usually serve one of the following three purposes: they help to clarify the facts of a case, they help to clarify the judge's reasoning, or they are used as literary embellishments. Her conclusion is that, with the growing tendency to use literary references in European international courts, legal education should put more emphasis on making students aware of the role that literature can have in legal argumentation. Some of Gadbin-George's observations will be referred to in the remaining part of the chapter, but it must be noted that she analyzes jointly separate opinions of the judges of the European Court of Human Rights and opinions of the advocate generals at the EUCJ who are not judges and whose opinions do not form part of the judgements.[6] The author seems to miss the specificity of the latter legal framework which undermines some of her claims.

Shakespeare in the Strasbourg Court

Using the HUDOC database we have identified nine references coming from Shakespeare's plays. Rather unsurprisingly, as many as five of these were taken from *Hamlet*.

---

5. For an annotated selection of books and articles on the topic, see D. Capri & J. Gaakeer (2015) and D. Capri (2018).
6. The judges of the EUCJ are not allowed to annex separate opinions to the Courts judgements.

Three were made by judge Boštjan Zupančič from Slovenia (in 2006, 2012, and 2015), and two by judge Iulia Motoc from Romania (in 2016 and 2021). Judge Loukis Loucaides from Cyprus referred to *Othello* (in 2007). Judge Ganna Yudkivska from Ukraine referred to Shakespeare twice, quoting *The Tempest* and *Richard II* (both judgements were issued in 2015). *Romeo and Juliet* was once referred to by a British judge, Sir Gerald Fitzmaurice (1978), a reference which, although it is the earliest, will be dealt with at the end of the analysis as it qualifies as a special case.

Judge Zupančič referred to *Hamlet* in three cases concerning insanity of the applicant. Criminal insanity is understood as a mental illness which makes it impossible for a defendant to know they were committing a crime or to understand that their actions are wrong. In all three cases, the judge supported his arguments referring to Hamlet asking Laertes for forgiveness in act five, scene two. In the earliest case, *Achour v. France*, he quoted the passage from the first quarto (what is known as the bad quarto), where it reads:

> If Hamlet in his madnesse did amisse,
> That was not Hamlet, but his madnes did it,
> and all the wrong I e're did to Leartes,
> I here proclaim was madnes.[7]

In the other two cases, *Ketreb v. France* and *Khan vs. Germany*, the judge quoted the text from the Arden Shakespeare 2006 edition of *Hamlet*, which contains the text of the authoritative second quarto with passages that are found in the first folio printed in an appendix. The passage quoted in the opinion reads:

> This presence knows, and you must needs have heard,
> How I am punished with a sore distraction.
> What I have done
> That might your nature, honour and exception
> Roughly awake, I here proclaim was madness.
> Was't Hamlet wronged Laertes? Never Hamlet.
> If Hamlet from himself be ta'en away
> And when he's not himself does wrong Laertes,
> Then Hamlet does it not; Hamlet denies it.
> Who does it then? His madness. If't be so,
> Hamlet is of the faction that is wronged—
> His madness is poor Hamlet's enemy. (5.2. 206–217)[8]

---

7. Here quoted after: *Hamlet* (Quarto 1, 1603). Internet Shakespeare Editions [online].
8. Here quoted after A. Thompson & N. Taylor (2016).

To shed some light on the judge's decision to opt for such quotations, it is necessary to outline what kind of cases these were, which will be done by summarizing the facts and the Court's reasoning in the *Khan v. Germany* case. The applicant moved from Pakistan to Germany in 1991 with her husband. Three years later, her son was born. The applicant obtained a permanent residence permit in Germany in 2001. Three years later, she committed manslaughter in a state of acute psychosis. She was diagnosed with schizophrenia and confined to a psychiatric hospital. In 2009, her expulsion from Germany was ordered as she was found to pose a danger to public safety because of the seriousness of the crime she committed. In the meantime, her mental health subsequently improved, she was granted days of leave and allowed to work full-time. The applicant questioned the domestic decision of expulsion in her application to the ECtHR and claimed that her expulsion would interfere with her right to respect for her private and family life under Article 8 of the Convention and that her specific circumstances had not sufficiently been taken into account by the German authorities. The domestic authorities found that, in addition to a risk of reoffending, the applicant was not integrated into German society since she spoke no German and basic medical care for psychiatric patients was available in big cities in Pakistan. So, weighing the impact on the applicant's private life against the danger posed to public safety, the Court did not find that the German authorities had overstepped their margin of appreciation. The case was decided under the necessity test, i.e., determining whether the interference had been necessary in a democratic society, among others, whether it is proportionate to the legitimate aim (public safety in the case concerned) pursued. In expulsion cases of migrants, the Court developed 10 criteria aimed at balancing the individual interest of the applicant on the one hand and the public interest on the other. The key criterion among the 10 was "the nature and seriousness of the offence committed by the applicant." This criterion was also applied by the Court in Ms. Khan's case (see especially, *Khan*, para. 45) and led the Court to the conclusion that "the applicant's expulsion from Germany would be proportionate to the aims pursued and can be regarded as necessary in a democratic society" (*Khan*, para. 56).

In other words, the Court (with six votes to one) supported the domestic authorities' conclusion that the expulsion would not constitute a violation of Article 8 of the Convention. Judge Zupančič was the only judge to disagree. He was of the opinion that, in the first place, no crime was committed because of the applicant's insanity, and therefore the criterion regarding the nature and seriousness of the offence was irrelevant. In his separate opinion he argued as follows:

> The question, therefore, is whether the insane person has or has not committed a criminal act. Since the basic criminal law doctrine requires that the act be a genuine emanation of the actor's personality, it is impossible to maintain that an actor who is of unsound mind has himself or herself committed the act. The causal link, as

required for the very establishment of an insanity defence, is to the mental illness. It follows logically that the mental illness is to blame. The actor is thus blameless, as indeed Shakespeare understood—and here comes the above-mentioned passage from the play. (*Khan...*, Dissenting opinion of Judge Zupančič)

What a Shakespearean scholar immediately finds intriguing in judge Zupančič's references is the source text quoted in the first reference. Why was the passage taken from the first quarto and why the second quarto text was the judge's second choice is impossible to establish. It might have been the judge's unawareness of the nature of the 1603 quarto, which was a corrupt unauthorized version of an abridged text of the play, or of the intricate differences between the three earliest printed versions.[9] A less probable conjecture is that he had a preference for the terser formulation of the bad quarto. But there is a more important problem with this reference, and this is where the Shakespearean matters overlap with the legal ones.

Judge Zupančič seems to ignore the fact that Hamlet's madness is pretended, that it is "a crafty madness," (3.1.8) as Guildenstern describes it. There is ample evidence in the text to support this—even if we are hesitant to trust Hamlet himself when he, for example, says to Gertrude: "I essentially am not in madness,/ But mad in craft" (3.4.188–9)—and to claim otherwise is to undermine the very core of the tragic developments of the play. As A. C. Bradley put it, "If Lear were really mad when he divided his kingdom, if Hamlet were really mad at any time in the story, they would cease to be tragic characters" (1991, p. 30). This does not mean, of course, that Hamlet is not subjected to extreme mental suffering. Bradley, again, with all his psychologizing, is very clear about this: "'Melancholy',... not yet insanity. That Hamlet was not far from insanity is very probable. His adoption of the pretence of madness may well have been ... an instinct of self-preservation .... But Hamlet's melancholy is ... a totally different thing from the madness which he feigns" (1991, p. 120). As Crawford (1916), succinctly put it, Hamlet

> did many things that the persons of the drama must construe as madness. His avowed intention was to throw them off the track. To understand the madness as real is to make of the play a mad-house tragedy that could have no meaning for the very sane Englishmen for whom Shakespeare wrote. (p. 65)

Actually, with Polonius's statement, "Though this be madness, yet there is method in't" (2.2.200) being one of the most famous quotations from the play, known also in translations into most languages of the world, it is very surprising that someone

---

9. For a thorough discussion of textual variations in the early editions, see, e.g., P. Edwards, (1997, pp. 8–32).

can see Hamlet's madness as real.[10] A reader of judge Zupančič's separate opinion is thus quite puzzled by this reference which, instead of supporting his argumentation, weakens it, in fact.

Another aspect that undermines the effectiveness of Judge Zupančič's literary reference is the context and meaning of the passage. Hamlet's pleading for forgiveness is not sincere. As Edwards argues:

> This is certainly disingenuous. Hamlet ... is making a public declaration to an audience, one of whom, Claudius, knows perfectly well why he killed Polonius. The furthest he dare go in apologizing to Laertes is to say that he never intended to kill his father.... In blaming his madness he knows that his audience (apart from Claudius) will believe him; he is continuing to play his part, and keeping up the long battle of wits with Claudius. (1997, p. 235)

Actually, Hamlet and Laertes do not reconcile until Claudius's treachery is revealed and Hamlet kills the king with the poisoned rapier, but that happens not earlier than in lines 306–311. This moment is marked by Laertes pleading:

> Exchange forgiveness with me, noble Hamlet.
> Mine and my father's death come not upon thee,
> Nor thine on me,

to which Hamlet responds: "Haeven make three free of it!" Surprisingly, Gadbin-George, who classifies judge Zupančič's use of the passage from *Hamlet* as a literary reference that helps to clarify the judge's legal reasoning (2013, para. 32 and 33), ignores the fact that the reference actually misses the point.

Another quotation from *Hamlet* is found in the partly dissenting opinion by judge Motoc. She criticized the way in which the Strasbourg Court had referred indirectly to some statements adopted earlier in the case law of the Supreme Court of the United States. The Strasbourg Court called them general statements developed previously in its own case law, instead of directly referencing the Supreme Court's case law, which the judge named as "a legal transplant." Judge Motoc wrote in her opinion, "As Shakespeare said in the words of Hamlet: Neither a borrower nor a lender be; for loan oft loses both itself and friend. I find that our Court is in exactly the situation described by Hamlet" (*Blokhin...*, Partly dissenting opinion of Judge Motoc). The judge used a well-known quotation that has become, at least for the native speakers of English, part of the proverbial language. The quotation is also quite adequate to her argumentation. But, contrary to what the judge said twice, these are not Hamlet's words. They are part of the famous speech by Polonius from act one, scene three, in which he

---

10. For an extensive discussion of the stories "about clever avenging sons who pretended to be stupid in order to outwit their enemies," which Shakespeare might have used as his sources, see A. Thompson & N. Taylor (2016, pp. 65–72).

advises his son before Laertes' embarking for France. Quite crucially for the dramatic effectiveness of the character, this is the first longer speech by Polonius, in a scene where he is busy instructing his children and trying to regulate their lives, a speech that reveals his suspicious and condescending nature, his logorrhea, as well as, on a different level, his potential as a comic character. Judge Motoc's blunder proves that, in the type of literary references we find in legal judgements, faithfulness to the literary work quoted or referred to is much less important than the very fact of referencing a commonly known and celebrated source which includes a situation most people can easily relate to. What is more, it seems that, in most cases, slight imprecisions—unlike considerable misinterpretations like Zupančič's—do not affect the reference's overall effectiveness. Transferring Shakespearean passages to new contexts utilizes their proverbial nature and endows them with new functions that compensate for misquoting.

The second time that judge Motoc referred to *Hamlet* was in the 2021 case of *N. v. Romania (No. 2)*. In her partly dissenting opinion the judge considered what she regarded as an insufficient use of Article 14 of the Convention in the Court's reasoning. Therefore, she begins her reasoning by stating that this article has often been referred to as "the Cinderella of the system" (para. 1). While such a comparison, albeit informal, can be accepted as illustrative of the judge's meaning, further analogies which she formulates are more than surprising. Judge Motoc claims that Cinderella can be compared to Hamlet due to the fact that both protagonists lose their parents and are mistreated by their step-parents, and that "[i]f Article 14 has been compared with Cinderella, following this logic we can also compare it to Hamlet, with an emphasis on its [sic] famous phrase 'to be or not to be'. Indeed, in the present case the Court found that there was no need to examine whether a violation has occurred" (para 1). Unfortunately, such reasoning is very awkward, and the use of literary references is based on sweeping generalizations. The whole catalogue of doubtfully accurate analogies seems to be only a pretext to mention the "to be or not to be" phrase, but all these rhetorical maneuvers only unnecessarily complicate the reasoning.

In the separate opinion by Judge Yudkivska, there is an interesting reference to *The Tempest*. It also relies on the proverbial potential of the employed phrase, but— first and foremost—displays the fact that such literary references, uprooted from their original contexts and functioning independently, acquire new meanings which are sometimes rather distant from the source. In her separate opinion concerning the case *Sargsyan v. Azerbaijan*, while commenting on the origin of the conflict in Nagorno-Karabakh, Judge Yudkivska wrote, "In Shakespeare's words, 'what's past is prologue'. The applicant's current situation is a result of the lengthy struggle between two Member States with no solution for past problems yet being found and new problems evolving" (*Sargsyan…*, Concurring opinion of Judge Yudkivska). This phrase from act two scene one of *The Tempest* is used in a way which does not require either pointing out to the character who pronounces it, nor to the circumstances in which it functions in the play-text. In fact, if these had been revealed, it would have necessitated a lengthy explanation because the context of the play's episode in which these words appear is not relevant for the judge's purposes. In Shakespeare's play, these words are part of the treacherous Antonio's speech in which he tries to persuade Sebastian "to perform an act / Whereof what's past is prologue" (2.1.252–3)[11], that is to kill Alonso, the king of Naples and take his crown. "Th'occasion" (2.1.207) to do this, as Antonio argues, has been produced by the recent circumstances, by what now belongs to the past—Alonso's only son has just drowned (as they believe), and his sister has been married to a Tunisian prince. In the judge's opinion the quotation became decontextualized, if only because the future promised by the prologue, as Antonio imagines, is a prosperous reign following the regicide he is ready to commit. While what Judge Yudkivska means is the need to consider the circumstances of the case before the Court in the context of the origins of the conflict between Armenia and Azerbaijan. Delving on the details of the original context would have obscured the judge's presentation of the facts of the case, instead of clarifying them, so she just took advantage of the proverbial conciseness and semantic clarity of the phrase. Yet, it is used not merely to embellish her reasoning with a literary reference, but also to uplift the pragmatic force of her language by making the message unambiguously communicative. Yudkivska's borrowing from *The Tempest* is evidence again that famous quotations from Shakespeare's plays are part of the cultural repertoire of the ECtHR judges, even if English is not their native tongue. If judges coming from civil law traditions imitate in this respect their colleagues from the United Kingdom and the US, as has been suggested by Gadbin-George (2013, section 5, para. 65–66), this is a culturally productive sociolinguistic phenomenon quite natural to environments where various cultures and discourses coexist and blend.

The second Shakespearean reference by Judge Yudkivska comes from *Richard II* act one, scene one, and was made in the case *Y. v. Slovenia* of 2015. The case regarded an alleged violation of the ECHR standards in the domestic criminal proceedings concerning the accusation of sexual assaults of a minor by a family friend in the context of inadequate provision of the minor's rights during the trial and the domestic court allowing the applicant to confront the accused (the personal cross-examination). In her reasoning, Judge Yudkivska considered the doctrine of "the right to confrontation" developed in the case law of the Supreme Court of the United States. Doing so, she extensively quoted one of the very well-known judges of this Court, the late Antonin Scalia and his stance of the matter in the judgement *Coy v. Iowa* (487 US 1012, 1016 /1988/):

In that judgment Justice Scalia traced the history of the right to confront as a "face-to-face encounter," illustrated in Shakespeare's *Richard II*:

---

11. *The Tempest* is quoted from V. M. Vaughan & A. T. Vaughan, Eds., (2001).

"Shakespeare was thus describing the root meaning of confrontation when he had Richard the Second say:

'"Then call them to our presence—face to face, and frowning brow to brow, ourselves will hear the accuser and the accused freely speak."'

He concluded that "there is something deep in human nature that regards face-to-face confrontation between accused and accuser as 'essential to a fair trial in a criminal prosecution.'"

Referring to Shakespeare's play via Scalia's judgement, Judge Yudkivska strengthened her argumentation with a double authority, that of Shakespeare and of the renowned American lawyer.

As it has been noted above, it is often the case with famous quotations that they best fulfil their role when they comment on a common situation or universally accepted values. Such is the case of Judge Loucaides's reference to *Othello* act three, scene three, made in a decision concerned with defamation. Criticizing what he sees as insufficient protection of human dignity provided by the Convention, he adds in a footnote:

In this respect the following well-known words of Shakespeare come to mind: "Good name in man and woman, dear my lord, is the immediate jewel of their souls ... who steals my purse, steals trash ... ; but he that filches from me my good name ... makes me poor indeed."

It may or may not be a coincidence that a Cypriot judge quotes this particular play in which Cyprus is the setting for a considerable part of important events. Gadbin-George, who assesses this reference as relevant in its function of clarifying the judge's legal reasoning (2013, section 3.2.2, para. 38) believes that the judge "seemed keen to show off his knowledge of *Othello*" (2013, section 4.1., para. 57), because there is a link between his native country and the location of the plot. We are of the opinion that a more important factor why this passage was quoted and how it functions is the fact that the character of Othello is generally remembered as a victim of slander. Gadbin-George has doubts whether the quotation is well-known enough to produce the intended associations, yet it is not so much the quotation that matters, but what the character stands for.

The earliest instance of using a Shakespearean quotation in the European Court of Human Rights' case law is going to be discussed as the last one because it is notably, and for our purposes importantly, different from the references analyzed above. It comes from a separate opinion written by a distinguished British lawyer, Sir Gerald Fitzmaurice, who was chosen judge to the ECtHR for years 1975–1980. Interestingly, his Shakespearean reference is found in one of the most famous and groundbreaking judgements in the whole history of the Court, the 1978 interstate case *Ireland v. the UK* which concerned violation of the conventional rights during "the Troubles." In this judgement the Court held that the use of the five techniques of interrogation (wall-standing, hooding, subjection to noise, deprivation of sleep, and deprivation of food and drink) used in August and October 1971 constituted a practice of inhuman and degrading treatment, in breach of Article 3 of the Convention, and that the said use of the five techniques did not constitute a practice of torture within the meaning of Article 3. Commenting on the meaning of the term prohibition of torture, inhuman or degrading treatment or punishment provided by this article, Fitzmaurice stated that

> Article 3 of the European Convention was not . . . intended to trade in paradoxes or propound conundrums such that it takes months of consideration in order to come to a final conclusion as to whether certain treatment can properly be said to attain the proportions of the inhuman. To my mind, that epithet should be kept for something that is immediately recognisable for what it is,—something much more than what occurred in the present case,—something different in kind. "What's in a name?" (*Romeo and Juliet*, 2.2.43)—it may be asked. The answer is "everything," if it involves placing a course of conduct in a wrong category, with consequences that are both inappropriate and unjust (*Ireland...*, Separate opinion of Judge Sir Gerald Fitzmaurice, para. 23.).

As Fitzmaurice is the only native speaker of English among the ECtHR judges discussed here, one feature of this reference to *Romeo and Juliet* is the naturalness and precision with which it is used.[12] Another, and a less obvious one, is that Judge Fitzmaurice, as a person brought up and educated in the United Kingdom and, therefore, conversant with Shakespeare's plays more thoroughly than any of the other judges, has the easiness to play with the possible answers to the "What's in a name" question so as to convincingly argue his point and criticize the Court for interpreting the meaning of Article 3 too extensively. To appreciate this, one needs to consider this question in a broader context of the tragedy's famous garden scene in which Juliet features a mini treatise on the meaning of words. She begins in a regretful tone: "O Romeo, Romeo, wherefore art thou Romeo?" (2.2.33)[13], but very soon, spurned by her youthful impatience and natural practicality, finds a solution which she boldly pronounces: "Deny thy father and refuse thy name./ Or if thou wilt not, be but sworn my love/ And I'll no longer be a Capulet" (2.2.34–36). This is a risky suggestion, one that in the feuding community of Verona would be judged as a betrayal of family allegiance, a disgrace, and an act of social self-annihilation. Perhaps aware of the naiveté of the proposition, Juliet attempts to justify her point of view by crafting an apparently logical argument:

> What's Montague? It is nor hand nor foot
> Nor arm nor face nor any other part

---

12. It must be noted that this reference is entirely misinterpreted by Gadbin-George (2013), section 3.2.3, para. 42.
13. The edition of the play quoted here is B. Gibbons (1980).

Belonging to a man. O be some other name.
What's in a name? That which we call a rose
By any other word would smell as sweet; (2.2.40–44).

An argument concluded by an offer whose unashamed openness (Juliet would certainly be more restrained if only she knew that Romeo is listening) can be explained only by "her youth and candour palpable in the clear, absolute quality of language and thought" (Gibbons, p. 48): "Romeo, doff thy name,/ And for thy name, which is no part of thee,/ Take all myself" (2.2.47–49). Juliet's passion and enthusiasm are contagious as is evident in Romeo's reaction to her offer: "Call me but love, and I'll be new baptis'd: /Henceforth I never will be Romeo" (2.2.50–51). Rejection of his name, however, creates a serious threat to Romeo's identity. There is clearly a conflict "between the social entity that that name designates and the individual's inner perception of him/herself" (Capri, 2015, p. 39), that is between Romeo's social obligations determined by his name and his private self-awareness. Stepping on the path suggested by Juliet would also mean that "he exists in pure negativity, in a nowhere land where he is no longer what he used to be and not yet what he aspires to be. But what is more, he no longer has legal identity" (Carpi, 2015, p. 41). In spite of all this, Juliet's answer is an enthusiastic and willful—nothing, as evidenced by the parallel with the rose. The name is of no importance, she argues, as it is not the thing it signifies. This is one answer to the question "What's in a name?"

The Court, Fitzmaurice claims in his separate opinion, came up with a different answer—everything: a word may or may not mean the thing it signifies, or it may mean many other things, depending on how we interpret it. Fitzmaurice disagrees with the Court's answer and postulates that the meaning of the phrase "prohibition of torture, inhuman or degrading treatment or punishment" should be self-evident. Citing Juliet's terse and vigorous question, the judge takes advantage of its status as a set phrase and a famous quotation to embellish his argumentation, but, more importantly, he depends on the fact that Juliet's question implies a debate on meaning in language. The quotation's rhetorical effectiveness relies on ascribing to the Court an answer which contradicts Juliet's answer.

When Fitzmaurice's use of the Shakespearean quotation is compared with the other references analyzed in this chapter, it turns out to be the most ingenious. Actually, the "What's in a name?" question raised by Sir Gerald Fitzmaurice at a time when the Convention as a "living instrument" was at the very beginning of its development[14]

---

14. The European Court of Human Rights referred *expressis verbis* to the concept of the Convention being a "living instrument" for the first time in another judgement from the same year, *Tyrer v. the United Kingdom* (25.04.1978 r., application nr 5856/72, esp. para. 31). By way of digr,ession it can be noted that also in this judgement Shakespeare is mentioned by Judge Fitzmaurice, although not in the form of a literary quotation, but rather as a cultural reference based on personal experience. The case concerned corporal punishment of juveniles. In his separate

still remains pertinent and essential in the context of the debates on the limits of the dynamic interpretation of the Convention, an issue as heatedly discussed in the Convention's beginning as it is now. And the risk that ECHR concepts may be interpreted to mean "everything" is even more challenging today than it was in 1978.

Concluding Remarks

The nine references discussed in this chapter give us an idea about the ways in which Shakespeare is present in the key institution of the European human rights protection system. The European Court of Human Rights is only one of several international adjudicating institutions and our tentative conclusions need to be verified with further research. But even this modest corpus of references reveals a number of interesting facts. As for the linguistic nature of the analyzed literary references, most of them have become set phrases, are of proverbial nature, pertain to issues of crucial and general importance and are characterized by conciseness. As for their cultural functioning, it is worth emphasizing that most of the Shakespearean references were included in opinions authored by judges who originated from outside the English-speaking culture, representing parts of Europe that geographically—and, especially from the point of view of western countries, culturally—can be perceived as peripheral. This is especially important if we remember that the European Convention of Human Rights was adopted under the auspices of the Council of Europe which, until the fall of the iron curtain, was an organization gathering the western democratic states. This changed in the 1990s only when new democracies from central-eastern Europe became member-states of the Council of Europe and parties to the Convention. New member states had to accommodate their human rights protection standards to the Conventional standards and judges coming from the new member-states started to have influence on the evolution of human rights protections in Europe.

One of the reasons for Shakespeare's popularity among lawyers in general can be that, because of the playwright's legal knowledge evident in the numerous references to law in his plays and sonnets, many practitioners of law "fancy Shakespeare as one of their professional colleagues" (Jenkin Chan, 2016, n. p.). Another reason "lies in Shakespeare's status as an embodiment of high culture; citing him seeks to invest the judgement with credibility and invoke a sense of history" (R. L., 2016, n. p.). In the context of the historical development of the ECtHR's case law and the Convention as a "living instrument," it is, indeed, apparent in most of the analyzed cases that Shakespearean references are used, more or less consciously, in an attempt to legitimize

---

opinion the judge, somewhat jocularly, noted that his point of view might be affected by his experience as a person educated in English schools, where students would consider corporal punishment much less severe than an alternative of being forced to learn by heart 500 lines from Shakespeare or Virgil (*Tyrer v. . . .*, Separate opinion of Judge Sir Gerald Fitzmaurice, para. 12).

the judges who come from what may be perceived as European peripheries. These references can be understood as a reminder that these judges share the European cultural heritage and use the same cultural codes. They constitute a manifestation of certain cultural aspirations and create a common ground of shared values and ideas. Last, but not least, they also reveal how much European languages and cultures are permeated with Shakespeare. Nevertheless, one must admit that in the Shakespearean references found in legal documents, literary historical rigorousness and linguistic accuracy are much less important than the intended, though not necessarily achieved, effect. And although, as has been demonstrated, the references can sometimes be counterproductive, lack of precision in quoting the plays seems to bother literary historians only.

References

Bradley, A. C. (1904/1991). *Shakespearean tragedy*. Penguin Books.
Button, A. (2001). Law. In M. Dobson & S. Wells (Eds.), *The Oxford companion to Shakespeare* (p. 252). Oxford University Press.
Carpi, D., & Gaakeer J. (2015). Focus: Shakespeare and the law, *Pólemos*, 9(1), 1–5.
Carpi, D. (2015). Romeo and Juliet: The importance of a name, *Pólemos*, 9(1), 37–50.
Carpi, D. (2018). Shakespeare and the law: State of the art. In D. Carpi & F. Ost (Eds.), *As you law it—Negotiating Shakespeare, law & literature* (Vol. 15, pp. 3–13). De Gruyter.
Crawford, A. W. (1916), *Hamlet, an ideal prince, and other essays in Shakesperean interpretation: Hamlet; Merchant of Venice; Othello; King Lear*. R.G. Badger.
Curran, K. (Ed.). (2017). *Shakespeare and judgment*. Edinburgh University Press.
Edwards, P. (1997). Introduction. In P. Edwards (Ed.), *Hamlet Prince of Denmark* (pp. 1–71). The New Cambridge Shakespeare. Cambridge University Press.
Gadbin-George, G. (2013).To quote or not to quote: "Literature in law" in European court decisions and legal English teaching, *ASp, 64,* http://journals.openedition.org/asp/3842; DOI: https://doi.org/10.4000/asp.3842.
Gibbons, B. (1980). Introduction. In *Romeo and Juliet*, B. Gibbons (Ed.), pp. 1–77. Methuen.
Jenkin, C. (2016). Shakespeare and the law. *Hong Kong Lawyer*. https://www.hk- lawyer.org/content/shakespeare-and-law
Kamień, J. (2024). *Prawo i literatura jako kierunek filozoficznoprawny* [*Law and literature as a legal-philosophical field*]. Wydawnictwo Uniwersytetu Gdańskiego, Wolters Kluwer.
Keeton, G. W. (1967). *Shakespeare's legal and political background*. Sir Isaac Pitman & Sons Ltd.
Kornstein, D. J. (1994). *Kill All the lawyers? Shakespeare's legal appeal*. Princeton University Press.
Kovler, A. (2021). Separate opinion: European Court of Human Rights (ECtHR). In *Max Planck Encyclopedia of International Procedural Law*, Oxford University Press. https://opil.ouplaw.com/display/10.1093/law-mpeipro/e3412.013.3412/law-mpeipro-e3412
Kowalski, M. (2024). Szekspir w Strasburgu—przyczynek do rozważań o literaturze w prawie [Shakespeare in Strasbourg—A contribution to studies on literature in law], *Ad Quem. Księga jubileuszowa z okazji 70. urodzin Profesora Jerzego Zajadło* [Ad Quem. Volume in honor of Professor Jerzy Zajadło], J. Kamień, S. Sykuna, & K. Zeidler (Eds.), pp. 355–366. Wydawnictwo Uniwersytetu Gdańskiego.

Maroń, G. (2019). Odwołania do literatury pięknej w orzecznictwie Europejskiego Trybunału Praw Człowieka [Literary references in the case law of the ECtHR]. *Ruch Prawniczy, Ekonomiczny i Socjologiczny*, 2, 67–82.

Meron, Theodor. (1993). *Henry's wars and Shakespeare's laws. Perspectives on the law of war in the later Middle Ages.* Clarendon Press of Oxford University Press.

Owen, H. P. (1972). *Shakespeare and the lawyers.* Methuen & Co.

Posner, R. A. (2009). Critical introduction. In *Law and literature* (pp. 1–18). Harvard University Press. https://doi.org/10.2307/j.ctvjhzpk6.4

R. L. (2016, January 8). Why lawyers love Shakespeare. *The Economist.*

Raffield, P. (2017). *The art of law in Shakespeare.* Bloomsbury.

Sokol, B. J., & Sokol, M. (2004). *Shakespeare legal language: A dictionary.* Bloomsbury Academic.

Thompson A., & Taylor N. (2016). Introduction. In A. Thompson & N. Taylor (Eds.), *Hamlet* (pp. 1–168). Bloomsbury.

Vaughan, V. M., & Vaughan, A. T. (Eds.). (2001). *The Tempest.* The Arden Shakespeare.

Ward, I. (1999). *Shakespeare and the legal imagination.* Butterworths.

Watt, G. (2016). *Shakespeare's acts of will.* Bloosmbury.

Ziemele, I. (2017). The nature and role of separate opinions. In I. Ziemele (Ed.), *Separate opinions at the European Court of Human Rights* (pp. 13–20). Riga Graduate School of Law.

Zurcher, A. (2010). *Shakespeare and the law.* Methuen.

Case Law of the European Court of Human Rights

Achour v. France, ECtHR (Grand Chamber), Judgment of March 29, 2006, Application no. 67335.

Blokhin v. Russia, ECtHR (Grand Chamber), Judgment of March 23, 2016, Application no. 47152.

Ireland v. the United Kingdom, ECtHR (Plenary), Judgment of January 18, 1978, Application no. 5310/71.

Ketreb v. France, ECtHR (Chamber), Judgment of July 19, 2012, Application no. 38447/09.

Khan v. Germany, ECtHR (Chamber), Judgment of April 23, 2015, Application no. 38030/12.

Lindon, Otchakovsky-Laurens and July v. France, ECtHR (Grand Chamber), Judgment of July 22, 2007, Applications nos. 21279/02 and 36448/02.

N. v. Romania (No. 2), ECtHR (Chamber), Judgment of November 16, 2021, Application no. 38048/18.

Sargsyan v. Azerbaijan, ECtHR (Grand Chamber), Judgment of June 16, 2015, Application no. 40167/06.

Tyrer v. the United Kingdom, ECtHR (Chamber), Judgement of 25 April 1978, Application no. 5856/72.

Y. v. Slovenia, ECtHR (Chamber), Judgment of May 28, 2015, Application no. 41107/10.

Case Law of the Supreme Court of the United States

Coy v. Iowa, Supreme Court of the United States, 487 US 1012, 1016 (1988).

CHAPTER THIRTEEN | WŁADYSŁAW WITALISZ

Troy as a Metaphor of Conflict: Trojan Allusions in Public Discourse About the War in Ukraine

Abstract

Narrations and commentaries of modern conflicts and wars are often framed by allusions to historical or literary narratives of the past. This allows the writers and commentators to tame and understand the present conflict and to cast the modern opponents (individuals or nations) in old recognizable roles. In the past three years, references to characters and episodes from the narrative of Troy have frequently reappeared in public discourse in reports and debates on the war in Ukraine. Although it should come as no surprise that Troy serves as a suitable reference in any debate on war, the number of Trojan allusions in texts on Ukraine is exceptionally high. In addition, they appear to have a consistent rhetorical and ideological purpose. This chapter attempts to identify and define that purpose by analyzing chosen examples of Trojan tropes found in texts on the tragic events in Ukraine. The texts referred to come from online newspapers, magazines, and book publications in English, French, Ukrainian, and Russian.

Keywords: Trojan war, Homer, reception, classical allusion, Russia, Ukraine

The initial idea of writing this text appeared a few weeks after the invasion of Russia on Ukraine in 2022, when all of us tried to understand what had just happened and searched for appropriate language to relate to it. The epic weight of the events, felt especially strongly by those of us living close to Ukraine, naturally invited epic parallels. For the present author, a scholar who used to research classical and medieval Trojan narratives, the verses of Homer and his followers narrating the anger of Achilles[1]

---

1. Homer's *Iliad* narrates the last phase of the late Bronze Age war between the Greeks (Achaeans), led by King Agamemnon, and the Trojans, led by King Priam and his son Hector. Homer presents the abduction of Helena, wife of the Greek King Menelaus, by the Trojan Prince Paris as the immediate cause of the war, but the history of the Greek Trojan conflict in the narrative is older. The anger of Achilles, caused by the death of his friend Patroclus from the hand of

helped to find words to name the political hubris of Putin's military invasion. Watching images of Russian tanks moving in the direction of Kyiv, I also recalled Simon Weil's famous essay "The *Iliad* or the Poem of Force" (Weil, 1991). The essay, originally written in French in 1939 and published in Nazi-occupied Paris in 1940, was Weil's own reassessment of her earlier pacifist philosophy and an attentively ethical but pessimistic rereading of the *Iliad* that questioned traditional heroic interpretations. "The true hero, the true subject, the centre of the *Iliad* is force. Force employed by man, force that enslaves man, force before which man's flesh shrinks away" (Weil, 1991, p. 3), she begins and clarifies her motivations to focus on the theme of force in the epic.

> For those dreamers who considered that force, thanks to progress, would soon be a thing of the past, the *Iliad* could appear as an historical document; for others, whose powers of recognition are more acute and who perceive force, today as yesterday, at the very centre of human history, the *Iliad* is the purest and the loveliest of mirrors. (Weil, 1991, p. 3)

In the early months of 2022, another brutal invasion called for Homeric parallels and made Weil's essay on force in human history and politics pertinent again. The *Iliad* can still serve as a mirror that helps us to understand and name the modern use of war in politics.

An additional encouragement to search for Trojan parallels in the public discourse about the military conflict in Ukraine came from an image illustrating an article I chanced to read in the English version of *Le Monde* on April 22, 2022: Nicolas Truong's "War in Ukraine and COVID-19: Europe is dealing with the 'return of tragedy'" (Truong, 2022). The deck of the article introduces the theme, "The afflictions of war and the pandemic appeared suddenly in our lives. Perceived as signs of 'historical comeback' on a continent that thought it was safe, these tragedies compel our societies to reinvent themselves." Truong expresses some sobering and disenchanting thoughts, similar to Weil's awakening to war's atrocities, about the state of the world:

> We thought war was over. Stored away with old documents and yellowed photographs in our cupboards, forgotten in the limbo of our memories, relegated to the dustbins of history. War had disappeared, occasionally rearing its head through our TV screens, emerging from the confines of distant countries. So much so that it had even become a metaphorical construct for some of our political elites. (Truong, 2022)

Hector, appears famously in the opening line of the poem and drives the Greek warrior to kill Hector in single combat and desecrate his body. The final fall of Troy is a result of the Greek stratagem that brings Greek soldiers into the city in a large wooden horse believed by the Trojans to be a votive gift to the Gods.

But the "punchline" of the article is for me the image by Christelle Enault[2] chosen by the *Le Monde* editors to illustrate the article. It represents a fragment of a human face—only one eye is visible—in the middle of the confusion of war, with fire, smoke, and explosions covering most of the picture's space. A hand, possibly the hand of the person whose eye we see in the picture, holds a mask. No, this is not the famous mask of Agamemnon, but clearly an ancient one, a mask of classical tragedy that reminds us of Greek theater masks. What is especially telling about the image is the act of donning the classical mask onto the face of a modern war, evoking the idea of a narrative or a rhetorical parallel between the past and the present. The eye in the picture will look at the modern war through the lens of the epic and tragic perspective that the classical mask represents. Conversely, the classical mask sitting on the face of the modern soldier will be seen in new contexts and will achieve new meanings, reminding us that history repeats itself. The image is an intriguing artistic projection of the major proposition of the text, but it may also be seen as an interesting comment on, indeed a problematization of its assumptions. One quoted above is that the tragedies we experience compel our societies to reinvent themselves. But does the Greek mask in the picture call for a reinvention that challenges the teachings of the ancient masters, suggesting that looking at the world from their ancient perspective is no longer adequate? Or does it invite us to do the opposite and recognize the epic and the tragic in the small events of the present? After all, the gaping mouth of the theatrical mask and its wide-open round eyes suggest a greater shock and a greater fear at the sight of war than belongs to the neutrally depicted modern human eye behind it.

My search for Trojan parallels in texts commenting on the war in Ukraine soon proved that writers and journalists still willingly don the ancient rhetorical mask and use Trojan allusions that, they believe, help to convey their meanings. Whether this is always so remains to be answered, as the adequacy of an allusion always rests on the cultural literacy of the authors and their readers. Of the dozens of examples found in newspapers, magazines, and online media, only several can be analyzed here. The aim of this paper is to identify Trojan references that are most frequently used in the analyzed discourse and to evaluate their semantic adequacy by comparing the contexts—ancient and modern—in which they are used. I will also try to reconstruct the aims for which the allusions are brought into the texts and consider their rhetorical effects on the reader. At the outset, it appears useful to briefly define the concept and function of any classical allusion used in modern discourse and to consider its communicative strengths and limitations.

A classical allusion is a specific reference to a character, an event, or a theme originating from classical literature. Allusions may invoke entire texts—often canonical works like those of Homer—or may consist of direct quotations or more subtle

---

2. Available at https://www.lemonde.fr/en/opinion/article/2022/04/29/war-in-ukraine-and-covid-19-europe-is-dealing-with-the-return-of-tragedy_5981946_23.html.

references to particular episodes or figures within those texts. Authors using references to classical myths, texts, and figures aim primarily to add an air of intellectual authority to their argument. Such references are meant to infuse the author's voice with a kind of gravitas that strengthens the message. By invoking classical sources, speakers or writers may also hope to align their thoughts with established wisdom or with longstanding principles known to everyone and generally accepted. The author's intent is then to establish a common ground with the reader or listener and to improve the credibility of his words. Once that credibility and authority are established, authors will use allusions to influence the readers' judgement of the represented reality. Allusions to particular classical characters who have grown to stand for established moral meanings can be used to suggest an evaluation of the characters and events in the current narrative. They influence, guide, or bias the reader's moral interpretation. For instance, comparing a modern political leader to a historical figure known for particular virtues or vices can shape public perception of that leader's qualities or actions.

Classical allusions connect the expressed ideas with a shared cultural heritage, a set of values, and ideals that resonate with audiences familiar with these references. They draw the audience closer to the text by appealing to their collective memory and cultural identity. This is possible only in communication with and within what Brian Stock (1983, pp. 88–240), discussing early forms of religious literacy, called a "textual community," that is, a group of people (readers or listeners) who share the same set of seminal texts and can therefore build their communication around them. However, Stock sees the role of shared textual references to be greater than just rhetorical facilitators of discourse. He believes that by establishing a common set of references patterns that carry important meanings, they contribute to the construction of the identity of the group and inform the self-representation of the group. In a chapter on the reception of Stock's concept in scholarly debate, Jane Heath summarizes Stock's argument. A textual community, she explains, is "a community whose life, thought, sense of identity, and relations with outsiders are organised around an authoritative text. The way it plays that role is through education and religion" (Heath, 2019, p. 5). Although sacred texts, especially those of established religions, are obvious to create and sustain the existence of textual communities within Stock's understanding, we believe that a recurring set of literary allusions to a certain text that appears over a period of time in a given culture can lead to the creation of a textual community whose self-expression becomes defined by meanings derived from that text. Further on we shall discuss an adequate example of this phenomenon referring to medieval historiography and political writing.

In summary, classical allusions can enrich an author's discourse by adding depth, connecting with historical and cultural values, and improving the rhetorical impact. Classical allusions used wisely and sparingly can strengthen the author's control over the reader's response. However, excessive or badly targeted use of classical allusions can sometimes alienate those who are not familiar with the references. The text becomes elitist and is accessible only to those with a certain level of education or cultural literacy.

One of the oldest sets of literary allusions used in the cultural discourse of the Western world, next to the Bible and classical mythology, is the narration of the Trojan War. The story has continued to inspire human imagination for millennia. Its characters and episodes have grown into a system of signs, which, through allusion or metaphor, helped to express meanings pertaining to historical periods and cultural regions other than Ancient Greece. Virgil's *Aeneid* reiterated Homeric Troy in the narrative act of *translatio studii et imperii* in which the identity of the new dynastic and political entity of Rome is defined by reference to the ancient heroic world. In Virgil's text, Rome becomes engendered in the founding myth of Aeneas and becomes endowed with the meanings and values contained in the narrative memory of the Trojan War and its aftermath. A few centuries later, medieval narrations of the history of the new political powers emerging in post-Roman Europe followed the example of Virgil and imagined successive generations of the Trojan diaspora founding new ruling dynasties and kingdoms. Thus, the 7th century chronicle of Fredegar (Fredegarius, Liber II, 4a–6), makes Francus, the son of Hector, found the kingdom of the Franks, while the 9th century Saxon history by Nennius (*Historia Brittonum* III, 7, 10) has Felix Brutus, the great-grandson of Aeneas, establish the city of Trinovantum, the New Troy, later known as London. The early founding stories were written to construct narrative frameworks of identities for the newly emerging political and national groups, while later narrations of Troy—written by Benoît de Sainte-Maure, Geoffrey Chaucer, or John Lydgate—would use the Trojan myth as a mirror set up to reflect or comment on current social and political reality (see Witalisz, 2011). While the new narratives of Troy mention Homer as a source of the tradition, they accuse the ancient author of confabulation[3] and a bias toward the Greeks.[4] The original Greek Homer was not accessible to the Latin authors of the pro-Trojan medieval world. They based their stories on the 1st or 2nd century Latin texts composed on the basis of Homer by Dares of Phrygia and Dyctis of Crete, whom the medieval writers believed to have been eyewitnesses of the Trojan War.[5]

---

3. The anonymous 14th-century author of the English *Gest Hystoriale of the Destruction of Troy* laughs at Homer saying that in his story "goddes foght in the filde, folke as thai were" (ll. 45).
4. "He with Grekis was allied, / Therfor he was to hem fauourable / In myche thing" (Lydgate, *Troy Book*, Prologue, ll. 280–283).
5. The historical veracity of Dyctis and Dares was taken for granted in the Middle Ages. The Latin *Ylias* by Joseph of Exeter (1190) thus dismisses Homer, and even Virgil: "Should I admire old Homer, Latin Virgil, or The Bard of Troy (unknown to tale), whose present eye, A surer witness of the truth, disclosed the war? (Joseph of Exeter, 2005, ll. 25–27).

The tradition, indeed, fashion, of the narration of the Trojan heritage continued well into the 17th century. James I of England still had his genealogical tree traced back to Felix Brutus, bringing even the Scots within the British and the Trojan pale. (Richards, 2002, p. 521) By retelling the story of the Trojan war, medieval writers supplied the founding fathers of the new lines of monarchs, as well as the coming generations of their children, with a history, an identity rooted in that history and an old heroic set of values and virtues. They also established Troy once and for all a common point of reference for any discourse of war, universal for the Western World. In the modern era, when the Greek text of Homer was finally made available and was translated into vernacular languages, the war at Troy remained a rich repository of well-known characters and episodes that continued to serve as points of reference and allusion in the neoclassical discussion of war and politics, but lost the earlier element of national, or political identification. In the 19th century, Heinrich Schliemann's discovery of Troy, followed by the popular sensational narration constructed around it, revived the old myths again and strengthened the iconicity of the Trojan war.

The ubiquity of Troy in texts on the war in Ukraine is overwhelming and highly evocative. It appears that the beginnings of the Trojan parallel in Russian-Ukrainian relations are much older than the full-scale war of 2022 and appeared in a Russian document planning the invasion as early as 2014. The Russian masterminds of the entire plan, Putin strategists led by Aleksei Muratov, later the official representative of the so-called Donetsk People's Republic in the Russian Federation, coded the original secret plan of the invasion with the name "Troy". In April 2018, *The Times* published a feature article "Operation Troy: Russia's blueprint for spreading chaos in Ukraine" revealing leaked information about the document. The codename "Troy" was certainly not chosen for rhetorical effect for the plan was to be seen by only a few of Muratov's cronies in the close command of the Russian forces. However, the decision to resort to this particular metaphor in a top-secret document describing strategy and military tactics reveals the authors' frame of mind and their understanding of the political importance of the operation.

In most rhetorical structures invoking Troy, the Russian forces are compared to the Greek invaders, while the Ukrainians become the defenders of Troy. The basic logic of the parallel is understandable. Like the Achaeans and the Trojans, the Russians and the Ukrainians are neighbors with a related and a troubled past, who, to some extent, shared the same language and the same religion. The larger hegemonic neighbor invades the smaller one, who has only recently built walls of independence and national identity to secure its safety. Similarly, the Greek attack on Troy narrated by Homer was not the first encounter between the Greeks and the Trojans. Troy had been burnt before and rebuilt. The Trojans had attacked Greek cities and islands. Decades of trouble had preceded the siege, which was meant to finally solve the Trojan problem. Agamemnon, encouraged by a false dream of easy victory sent to him by

Zeus, plans to take Troy in one battle (Book II, 1–47). The dream feeds his hubris and drives his rash military decisions. He knows that his soldiers outnumber the troops of the enemies and accuses the Trojans of allying themselves with their neighbors to confound the Greeks (Book II, 109–154). He believes that it is his duty to defeat Troy to put an end to the ongoing trouble. Homer adds to this the grand romantic story and turns the abduction of Helena, Agamemnon's brother's wife, by Paris into the immediate cause of the war. Although there is no romance in the modern act of war, Putin's infamous speech (Putin, 2022) preceding the invasion of 2022 echoes many of Agamemnon's arguments in waging his war. He denies Ukrainians their ethnic and political identity and represents his "special military operation" as a necessary act of justice. He maintains that Russia is seeking peace and has a moral obligation to establish security in the region. He accuses Ukraine of being aggressive and attempts to associate Ukrainians with terrorism and Nazism. He denounces Ukraine's aspiration to NATO and calls it "a puppet of the West." Putin's dream of greatness was not sent by Zeus but is fed by nostalgia for the Russian and Soviet empires and spiritually inspired by his alliance with the Orthodox Church.[6]

The Putin-Agamemnon parallel continues in an article published by the Greek-Australian news portal "NEOS KOSMOS" on April 26, 2022. Joel Christensen's[7] commentary "Epic glory and modern war: From the walls of Troy to the defence of Kyiv" is accompanied by an image linking a portrait of Putin with the famous golden mask found by Heinrich Schliemann at Hissarlik, named by the archaeologist the mask of Agamemnon. Following the anti-heroic reading of the *Iliad* by Simone Weil, Christensen uses the Trojan framework to engage in an ethical argument that reveals the "fraught notion of glory and fame" and shows that "there is no glory or fame in bloodletting" at any historical time.

With Agamemnon standing for Putin, one would expect Priam, the king of Troy, to be a suitable analogue to President Zelensky, but in his case the most frequent character referred to in the allusive discourse is the figure of Hector, the oldest son of Troy's King Priam, indeed the leader of the Trojan forces. Hector is primarily a man of war in the Homeric tradition, a loyal warrior devoted to his family and his city who dares Achilles to a single combat and dies a heroic death. The choice of this parallel for Zelensky is certainly an empowering device that goes along with the image of the president as a leader of a nation at war, a soldier himself. It is probably Zelensky's military look that informs the comparison. But if Zelensky is Hector, then his opponent must be Achilles, and indeed we do find individual texts where Putin is represented as Achilles, though this is not frequent (De la Porte, 2022). In Homer, from the moment

---

6. For a discussion of Putin's religious inspirations see G. Przebinda (2014).
7. Joel Christensen is a renowned classical scholar from Brandeis University (USA) who often comments on current issues looking at them through the lens of classical literature.

that he forgets his infatuation with Briseis and loses his friend Patroclus by the hand of Hector, Achilles is represented primarily as a brave warrior driven by a particular rage that comes from his loss, a true hero among the Greeks and a worthy opponent of Hector. Both Hector and Achilles are narrated by Homer as fearless heroes, loyal to their causes though brutal in their combat. However, Achilles magnanimously returns the body of Hector to his father and receives the grieving Priam with respect due to a king. Although the Homeric narrative makes the Achilles/Putin-Hector/Zelensky parallel possible, the way that the two presidents are represented by the western media makes it less acceptable. Zelensky, a leader of his people, usually in military fatigues, alone and central to the image, looking directly at the camera, speaking with the harsh voice of an experienced soldier; and Putin, an alleged war criminal, always surrounded by his guards, as if needing protection, overpowered by the byzantine interiors of his palaces, his uneasy smile turning into a grin, his small eyes always looking for trouble. This of course is a biased picture created by the media, but such a picture excludes a parallel between Putin and Achilles. Especially that this parallel would imply a rather grim end to the fate of the Ukrainian Hector.

Another interesting use of the figure of Achilles in the language of the modern conflict appears in military nomenclature. The first Ukrainian drone battalion was proudly called "Achilles," clearly alluding to the combat skills and effectiveness of the Greek warrior. Interestingly, this allusion overlooks the national identification found in most of the Trojan-Greek references and appropriates the prowess of the Greek hero into the Trojan context. Pursuing the attributes of the Achilles allusion, another text talks of the Ukrainian drones that expose the Achilles' heel of the enemy (Daniels, 2025).

Probably the most common phraseological unit based on a classical allusion which functions in everyday language is the Trojan horse. Used to convey the meaning of a deceptive strategy or trick, the phrase alludes to the huge wooden horse left by the Greeks at the gates of Troy as they seem to depart, leaving the city unconquered. The Trojans are uncertain about its function and use, but in the end, they decide to bring it within the city walls. Sabotage and diversionary action are routine tactics of Putin's warfare. The coded document "Operation Troy" mentioned above speaks of secret actions behind the scenes geared toward destabilizing Ukraine through propaganda and misinformation, the new form of the wooden horse. The trope itself appears in many contexts commenting upon the war but was used for the first time as early as 2014 when Putin sent Russian humanitarian aid to the newly annexed territories of Donbas. *BBC News* correspondent Daniel Sandford expresses doubts about the contents of the dozens of trucks entering Eastern Ukraine with humanitarian aid. "Ukraine conflict: Russian aid or Trojan Horse?," he openly asks in his title (Stanford, 2014).

Some of the authors searching for Homeric parallels do not stop at allusions to individual characters. On *Medium*, a social publishing platform that prioritizes quality writing, Nicolae Pirvu (2024) builds a complete Trojan allegory to explain his interpretation of Russian-Ukrainian relations. In this text, Ukraine is compared to Helen and Russia to her husband Menelaus.

> Today's Ukraine, like Helen from the myth, is extremely attractive on the international stage, thanks to the wealth of its agricultural sector. […] Up until 2008, Ukraine (our modern Helen) and Russia (our Menelaus) were close partners, getting along quite well. However, things took a dramatic turn at the NATO summit in Bucharest when the USA (our Paris) made its presence known to Helen (Ukraine) and, blinded by her beauty, set his mind on having her only for himself.
> In 2014, Ukraine (Helen) broke ties with Russia (Menelaus) and sided with the USA (Paris). Refusing to accept this new reality, Russia (Menelaus) launched a war against them. […] Like its ancient counterpart, this modern conflict seems destined to be long and devastating. It could drag on undecided until Russia (Menelaus) might win it through a shrewd move, kind of modern "Trojan Horse."

Although the article certainly cannot be called choice political commentary, it makes creative use of a set of classical allusions to drive home the author's ideas. It is important to remember that this text comes from a social platform and should therefore be seen as written in a language that is used by ordinary people. Troy is still part of our language and our imagination. We understand Menelaus's rage over Helen's abduction and recognize the irrational infatuation of the youthful Paris with the divine beauty of Zeus's daughter. On the one hand, we still belong to the Trojan textual community, but on the other, the allusions we construct use and transfer only some of the meanings of the original character or event and are based on simplified and conventionalized senses of the old texts, constructed by centuries of tradition and re-narration. In Homer's world, the relationship between Menelaus and Helen was complicated. Although we still remember the jealous rage of the husband at the loss of his wife, we forget that Helen's union with Menelaus was not the result of mutual love, but an effect of a political settlement designed by Helen's father, Tyndareus, that aimed to prevent war between many of Helen's suitors. But this forgetfulness serves the purpose of the allusion perfectly well. The author of the *Medium* text does not seem to remember either that the history of Ukrainian-Russian relations, as complicated as the marriage of their classical counterparts, did not begin in the 20th century when he believed that they were "close partners, getting along quite well." Like other parallels based on a long narrative work with an even longer history of literary and cultural reception, Trojan allusions to Ukraine must be constructed by choosing only one or some of the many meanings contained in the classical referent.

As stated at the beginning of this paper, the power and universal nature of the Trojan narrative makes it a handy parallel to the discourse of any war. But in reports and commentaries on the war in Ukraine written in many different languages and published in numerous media outlets, the frequency of Trojan allusions is such that we cannot treat it merely as a coincidence of rhetorical styles. Some of that popularity may have come from the historical moment's special need for epic language, a moment defined by the geography and the size of the conflict. The Western world has not experienced an extended full-scale war so close to its borders since the end of World War II and possibly needed the powerful tropes of Homer to be reawakened from Simone Weil's pacifist dream once again.

In search of other explanations for Troy's pertinence for the war in Ukraine, we must turn back to the concept of *translatio imperii* mentioned above. The tradition of Troy has been annexed by many young and emerging nations that built around the heroic narratives, myths, and official histories of their own identity. Although modern scholarly historiography would not allow such narrations to be created today, folk history and urban legend traditions will have no qualms. The narration of folk history, which appeared to have died with the demise of popular oral narration, is on the rise again due to the availability of digital channels of expression and communication. For some time already, this popular historical tradition has been making forays into a narration that brings Ukraine and Troy surprisingly close to each other. Significantly, the first work of literature that established Ukrainian as a literary language was a free heroicomical travesty of Virgil's *Aeneid*, entitled *Енеїда* and published by Ivan Kotliarevsky (Котляревський) in 1798. This mock-heroic poem satirizing life in 18th-century Ukraine made the story of Troy, even though parodied, bedtime reading for Ukrainians and created a textual community that understands classical allusion. Until today, the poem has been considered a kind of Ukrainian epic.

Another source of popular Trojan-Ukrainian associations has been archaeological excavations carried out in southern and south eastern Ukraine (the area of Mykolaiv), which rendered numerous bronze age artifacts dated around 13th–12th centuries BCE. In recent years, there have been clear attempts by both non-scholarly writers and scholars, however cautious, to connect these sites with the archaeology of Troy. The article "Exploring the Ukranian Troy" on the website of the German-Ukrainian Academic Society speaks with enthusiasm of the excavation sites around Mykolaiv. "Archeological treasure trove points to Mykolaiv's ancient origins and has a potential to rewrite history books, but underfunding prevents full analysis of this exciting site." Vitaliy V. Otroshchenko (Отрощенко) from the National Academy of Sciences of Ukraine uses the name of Troy to refer to the excavations.

The possibilities of the participation of the Late Bronze Age steppe tribes in the campaigns of the 'Sea Peoples', which also touched the inhabitants of Troy in the

13th—12th centuries BCE now are under discussion. The concretisation of the cultural connections between the bearers of archaeological cultures of the Bronze Age steppe zone and the appropriate cities of Troy is now acquiring a certain dynamic. [...] Attention to the cultural complexes of Troy increased during the period of the restoration of Ukraine's independence due to the discovery and excavation of fortified settlements of the Final Bronze Age along the North Pontic area and the Lower Dnieper basin. (Отрощенко, 2018, p. 10)

Otroshchenko himself links the increasing interest in Trojan archaeology with Ukraine's independence but concludes with a warning. "The author warns native archaeologists against the abuse of the Troy name during the presentation of archaeological sites of our country" (Отрощенко, 2018, p. 10).

Of course, nothing inspires popular imagination and folk history better than such warnings. Home grown historians and archaeologists run internet sites and publish books in which links between Troy and early Ukrainian history are a foregone conclusion. In a preface to a self-published internet book entitled *Ukrainian Troy. Discovery*, Vsevolod Pavliuk writes, "There are good reasons to identify the historic fortress of Troy with the modern village of Parutyne, which is home to the National Historical and Archaeological Reserve 'Olbia'" (Pavliuk, 2019, p. 5). Although scholarly books differentiate between myth and history, they often refer to the folk Trojan narration of Ukraine as an element of communal memory, and thus also contribute to keeping it alive. Andrew Wilson's *The Ukrainians. Unexpected Nation*, an excellent cultural and political history of Ukraine, contains the following:

[...] Some have claimed that Troy was a Ukrainian city, at or near the site of the later Greek city of Olbia or Olviia, near the mouth of the southern Buh river in what is now Mykolaiv oblast. Alternatively, Troy may have been near Tenedos, now the Tenderivska spit in the estuary of the Buh and Dnieper. The grave of Achilles is therefore also to be found somewhere on a small Black Sea island in the Buh delta, although it has escaped the attention of archaeologists to date. (Wilson, 2015, p. 38)

Willson's acceptance of the alternative mythical history of Ukraine and his inclusion of the story of the Trojan roots of her people in a scholarly monograph are gestures of respect for a cultural narrative that is born of the aspirations of an emerging nation. We are obviously dealing here with modern echoes of the concept of the translation of empire that early Rome and then the new mediaeval dynasties staged by allying themselves with Troy. Today, this narration is not a propagandist strategy dictated by official historical politics as it was in Lancastrian England and many other European countries at the time, but it may be as effective in a world of the internet and social media where historical narration is no longer the sole privilege of the political center. As in the Middle Ages, the fantastical narration aids realistic political aims, the building of a state needs a narrative, and a mythical narrative can be more evocative than one based on verifiable historical facts.

Conclusion

The recurrence of Trojan allusions in public discourse surrounding the war in Ukraine reveals not only the enduring rhetorical power of classical narratives, but also the cultural mechanisms through which societies interpret contemporary conflict. As this study has demonstrated, references to Homeric characters and episodes—whether invoked in journalistic commentary, political rhetoric, or popular media—serve as more than ornamental devices. They function as interpretive frameworks that shape moral evaluations, historical analogies, and national self-representations. The Trojan myth, with its rich tradition of reception and re-narration, offers a flexible yet authoritative vocabulary for articulating the complexities of war, heroism, and identity.

The rhetorical deployment of figures such as Hector, Achilles, Agamemnon, and Helena in the context of Ukraine and Russia underscores the selective nature of classical allusion. These references are not neutral; they are ideologically charged and culturally contingent, often reflecting the values and aspirations of the communities that employ them. The notion of a "textual community," as articulated by Brian Stock, provides a useful lens to understand how shared literary heritage can inform collective identity and political discourse. In Ukraine's case, the appropriation of Trojan motifs—whether through literary parody, archaeological speculation, or folk historiography—signals a desire to inscribe national resilience and historical legitimacy within a venerable epic tradition.

Ultimately, the prominence of Trojan allusions in the discourse on Ukraine suggests that classical narratives continue to offer a potent means of engaging with the ethical and existential dimensions of war. They allow authors and audiences alike to navigate the trauma of conflict through familiar archetypes, while also reconfiguring those archetypes to reflect the realities of the present. In doing so, they reaffirm the relevance of ancient texts in shaping modern consciousness and underscore the dialogic relationship between myth and history in times of crisis.

References

Christensen, J. (2022, April 26). Epic glory and modern war: From the walls of Troy to the defence of Kyiv. *Neos Cosmos*. https://neoskosmos.com/en/2022/04/26/dialogue/opinion/epic-glory-and-modern-war-from-the-walls-of-troy-to-the-defence-of-kyiv/

Cook, E. (2024, November 3). Ukraine "Achilles" battalion officer issues warning about Western drones. *Newsweek*. https://www.newsweek.com/urkaine-achilles-battalion-drones-electronic-warfare-russia-kharkiv-kupiansk-1979304

Daniels, M. (2025, June 5). Ukraine's drone attack exposes Achilles' heel of military superpowers. *The Wall Street Journal.* https://www.wsj.com/world/ukraines-drone-attack-exposes-achilles-heel-of-military-superpowers-75d1d79c

Dares Phrygius. (1966). De Excidio Troiae. In R. M. Fraser (Trans.), *The chronicles of Dictys of Crete and Dares the Phrygian.* Indiana University Press.

de la Porte, Xavier. (2022, March 28). Poutine et Zelensky s'apparentent aux Achille et Hector de l'*Iliade. Le Nouvel Obs.* https://www.nouvelobs.com/idees/20220328.OBS56313/poutine-et-zelensky-s-apparentent-aux-achille-et-hector-de-l-illiade.html

Dictys Cretensis. (1966). Ephemeris Belli Troiani. In R. M. Fraser (Trans.), *The chronicles of Dictys of Crete and Dares the Phrygian.* Indiana University Press.

Exploring the Ukrainian Troy. *Ukrainet.* https://ukrainet.eu/2017/08/15/exploring-the-ukrainian-troy/

Fredegarius Scholasticus. (1888). Chronicle of the Franks. Liber II, 4a-6. In Bruno Krusch (Ed.), *Monumenta Germaniae Historica. Scriptores rerum Merovingicarum* (Vol. II, pp. 1–168). Hanover.

Heath, Jane. (2019). "Textual Communities": Brian Stock's concept and recent scholarship on antiquity. In Florian Wilk (Ed.), *Scriptural Interpretation at the Interface between Education and Religion* (pp. 5–35). Brill.

Homer. (2016). *Iliad* (Samuel Butler, Trans.). Neeland Media.

Joseph of Exeter. (2005). *Iliad (Daretis Phrygii Ylias)* (A. G. Rigg, Trans). Centre for Medieval Studies, University of Toronto. https://ylias.medieval.utoronto.ca/web-content/JOSEPH%20OF%20EXETER.pdf

Котляревський, І. П. (1969). Енеїда. [In] І. П. Котляревський. *Повне зібрання творів, підготовка текстів та коментарів Б. А. Деркача.* Київ.

Lydgate, John. (1998). *Troy book* (R. R. Edwards, Ed.). Western Michigan University.

Nennius. (1948). Historia Brittonum. In J. A. Giles (Ed.), *Six Old English Chronicles* (pp. 381–416). Henry G. Bohn.

Отрощенко, В. В. (2018). Троя В Дискурсі Української Археології. *Археологія* 4, 5–10. https://arheologia.com.ua/index.php/arheologia/article/view/34/33

Parfitt, T. (2018, April 2). Operation Troy: Russia's blueprint for spreading chaos in Ukraine. *The Times.* https://www.thetimes.com/uk/politics/article/operation-troy-russia-s-blueprint-for-spreading-chaos-in-ukraine-x2bqv7hbg

Richards, J. M. (2002). The English accession of James VI: 'National' identity, gender and the personal monarchy of England. *The English Historical Review*, 117(472), 513–535.

Panton, G. A., & Donaldson, D. (Eds.).(1869). *Gest Hystoriale of the Destruction of Troy.* EETS o.s. 39, 56. N. Trübner.

Pirvu, N. (2024, February 12). Troy relocates to Ukraine. *MEDIUM.* https://medium.com/@nicolaepirvu/troy-relocates-to-ukraine-68a94961848a

Przebinda, G.(2014). The third baptism of Rus. The participation of Moscow orthodox church in Putin's expansion in Ukraine. *Przegląd Rusycystyczny*, 4(148), 5–15.

Putin, V. (2022, February 24). *Address of the president of the Russian Federation.* http://en.kremlin.ru/events/president/news/67843

Sandford, D. (2014, August 22). Ukraine conflict: Russian aid or Trojan horse? *BBC News.* https://www.bbc.com/news/world-europe-28752878

Stock, B. (1983). *The implications of literacy: Written language and models of interpretation in the eleventh and twelfth centuries*. Princeton University Press.

Truong, N. (2022, April 29). War in Ukraine and Covid-19: Europe is dealing with the "return of tragedy." *Le Monde*. https://www.lemonde.fr/en/opinion/article/2022/04/29/war-in-ukraine-and-covid-19-europe-is-dealing-with-the-return-of-tragedy_5981946_23.html

Weil, S. (1991). *The Iliad or the poem of force*, (12th reprint ed.) Pendle Hill.

Wilson, A. (2015). *The Ukrainians. Unexpected nation* (4th ed.). Yale University Press.

Witalisz, W. (2011). *The Trojan mirror. Middle English narratives of Troy as books of princely advice*. Peter Lang.

SECTION FIVE

Conflict in Interactions: Avoidance, Identity, Messages, and Consensus

CHAPTER FOURTEEN | **SACHIYO SHEARMAN AND KUMI ISHII**

Conflict Avoidance Experiences in Family and at Work

Narrative Analysis of Avoidance Motives, Strategies, and Impacts

Abstract

The Dual Concern Model explains that conflict management strategies can be explained by one's degree of concern for self and concern for the other and that conflict avoidance can be explained with low concern for self and the other (De Dreu et al., 2000). Thus, avoiding conflict is often perceived negatively. The recent research, however, indicates that conflict avoidance can positively impact relationships (e.g., Sun & Slepian, 2020; Thornton & Flechter, 2024). The current study examined the prevalence of conflict avoidance and its narratives. We surveyed 150 participants' experiences of conflict avoidance in family and at work. Their responses were coded in terms of topic, interactants, avoidance behaviors, motivations for avoidance, and its impact on their relationship. The majority of participants reported conflict avoidance experiences at work (91%, $n = 131$) and in family (79%, $n = 118$). The topics of conflict avoidance and avoidance strategies used at work and family are reported. Avoiding conflict in the family is associated with positive or neutral relational outcomes, while avoidance at work is met with negative relational outcomes. Conflict avoidance was not associated with low concern for self and the other, as the Dual Concern Model predicts. Rather, current participants associate conflict avoidance with high concern for self. These results indicate that avoidance is not the mere absence of the lack of concern for self and the other, but it can be considered as a strategic approach to managing conflict.

Keywords: conflict avoidance, conflict management, Dual Concern Model, narrative analysis

Conflict is ubiquitous, and despite its intensity level, we all face conflict in our daily lives. When facing conflict, we make choices to manage it in a variety of ways. Previous research explained people's choices in conflict management based on two-dimensional models: levels of assertiveness (i.e., emphasizing your needs or concern for self) and cooperativeness (i.e., showing understanding for others' needs, or concern for others) (Ruble & Thomas 1976; Thomas, 1976).

In this two-dimensional model of conflict management, people's choices in dealing with a conflict can be explained with the combination of the degree of concern for self (i.e., assertiveness) and concern for the other (i.e., cooperativeness) (Blake & Mouton, 1964; De Dreu et al., 2000; Rahim, 1983). When individuals are highly concerned for their own needs and those of others, they may try to engage and manage conflict with problem-solving attitudes to meet both parties' needs. Individuals with high concern for self, but not for the other, may assert and compete to achieve one's own goals out of a conflict situation. Individuals with high concern for the other and low concern for self would choose to accommodate the other's wish in a given conflict. When individuals do not have enough motives for self or the other, they may avoid the ongoing conflict. This last choice, conflict avoidance, is considered to be the least productive approach to conflict management because individuals choose not to engage, and the course of conflict is often not dealt with (e.g., Blake & Mouton, 1964; Thomas, 1976; Pruitt & Rubin, 1986).

Conflict Avoidance

More recent research, however, suggests that people strategically choose to avoid conflict for various reasons. Although research traditionally considered avoidance in a conflict as an "undesirable option," scholars have reported that conflict avoidance can be useful and constructive, showing concern for the other's face as well as mutual face and reaffirming existing relationship (Oetzel et al., 2000; Oetzel et al., 2001; Ting-Toomey, 1988; Tjosvold & Sun, 2002; Sun & Slepian, 2020).

Conflict avoidance behaviors were studied across various contexts including the workplace. Previous studies indicate that avoidance is primarily used to maintain work relationships (Lussier, 2010). For instance, Tjosvold and Sun (2002) surveyed Chinese workers and found that many managers employ avoidance strategies, including withdrawal, disengagement, accommodation, and outflanking. They report that the complexities of avoidance strategies and claims that the avoidance technique is used not only to maintain the relationship but also to be proactive to avoid retaliations from the other party, and to outflank the other party while maintaining the harmony. Additionally, the association between avoidance strategies and cooperative relation and productivity at the workplace is reported (Tjosvold & Sun, 2002).

In addition to work relationships, later studies on conflict avoidance indicate more positive outcomes. For instance, in Yang and Li's (2017) study in China, leaders' conflict avoidance relates to followers' perceived trust in leaders, perceived justice, and emotional well-being. As the authors explain that their findings may be influenced by their national culture, it exhibits positive effects of avoiding behaviors in conflict situations. Ohbuchi and Atsumi (2010) argue that avoidance in conflict situations is used as a strategy among organizational members. They have found that avoidance is effective for achieving collectivistic goals (e.g., interdependent identity, group harmony), whereas it is ineffective for achieving individualistic goals (e.g., self-interest, fairness, independent identity). Their findings can explain why conflict avoidance is often seen in collectivistic culture.

Conflict avoidance has been also reported in family contexts. The literature on family communication generally presumes that engaging in conflict is more preferrable than avoidance. However, Roloff and Wright (2015) suggest that individuals' engagement in verbal conflict is rare in close relationships. For instance, among the romantic partners' interactions, only 1% of the daily conversations of romantic partners involve conflict interactions, and many people tend to observe behaviors, activities, and mediated discussions rather than interacting for solutions directly.

Additionally, Caughlin et al. (2012) claims that conflict avoidance can be functional in family relations, noting that conflict avoidance is seen as common tactics such as changing subjects or leaving the site of discussion, and can be beneficial at times, in particular, in toxic marital relations. Likewise, Lau (2007) found that an avoidance pattern of parental relationship is beneficial for well-being of children.

Thus, although avoidance is often explained from the mere absence of concern for self and the other, it is not ineffective, and it can be used as a strategic approach to managing conflict (Small et al., 2024; Wang et al., 2012). The current study collected individuals' narratives of conflict avoidance in two contexts (workplace and family), in order to enhance our understanding of interpersonal conflict management using avoidance. In the given narratives of conflict avoidance, we examined the individuals' motives for avoidance, various types of avoidance behavior in a conflict situation, and the individuals' perception of the impact of conflict avoidance on the existing relationship. We also examined the association between two types of motives and the choice of avoidance strategies.

The Dual Concern Model and Conflict Avoidance

The Dual Concern Model argues that people's conflict management strategies can be predicted based on the combination of varying levels of self-concern and other concerns (De Dreu et al., 2000; Pruitt & Rubin, 1986; Rubin et al., 1994). This model posits that individuals have varying degrees of self-concern (i.e., the level of assertiveness to achieve one's own motive) as well as other-concern (i.e., the level of cooperativeness to achieve other's concern) in a conflict situation. The combination of the two motives predicts one's tendency to choose five major strategies: (1) problem-solving or integration, (2) compromise, (3) competition, (4) accommodation, and

(5) avoidance (De Dreu, et al., 2000; Pruitt & Rubin, 1986). For instance, when one's concern for both self and the other are high, a problem-solving approach will be taken, in an attempt to achieve a mutually acceptable agreement. When one's concern for self and the other is moderately high, one may choose a compromise approach where both parties' needs are moderately met. When one's concern for self is high but concern for the other is low, one would likely choose a competitive approach in negotiation to win. If a negotiator is high in concern for the other but low in concern for self, then they would likely move to accommodate the other's needs and make concessions. An individual with a low concern for both self and the other would likely do the bare minimum in the situation. The person may choose to avoid or withdraw from the engagement in a conflict or a negotiation, or from the situation.

The Dual Concern Model explains conflict management well, inspired a variety of research studies, and is applied in various contexts (e.g., Rhoades & Carnevale, 1999). There have been some findings that only partially support the Dual Concern Model. For example, Davis et al. (2023) recently reported strong evidence in support of predicting people's tendency to engage in dominating, obliging, and integrating using the two dimensions of the Dual Concern Model, but no support was found for the avoidance style. Other research reports that gender and age affect avoidance behavior in conflict (e.g., Asma, 2024). These imply that an individual's choice to avoid conflict is not easily explained just by low concerns for self and the other.

Conflict avoidance is not the mere absence of concern for self and others, but rather it can be used as a strategic approach to manage conflict (Sun & Slepian, 2020; Thornton & Fletcher, 2024; Wang et al., 2012). These avoidance behaviors occur when people face unwanted conversation topics such as politics and personal issues, including financial status and privacy concerns (Small et al., 2024; Sun & Slepian, 2020). Thus, individuals choose topic avoidance, a type of avoiding tactics in dealing with a conflict. Previous studies have reported that individuals choose to avoid conflict to maintain harmonious relationships (e.g., Caughlin & Afifi, 2004; Caughlin & Golish, 2002), to maintain relational closeness and satisfaction (e.g., Dailey & Palomares, 2004), or to focus on what is more important than engaging in the conflict (e.g., Thornton & Fletcher, 2024; Zhang & Wei, 2017). Scholars have argued that the behavioral choice to practice topic avoidance is associated with individual and relational goals, and people may choose avoidance strategically to obtain relational bonding (Roloff & Ifert, 2000).

Avoiding behavior can be motivated from a concern for the other's face. An individual may avoid conflict to protect the other person's face or to protect relationships, and this is particularly common among people who have collectivistic tendencies (Chen et al., 2018; Tjosvold & Sun, 2002). Chen et al. (2018) reported that managers who work in public sectors in China used avoiding and obliging strategies as well as integrating strategies. These are consistent with Ting-Toomey's (1988) position in her face negotiation theory that people in a group-based society tend to avoid conflicts to save the other's face. Similarly, Oetzel et al. (2000) have reported that avoidance is selected to save the other's face as well as mutual face.

The current study, therefore, attempted to enhance the understanding of one's motives (i.e., concern for self and the other) for avoidance behavior in a conflict situation by examining participants' narratives of conflict avoidance experience. Thus, we proposed the following research questions:

Research Question 1: What are (a) topics, (b) interactants, and (c) avoiding strategies reported by individuals who experienced conflict avoidance in the workplace and with family?
Research Question 2: How are the concerns for self and the other manifested in the conflict avoidance narratives, and how are they associated with conflict avoidance?
Research Question 3: What do the participants report as the impact of conflict avoidance at work and in family?

Methods

A total of 150 undergraduate students from two state universities in the Southern region of the United States participated in this study. About half ($n = 74$; 49%) of the participants were from the Mid-South, and the rest were from the Southeast ($n = 76$; 51%). There were more female ($n = 97$; 65%) than male ($n = 47$; 31%) participants, and about 10% of the participants ($n = 11$) did not report their sex. Their ages ranged from 18 to 56 years old ($M = 23.6$, $SD = 7.52$). Most of them were white/European American ($n = 109$; 73%), followed by Black/African American ($n = 24$; 16%), Asian/Asian Americans ($n = 7$; 5%), Hispanic/Latino Americans ($n = 1$; 0.7%), and American Indian/Alaska Native ($n = 1$; 0.7%), while the rest of the participants ($n = 11$; 7%) did not report their ethnicity.

This study employed an online survey questionnaire to ask for participants' conflict experience of avoiding conflict at work and/or conflict with family. The survey started with a definition of conflict avoidance—"not directly engaging in a conflict or actively withdrawing from a conflict situation." Avoiding conflict can be shown in various actions, such as by not responding, not communicating, shifting the topic, walking away, or physically avoiding or ignoring the person or the relationship. The survey also included two established measurements: (a) the Taking Conflict Personally Scale (Hample & Dallinger, 1995) and (b) the Vertical/Horizontal Individualism and Collectivism Scale (Singelis et al., 1995). The current paper's emphasis is on the avoidance of narrative analyses and includes an analysis of these measures. After obtaining approval from the Institutional Review Board (IRB), we recruited participants from communication classes in two universities by offering extra credit by each instructor.

After reading the definition of conflict avoidance, participants were asked if they have experienced conflict avoidance at work and in the family. Participants had to select yes or no to this question. The participants who answered yes were then asked to recall a previous experience of conflict avoidance in the workplace and in the family. In each context, participants are asked to report their experience of conflict avoidance in four categories: (a) conflict interactant, (b) conflict topic, (c) conflict avoidance tactics used, and (d) avoidance motivations. Their narratives were coded by two trained research assistants using the following five categories: (a) who was involved in the conflict that they avoided, (b) what the conflict was about, (c) how they avoided the conflict situation, (d) their reasons for conflict avoidance, and (e) the impact of conflict avoidance on their relationship. These categories are created to understand the conflict avoidance motivations employing a modified version of Cupach and his colleague's conflict analysis framework involving distal and proximal contexts and outcomes (Cupach et al., 2009).

Using the mixed data coding process described by Saldana (2021), the descriptive coding (i.e., coding of a word, a short phrase, or a basic topic) and structural coding (i.e., coding of topics of inquiry in relation to specific research question in a study) methods were employed to rate the conflict interactant, conflict topics, and conflict avoidance. Specifically for the reasons of conflict avoidance, we created categories based on the previous research literatures as a framework for guiding initial coding categories (Sun & Slepian, 2020; Wang et al., 2012). Intercoder reliability scores for each category were calculated using the 25.3% (n = 38) of the sample. All reliabilities were satisfactory: Conflict interactant (α = .80), conflict topic (α = .76), conflict avoidance tactics (α = .84), and avoidance motivations (α = .78).

Additionally, participants reported their levels of self and other concerns in regard to the conflict avoidance experience that they had reported by responding to the five items with a four-point Likert scale from 1 = not at all, 2 = just a little, 3 = somewhat, to 4= a lot. Examples are: When you avoided this specific conflict, how much have you considered the following? Self-concern included my time, my energy, my emotion, my impression, and what I gain from this conflict, and other concerns were measured with the other person's time, the other person's energy, the other person's impression, and what the other person gained from your avoidance. These self and other concerns in two contexts yielded high reliability, reported self-concern for the workplace conflict avoidance, α = .76, other-concern for the workplace conflict avoidance, α = .85, self-concern for family conflict avoidance, α = .84, and other-concern for family conflict avoidance, α = .90.

Results

Preliminary Analysis

Out of the 150 participants, most participants (85%) reported having experienced conflict avoidance in both workplace and family contexts. In the workplace, 136 participants (91%) reported experiencing conflict avoidance, 14 participants (9%) stated that they had not experienced conflict avoidance, and one (0.6%) did not respond. In the family context, 118 participants (79%) reported conflict avoidance in the family, 34 participants (23%) had not experienced conflict avoidance, and four participants (3%) did not respond. When we asked participants to report their experiences of conflict avoidance, many of them could think of an experience of avoidance. Those who could not or did not report conflict avoidance are those who could not think of anything or those who reported active engagement of a conflict instead of avoidance.

Findings from the Conflict Avoidance Narratives

We answer the first research question by reporting the frequency of the participants' avoiding experience regarding (a) interactants, (b) topics, and (c) avoidance strategies used in the workplace and family contexts, respectively, in the following sections.

Conflict Avoidance in the Workplace

Interactants. For the conflict interactant at work, four categories were created: coworker, boss/supervisor, subordinate, and the other category. After completing the coding, we added an extra category of multiple parties to our coding, since many participants reported such situations. Out of the 136 conflict avoidance narratives, the interactants in the conflict situation were their coworker ($n = 56$; 41%), boss/supervisor ($n = 38$; 28%), multiple parties ($n = 15$; 11%), subordinate ($n = 7$; 5%), and other ($n = 20$; 15%). The other category included participants such as customers, clients, or coworkers in different divisions. The multiple parties included more than two parties, such as a subordinate and a coworker.

Topic. The participants avoided conflict about job or task allocation (n = 50, 38.2%), rules and ethics ($n = 28$, 21.4%), opinions and reviews ($n = 21$, 16%), work progress ($n = 17$, 13%), relationship ($n = 10$, 7.6%), and other topics ($n = 5$, 3.8%). The job and task allocation refers to the conflict regarding the division and assignment of a shared task. The rules and ethics category refers to the conflict in the interpretation of company regulations or the perception of ethical standards at work. Work progress refers to a conflict about the timeline and scheduling relating to the shared tasks that they have to work on. Relationship refers to a conflict about the interpersonal relationship. The other topics refers to any other conflict issues that did not fit in to other categories such as how to talk to a customer, or how to navigate a complaint.

Avoidance strategies. The avoidance strategies used in the workplace were coded with the following categories: (a) leaving the job or terminating the relationships, (b) withdrawing from the responsibility temporarily, (c) avoiding interaction temporarily, (d) appealing to third parties (e.g., supervisor, coworker), (e) keeping the status quo and accepting as is. Leaving a job or terminating the relationship indicates that a participant's choice to quit their job or to terminate work relations to avoid a conflict at work. Withdrawing from the responsibility temporarily refers to a participant's choice to disengage from a role, specific tasks, or work to avoid a conflict. Avoiding an interaction temporarily indicates to avoiding the specific individual(s) involved in a conflict temporarily. Appealing to third party refers to a person not engaging directly but asking a third party such as a coworker or a supervisor to intervene. Lastly, keeping the status quo is to choose to not to engage in a specific conflict while maintaining the current situation, even though a person may not be happy about the situation. Although we requested participants to report their avoidance behavior, some of their narratives unexpectedly showed engagement, such as confronting them after taking some time. Thus, an additional category of (f) not avoiding was added for such cases. The frequency of these five categories were: no contact or terminating the association ($n = 9$; 7.1%), avoiding interaction temporarily ($n = 51$; 40.2%), appealing to the third party ($n = 19$; 15%), keeping the status quo and accepting as is ($n = 35$; 27.6%), and not avoiding or other ($n = 13$; 10.2%).

Conflict Avoidance with Family

Interactant. For the conflict interactant at family conflict, we created four categories: family, parents, siblings, child, and other family members. The multiple party option was added since a few participants reported different combinations of such conflict avoidance experience. Out of the 118 conflict avoidances reported, the interactants were parents ($n = 61$; 51.7%), siblings ($n = 19$; 16.1%), multiple parties (among family members) ($n = 19$; 16.1%), child (daughter/son) ($n = 1$; 0.7%), and other family members (i.e., extended family, grandparents, relatives) ($n = 20$; 15.3%). Multiple parties refer to cases where more than two individuals, such as a mother and an aunt, are reported.

Topic. Conflict topics avoided in the family context included daily life in family ($n = 25$; 23.6%), personality ($n = 25$; 23.6%), social relation (e.g., dating) ($n = 13$; 8.7%), money and finance topic (e.g., tuition payment) ($n = 13$; 8.7%), opinions (e.g., politics) ($n = 11$; 7.3%), work, career, and education (n = 9; 6%), and other ($n = 10$; 6.7%). The daily life in a family refers to disagreements about daily behaviors such as cooking or watching television. Personality refers to a conflict regarding a family member's habit or individual idiosyncrasy such as gossiping or complaining too frequently. Social relation refers to a conflict about a family member's choice of social life, hanging out with a specific group of people, or going out too much. Money and finance topic refers to the conflict regarding how money is spent or handled. Opinions refers to a conflict regarding family members' political views or social opinions. Work, career, and education category deals with a conflict about family members' choice or decision regarding where to study or not study, where to work or not work.

Avoidance strategies. The avoidance strategies in the family context were coded with the following created categories: (a) no contact or terminating the association, (b) avoiding interaction temporarily, (c) appealing to the third party, (d) keeping the status quo and accepting as is. In addition, we have added (e) not avoiding because, similar to the workplace context, some participants also reported indirect engagement as their conflict avoidance with family. The frequency of these six categories were: (a) no contact or terminating the association ($n = 5$; 4.7%), (b) avoiding interaction temporarily ($n = 81$; 75.7%), (c) appealing to the third party ($n = 3$; 2.8%), (d) keeping the status quo and accepting as is ($n = 12$; 11.2%), and (e) not avoiding or other ($n = 6$; 5.6%). No contact or terminating the relationship indicates that a participant's choice to choose not to be in touch with or to terminate association with the specific person to avoid a conflict. Avoiding an interaction temporarily refers to not getting in touch with the specific family member(s) who are involved in a conflict temporarily. Appealing to third party refers to a person not engaging directly but asking a third party such as a grandmother or a priest to intervene. Lastly, keeping the status quo is to choose to not to engage in a specific conflict while maintaining the current situation, even though a person may not be happy about the situation.

Motivations for Avoidance

To answer the second research question, we report the frequency of two concerns (i.e., concern for self and concern for the other) in the conflict situation at work and with family, respectively. The mean score of self-concern ($M = 3.0$, $SD = .71$) was higher than that of other-concern ($M = 2.3$, $SD = .94$) in the workplace. A similar pattern was observed in the family context, with self-concern ($M = 3.1$, $SD .86$) and other-concern ($M = 2.7$, $SD = 1.0$). The variance was highest in the other concern in family, and smallest in the self-concern at work (see Table 1).

Motivations for avoidance in the workplace. Most participants reported that avoidance was selected because of their high self-concern ($n = 86$; 67.2%). About one-fifth of participants reported having both self and other concerns ($n = 24$; 18.8%), and one-tenth of participants reported high other concerns ($n = 12$; 9.4%). Only less than one-tenth of participants ($n = 6$; 4.7%) reported neither concern for self nor the other.

Motivations for avoidance with family. Many participants ($n = 59$; 57.8%) reported that the choice was from their high self-concern. About one-fifth of participants reported having both self and other concerns ($n = 22$; 21.6%), and one-tenth of participants reported high other concerns ($n = 14$; 13.7%). Only less than one-tenth

Table 1. Descriptive Statistics of Two Concerns at Work and in Family

	Workplace		Family	
	Self-Concern	Other-Concern	Self-Concern	Other-Concern
N	127	129	103	105
Mean	3.06	2.30	3.10	2.71
Median	3.20	2.25	3.20	2.75
Std. Deviation	.706	.947	.858	1.01
Variance	.49	.89	.73	1.02
Skewness	-.80	.12	-.69	-.31

of participants ($n = 7$; 6.9%) reported having motivations for conflict avoidance that did not include concerns for self or the other.

Two Motives and Avoidance Tactics

A chi-square test was conducted to examine if the two types of motives differentiate the avoidance strategy choices in the workplace. The result was not significant in the workplace context (χ^2 (12, 124) = 7.30, p = .837). Likewise, another chi-square test was run to examine if the two types of motives differentiate to use the avoidance strategy in conflict avoidance with family. The results also indicated no significant difference between the type of motives and the avoidance strategy in the family context (χ^2 (12, 102) = 18.36, p = .105). The association between two types of motives (self and other concerns) with avoidance strategies can be seen in two figures (See Figure 1 and 2).

Impact of Avoidance on Relationships

Research question three asked what the participants report as the impact of conflict avoidance at work and in family. Participants in the current study reported conflict avoidance narratives at work and in family. They were asked how they perceive the impact of avoiding conflict on their work relationship and interpersonal relationship in family.

Impact on relationships at work. Participants were asked if their relationship with the person involved in the conflict has changed in terms of its closeness and contact. Roughly one-third of participants reported that the relationship had ended with no further contact ($n = 41$; 27.3%). The remaining individuals reported having moderately negative impacts, including "more distant" relationships ($n = 23$; 15.3%) and "limited contacts" ($n = 17$; 11.3%) after the conflict avoidance. This indicates that participants' choice of conflict avoidance resulted in negative relational consequences—either no

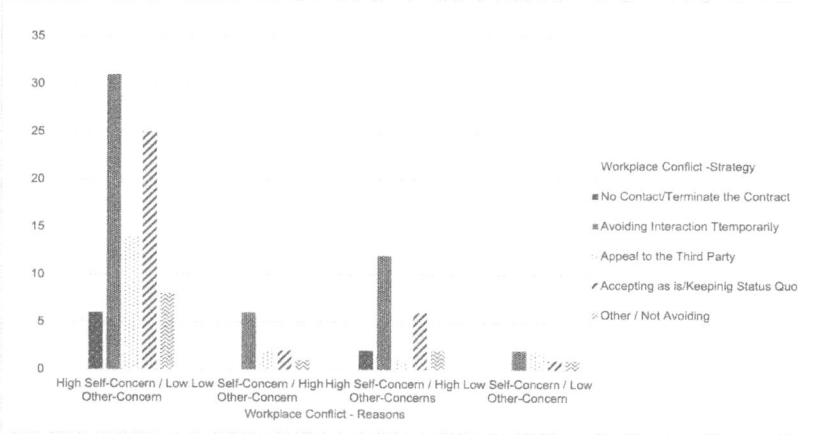

Fig 1. Bar graph of workplace conflict avoidance strategies and two concerns

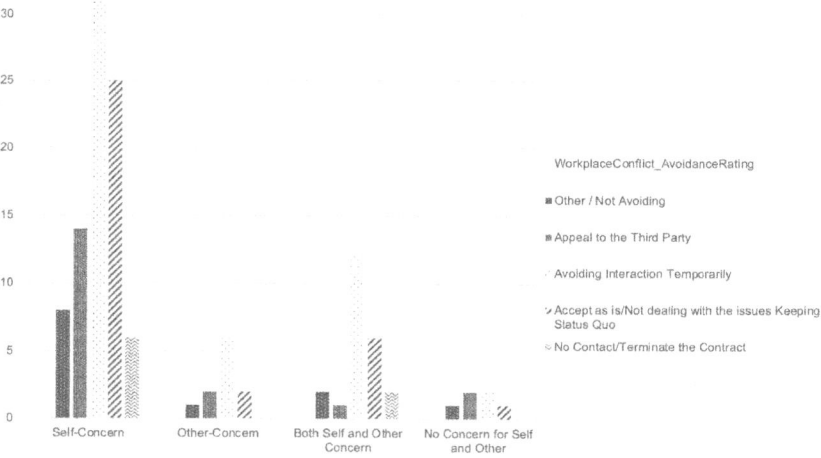

Fig 2. Bar graph of family conflict avoidance strategies and two concerns

further contact, limited contact, or more distant contact for the majority of the time ($n = 81$; 53.9%). On the other hand, the other half of the individuals who avoided the conflict reported either a positive impact stating "relationship has increased closeness" ($n = 7$; 4.7%) or a neutral impact, stating that "the relationship has remained the same" ($n = 38$; 25.3%).

Impact on relationships in family. When asked about avoidance's impact on relationships in the family, the majority of the participants reported a neutral or positive impact. Participants stated that the relationship has "remained the same" ($n = 51$;

34%) or "increased closeness" ($n = 26$; 17.3%) after they avoided a conflict. Only a few reported that the relationship has "ended with no further contact" ($n = 2$; 3.3%) or that the relationship ended with "limited contacts" ($n = 2$; 1.3%), while others reported that the "relationship got more distant" ($n = 21$; 14%). A majority of participants reported that conflict avoidance in family contexts resulted in either neutral or positive relationship outcomes ($n = 77$; 51.3%).

Discussion

The current study examined the participants' narratives of conflict avoidance episodes in the workplace and with family. The Dual Concern Model (e.g., De Dreu et al., 2000) implies that avoidance is an undesirable strategy, as explained with low concern for self and the other. This perception is partly due to the strong emphasis on engagement and constructive management of conflict, as many people perceive conflict avoidance as an ineffective strategy (e.g., Gross & Guerrero, 2000). Although we may perceive avoidance as undesirable, the majority of participants (91% at work and 79% in family) in the current study reported using conflict avoidance.

At work, individuals reported avoiding conflict on topics such as task allocation, rules/ethics, opinions/reviews, work processes, and work relationships. Participants reported avoiding conflict with their coworkers, supervisors, subordinates, and multiple parties at a time. In family, individuals reported avoiding conflict on topics such as daily life issues, work/career/education choices, personality, social relations, money/finance issues, and attitudes/opinions. Participants avoided conflict with parents, siblings, children, other extended family members, and multiple parties at a time.

Participants reported using a variety of avoidance strategies ranging from terminating the contact/relationship, temporarily avoiding interaction, pretending the issues do not exist (accepting the status quo), or appealing to a third party. This indicates that many people use conflict avoidance as a strategy of their choice both in the workplace and with family. Our results were consistent with previous studies that reported strategic use of avoidance in dealing with conflicts (e.g., Cai & Fink, 2002; Kim & Leung, 2000; Sun & Slepian, 2020).

Regarding the association between avoidance tactics and self and other concerns, there were no significant results in the current study. Although it was nonsignificant, many of the avoidance strategies co-occur with both high level of self-concern and other-concern. This indicates that the low concern for self and the other is not necessarily the needed condition for the avoidance tactic. Even though the significance results are not reported, the presence of self and other concerns can be motivations for the choice of conflict avoidance.

Additionally, our results showed the complexity of avoidance tactics. For instance, some participants reported appealing to a third party as one of their avoidance strategies. Appealing to a third party can be considered as an avoidance tactic because this person avoided facing another party directly. It can be said, however, that a certain level of conflict engagement still exists, depending on the level of involvement provided by the third party. Likewise, some participants reported that they would avoid the other individual temporarily. If individuals later confront each other, this can be considered an engagement after taking a break. Individuals may be temporarily avoiding the other person in conflict, although this can be considered as a case of conflict engagement over time.

Notably, participants reported a diverse range of impacts of avoidance in relationships. The impact of avoidance in family contexts resulted in rather positive and neutral relational outcomes, while at work the majority of people reported that the impact of conflict avoidance at work is met with rather negative relational outcomes such as terminating the relationship, limiting contact, or distancing. The participants intentionally select avoiding strategies when relationships are valued or permanent such as with family members. The avoidance strategy may be conveniently used in family contexts where the relationship is more permanent and is expected to survive conflict negotiation, rather than in the workplace where relationships can be transitory. This result may give us insights as to when an avoidance strategy can be effective or meaningful. As previous studies have reported, avoidance tactics can result in focusing on other important issues (e.g., Thornton & Flechter, 2024).

Limitations/Suggestions for Future Studies

There are several limitations to the current study. The current data are from a small number of college students in the southern regions of the United States. In addition, we solicited conflict avoidance experiences in only two contexts, workplace and family, but did not consider other contexts of interpersonal conflict such as personal friends and neighbors. The participants of the study were college students, and they may have had limited work experience to report in this study. Since we are providing quantitative analyses of avoidance narratives, we failed to provide in-depth interpretations of each conflict avoidance narrative. For instance, in the current study, we did not consider the intensity levels of avoidance in this study, because our purpose was to examine the types of avoiding behaviors in their conflict avoidance narratives. However, we have found that some avoiding behaviors are stronger than others. For instance, a relationship termination can be viewed as a higher level of avoidance than avoiding interaction temporarily, avoiding specific topics, or pretending the issue does not exist by not taking any actions. Consideration of avoidance tactics in terms of their intensity may contribute to a deeper understanding of avoidance strategies. Additionally, the current study failed to account for the participants' shift with their strategies. A longitudinal study examining the continuum of engagement and avoidance on a timeline may provide a better understanding. Additionally, we believe that further exploration of avoidance types and their intensity might be helpful in advancing this important research area.

Conclusion

The current study examined the narrative analyses of participants' experiences of conflict avoidance in family and at work. Their responses were coded in terms of topic, interactants, avoidance behaviors, motivations for avoidance, and its impact on relationships. This study provides a snapshot of people's avoidance behaviors at work. Additionally, participants report how avoiding conflict in the family is associated more so with positive or neutral relational outcomes, while avoiding conflict at work is met with negative relational outcomes. Consistent with the previous studies, conflict avoidance was not associated with low concern for self and the other, as the Dual Concern Model posits, but rather with high concern for self. These results indicate that avoidance is not the mere absence of concern for self and the other, but it can be considered a strategic approach to managing conflict. The further analysis on conflict avoidance may be meaningful for understanding constructive ways of dealing with conflict in the family and at work.

References

Asma, M. (2024). Age and gender differences in conflict resolution styles among adults. *Asian Journal of Integrated Social and Behavioral Sciences, 1*(1), 31–36.

Blake, R. R., & Mouton, J. S. (1964). *The managerial grid.* Gulf.

Cai, D. A., & Fink, E. L. (2002). Conflict style differences between individualists and collectivists. *Communication Monographs, 69,* 67–87. https://doi.org/10.1080=03637750216536

Caughlin, J. P., & Afifi, T. D. (2004). When is topic avoidance unsatisfying? Examining moderators of the association between avoidance and dissatisfaction. *Human Communication Research, 30,* 479–513. https://doi.org/10.1093/hcr/30.4.479

Caughlin, J. P., & Golish, T. D. (2002). An analysis of the association between topic avoidance and dissatisfaction: Comparing perceptual and interpersonal explanations. *Communication Monographs, 69,* 275–295. https://doi.org/10.1080/03637750216546

Caughlin, J. P., Hardesty, J. L., & Middleton, A.V. (2012). Conflict avoidance in families. In P. Noller & G.C. Karantzas (Eds.), *The Wiley-Blackwell handbook of couples and family relationships.* https://doi.org/10.1002/9781444354119.ch8

Cupach, W. R., Canary, D. J., & Spitzberg, B. H. (2009). *Competence in interpersonal conflict.* Waveland Press.

Davis, M. H., Duggan, J., Gumprecht, M., Loll, O., & Poulo, B. (2023). Testing the assumptions underlying the Dual Concerns Model: Need for dominance, narcissism, and emotion regulation also play a role. *Negotiation & Conflict Management Research, 16*(3), 230–246. https://doi.org/10.34891/xh7x-zf94

De Dreu, C.K.W., Weingart, L. R., & Kwon, S. (2000). Influence of social motives on integrative negotiation: A meta-analytic review and test of two theories. *Journal of Personality and Social Psychology, 78*(5), 889–905. https://doi.org/10.1037/0022-3514.78.5.889

Hample, D., & Dallinger, J. M. (1995). A Lewinian perspective on taking conflict personally: Revision, refinement, and validation of the instrument. *Communication Quarterly, 43*, 297–319. https://doi.org/10.1080/01463379509369978

Hample, D., & Richards, A. S. (2019). Personalizing conflict in different interpersonal relationship types. *Western Journal of Communication, 83*(2), 190–209. ttps://doi.org/10.1080/10570314.2018.1442017

Kim, M. S., & Leung, T. (2000). A multicultural view of conflict management styles: Review and critical synthesis. *Communication Yearbook, 23*, 227–269.

Kilmann, R. H., & Thomas, K. W. (1977). Developing a forced-choice measure of conflict-handling behavior: The "MODE" instrument. *Educational and Psychological Measurement, 37*, 309–325. https://doi.org/10.1177/001316447703700

Lau, Y. K. (2007). Parent-child relationships, parental relationships and children's self-esteem in post-divorce families in Hong Kong. *Marriage & Family Review, 42*(4), 87–103. https://doi.org/10.1300/J002v42n04_05

Leung, K. (1988). Some determinants of conflict avoidance. *Journal of Cross-Cultural Psychology, 19*(1), 125–136. https://doi.org/10.1177/0022002188019001009

Lussier, R. N. (2010). *Human relations in organizations: Applications and skill building.* McGraw Hill.

Oetzel, J., Ting-Toomey, S., Masumoto, T., Yokochi, Y., Xiaohui, P., Takai, J., & Wilcox, R. (2001). Face and facework in conflict: A cross-cultural comparison of China, Germany, Japan, and the United States. *Communication Monographs, 68*(3), 235–258. https://doi.org/10.1080/03637750128061

Oetzel, J. G., Ting-Toomey, S., Yokochi, Y., Masumoto, T., & Takai, J. (2000). A typology of facework behaviors in conflicts with best friends and relative strangers. *Communication Quarterly, 48*(4), 397–419. https://doi.org/10.1080/01463370009385606

Ohbuchi, K., & Atsumi, E. (2010). Avoidance brings Japanese employees what they care about in conflict management: Its functionality and "good member" image. *Negotiation & Conflict Management Research, 3*(2), 117–129. https://doi.org/10.1111/j.1750-4716.2010.00052.x

Pruitt, D. G., & Carnevale, P. J. (1993). *Negotiation in social conflict.* Brooks/Cole.

Pruitt, D. G., & Rubin, J. Z. (1986). *Social conflict: Escalation, stalemate, and settlement.* Random House.

Rahim, M. A. (1983). A measure of styles of handling interpersonal conflict. *Academy of Management Journal, 26*, 368–376. https://doi.org/10.2307/255985

Rhoades, J. A., & Carnevale, P. J. (1999). The behavioral context of strategic choice in negotiation: a test of the dual concern model 1. *Journal of Applied Social Psychology, 29*(9), 1777–1802. https://doi.org/10.1111/j.1559-1816.1999.tb00152.x

Roloff, M. E., & Ifert, D. E. (2000). Conflict management through avoidance: Withholding complaints, suppressing arguments, and declaring topic taboo. In S. Petronio (Ed.), *Balancing the secrets of private disclosures* (pp. 151–179). Lawrence Erlbaum.

Roloff, M. E., & Wright, C. N. (2015). Conflict avoidance: A functional analysis. In *Uncertainty, information management, and disclosure decisions* (pp. 320–340). Routledge.

Ruble, T. L., & Thomas, K. W. (1976). Support for a two-dimensional model of conflict behavior. *Organizational Behavior and Human Performance, 16*(1), 143–155. https://doi.org/10.1016/0030-5073(76)90010-6

Saldaña, J. (2021). *The coding manual for qualitative researchers*. Sage.

Schrodt, P. (2005). Family communication schemata and the circumplex model of family functioning. *Western Journal of Communication, 69*(4), 359–376. https://doi.org/10.1080/10570310500305539

Sillars, A. L., Coletti, S. F., Parry, D., & Rogers, M. A. (1982). Coding verbal conflict tactics: Nonverbal and perceptual correlates of avoidance-distributive-integrative strategies. *Human Communication Research, 9*, 83–95. https://doi.org/10.1111/j.1468-2958.1982.tb00685.x

Singelis, T. M., Triandis, H. D., Bhawuk, D. P., & Gelfand, M. J. (1995). Horizontal and vertical dimensions of individualism and collectivism: A theoretical and measurement refinement. *Cross-Cultural Research, 29*(3), 240–275. https://doi.org/10.1177/106939719502900302

Small, M. L., Brant, K., & Fekete, M. (2024). The avoidance of strong ties. *American Sociological Review, 89*(4), 615–649. https://doi.org/10.1177/00031224241263602

Sorenson, R. L., Morse, E. A., & Savage, G. T. (1999). A test of the motivations underlying choice of conflict strategies in the dual-concern model. *International Journal of Conflict Management, 10*(1), 25–44. https://doi.org/10.1108/eb022817

Sun, K. Q., & Slepian, M. L. (2020). The conversations we seek to avoid. *Organizational Behavior and Human Decision Processes, 160*, 87–105. https://doi.org/10.1016/j.obhdp.2020.03.002.

Thomas, K. W. (1976). Conflict and conflict management. In M. Donnette (Ed.), *Handbook of industrial and organizational psychology* (pp. 889–936). Rand McNally.

Thornton, K.R.V., & Fletcher, S. (2024). Two workplace behaviors to effectively navigate conflict in today's workplace. *Negotiation and Conflict Management Research, 17*(3), 208–228. https://doi.org/10.34891/70t1-s146

Ting-Toomey, S. (1988) Intercultural conflicts: A face-negotiation theory, in Y.Y. Kim & W. Gudykunst (Eds.), *Theories in intercultural communication* (pp. 213–235). Sage.

Tjosvold, D., & Sun, H. (2002). Understanding conflict avoiding: Relationship, motivation, actions, and consequences. *International Journal of Conflict Management, 13*(2), 142–164. https://doi.org/10.1108/eb022872

Wang, Q., Fink, E. L., & Cai, D. A. (2012). The effect of conflict goals on avoidance strategies: What does not communicating communicate? *Human Communication Research, 38*(2), 222–252. https://doi.org/10.1111/j.1468-2958.2011.01421.x

Yang, I., & Li, M. (2017). Can absent leadership be positive in team conflicts?: An examination of leaders' avoidance behavior in China. *International Journal of Conflict Management, 28*(2), 146–165. http://dx.doi.org.wku.idm.oclc.org/10.1108/IJCMA-12-2015-0083

Zhang, Z-X., & Wei, X. (2007). Superficial harmony and conflict avoidance resulting from negative anticipation in the workplace. *Management and Organization Review, 13*(4), 795–820. https://doi.org/10.1017/mor.2017.48

CHAPTER FIFTEEN | ANITA BUCZEK-ZAWIŁA, KRZYSZTOF IDCZAK,
EMILIA JANUŚ, ERYK KOWALCZYK,
AND WIKTORIA KOZIEŁ

GIFference Conflict?
The Use of GIFs Among Generations

Abstract

GIFs (short for Graphics Interchange Format) are image animated-format files, which are typically used to express humor or other emotions, mainly by referencing memes or memorable tropes from TV shows and movies. The format is currently deemed passé and apparently doomed to vanish from the public domain and popular use. This seems to permeate the web, where it is also emphasized that there appears to be a generational divide reflecting polarized attitude to using animated GIFs, with the youngest users claiming that GIFs are dated, "cringe," and good only for baby boomers and millennials. However, an examination of numerous websites and personal exchanges of TMC participants seems to call that claim into question. The present paper aims to address conflicting views on using GIFs by members of various generations, as well as to explore the communicative potential they offer in specific, emotionally-charged exchanges. The evidence was collected via two quantitative instruments (two online surveys, with 66 and 22 participants respectively), and one qualitative instrument (a personal interview with a single interviewee). The findings indicate that the use of GIFs has become largely generationalized; nonetheless, they are still used communicatively by the general public. One of the contexts where GIFs are still functional is when they are used as a response in a (TMC) argument or conflict situation, where such files substitute for an actual verbal reaction (Quantitative Instrument 2). Respondents in Online Survey 1, i.e., members of the youngest generational cohort, use the formula slightly less frequently, but they do not hold any substantial negative feelings toward GIFs. For baby boomers, they provide a means to develop and sustain interpersonal relations. Therefore, the data gathered appear to suggest that even though this specific format has possibly lost some of its former currency, the probability of GIFs causing (intergenerational) misunderstandings and conflict is rather remote.

Keywords: GIFs, TMC communication, intergenerational conflict, emotional response

"A GIF—which is short for Graphics Interchange Format—is an image file. GIFs, unlike other image formats, are frequently animated" (Heinzman, 2019, para.1). Characteristically, they are often used to express humor or a plethora of emotions, mainly through referencing memes or memorable tropes from TV shows and movies. For several years now, the format appears to have been deemed not modern and is apparently doomed to disappear from public use. This view is also extensively propagated on the web, not least so by big companies crucially invested in the business (e.g., Giphy). In a September 16, 2022, article published by the *The Guardian*, "'Gifs are cringe': How Giphy's multimillion-dollar business fell out of fashion," for example, Alex Hern maintains that there appears to be a generational demarcation line in terms of who is still in favor of using animated GIFs, with the youngest users claiming GIFs are dated, cringe, and good only for baby boomers and millennials.

Yet, there is evidence to challenge this claim. GIFs are used still on a variety of websites of different provenance and themes, as well as in personal exchanges of technology-mediated communication (TMC) participants. While it may be true that the use of GIFs has become largely generationalized, they are still used communicatively in a number of contexts, for example, as a response in an (TMC) argument or conflict situation, where they substitute for an actual verbal reaction.

It is such issues that the present paper aims to address, namely, the conflicting views on using GIFs by members of various generations, as well as exploring the clear potential to keep them functional in specific, emotionally-charged communicative exchanges. Evidence collected through two surveys and a semi-structured interview appears to suggest that this specific format is possibly slightly less popular than previously, nonetheless the concerns for GIFs causing (intergenerational) misunderstandings and conflict are unfounded. This is the thread we would like to explore to be able to demonstrate that GIFs may not be as dead as it has been suggested.

The paper is structured in the following manner: after an introduction to the format known as a GIF and a discussion of GIF types and characteristic uses, the study follows. It represents a mixed quantitative-qualitative methodology design, with three distinct instruments used to collect the data. These comprise: an online survey into GIFs use among the younger population cohort (Quantitative Instrument 1), a case study of GIF use among baby boomers, based on a semi-structured interview with one subject (Qualitative Instrument 1), and a mini online survey among Gen X female TMC participants (Quantitative Instrument 2). The research questions can be worded as follows:

RQ1: Is there a distinct unwillingness to use the GIF format in TMC contexts in the group of young people?
RQ2: If so, for what reasons?

RQ2: Is there still a potential for GIFs to be used by members of generations other than Gen Z?

RQ4: If so, in what manners and for what reasons?

The analysis and discussion of the results conclude the paper.

GIFs in Online Communication

Graphics Interchange Formats (GIFs) represent a kind of format that utilizes animated images or soundless videos which are looped. These looped animations of embodied actions are often derived from movies, television, and other forms of multimedia such as YouTube. The feature was created in 1987 by CompuServe engineer Steve Wilhite and promptly became an ideal way of adding visual content and movement to a website at a time of the early, less advanced web (Miltner & Highfield, 2017).

In the modern age, they are an ever-present form of self-expression that is most often used as, but not limited to, a means of communication. "GIFs are now ubiquitous in contemporary Internet-based communicative environments, including text messaging, email, social media, dating apps, and workplace management software (Miltner & Highfield, 2017, p. 4). GIFs are meant to help with expression of various emotional states, actions, and reactions in a way that engages the viewer (Liz R., 2023, para. 2–5) and are seen as a suitable resource to generate emotionality precisely because they can represent a plethora of feelings (Rúa-Hidalgo et al., 2021). Their popularity can be attributed to their ability to engage the viewer with captivating visuals and ability to convey ideas and emotions in an effective manner (Liz R., 2023, para. 6–7). Therefore, one of the most common communicative affordances of GIFs is the performance of affect. Tolins and Samermit (2016, p. 76) claim that "the use of GIFs presents the reproduced action as the texter's current embodied action, which would otherwise be prohibited by the written format". In this sense, GIFs help define how people act on everyday experiences, and how these affective performances are further shaped and augmented. People use GIFs as embodied enactments to display their affective stances to prior text as well as depict a potential action that emphasizes that stance (Tolins & Samermit, 2016). In this way, in technology-mediated communication the format may function as surrogate for verbal as well as nonverbal signals, e.g., phonic gestures, smiling, nodding, looking confused, normally found in face-to-face conversations. Tolins and Samermit (2016, p. 88) point out that GIFs generally originate from source material on the internet or in visual media, arising from internet culture, and thus they interact across mediums, yet they are considered most successful in their discursive appeal when the original source is ignored in the light of widespread distribution.

Therefore, in communication GIFs serve a similar role as memes and emojis—they are used as an enhancement for communication by underlining emotions contained in a given conversation, frequently adding the element of humor. As GIFs use multiple semiotic utterances (language, image, video), they, similarly to memes, are intertextual and interdiscursive, borrowing from other texts and references while displaying a new message, and implicitly combining various language conventions (discourses, styles, and genres) in order to convey a new message in creative ways (Wagener, 2020).

> GIFs are used by individuals in order to not only express a view of the world drawing on pop culture references (like memes) but also appear in contexts where reenactments of emotions and mental states need to be communicated within interactions. (Wagener, 2020, p. 839)

They are a perfect tool for expressing a lot of information with the least effort, and in addition, they do it in an engaging manner, and are "a good tool for sensory appeal through the use of movement, color and repetition" (Rúa-Hidalgo et al., 2021).

As a nonverbal form of communication, GIFs may occasionally introduce ambiguity, thus causing the viewer to misinterpret the intention of the sender. As Jiang et al. (2018, p. 5) warn "while GIFs' capacity for multiple meanings and cultural references make them an appealing media to use, these same characteristics also introduce potential for miscommunication", so that grounding in participants' communication may be both positively and negatively impacted by the particular GIFs used. Just like other forms of TMC, they convey significantly less contextual cues, which makes it harder for a viewer to fully interpret the message. However, the scarcity of contextual cues does not pose a big problem in cases of prolonged use of such a form of communication. Over time using and interpreting GIFs becomes easier, as the users usually build a relationship and can better understand what cues they should look for, possibly making this form of TMC a more efficient way of communicating than even face-to-face communication (Jiang et al., 2018, pp. 2-3).

Two main types of GIFs can be distinguished (Tolins & Sammermit, 2016; Church et al., 2023): the idea-expressing GIF and the reaction GIF. The former is used to report news, to convey more elaborate speeches or to simply present data. The latter category is a bit more complex, having three distinct sub-varieties: actual, hypothetical, and argumentative.

> An *actual reaction* GIF demonstrates a feeling that the user is experiencing in the moment as a response to something said. [...] The *hypothetical reaction* GIF can be used in situations where the user wishes to portray an emotion that they would feel in a hypothetical situation, known on Tumblr as MRW(My Reaction When) and HIFW (How I Feel When) situations [...]. The least-recognized reaction GIF

within the literature is the *argumentative reaction* GIF, which is essentially used as a means of arguing. (Church et al., 2023, p. 3)

A slightly different distinction is found at the Superpixel website (SuperpixelSG, 2022) as well as in Yao (2018). They recognize, maybe as the most well-known genre, the Reaction GIFs, which primary function is to express reactions and feelings. They tend to focus on portraying a single emotion to encapsulate the state of mind of the person that sends it in order to avoid using a plethora of words to do the same thing (Yao, 2018, para. 12). Film and television are the sectors most responsible for the content shown in most reaction GIFs. Outside of Hollywood, such GIFs are used in online marketing by replacing textual responses with animations. Reaction GIFs are also often used to add weight and substance to a user's online comment. Additionally, they are meant to focus on the visuals instead of their potential intricacies of meaning. They are supposed to provide the viewer with a quick reaction of connecting the visuals to the attitude of the sender, and although it often proves to be efficient, it can also lead to misunderstandings (Sasamoto, 2023, p. 408).

The Cinemagraph GIF, which is essentially a hybrid of photography and animation, has a quiet, peaceful quality since they only include one or two elements, usually slight areas of motion, such as distant waterfalls or city streets. Because of its professional appearance and peaceful tone, travel and fashion industries use cinemagraph GIF.

In contrast, the Perfect-loop GIF is more lively, being a recording of an event that has been smoothly and seamlessly looped to provide users with satisfying visuals, which can be used in almost any type of digital content, making it more dynamic (Jitter, 2022). They are distinct from the fourth subcategory, the Technical GIF, the job of which is to transform dull data into interesting information. This type of GIF is particularly convenient for marketers who wish to integrate data, diagrams, or graphs into product descriptions (SuperpixelSG, 2022).

The way that a GIF is made can also differ, with three main types being the most prevalent—video-based GIFs, animation-based GIFs and GIF stickers. Video based GIFs are created out of short clips of popular films, TV series or any other kind of video. Animation-based GIFs are made with the use of illustrations that are animated with the use of additional software. GIF stickers are similar to animation-based GIFs, as they are made out of animated illustrations, with the main difference being that they possess transparent backgrounds (Giflytics, n.d.).

The ability to easily engage viewers made GIFs a perfect tool for marketing. Younger internet users are drawn to this kind of promotion as they can quickly comprehend the idea behind a given product without reading its description. In marketing, GIFs are cheaper than more elaborate forms of promotion like videos, they load quicker, and their playful nature helps humanize the brand that decides to use them (Liz R.,

2023, para. 12). This use testifies to the versatility of the format and underscores functions unrelated to textual communication.

The Study

The study reported on in this paper is based on three research instruments: an online survey among Gen Z (Quantitative Instrument 1), aiming to identify certain observable regularities pertaining to GIF use in this age group; a semi-structured interview with a member of the baby boomer generation, who is an avid enthusiast of using a very specific type of the format (Qualitative Instrument 1), and an online mini-survey probing the use of reaction/argumentative GIFs among female Gen Xers (Quantitative Instrument 2). The research was conducted independently for each instrument, and the results analysis is a synthesis of the outcomes that transpired. The results are discussed in the following subsections.

Do Young People Still Use GIFs in TMC: Quantitative Instrument 1

The use of GIFs in technology-mediated communication (TMC) has become a significant aspect of digital interactions. However, questions remain about the extent to which young people incorporate GIFs into their communication practices, the reasons behind their use or avoidance, and their general perception of this medium. To address these inquiries, as defined in RQ1 and RQ2, a survey was conducted among 66 participants, initially from undefined diverse age groups, to examine their habits and opinions regarding GIF usage in TMC.

The questionnaire[1] consisted of 11 questions: 5 single-choice closed questions, 5 multiple-choice questions, and 1 open-ended question. Several of the multiple-choice questions included an "Other" option, making them semi-open. The survey was distributed online via Google Forms and promoted among friends and acquaintances, with a "snowball effect" encouraged for further participation. It was open from September 11–September 13, 2024. Let us begin by presenting the basic facts about our respondents.

The survey was responded to by 66 participants. Among the four provided age groups, the majority of respondents (97%—64 people) belonged to the younger digital generation, consisting of individuals under 26 years old. The remaining participants (3%—2 people) were between 44 and 60 years old. No respondents fell within the 27–43 or above 60 age groups. It therefore transpires that the largest group of 64 respondents fall into the desired age cohort, commonly labeled as Gen Z (Shorey et

---

1. The questionnaire is located in Appendix A at the end of the text.

al., 2021). This is, as of now, the second youngest of the age groups, born between 1997 and 2012 (Slepian et al., 2024).

Among the 66 individuals who participated in the survey, a total of 40 (60.6%) respondents were female, making up the majority of the sample. Approximately 30% of the participants (22 people) were male, whereas four respondents (6.1%) selected the third option, "other," indicating a diverse range of gender identities within the sample.

The following two questions investigated the respondents' participation in TMC, and the potential use of GIFs while engaged in online communication. Nearly all respondents—63 out of 66—confirmed their participation in TMC, which highlights its widespread usage among those surveyed and suggesting that digital communication tools are an integral part of their daily interactions. Slepian et al. (2024) observe that for Gen Z the digitally dominant world is the primary point of reference, with technology, smartphones, and the internet constantly on hand. Dimock (2019) adds that these youngsters have been growing up in an "always on" technological environment, and this is why TMC is a regular fixture for them.

What is of more relevance for the present paper is that a substantial proportion of respondents (80.3%—53 people) reported actively incorporating GIFs into their digital conversations. However, 13 participants (19.7%) indicated that they do not use GIFs at all.

Among those who actively use GIFs, the primary recipients are friends (77.3%—51 people), romantic partners (37.9%—25 people), and family members (43.9%—29 people). Only a few participants (12.1%—8 people) admitted to using GIFs when communicating with strangers. This was a multiple-choice question, allowing respondents to select more than one category of recipients, which is why the total percentage exceeds 100%. The answers reflect the diverse contexts in which GIFs are shared.

In the previous question, 13 respondents stated that they do not use GIFs, while only 12 made the same declaration in this question. This discrepancy suggests that one respondent may have changed their answer after seeing the available options, possibly due to a lack of full understanding of the previous question, which did not include a practical example.

Additionally, a few respondents introduced new response options in the survey, namely: "posts" (1.5%—1 person), "only on Discord to a friend" (1.5%—1 person), and "coworkers" (1.5%—1 person).

The study revealed different motivations for using GIFs in TMC. In another multiple-choice question, participants could select more than one reason from the ones provided or could offer their own insights. According to the two most common responses, 48 people (72.7%) use GIFs to make conversations more fun, while 42 people (63.6%) use GIFs as a medium to express their authentic reactions. The third group consists of 9 respondents (13.6%) who claim to use GIFs "to break the long chain of

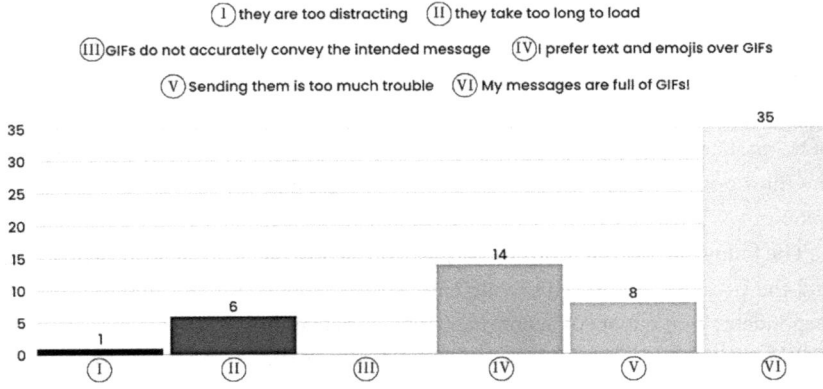

Fig 1. "If you do not use GIFs, why?"

written messages," suggesting that GIFs have a tension-reducing value in TMC. Similarly to previous questions, new answer options were added to highlight the humorous value of the medium, with 3% (2 people) selecting this option. The remaining 12 participants (18.2%) still claim not to use GIFs in their TMC communications.

The next question was designed to establish the reasons against using GIFs. The answers revealed several of them, including among those who actually use them, even if only occasionally. Due to the multiple-choice format, which leads to overlapping answers, it is impossible to derive an exact percentage for the general result. Figure 1 below shows the breakout of provided options.

The chart depicts only the answers based on the options originally provided in the questionnaire, while the table below lists the additional insights provided by the respondents, categorized into several sub-motives.

Table 1 includes the contributions submitted in the rubric "other", categorized for common themes, developed inductively through data-driven coding (Kuckartz, 2019, p. 184), as the focus of the paper is on interpreting and understanding patterns and trends, and not just on quantifying the occurrence of certain words (Oberoi, 2025).

Apart from people who use GIFs, either often or rarely (as seen in responses such as "My messages are full of GIFs" and "I use GIFs sometimes," representing 16.5% or 11 people), many participants shared reasons for not using them. These include: "they are too distracting" (1.5%, 1 person), "they take too long to load" (9.1%, 6 people), "I prefer text and emojis over GIFs" (21.2%, 14 people), and "sending them is too much trouble" (12.1%, 8 people).

The question about the favorite type of GIFs was multiple choice, another one where respondents could mark several options among those provided. The survey responses reveal clear trends in GIF preferences. Meme GIFs, based on internet trends, turn out to be the most popular, preferred by 45 respondents (68.2%). Reaction GIFs, used to

Table 1. "Other" reasons for not using GIFs in TMC

acknowledging GIF infrequent use	simply acknowledging use	other problematic aspect
I sometimes use them (sparingly)	I use gifs sometimes	It's kinda embarrassing, that's why I only send it if it's a meme
I use them sparingly often as a punchline to a joke	I sometimes use GIFs, but not too often	My friends don't use gifs
I use GIFs, although quite rarely!	I do use them	I often forget about them and I always forget where to find gifs on messenger
	usually I use gifs	
	I use gifs	
	I use them	

express emotions like laughter or surprise, follow closely with 37 preferences (56.1%). Pop Culture GIFs, featuring scenes from movies or shows, were chosen by 29 respondents (43.9%). Less favored categories include Celebration GIFs (21.2%—14 people), Animated Text GIFs (13.6%—9 people), and Looping GIFs (12.1%—8 people). Inside Joke GIFs were the least popular, with only 1 response (1.5%) in this category.

The survey also explored whether participants frequently receive GIFs from others in their interactions. The findings indicate that the majority of respondents reported receiving GIFs (87.9%—58 people), with only 8 individuals (12.1%) stating that they did not.

The primary senders include friends (87.9%—58 people), partners (34.8%—23 people), and family members (42.4%—28 people), mirroring the groups identified as recipients. Seven of the respondents admitted to not receiving any GIFs (10.6%), and only six (9.1%) received GIFs from strangers. Additionally, two respondents introduced new response options in the survey, namely: "People from servers on *Discord*" (1.5%—1 person), and "coworkers" (1.5%—1 person).

To gain insight into the broader perception of GIFs, in the final question respondents were asked to describe their opinions using a single word in an open-ended question. Their answers were coded for common themes through pattern coding strategy (Miles et al., 2014).

The most popular response was "Fun" (22%, 11 people) and its variations, such as "Funi," "Funny," and "Funny pictures go brrrrr" (8%, 4 people). Other common descriptors that received more than one vote included: "Cool" (6%, 3 people), "Cringe" (4%, 2 people), "Slay" (4%, 2 people), and "Expressive" (4%, 2 people).

Table 2. Participants' responses coded for common sentiments and themes

Emphasizing the fun element	Emphasizing the communicative potential	Balanced opinions	Negative opinions
fun / funny	expressive	neutral	old fashioned
funi	creative	underutilized	sparse
funni picture go brrrrr	effort	underrated	overrated
cool	versatile	relatable	cringe (2) (+ but who cares)
amusing	useful	interesting	slay
entertaining		Me-core	
gay			
Hehe			

The colloquial character of the actual words used testifies to the authenticity of the responses in the sample.

There were two responses: "Bayle," and "Jiffs" which were ambiguous and challenging, and therefore impossible to categorize, though the second item can be speculated to be an instance of play on the ambiguous pronunciation: [gɪf] or [dʒɪf].

The findings obtained through conventional content analysis (Hsieh & Shannon, 2005) suggest that GIFs are widely used by younger individuals as a means of enhancing communication through humor and emotional expression. However, they are not universally embraced, as some users find them troublesome or prefer alternative forms of interaction.

Baby Boomers and GIFs: Qualitative Instrument 1

The use of GIFs by younger generations prompted the question of whether older generations also use them, and if so, why and how significant their usage is (RQ3 and RQ4, respectively). To answer these queries, in part, a qualitative content analysis (Hsieh & Shannon, 2005; Oberoi, 2025) of a case study was conducted, based on an interview with the representative of the baby boomer generation, namely people born between approximately 1945 and 1965 (Slepian et al., 2024; Allison, 2013). The interview was conducted in Polish and later translated into English. The interviewee was a 67-year-old Polish woman, who will be referred to as "Jane" for the rest of this article.[2]

---

2. The actual questions asked during the interview are listed in Appendix B, both in Polish, the language of the interview, and translated into English for easier reference.

After being asked for the definition of GIFs, Jane referred to them as "welcoming postcards." This immediately suggests that the members of the baby boomer generation are aware of the existence of GIFs and know how to use them, so that they can fall into the category of GIF enthusiasts, as defined by Church et al. (2023). However, this also indicates that the baby boomers do not view GIFs as an image format, but rather as a form of greeting or addressing their conversation partner. She continued by explaining that she does not comprehend what exactly GIFs are or how they are created but believes that their invention was a *splendid idea*[3] and that she was *glad* to receive them. She also expressed her *gratitude* for receiving them and that she "always tries to *reciprocate*" by sending a GIF back to her converser. Her answers straightforwardly represent the context in which GIFs are used by the baby boomer generation and that she mainly associates GIFs with positive feelings. This will be a continuing trend in the entirety of the interview.

Labeling GIFs as "welcoming postcards" by Jane can be explained by the types of GIFs she and her friends of the same age use.[4] One of her examples is a GIF that incorporates greetings—"Dzień Dobry" (Eng: Good Morning) and a short poem with good wishes, that translates to "I wish to offer you a flower of friendship, so that your world may be more beautiful. May a smile always shine in your life, bringing you joy and delight." Another one contains two wishes—"Smacznej Kawusi" (Eng: Enjoy Your Coffee) and "Miłego Dnia" (Eng: Have a Nice Day). It is easy to see why these types of GIFs can be used as conversation starters. Jane later reflected on the beginnings of her GIF-using experience:

> My friends started sending GIFs to me and I wanted to show them my *gratitude* by doing the same. The problem was, I did not know how. Luckily my grandson is kind of tech-savvy and showed me how to send GIFs like "enjoy your coffee." (Pl: smacznej kawusi)

This answer underlines the most fundamental motive behind sending a GIF by a baby boomer, this being reciprocity. After being asked if she knew how her friends learned how to use GIFs, she expressed uncertainty but theorized that they probably went through a similar experience, that is being helped by a younger member of their family. Jane was later asked to describe her process of sending a GIF:

> I enter *greetings* like 'have a nice day' and then put "gif" into Google on my phone and then find the one I think is nicely decorated. I download it and then through Messenger I send it to my friends or to my family's group chat. Sometimes I search

---

3. The italics in this section highlight the words or expressions Jane used in the interview to repeatedly communicate the primary motives for using GIFs.
4. The examples of baby boomer GIFs have been provided by the respondent herself, as those she actually used in online exchanges.

for a GIFs related to a specific day or time of day to show them I think about them right now.

The aforementioned GIFs not only feature various wishes, but they also include messages that relate to a specific day/season of the year—"Letnia Środa" (Eng: Summer Wednesday) or to a specific time of day—"Dobranoc" (Eng: Goodnight). Jane's desire to send a GIF that relates to the exact time the conversation is taking place additionally proves that for her generation GIFs are an important means of showing affection and fostering social connections.

After being asked from whom she receives these types of GIFs most often, she responded that she mainly receives them from her family and friends; however, she emphasized that the number of friends she received these types of messages from has significantly decreased throughout the years. Jane explained that the reason behind this occurrence was the lack of interest of her friends in sending a GIF back. "I will not *show affection* to someone who does not want it," she stated. This again proves the importance of reciprocity (or lack thereof) in relation to using GIFs by baby boomers, as they are also used as a tool for maintaining social relationships (Jiang et al., 2018).[5]

The interview concluded with Jane's final comments on the concept of GIFs. She again expressed her contentment related to the existence of GIFs and underlined the importance of them, as they are "a quick and easy way to *show someone they are not alone*." Jane's comments highlight that baby boomers mainly associate GIFs with positive emotions and use them as a way of greeting their conversation partners or showing affection to their close ones. They use GIFs designed to improve the mood of their addressee and those that relate to the time the conversation is taking place. Although baby boomers may not know the exact definition of a GIF, they still see it as an important communication tool, used for maintaining their social status and relationships, which are all important for them.

GIFs as a Response Tactic in TMC Conflict Among Gen X: Quantitative Instrument 2

To further investigate the matters defined in Research Questions 3 and 4, another small-scale survey was prepared and distributed.

---

5. Dr. S. Johnson (personal communication, February 18, 2025), another representative of the baby boomer generation, who as a native English speaker, originally from Texas, proofread the paper, stated that she also receives those types of GIFs from her friends and colleagues, but unlike Jane, she replies to those messages via text, not GIFs. This proves that the phenomenon of highly decorated GIFs being used as "welcoming postcards" is not limited to Poland and that replying to a message with another GIF is optional, as some prefer responding with a textual message. Still, reciprocity is taken care of.

Table 3. Quantitative instrument 2 – descriptive statistics

Number of respondents	22
Gender	female
Age	45 - 55
GIF users	18
Argumentative reaction GIF users	14

GIFs seem to be popular with a specific group of people who use them most frequently as a response tactic in an (TMC) argument or conflict situation. These are argumentative reaction GIFs (Church et al., 2023), which substitute for an actual verbal reaction. The research started with casual discussion on using the "Smacznej Kawusi" (*SK* henceforth) "welcoming postcard," discussed in the previous section, then was adapted into a mini-survey, consisting of four major questions[6], in several cases followed by personal communication offline to clarify or elaborate on the responses.

The sampling was not fully random, as the survey was distributed among small community of colleagues and friends, all females, who fell into the designated age cohort (over age 45) and were known to be avid users of online communicators. All in all, 22 people were recruited to respond to the questionnaire. In this group, 4 said they did not use GIFs at all when engaged in online exchanges. Among the reasons for non-use, the recurring ones involved: no need, never use anything except words (2) and emojis being sufficient (2).

The remaining respondents and GIF-users (N=18) would normally respond with a GIF to one sent to them (cf. the reciprocity underlined in the baby boomer study above), rather than initiate a communicative exchange with this format. A substantial majority (N=14) frequently send a specific type of argumentative reaction GIFs (Church et al., 2023), but exclusively in female-to female exchanges only, characteristically in dyadic conversations, and when TMC-conversing with friends, adult daughters, colleagues, and rarely—elderly parents.

While the elaborate, ornate, colorful GIFs of *SK* type are not appealing or downright over-the-top for them, others that can function as conversation ending measures are used willingly, if not entirely frequently. They require particular conversational contexts. Some discussions may turn out particularly difficult, with no "let's agree to disagree" attitude. In such contexts, rather than verbally expressing disagreement, or

---

6. The actual questions are listed in Appendix C: Quantitative Instrument 2.

stressing the interlocutor's lack of logic, animated GIFs appear useful. The use of the GIF may also mark the end of the conversation.

Although they were unwilling to share the actual conversations, they provided the GIFs used there. Most of these have image as well as words (*Seriously?; I've had enough; It doesn't make sense; Leave it; I give up; Whatever*) since those with animated images only have been deemed not straightforward or communicative enough.

The primary reason for the use, as intimated by the respondents, is the belief that it would be offensive to leave the conversation without a word or to use abusive words. When no more sensible and appealing arguments can be put forward, with unwillingness to offend or hurt, they resort to measures other than verbal only, with the view to preventing conflict escalation. On the other hand, in that manner, they are still able to express the disagreement, dissatisfaction, nonsense, etc. In these interactions animated GIFs display the user's negative uptake of a comment as well as/or their stance toward previously texted declarations or opinions. These may range from annoyance, indifference, lack of acceptance, opinion rejection to impatience. Due to such considerations, the respondents uniformly rejected the likelihood of dropping out of using GIFs in the above manner and situations.

Analysis and Discussion

GIFs allow for emotional expressions within contexts and exchanges that work dynamically in interactions and communication. They are used by individuals in order to not only express a view of the world but also appear in contexts where reenactments of emotions and mental states need to be communicated within interactions (Wagener, 2020). In the three investigated groups/cases, emotional responses were at the core of the motivation for individuals to engage in and maintain communication and social interaction. In that sense, GIFs act as surrogates or proxies for expressing emotion and affect. GIFs remain more appropriate in contexts where emotional and cognitive reactions need to be expressed in a condensed manner, which may be particularly useful in the field of digital communication and interactive exchanges to sustain them efficiently and make it somehow more entertaining (Gen Zs—RQ1) and suitable (others—RQ3 & 4).

In relation to Research Question 1, the answers provided in the survey imply that GIFs are used extensively by Gen Zers, and that they see their potential as well as problematic aspects. The insights coming from the "other" answers, as well as in the last open question testify to conscious and deliberate choices, ignoring the potential negativity and outdatedness. The expression that succinctly expresses the attitude that seems to prevail in this group is "cringe, but who cares." As Miltner and Highfield (2017) observed, the timing and placement of the GIF's meaning is influenced by the context in which it is placed, leaving open a possibility for varied meanings to emerge, allowing for different interpretations by different audiences. This must be an attractive and appealing aspect, especially when a GIF does not exactly match the situation, and the incongruity adds humor and fun (cf. Table 2 above) to the conversation. It can be speculated that this is the affordance that remains most appealing for the youngest cohort of respondents, also because they expect instant communication through various digital channels, with authentic, (nearly) real-life feedback (Harris, 2023). With reference to Research Question 1, it can be assumed that there does not seem to be any substantial unwillingness to cease incorporating GIFs into communicative exchanges among the younger TMC users. As a result, Research Question 2 simply does not apply.

Research Question 3 aimed to uncover the potential appeal of GIFs in groups other than the younger generation. Such appeal and attractiveness were revealed in the case study of Jane, a baby boomer, as well as in the small-scale survey pertaining to argumentative GIFs use in interpersonal conflict contexts by representatives of Generation X.

Finally, Research Question 4 aimed to probe into the reasons for which GIFs are used by non-Gen Zers, and the manners through which the motives are executed. The respondents forwarded numerous illuminating insights.

Fostering relationships, also with the *SK*-type GIFs, was underscored in the interview with the baby boomer. Baby boomers in general prioritize personal connections and inclusive language, which are believed to foster effective communication (Harris, 2023). It is interesting to note that for members of the oldest cohort, the positivity embodied in the specific GIF type they use is the key element to transmit emotionally-charged concepts such as gratitude, affection, new beginnings, reciprocity, etc. Admittedly, it is a case study only, however, extrapolating from the active involvement in online interactions with people of her age group, as well as the clear positive motivation for using "welcoming postcards" for maintaining and enhancing relationships, GIFs demonstrate the potential to be a constant feature of TMC exchanges in the baby boomer generational cohort, possibly also with members of other age groups.

Members of Gen X, adaptable as they are, prefer efficient communication that respects their time and value a results-driven approach (Harris, 2023), hence GIF-based responses appear well-suited to their communicative styles. GIFs are a powerful means for displaying emotions and they are also used to provide a visual elaboration on one's own declared affective stance. Their communicative properties typically rely on conveying body language and emotions, identified as embodied response, co-speech and performance affect (Church et al., 2023, p. 733). In that sense, the way they are used in conflict or argument exchanges exaggerates the emotion, making them even more communicatively effective. Thus, GIF use has the potential to change the course of a conversation, even when used as an ending remark or a visual affective punchline. Even with argumentative reaction GIF (Church et al., 2023), which is essentially used as a means of arguing, it is possible to augment and shape our affective performances, or at a minimum, to avoid awkwardness. Sasamoto (2023, p. 410) notes that, similar to irony, "reaction GIFs often involve the communication of an attitude via the echoic use where the communicator expresses their dissociative attitude to the attributed thought delivered by the image of a particular GIF." This may be the prototypical reason for using the images as a (mild) conflict response tactics by (female) members of Generation X.

It can therefore be extrapolated that the potential in varied GIF uses, such as, among others, for fostering relationships, releasing tension, meaning making or shaping interpersonal exchanges, is both noticed and creatively utilized by members of other generational cohorts.

Conclusion

As digital communication continues to evolve, the role of GIFs may shift further, prompting the question of whether they will remain an integral component of TMC or gradually decline in relevance. Future research should explore how emerging technologies influence the use of GIFs across various age groups, and whether new forms of digital expression will eventually replace them. GIFs are an attractive option when it comes to generating emotions, which can translate into higher conversions on social networks so that users become more effective in communicative terms (Rúa-Hidalgo, 2021).

It ought to be acknowledged that, admittedly, the research did not even attempt to investigate millennials' attitudes toward GIF use. The reason for this conscious omission is the conviction expressed in the original *Guardian* article: "So now they are basically the cringe reaction image your millennial boss uses in Slack." It has been a widespread view that GIFs remain the most popular with members of this generation, as these are the people who came of age during the internet explosion (Dimock 2019). It can, though, tentatively be assumed that the contexts—if not the frequency—in which they would use this element of digital communication would mirror that of both the younger and older TMC participants.

> Diverse applications of the GIF underscore how the format's polysemy and affective capacity afford users with the opportunity to provide heightened and layered communication, demonstrate cultural knowledge, and occasionally engage in displays of resistance to certain ideologies and actors. (Miltner & Highfield, 2017, p. 9)

This specific format is possibly less popular than previously, yet the probability of GIFs causing (intergenerational) misunderstanding and conflict is remote. More so, though the workplace styles and values between members of different age cohorts differ, their communication styles are actually similar (See Hee & Yeojin, 2024), so that potentially GIFs may reduce the generational gap through communication. Rather than generating conflict, they can assist in conflict management.

References

Allison, D. A. (2013). *The patron-driven library. A practical guide for managing collections and services in the digital age* (Vol. 2: A culture of technology). Chandos Information Professional Series, Woodhead Publishing Limited. https://doi.org/10.1016/B978-1-84334-736-1.50002-7

Church, S. H., King, J., Robinson, T., & Callahan, C. (2023). Relating, searching, and referencing: Assessing the appeal of using GIFs to communicate. *Convergence: The International Journal of Research into New Media Technologies, 29*(3), 730–745.

Dimock, M. (2019, January 17). *Defining Generations: Where Millennials End and Generation Z Begins*. Pew Research Center. https://www.pewresearch.org/fact-tank/2019/01/17/where-millennials-end-and-generation-z-begins

Giflytics. (n.d.). Which type of GIF is best for your brand? Accessed February 12, 2025, https://www.giflytics.com/blog/type-of-gifs#:~:text=There%20are%20a%20lot%20of,short%20clips%20of%20video%20content

Harris, Y. (2023, August 16). Communication styles of Gen Z to boomers & beyond in the workplace. Powell. https://powell-software.com/resources/blog/communication-styles/

Heinzman, A. (2019, September 25). What is a GIF, and how do you use them?. How-to-Geek. https://www.howtogeek.com/441185/what-is-a-gif-and-how-do-you-use-them/

Hern, A. (2022, September 16). "Gifs are cringe": How Giphy's multimillion-dollar business fell out of fashion. *The Guardian*.

Hsieh, H-F., & Shannon, S. E. (2005). Three approaches to qualitative content analysis. *Qualitative Health Research, 15*(9), 1277–1288. https://doi.org/10.1177/1049732305276687

Jiang, J. A., Fiesler, C., & Brubaker, J. R. (2018). "The perfect one": Understanding communication practices and challenges with animated GIFs. *Proceedings of the ACM on Human-Computer Interaction, 2*/CSCW, Article No. 80, 1–20. https://doi.org/10.1145/3274349

Jitter. (2022, Jan 28). How to make perfectly looped GIFs. Jitter. https://blog.jitter.video/perfectly-looped-gifs/

Kuckartz, U. (2019). Qualitative text analysis: A systematic approach. In G. Kaiser & N. Presmeg (Eds.), *Compendium for early career researchers in mathematics education* (pp. 181–197). ICME-13 Monographs, Springer, https://doi.org/10.1007/978-3-030-15636-7_8

Liz R. (2023, August 31). The role of GIFs in modern content strategies. https://ranking-articles.com/the-role-of-gifs-in-modern-content-strategies/

Miles, M. B., Huberman, A. M., & Saldaña, J. (2014). *Qualitative data analysis. A methods sourcebook*. Sage.

Miltner, K. M., & Highfield, T. (2017). Never gonna GIF you up: Analyzing the cultural significance of the animated GIF. *Social Media + Society, 3*(3). 1–11. https://doi.org/10.1177/2056305117725223

Oberoi, A. (2025, January 20). Types of content analysis in qualitative research. Looppanel. https://www.looppanel.com/blog/types-of-content-analysis-in-qualitative-research

Rúa-Hidalgo, I., Galmes-Cerezo, M., Cristofol-Rodríguez, C., & Aliagas, I. (2021). Understanding the emotional impact of GIFs on Instagram through consumer neuroscience. *Behavioral Sciences, 11*, 108. https://doi.org/10.3390/bs11080108

Sasamoto, R. (2023). Perceptual resemblance and the communication of emotion in digital contexts. *Pragmatics, 33*(3), 393–417. https://doi.org/10.1075/prag.21058.sas

Shorey, S., Chan, V., Rajendran, P., & Ang, E. (2021). Learning styles, preferences and needs of generation Z healthcare students: Scoping review. *Nurse Education in Practice, 57*, 103247. https://doi.org/10.1016/j.nepr.2021.103247

Slepian, R.C., Vincent, A.C., Patterson, H., & Furman, H. (2024). Social media, wearables, telemedicine and digital health,"—A Gen Y and Z perspective. In K. S. Ramos (Ed.), *Comprehensive precision medicine* (pp. 524–544). Elsevier. https://doi.org/10.1016/B978-0-12-824010-6.00072-1

So Hee, L., & Yeojin Y. (2024). Work values and communication styles among Generation X, Y, and Z nurses: A cross-sectional study. *International Nursing Review, 71*(1), 115–121. https://doi.org/ 10.1111/inr.12863

SuperpixelSG. (2022, July 7). GIF 101: Definition, types, and its purpose. Superpixel. https://superpixel.sg/blog/gif/

Tolins, J., & Samermit, P. (2016). GIFs as embodied enactments in text-mediated conversation. *Research on Language and Social Interaction, 49*(2), 75–91. https://doi.org/10.1080/08351813.2016.1164391

Wagener, A. (2020). The postdigital emergence of memes and GIFs: Meaning, discourse, and hypernarrative creativity. *Postdigital Science and Education, 3*(10), 831–850. https://doi.org/10.1007/s42438-020-00160-1

Yao, R. (2018, April 5). The surging popularity of GIFs in digital culture. Medium. https://medium.com/ipg-media-lab/the-enduring-popularity-of-gifs-in-digital-culture-54763d7754aa

Appendix A
Quantitative Instrument 1

GIFS IN CONFLICTS—A CONFLICT WITH GIFS

🎉 Thanks for joining in on the fun! We're curious about how you sprinkle GIFs into your everyday chats—whether you're lighting up social media, keeping the group chat alive, or even using them at work (yes, we see you!). Your feedback will help us dive into the world of GIFs and see how they spice up the way we express feelings, share info, and connect with people online.

This quick survey should only take about 5 minutes of your time, and we promise—your answers are totally anonymous. There's no right or wrong here, just your genuine thoughts and GIF-filled stories!

Ready to GIF it a go? Let's do this! 🎬 ✨
* Mandatory question

1. Your age? *
   Mark one answer only
   ☐ < 26
   ☐ 27–43
   ☐ 44–60
   ☐ 60 >

2. Your gender? *
   Mark one answer only.
   ☐ female
   ☐ male
   ☐ other

3. Are you an active user of TMC (=technology-mediated communication)?
   Mark one answer only.
   ☐ Yes
   ☐ No

4. Do you send GIFs in TMC? *
   Mark one answer only.
   ☐ Yes
   ☐ No

5. If yes, to whom? *

   Mark all answers that apply.
   - ☐ friends
   - ☐ partners
   - ☐ family members
   - ☐ strangers
   - ☐ I do not use GIFs
   - ☐ Other: _____

6. Why do you use GIFs? *

   Mark all answers that apply.
   - ☐ they make conversations more fun
   - ☐ to mirror my reactions
   - ☐ to break the long chain of written messages
   - ☐ I do not use GIFs
   - ☐ Other: _____

7. If you do not use GIFs, why? *

   Mark all answers that apply.
   - ☐ they are too distracting
   - ☐ they take too long to load
   - ☐ GIFs do not accurately convey the intended message
   - ☐ I prefer text and emojis over GIFs
   - ☐ Sending them is too much trouble
   - ☐ My messages are full of GIFs!
   - ☐ Other: _____

8. Your favorite types of GIFs? *

   Mark all answers that apply.
   - ☐ Reaction GIFs: Express emotions or reactions (e.g., laughter, surprise)
   - ☐ Meme GIFs: Based on popular memes or internet trends
   - ☐ Pop Culture GIFs: Scenes from movies, TV shows, or music videos
   - ☐ Animated Text GIFs: Short phrases or words with motion effects
   - ☐ Looping GIFs: Seamlessly repeating animations or visuals
   - ☐ Celebration/Party GIFs: Festive or congratulatory animations (e.g., confetti, dancing)
   - ☐ Other: _____

9. Do you receive GIFs in TMC? *

   Mark one answer only.
   - ☐ Yes
   - ☐ No

10. If yes, from whom? *
    Mark all answers that apply.
    ☐ friends
    ☐ partners
    ☐ family members
    ☐ strangers
    ☐ I do not receive any
    ☐ Other:_____

11. If you were to use 1 word to describe your opinion on using GIFs, what would it be?

    _____

Appendix B
Qualitative Instrument 1

- Jak się nazywasz, ile masz lat oraz skąd pochodzisz?
  (Eng: What is your name, age, and nationality?)
- Czy wiesz czym są GIFy?
  (Eng: Do you know what GIFs are?)
- Czy znasz dokładną definicję GIFa?
  (Eng: Do you know the exact definition of a GIF?)
- Jak zaczęłaś używać GIFów?
  (Eng: How did you start using GIFs?)
- Czy wiesz jak twoi znajomi zaczęli używać GIFów?
  (Eng: Do you know how your friends started using GIFs?)
- Czy możesz mi przedstawić swój proces wysyłania GIFa?
  (Eng: Can you tell me your process of sending a GIF?)
- Od kogo najczęściej dostajesz tego typu GIFy?
  (Eng: From whom do you receive these types of GIFs the most?)
- Czy masz jakieś ostatnie komentarze na temat GIFów?
  (Eng: Do you have any final comments on the concept of GIFs?)

Appendix C

Quantitative Instrument 2

Would you please provide information to the following questions:

1. Do you use GIFs in online communication (mobile, computer mediated, etc.)?
   YES   NO

2. If no, why (please state your reasons, succinctly)

3. If yes,
   a. With whom?

   b. To communicate what?

4. If yes, how likely are you to drop using them?
   a. Very
   b. Not likely
   c. Hard to say
   Would you be willing to share the GIFs used?

CHAPTER SIXTEEN | **YOUSIF AL-NADDAF AND ROMUALD GOZDAWA-GOŁĘBIOWSKI**

Between Borders and Identities

(How) Arab EFL Learners Engage with Global English

Abstract

English holds an undeniable global utility, yet its cultural connotations often clash with deeply ingrained religious and societal norms in Arab contexts. This study reinterprets data from 21 Arab EFL learners to investigate how they reconcile the academic and professional benefits of English with perceived threats to their cultural or religious identity. Questionnaire findings reveal that while many learners view English as essential for success—particularly career or academic mobility—they are anxious about adopting Western cultural elements that conflict with local traditions. Some learners selectively engage with beneficial language skills and what they deem 'safe', while filtering out content they find culturally incompatible, others, however, resist Western norms more firmly. These strategies demonstrate a balancing act between instrumental motivation and cultural preservation, aligning with prior research on selective borrowing. The results stress the need for multiple pedagogical strategies, including culturally responsive teaching, transcultural approaches that blend cultural norms, and a culture-free (lingua franca) perspective. Collectively, these methods can reduce cultural tensions, help students maintain their identities, and sustain motivation in Arab EFL contexts. Overall, this study highlights that language instruction need not—and should not—come at the expense of learners' deeply held cultural values.

Keywords: Arab EFL learners, cultural identity, motivation, western norms, selective adaptation

Introduction

English was given the global "lingua franca" title for a reason; it is the most widely utilized language as a means of inter-community communication. It is the current medium of instruction and communication for a wide variety of domains—encompassing international business, education, science, academia, technology, entertainment, radio, and aviation, to name but a few (Crystal, 2003). As a result, proficiency in English has become increasingly in demand as it provides access to a wide range of opportunities in a globalized world, from securing education and better jobs to international research and cultural media accessibility. However, despite these countless instrumental opportunities English provides, the widespread use of English also poses an essential question about cultural identity, values, power, and tradition, especially when English intersects with communities that hold strong religious, cultural, and linguistic traditions, such as the case of the Arabic world.

In Arab EFL contexts, the motivation to learn English for academic and professional purposes can conflict with deeply held cultural and religious norms (Sadek, 2007; Elshenawy, 2017) that differ significantly from the Western values often present in English language textbooks, media, and classroom activities. While learners gain increased career opportunities and enhanced education, they may also face tensions when encountering cultural references or practices that clash with their culture and religion (Ateyat & Gasaymeh, 2015). Thus, for some EFL learners, the journey of acquiring English extends beyond simply learning vocabulary and grammar—it transforms into a balancing act, where students endeavor to uphold their cultural and religious values while engaging with a language that dominates global communication and discourse.

These conflicts have practical implications beyond academic interest. On an educational level, unresolved cultural frictions may alter learners' motivation, classroom participation, and overall language achievement. Socially, recognizing and addressing these challenges can foster intercultural understanding and tolerance, contributing to more harmonious interactions between local traditions and global influences. Therefore, to develop a culturally responsive curriculum, educators and policymakers need to have a robust comprehension of how learners negotiate potential conflicts arising from English's global status. This insight could also shed light on the evolving role of English in societies where religion is a defining element of cultural life, helping strike a balance between embracing a global lingua franca and respecting deeply held traditions.

Recent research on language, culture, and identity showcases the extent to which learners' backgrounds shape their attitudes toward a foreign language (Gardner, 1985; Hofstede, 2011; Elshenawy, 2017; Ateyat & Gasaymeh, 2015). In the context of Arab EFL learners, Sadek's (2007) findings illustrated that students' desire to learn for instrumental reasons often clashed with fears of adopting Western cultural norms. Similarly, Elshenawy (2017) observed that although the dominance of English in Qatar opens doors to international education and business opportunities, it can also undermine local traditions and cultural values. In the same vein, Ateyat and Gasaymeh (2015) contend that many Arabs regard English as a potential threat to their cultural identity, which essentially gives rise to ambivalent feelings regarding engaging with

Western cultural elements when learning English. Yet, not all researchers perceive Western cultural references as purely detrimental; introducing the target culture can, under certain circumstances, increase students' curiosity, motivation, and interest in both the language and the cultures that speak it (Genc & Bada, 2005).

In these "contested" cultural spaces—what might be called "difficult neighborgoods"—global English (i.e., English as an influential worldwide medium of communication) and local Arabic values intersect, collide, and sometimes converge. Global English here refers to more than just grammar and vocabulary; it encompasses Western sociocultural norms that often appear in textbooks, media, and classroom activities. In such contexts, learners may adopt strategies like selective borrowing (where they filter out incompatible norms) or outright resistance, illustrating a balancing act between linguistic proficiency and cultural preservation.

Building upon these insights, this study examines such a neighborhood of cultural conflict, revealing how Arab EFL learners navigate these intersecting forces while in pursuit of linguistic proficiency and cultural preservation. Specifically, it addresses two central questions:

1. How do Arab EFL learners reconcile the academic and professional advantages of English with the cultural tensions they experience when encountering Western norms?
2. What strategies—such as selective adoption, resistance, or negotiation—do learners use to manage these tensions and maintain their cultural or religious identities?

The term "Western norms" here refers to cultural practices and assumptions that may differ substantially from local Arab traditions, sometimes causing internal conflict for learners attempting to integrate the language into their daily lives.

By reinterpreting data originally collected for my MA thesis at the University of Warsaw—which primarily focused on learner motivation and attitudes—this study investigates the human dimension of cultural conflict (rather than implying that language or values themselves "conflict"). It demonstrates that Arab EFL learners often view English not only as a set of linguistic skills but also as a culturally charged space where personal values and educational objectives intersect. Section 2 of this paper reviews key literature on the interplay between language, motivation, and cultural identity, outlining relevant frameworks from previous research on Arab EFL contexts. Section 3 introduces the study's methodology, participants, and data collection procedures. Section 4 presents the core findings, highlighting the various ways learners adopt, modify, or resist Western cultural elements while pursuing English proficiency. Section 5 interprets these findings within the context of broader debates on language education policy and teaching practices. Lastly, Section 6 concludes by reflecting on how the tensions highlighted in this study underscore the importance of balancing local values with the undeniable global utility of English.

Conceptual Framework

Language, Culture, and Conflict

Before exploring the cultural conflicts that may arise between widely distinct cultures, it is helpful to establish the connection between language and culture. The notion that language shapes identity is widely accepted among scholars in language education and second language acquisition (Kramsch, 1998; Brown, 2007). Similarly, numerous scholars including Brown (2007), Kuang (2007), Tang (1999), Ardila-Rey (2008), Damen (1987), and Kramsch (1998) agree that language and culture are inseparable.

For instance, Brown (2007, pp. 189–190) points out that language and culture cannot exist without each other because "the two are intricately interwoven, so that one cannot separate them without losing the significance of either language or culture." A helpful way to conceptualize the relationship between the two is through Jiang's (2000, p. 328) metaphor: language and culture together compose "a living organism; language is flesh, and culture is blood. Without culture, language would be dead; without language, culture would have no shape." In this sense, one could argue that language is a product of culture (Miur, 2007), and culture is manifested through language; it is through language that concepts, traditions, values, and culture are communicated. Essentially, language becomes inseparable from culture when used for communication purposes (Kramsch, 1998), especially considering that language often carries dynamic or associative meanings shaped by a given cultural context.

For example, in English, the word "dog" often connotes a loyal companion or pet. By contrast, in many Arab societies, the word "kalb" (dog in Arabic) typically evokes associations with watchdogs, thieves, or impurity—an association partly tied to religious teachings that discourage close contact with dogs. A similar argument could be made for food items that may seem neutral or even positive in English, whereas their Arabic counterparts may trigger strong negative reactions due to cultural or religious prohibitions. This illustrates how the same referent (e.g., an animal or a type of food) can be perceived quite differently depending on the cultural values embedded in each language.

Because language is profoundly interconnected with cultural values and practices, tensions could emerge when learners stumble upon values and norms that significantly differ from their own. In the context of Arab EFL learners, these major cultural differences could manifest not only in classroom materials but also in social expectations. This essentially creates conditions of conflict for students attempting to reconcile two distinct sets of cultural norms. The following section explores how these cultural frictions arise, drawing on the concept of acculturation challenges and frameworks such as Hofstede's (2011) cultural dimensions to explain why these tensions are particularly evident in Arab-Western interactions.

Acculturation and Cultural Conflict

While acculturation is traditionally defined as the process whereby an individual adapts to a new culture after physical relocation (Berry, 1997), in this study, the term is used more broadly to describe the psychological and social adaptation that occurs when Arab EFL learners encounter Western cultural norms while learning English. Even in the absence of direct migration, learners experience cultural exposure through textbooks, classroom discussions, and media, which can produce similar forms of cultural tensions and negotiation.

In Arab EFL contexts—where religious and societal norms differ profoundly from those that are evident in Western cultures—this transfer of cultural content can lead to acculturation challenges. As Cormoş (2022, p. 1) explains, acculturation is "the process by which an individual acquires and adapts to a new cultural environment as a result of being placed in a new culture." Here, however, the new cultural environment is not a country, but the classroom and the resources that carry Western values. Essentially, this means that learners have to learn not only the language but also the cultural norms—such as forms of greetings, invitations, and customary speech acts—that are associated with it. Without cultural competence, effective communication with native speakers could potentially be hindered (Brown, 2007; Lanucha, 2018).

It is essential to mention the distinction between acculturation and assimilation. According to Lustig and Koester (1999, p. 341), acculturation as the "culture change that results from continuous, firsthand contact between two distinct cultural groups," which occurs without the complete loss of the learner's own culture. In contrast, assimilation involves adopting the dominant culture to such an extent that the learner becomes indistinguishable from its members (Pauls, 2008). Assimilation typically occurs when individuals actively reject their heritage culture. However, for Arab EFL learners, the process is more about negotiating and balancing two sets of cultural values rather than completely abandoning one for the other (Sadek, 2007; Bataineh & Reshidi, 2017).

Researchers have observed that learners tend to pass through several stages when adapting to a new culture (Education at a Glance, 2021). While the traditional "honeymoon," "distress," "adjustment," and "acceptance" phases are more commonly discussed in the context of migration, similar processes can be observed when learners encounter a new culture even without physical migration; a study on Zambian adolescents demonstrated that exposure to Western cultures via media led to the formation of distinct cultural identities, with some adolescents becoming more "Westernized" (Ferguson et al., 2015). In the Arab EFL setting, initial enthusiasm about learning

English may be followed by discomfort when confronted with unfamiliar Western social norms, eventually leading to a phase of selective adaptation or negotiated acceptance (Sadek, 2007; Diallo, 2014).

The cultural friction and acculturation challenges mentioned above do not only have an impact on how Arab EFL learners adapt to Western norms, but they also have effects on learners' motivation and attitudes toward English (Sadek, 2007; Elshenawy, 2017; Ahmed, 2011). While encountering unfamiliar cultural norms in classrooms, learners often find themselves caught between wanting to learn English for pragmatic reasons on the one hand and wanting to preserve their cultural heritage on the other (Ateyat & Gasaymeh, 2015). This dynamic tension—where concerns about cultural assimilation intersect with instrumental and integrative motivations—shapes how students engage with language. The next section will draw on Gardner's framework to explore Arab students' motivation and attitude toward English language learning in the face of these conflicting challenges.

Motivation and Attitude

Motivation and attitude play a key role in language learning, essentially shaping learners' success and engagement in EFL classrooms (Ellis, 1994). Motivation is particularly complex for Arab EFL learners because it intersects pragmatic benefits and concerns about cultural preservation when learning English through Western culture (Ateyat & Gasaymeh, 2015; Elshenawy, 2017). If the aim is a smooth learning process, instructors must examine students' attitudes and motivation toward the target language (Getie, 2020).

According to Gardner's (1985) socio-educational model, for a learner to be motivated, a combination of desire, effort, and a positive attitude toward both the language and its cultural community is needed. However, in contexts where cultural preservation is a concern, learners may develop ambivalent attitudes—valuing English for academic and career development while remaining cautious about its cultural components (Sadek, 2007; Asraf, 1996). Gardner and Lambert (1959, 1972) divided motivation into instrumental motivation (driven by pragmatic needs like securing better jobs and academic opportunities) and integrative motivation (reflecting a learner's desires to learn about the target culture and connect with the target language community). While SLA literature suggests that integrative motivation leads to greater long-term success (Suliman et al., 2024; Gardner & Lambert, 1972), research has also illustrated that instrumental motivation can be a significant driver (Lukmani, 1972; Roman & Nunez, 2020). In practice, many learners fall between the two, often mixing career-focused goals with varying degrees of cultural curiosity (Wadell & Shandor, 2012).

In the case of Arab EFL learners, studies indicate that instrumental motivations often dominate (Al-Ta'ani, 2018; Aljuaid, 2021), with learners primarily regarding English as a tool for professional and academic growth rather than as a means of cultural integration (Sadek, 2007). At the same time, some learners regard Western cultural elements embedded in textbooks or media as potentially threatening to local religious or social norms (Ateyat & Gasaymeh, 2015). Scholars warn against forcing target-culture assimilation in EFL classrooms given that it can alienate students who feel uneasy about Western values (Zaid, 1999; Baker, 2015). Instead, a middle ground approach encourages teachers to promote communicative competence while allowing learners the autonomy to adopt or reject specific cultural aspects (Asraf 1996; Sadek, 2007).

Nonetheless, some concerns remain regarding how far cultural influences should extend in language education, especially when learners feel that English may threaten their core beliefs (Elshenawy, 2017). For instance, English's dominance in Qatar's education system has led to ambivalent attitudes—students recognize its benefits yet remain concerned about its cultural implications (Elshenawy, 2017). This tension—where instrumental benefits collide with the perceived risk of cultural assimilation—ultimately shapes how Arab EFL learners approach English. Drawing on Hofstede's cultural dimensions, the next section will examine how the inherent differences between Western and Arab cultural values further ignite these conflicts in the classroom.

Hofstede and Western Cultural Norms

While the previous discussion demonstrated how Arab EFL learners navigate the tension between the instrumental benefits of learning English and the need to protect their cultural values, this section will examine how the specific Western cultural elements in English materials contribute to these conflicts. Scholars argue that conflicts are more likely between culturally distant communities (Bove & Gokemen, 2016), especially if the source culture contains norms that differ significantly—or do not exist at all—in the target culture (Brown, 2000). In practice, this often manifests when English textbooks and classroom activities introduce Western holidays, social practices, or everyday behaviors that reflect predominantly individualistic, secular values. In contrast, many Arab contexts are characterized by strong religious traditions, and more of a collective ethos, thereby increasing the potential for misunderstandings or discomfort between the two cultures.

A useful framework for interpreting these possible clashes is Hofstede's cultural dimensions. Essentially, the framework categorizes societies along axes such as individualism vs. collectivism and indulgence vs. restraint (Hofstede, 2011). According to Hofstede, Western societies generally exhibit high levels of individualism and indulgence, promoting self-expression and personal achievement, whereas Arab societies typically feature collectivism, tradition, and restraint, with religious norms and family cohesion playing essential roles. This discussion focuses on indulgence vs. restraint, where:

1. Indulgent societies place a high value on personal enjoyment and leisure, with the belief that they are largely in control of their own actions.
2. Restrained societies tend to limit such indulgence, often attributing actions and lifestyle choices to larger moral or religious frameworks (Hofstede, 2011).

A comparison between Arab and Western culture using Hofstede's indulgence-versus-restraint dimension renders "Western culture" (admittedly a broad label) more indulgent than "Arab culture" (another overarching category), especially regarding practices like casual alcohol consumption or partying. For instance, an utterance such as "would you like to go for a pint?," essentially inviting someone for a pint of beer, might be an innocent invitation or otherwise culturally appropriate in many Western communities, but could be perceived as inappropriate or offensive in a context where religious prohibitions discourage alcohol use, such as an Arab Muslim community (Baron-Epel et al., 2014). Although not every "Western" community is equally indulgent, nor every "Arab" society uniformly restrained, the generalized contrast helps explain why some Arab EFL learners may reject or question certain cultural references embedded in English materials.

This gap could contribute to learners feeling pressured to assimilate or resist aspects of the target culture, in fear of losing their own cultural identity. Yet, EFL pedagogy should not require approaches in which every lesson references Western norms or assumptions. Instead, some scholars advocate a selective cultural adaptation model (Asraf, 1996; Sadek, 2007), in which students maintain their religious and social values while learning the language. Alternatively, intercultural approaches allow teachers to use English to describe learners' local realities, limiting potentially controversial Western cultural content (Baker, 2015; Zaid, 1999).

Insights drawn from Hofstede's cultural dimensions showcase how varying degrees of indulgence vs. restraint or individualism vs. collectivism may affect learners' comfort with Western-based English materials. Through being aware of these broad cultural tendencies, educators can adapt lessons to reduce cultural friction, encourage respectful curiosity about unfamiliar norms, and focus on language proficiency rather than cultural homogenization. Such an approach could potentially yield more inclusive and effective EFL classrooms.

The Arab EFL Context

The Arab EFL context can be further complicated by the cultural conflicts outlined above. For instance, in some Gulf countries, the dominance of English in curricula has led to the marginalization of Arabic culture. Ahmed's (2011) analysis found that many EFL textbooks reduce Arab traditions to superficial mentions, thereby effectively casting local tradition as the "other" while sidelining the Arabic language and identity. Similar concerns are raised by Ateyat and Gasaymeh (2015), Sadek (2007), and Elshenawy (2017), which indicates that an uncritical adoption of English comes at the expense of cultural integrity in Arab EFL settings.

For instance, Sadek (2007) found that many Arab learners prioritize English for instrumental (e.g., career) reasons but simultaneously worry that the integration of Western cultural elements in EFL classrooms could threaten their cultural and religious values—a trend similarly reported by Ateyat and Gasaymeh (2015). Elsehnawy (2017), focusing mostly on Qatar, observed that the global reach of English introduces a dichotomous pressure on Arab students: on the one hand, the drive to succeed in an increasingly globalized world, and on the other, a need to preserve their cultural identity.

This duality is essential because it illustrates that Arab EFL learners are not simply acquiring a new language; they are also navigating complex cultural negotiations, with their decisions affecting both how they engage with English education and how they protect their own cultural values (Elsehnawy, 2017; Sadek, 2007). As such, educators in Arab EFL settings must design a curriculum and teaching methods that include local culture while still equipping students with the skills needed for international opportunities.

The literature reviewed thus far illustrates that Arab EFL learners face a challenge when it comes to balancing the practical benefits of English with the risk of leaving elements of their culture behind. Although English is valued for its academic and professional advantages, many learners remain cautious about Western cultural elements prevalent in textbooks and classroom materials. As such, many learners often adopt strategies of "selective borrowing" or resistance in an attempt to preserve their cultural and religious identities while learning English. The following section outlines the methodology originally used in my MA research, which I have reinterpreted for this study to explore how Arab EFL learners navigate the tensions inherent in English language education.

Research Methodology

This study employs a quantitative research design adapted from data collected for my MA thesis at the University of Warsaw. While the original purpose of my thesis was to examine motivation and attitudes among Arab EFL learners—specifically investigating whether they were primarily instrumentally or integratively motivated, their attitudes toward Western culture, and their perceptions of cultural interference—this present study reinterprets those findings to explicitly focus on the cultural tensions and conflicts that emerge when Arab learners engage with English-language materials containing Western cultural norms.

Participants completed a questionnaire that included demographic questions, items assessing motivational orientations, and sections evaluating students' attitudes toward both their own Arabic identity and Western cultural norms. For this study, the analysis centers on how learners view Western cultural references as a potential source of conflict and the strategies they adopt (e.g., partial acceptance or resistance) to maintain their cultural and religious values while engaging with English. Additionally, this study examines how Arab learners negotiate between their cultural values and the linguistic expectations of English environments.

Participants and Data Collection

This study was conducted with 21 Arab EFL learners who completed a questionnaire designed to examine their attitudes, motivation, and perceptions of cultural influence in English language learning. The participants were not recruited from a single institution but rather represented a diverse group of learners studying English in various academic and professional settings. Given the crucial role of English in education, career advancement, and global communication, these learners often engaged with the language in university courses, private language institutes, or self-directed learning programs.

The participants had been learning English for approximately 10 years, but their proficiency varied. All were native Arabic speakers, with gender balance nearly even (11 male, 10 female). They also varied in age, ranging from 20 to 44 years old. However, the sample was relatively homogenous in nationality, as 18 of the 21 respondents were Jordanian, with one participant from Palestine and two from Morocco. Many respondents were living in Qatar at the time of the study.

Data was collected through an online questionnaire distributed via Google Forms. Participants were recruited online, to ensure accessibility to a wider sample of Arab EFL learners. Anonymity was maintained, and all participants were informed of the research objectives and their right to withdraw at any time before completing the survey.

By examining participants from various countries, educational levels, and language proficiency bands rather than a single institutional setting, this study provides a broader lens on how Arab EFL learners navigate cultural tensions while acquiring English. The diversity of the respondents allows for an exploration of how different personal, social, and religious factors influence their attitudes, learning experiences, and coping strategies in balancing linguistic proficiency with cultural identity.

Questionnaire Structure

The questionnaire for this study was designed to assess multiple aspects of Arab EFL learners' motivations and attitudes, including how they perceive Western cultural elements in English learning and whether those elements contribute to cultural tensions or conflicts.

The questionnaire consisted of four main sections, each designed to capture different aspects of learners' experiences:

1. Demographic Information:
   - Age, gender, and country of origin.
   - Level of English proficiency.
   - Educational background and current English-learning context (e.g., university, private language courses, or self-study).
2. Motivation to Learn English
   - Instrumental vs. integrative motivation (based on Gardner's socio-educational model).
   - Practical reasons for learning English (e.g., career opportunities, academic success).
   - Desire to engage with English-speaking communities or Western culture.
3. Attitudes Toward English and Western Culture
   - Perceptions of Western cultural values embedded in English language materials.
   - Whether participants perceive Western cultural elements as a benefit or threat to their own cultural identity.
   - Comfort level with cultural references in textbooks, media, and classroom activities.
4. Cultural Identity and Negotiation Strategies
   - Whether participants feel they can maintain their Arabic cultural and religious identity while learning English.
   - Strategies used to navigate cultural conflicts (e.g., selective-borrowing, resistance, or acceptance of Western norms).
   - Preferences regarding the integration of Arabic cultural elements into English language learning materials.

The questionnaire utilized Likert-scale questions, multiple choice items, and open-ended responses. By focusing on how Arab EFL learners balance linguistic proficiency with cultural identity, this study provides insights into broader sociocultural challenges of English education in the Arab world.

Findings and Analysis

This section presents the key findings from the questionnaire responses collected during my MA thesis, reinterpreted to focus on the cultural tensions Arab EFL learners face when in contact with English. The results analyzed in relation to the study's research questions are:

1. How do Arab EFL learners reconcile the academic and professional advantages of English with the cultural tensions they experience when encountering Western cultural norms?
2. What strategies—such as selective adoption, resistance, or negotiation—do learners use to manage these tensions and maintain their cultural or religious identities?

The findings are categorized into four main themes that emerged from the responses: (1) Attitudes Toward Western culture in English Language Learning, (2) The Role of Motivation: Instrumental vs. Integrative, (3) Cultural Conflict and Identity Negotiation, and (4) Coping Strategies: Selective Adaptation vs. Resistance.

Attitudes Toward Western Culture in English Language Learning

One of the primary areas of exploration in this study is how Arab EFL learners perceive Western cultural elements in English education. The data collected from the questionnaire revealed a rather complex and often ambivalent relationship with these cultural elements, essentially showcasing a spectrum of attitudes ranging from acceptance and selective integration to skepticism and resistance/rejection. The findings illustrate that while some learners view Western cultural exposure as a valuable component of English education, others perceive it as a cultural threat that could interfere with their Arabic identity and values.

Responses to statement 14, "*I feel that learning about Western culture interferes with my culture*," are summarized in Table 1.

Response Category	Frequency	Percentage (%)
Strongly agree	3	14.3
Agree	7	33.3
Disagree	5	23.8
Strongly disagree	6	28.6
Total	21	100

Responses to statement 15, "*I think Western people...*" are summarized in Table 2.

Response Category	Frequency	Percentage (%)
Have extremely different values that do not overlap with Arab values	18	85.7
Have almost the same values as Arabs	2	9.5
Other	1	4.8
Total	21	100

Perceived Differences Between Western and Arab Culture

As indicated in Table 1, responses to question 14 revealed significant concerns about cultural interference. While some students were neutral or disagreed, a significant portion of 46.7% (10 participants) either strongly agreed or agreed that learning Western culture could interfere with their Arabic cultural identity.

Building on these findings, Table 2 shows that participants perceived Western culture as significantly different from their own. Responses to question 15 indicated that an overwhelming majority (85.7%, 18 participants) believed that Western people uphold values that do not overlap with Arab values. This perception reinforces the notion that many Arab learners see English as not only a linguistic tool but also a carrier of cultural values distinct from their own.

These cultural tensions were evident in participants' comments. One respondent stated: "Most of the time, I feel as though learning about Western culture equates to putting my own culture at risk because, from my perspective, they are complete opposites." However, others expressed a more open approach, emphasizing that learning about different cultures does not necessarily mean adopting them: "not really, in my culture we are open to learning about different cultures and different languages… However, not to a point where we have to leave what we believe in and sacrifice it for our interest in other cultures."

These responses reflect an internal negotiation process, whereby students attempt to balance their exposure to English with the need to preserve their Arabic identity.

Impact of Western Culture on Motivation

The potential for cultural conflict appears to have a tangible impact on students' motivation to learn English. Responses to question 22 ("What would hinder your motivation to learn English?"; see Appendix A) revealed that 66.7% (14 participants) stated that excessive exposure to Western culture in English instruction would negatively impact their motivation to learn.

This finding suggests that while Arab learners value English for its practical benefits, they remain wary of an overemphasis on Western cultural elements in the curriculum. One participant elaborated on this perspective: "I enjoy learning about their culture, but only to a certain degree. I wouldn't enjoy being taught only about Western culture because I feel like there is a lot of differences between us and them…"

This response further strengthens the need for a balanced curriculum that integrates both linguistic proficiency and cultural sensitivity, a recommendation also put forth by scholars like Asraf (1996), who emphasized the importance of including learners' native culture in EFL education.

Selective Engagement and Cultural Filtering

Although some learners viewed Western culture as a potential threat, others demonstrated a more selective approach. Many students reported engaging with English language content that aligned with their values while disregarding elements they deemed inappropriate or culturally incompatible.

For instance, when discussing their preferred exposure to Western culture in language learning, some respondents repeatedly noted the need to filter out holidays, alcohol, and relationship norms. One participant emphasized that they prefer a moderated approach to Western cultural content, given that full immersion felt overwhelming. This approach aligns with findings from Sadek (2007) and Asraf (1996), who noted that Arab EFL learners often adopt a "selective borrowing" strategy, in which learners acquire English for practical purposes while resisting cultural assimilation.

The Need for Balanced Cultural Representation

The findings underscore the necessity of a balanced approach to English language learning that could potentially accommodate cultural sensitivities. A considerable 76.2% (16 participants) believed that they could have learned English without learning about Western culture. One participant stated: "it is not necessary to learn Western culture to learn the language." However, other students acknowledged that cultural awareness can enhance language learning. Some 52.4% (11 participants) agreed that understanding Western culture can aid in mastering the language. As one respondent stated: "Knowledge of cultural contexts that underpin the language you're learning can provide you with invaluable insights into certain phrases that are often spoken by natives of a particular cultural group." This suggests that while many Arab learners prefer a linguistic-focused approach, a moderate inclusion of cultural content could be beneficial—provided it does not overshadow their own cultural identity.

The Push and Pull of English Learning: Motivation vs. Cultural Identity

Apart from the attitudes toward Western culture in English language education, this study explores how cultural tensions influence learners' motivation to acquire English. The questionnaire findings showcase that Arab EFL primarily exhibit instrumental motivation; that is, they view English as a tool for academic, professional, and economic success. However, a large number of participants also raised concerns about cultural interference, essentially highlighting an ongoing tension between pragmatic benefits and cultural preservation.

Dominance of Instrumental Motivation

The findings revealed that a majority of Arab EFL learners are motivated to learn English for practical reasons rather than cultural integration. Responses to statement 1, "I think English is necessary for my success (work, social status, family)" received the highest score in the entire survey:

- 85.7% (18 participants) strongly agreed
- 14.3% (3 participants) agreed
- Total agreement: 100% (21 participants)

Similarly, responses to question 21, which asked participants what motivates them to learn English (see Appendix A), revealed that 81% (17 participants) viewed English as an essential skill for success in a globalized world. This finding supports previous research by Gardner (1985) and Sadek (2007), which suggests that instrumental motivation tends to dominate in non-western EFL settings, particularly when English is seen as a necessity rather than a cultural gateway.

This data suggests that Arab EFL learners do not see English as a means of assimilating into Western society; rather, they prioritize its practical benefits.

Cultural Concerns and the Fear of Language Domination

Despite this strong instrumental motivation, many participants expressed concerns about potential cultural conflicts arising from prolonged exposure to Western cultural elements embedded in English learning.

For instance, responses to statement 7, "I feel as though English is dominating the world," reflect this concern:

- 71.4% (15 participants) strongly agreed
- 28.6% (6 participants) agreed
- Total agreement: 100% (21 participants)

When asked to justify their responses, participants provided a range of perspectives; some viewed the dominance of English positively, mentioning its practicality and ease of learning: "it's a good thing because English is needed everywhere." Others, however, expressed unease about the diminishing role of Arabic:

> I strongly agree, because nowadays I'm using English more than I am using my own language and that is not something good because I am afraid in the future we will stop using our language because we will all be speaking English.

This internal struggle reinforces the "push and pull" dynamic—where Arab learners are essentially grappling with the need to master English for practical purposes while simultaneously striving to protect their native language and cultural identity.

Cultural Tensions as a Demotivating Factor

An overemphasis on Western cultural content in English language teaching and learning can act as a demotivating factor for some learners. Building on earlier findings about cultural demotivation, responses to question 22 revealed a clear pattern: while the majority of participants viewed excessive Western cultural content as demotivating, only 14.3% (3 participants) stated that not being taught about Western culture would hinder their motivation. Additionally, 19% (4 participants) provided other reasons for decreased motivation, including being forced to learn English exclusively through Western culture and having limited opportunities for communication with English speakers.

This suggests that while some learners appreciate a degree of cultural exposure, an overemphasis on Western norms can be perceived as intrusive and discouraging. One respondent elaborated: "I like learning the good parts of their culture, but not the ones that contradict my own values." This further supports Asraf's (1996) argument that culturally sensitive language education is crucial for sustaining motivation among non-Western EFL learners.

The Push and Pull of English Learning

The findings paint a clear picture of the tension between the instrumental benefits of English and concerns about cultural preservation; on the push side, learners are motivated by the academic, professional, and social mobility that English provides. On the pull side, concerns about cultural interference, language loss, and excessive exposure to Western cultural norms create barriers that lead to learners' disengagement. This tension raises important pedagogical considerations. How can English be taught in a way that maximizes motivation while minimizing cultural resistance? Can English education be structured to allow learners to engage selectively with cultural elements?

The next section will illustrate the strategies Arab EFL learners have developed to navigate these tensions—from selective adaptation to outright resistance.

Coping Strategies: Selective Adaptation vs. Resistance

Building upon the previous discussion of cultural tensions in English learning, this section aims to explore how Arab EFL learners actively navigate and negotiate their engagement when faced with Western cultural elements. While some learners adopt a selective adaptation strategy, engaging with aspects of Western culture they deem "safe" and beneficial while filtering out others, others express resistance to Western cultural exposure in English language learning.

Selective Adaptation: Engaging with Beneficial Aspects of English While Maintaining Cultural Identity

A significant number of Arab EFL learners strategically engage with English by selectively adapting some of its cultural elements instead of fully embracing or rejecting Western cultural norms. These learners adopt aspects they find useful—particularly those related to professional, academic, or communication skills—while consciously filtering out content that contradicts their beliefs. This approach essentially allows students to maximize the instrumental benefits they receive from English while avoiding cultural assimilation.

Responses to multiple questionnaire items reinforce this perspective. Building on earlier findings about students' preference for learning English without Western cultural content, participants demonstrated clear patterns of selective engagement with cultural content. One participant stated, "It is not necessary to learn Western culture to learn the language." Similarly, another respondent emphasized their selective engagement, saying that they focus only on cultural elements that align with their values. Many participants described actively filtering out Western cultural content that they deemed irrelevant or conflicting with their values. Among the most commonly rejected cultural elements were:

1. Western holidays and celebrations (e.g., Christmas, Halloween, Thanksgiving)
2. Alcohol consumption in social contexts
3. General cultural and religious practices

One participant described this filtering process as follows: " I like to have a diversity of options, however, if the place serves pork or alcohol, I wouldn't enjoy it let alone visit it." Similarly, in response to statement 14, "I feel learning about Western culture interferes with my culture," one participant voiced their concern stating, "Yes, because I don't want to be learning about holidays and celebrations that are not in my own culture…" In the same vein, one participant, when asked to justify "disagreeing" with the statement 2 "I enjoy listening to Western music," noted "I don't like the things that are often referred to in western music because it goes against my religion." In statement 16, when asked about whether Arabs should learn more about their own tradition instead of adopting Western traditions, one respondent stated: "I agree, but I also think that it wouldn't be too bad to learn or adopt the good parts of Western traditions."

These responses reinforce Sadek's (2007) and Asraf's (1996) findings, which showcase how Arab EFL learners often adopt a "selective borrowing" strategy—engaging with English as a practical tool while resisting cultural assimilation. This underlines the agency that learners go through when navigating the tension between linguistic necessity and cultural preservation.

Cultural Resistance: Rejecting or Minimizing Engagement with Western Cultural Elements

While many learners adopted more of a pragmatic, selective approach, a notable number of students expressed resistance toward the integration of Western culture in English learning materials. These learners perceived Western cultural elements as a threat to their identity and actively rejected engagement with them.

This resistance to excessive Western cultural content, as demonstrated in the earlier motivation findings, manifested in students' broader attitudes toward cultural integration in language learning. Students expressed clear preferences for maintaining their cultural identity while learning English, emphasizing the importance of balanced cultural representation in their language education journey.

One participant expressed strong concerns about cultural interference, stating: "When I learn about Western things specifically, I feel uncomfortable because our culture doesn't align with theirs, so I feel like I have to puy my culture aside and swallow my pride and learn this new culture." Another participant wrote:

> In many ways; Arabic and western cultures are essentially vastly different than each other. Western people hold quite different values than Arabic people. Going clubbing, dancing, dress codes are extremely different than ours and not in a good way because it goes against our religion as muslims.

Similarly, in response to statement 4 "I enjoy learning about the Western culture while learning English," one student disagreed noting: "Because our culture do not fit their culture and their traditions." Another participant voiced their resistance about Western fashion claiming: "because its contrary to our costumes and religion." This is reinforced by another student who voiced their concerns about Western cultural elements: "… So when the teacher teaches my about Christmas or New Years eve or easter, all of these celebrations we do not have nor do we accept so I don't want to learn about these things." Another respondent raised concerns about the preservation of their identity postulating: "Adopting Western culture and values means abandoning my own, and that's why I think it is much better for Arabs to learn and enrich their knowledge about their own culture."

This sense of cultural intrusion aligns with research by Ateyat and Gasaymeh (2015), who found that Arab learners often associate English education with Westernization, leading to concerns about losing their cultural and religious identity. Similarly, Elshenawy (2017) observed that students in Qatar were often reluctant to engage with Western norms in English learning due to fears of cultural erosion.

Having presented the core findings from this study, illustrating how Arab EFL learners navigate their cultural tensions through selective adaptation and resistance, the following section will interpret these findings by placing them in dialogue with existing literature. Specifically, this discussion will showcase how these learner strategies align or contrast with theoretical frameworks. It will also highlight the practical implications for language education policies and pedagogical practices in Arab contexts.

Discussion

Revisiting the Research Questions

The findings presented in the previous section shed light on 1) How Arab EFL learners reconcile English's academic and professional advantages with cultural tensions, and 2) The strategies they employ to maintain cultural and religious identities while engaging with English. Overall, the data illustrated a complex interplay between instrumental motivation, cultural preservation, and the selective adoption or resistance of Western cultural norms.

Interpretation of Key Findings

Cultural Tensions and Instrumental Priorities

Participants consistently perceived English as a crucial tool for academic, professional, and socioeconomic mobility, thereby aligning with Gardner's (1985) concept of instrumental motivation. However, the data also highlighted that instrumental motivation cannot be understood, nor does it operate in isolation; concerns about cultural identity make the learning process more ambivalent. This parallels Elshenawy's (2017) and Sadek's (2007) findings, which document how Arab learners perceive and value English for its global utility but remain anxious about adopting the cultural norms they perceive as opposing or unethical to their own.

An essential element of this research lies in how Arab EFL learners experience Western norms as culturally intrusive. Many respondents were aware that some exposure to Western culture can aid them in mastering the linguistic subtleties, yet they also voiced strong preferences by setting boundaries around culturally sensitive topics (e.g., alcohol consumption, certain holidays, dating norms). Such selective engagement showcases how learners engage with English while choosing which cultural components to incorporate or reject (Asraf, 1996; Khuwaileh, 2000; Uddin, 2017).

This selective stance strengthens Kramsch's (1998) argument that language is inextricably linked to culture—but that linkage does not require full cultural assimilation. Instead, learners can develop what Byram (2021) calls "intercultural competence," essentially using English to communicate effectively across cultures, but without abandoning their original identity or cultural values. In other words, learners acknowledge that language cannot be learned without its cultural origins, but deliberate decision making—what might be termed "selective-borrowing" (Asraf, 1996)—allows students to maintain cultural integrity while benefiting from the instrumental values of English. By establishing boundaries, learners can actively manage both linguistic gains and cultural preservation—such as traditions, values, and beliefs—rather than adopting every element of the target language's culture, thereby reflecting a contemporary understanding of EFL education—one that facilitates cross-cultural communication without the need for learners to adopt all cultural norms of native speakers. This dynamic is particularly prevalent in Arab EFL contexts, where religious and social factors strongly influence which cultural elements learners accept or reject.

Negotiation of Identity in the EFL Classroom

The findings also illustrate how learners actively negotiate and construct their cultural identities while engaging with English and Western cultural elements. Responses suggest that many participants perceive Western norms and values as distinct, if not in direct conflict with traditional Arab or Islamic teachings. It is rather interesting that although religion was not explicitly mentioned in the survey, many participants mentioned it as a bone of contention; that is, their religion (Islam) forbids them from learning about elements directly opposing it. This aligns with Hofstede's (2011) cultural dimensions framework, in which Western societies often rank higher on individualism and indulgence, whereas Arab societies emphasize collectivism and restraint. More specifically, religion does indeed seem to be one element that guides Arab EFL learners' ways of living. The resulting "clash" echoes what Berry (1997) describes as acculturation stress—though it is important to note that I did not directly observe or measure participants' experiences of acculturation stress in the classroom. Any suggestion of "clash" thus stems from self-report, emphasizing the subjective dimension of cultural tensions rather than a documented classroom phenomenon.

Learners are not merely passive recipients of cultural content; instead, I would argue that students actively choose selective adaptation as a strategy to interpret and modify cultural content based on their needs, interests, and contexts. Building on Asraf's (1996) and Sadek's (2007) notion of "selective borrowing," participants often filter or reject cultural elements they deem incompatible with their beliefs. This adaptation helps reconcile the dual aims of 1) benefiting from English's practical advantages, and 2) protecting core aspects of Arabic identity. Remarkably, a subset of participants engaged in more active resistance, expressing a clear stance that Western content might "erode" their cultural traditions and values—reflecting the essential role of religion and social norms in shaping attitudes toward language education.

Alignment with Existing Literature

These findings resonate with a broader body of work on language and cultural conflict in non-Western EFL settings. Similar to Ahmed's (2011) work in the Gulf, the current results emphasize the apprehensions around the "marginalization" of Arabic culture when English materials privilege Western perspectives. At the same time, they confirm Gardner and Lamber's (1972) distinction between integrative and instrumental orientations—albeit with an essential caveat in mind: in heavily tradition-oriented societies, cultural integration is not always a desired or viable goal. Instead, learners often gravitate toward a "third path," whereby they obtain the practical advantages of learning English while selectively distancing themselves from Western influences that oppose their values.

Implications for Pedagogy and Policy

Based on these findings, EFL educators and curriculum developers in the context of Arab EFL learners could benefit from:

1. *A balanced cultural representation* wherein they incorporate examples and texts that reflect both Western and Arabic perspectives, thereby normalizing local cultural experiences in the English classroom. This could potentially reduce students' constant worry about the preservation of their culture.
2. *Context-sensitive approaches*; that is, rather than forcing alignment with Western holidays and social norms, materials can promote comparative or neutral scenarios. Models like CBI (Content-Based Instruction), EMI (English-Medium Instruction), CLIL (Content and Language Integrated Learning), or an EIL/ELF (English as an international/Lingua Franca) approach may help focus on local or universal content rather than exclusively Western topics. This could facilitate a safer space for students to practice their language skills without feeling pressured to adopt unfamiliar customs.
3. *Selective cultural content*: teachers could offer optional or elective modules focusing on cultural exploration that allows learners to self-select based on their interest and comfort level. This aligns with the "filtering" strategy many already employ. This would essentially allow learners to explore the beneficial aspects without putting their own values at risk.
4. *Teacher training in intercultural competence*: instructors should learn how to negotiate sensitive cultural topics and be aware of the strong religious and societal norms at play in many Arabic contexts. Awareness of potential areas of conflict—such as alcohol or clothing—can help teachers avoid alienating learners. Alternatively, one intercultural approach envisions students as "intercultural mediators," that not only learn how to communicate, but also develop the ability to interpret, mediate, and negotiate cultural meanings (Byram, 2021).
5. *Material centered on source culture*: curriculum designers could integrate Arabic values, traditions, and content in English learning, reinforcing learners' sense of identity while teaching the target language. This could potentially address concerns about the marginalization of Arabic culture; it emphasizes that English is a global tool rather than a vehicle for unwanted or forced assimilation.

Limitations and Future Research

Before moving forward, it is crucial to mention the limitations of this study. Since the data was originally collected for my MA thesis at the University of Warsaw, it was primarily designed to examine motivation and attitudes among Arab EFL learners rather than focusing exclusively on cultural conflict. While the questionnaire data has been reinterpreted to explore tensions between Western cultural norms and Arabic values in English language learning, certain nuances may not have been fully captured.

Additionally, the study relies on self-reported data—an approach prone to several biases and validity concerns (Grimm, 2010; Miller, 2012). Social desirability bias can arise if participants adjust their answers based on what they believe is expected of them rather than their true opinions (Miller, 2012). Recall bias may also affect how accurately respondents remember and report past experiences or attitudes (Raphael, 1987).

Building on present findings, future research could expand the participant pool and employ qualitative methods, such as interviews, classroom observations, or focus groups to capture in-the-moment negotiations of identity and culture in EFL classrooms. It could also examine how different age groups or educational settings (e.g., high school vs. university) vary in their approaches to selective adaptation or cultural resistance, whether teacher perceptions align with students' perceptions regarding cultural content, and how any discrepancies shape classroom dynamics. Lastly, considering the role of digital media, future research might investigate how learning English through AI-based platforms might influence cultural adaptation or resistance among Arab EFL learners.

Conclusion

This study investigated how Arab EFL learners reconcile the academic and professional benefits of English with their cultural and religious values. Additionally, it sheds light on the subtle interplay Arab EFL learners navigate. They actively pursue the instrumental benefits of English while protecting and reasserting their cultural and religious identities. Rather than viewing some cultural elements as incompatible, many learners adopt flexible strategies to help them advance in a global world inseparable from English while remaining rooted in their own traditions. This tension points to the importance of culturally responsive pedagogies that respect learners' values while supporting their linguistic and professional goals. English education need not—and should not—come at the expense of a learner's cultural identity and values.

Although the sample was relatively small and relied on self-report, the results offered a foundation for future research to further explore these dynamics in larger—and perhaps—more diverse Arab populations and through qualitative designs such as classroom observations. Overall, the core takeaway from this study is that language educators and policymakers must tend to more than merely grammar and vocabulary; fostering mutual respect for cultural identities is just as essential in helping Arab learners thrive in English language settings.

References

Ahmed, K. (2011). Casting Arabic culture as the "other": Cultural issues in the English curriculum. In C. Gitsaki (Ed.), *Teaching and learning in the Arab world* (pp. 119–137). Peter Lang.

Al-Naddaf, Y. (2023). *Teaching language through culture to Arab learners of English: A study of motivations and attitudes* [Unpublished master's thesis]. University of Warsaw.

Al-Ta'ani, M. H. (2018). Integrative and instrumental motivations for learning English as a university requirement among undergraduate students at Al-Jazeera University/Dubai. *International Journal of Learning and Development*, 8(4), 89–105. https://doi.org/10.5296/ijld.v8i4.13940

Aljuaid, H. (2021). Students' motivation to learn English as a foreign language in the context of Saudi Arabian learners. *Arab World English Journal*, 12(3), 242–256. https://doi.org/10.24093/awej/vol12no3.17

Ardila-Rey, A. (2008). Language, culture, policy, and standards in teacher preparation: Lessons from research and model practices addressing the needs of CLD children and their teachers. In M. E. Brisk (Ed.), *Language, culture, and community in teacher education* (pp. 331–351). Lawrence Erlbaum.

Asraf, R. M. (1996). Teaching English as a second or foreign language: The place of culture. *Proceedings of the International Conference "English and Islam: Creative Encounters 96" December 20–22, 1996*. Retrieved April 15, 2006, from http://www.tesolislamia.org/articles.html

Ateyat, K., & Gasaymeh, M. (2015). A Study of Faculty Members' Perceptions of the Effect of the Globalization on Higher Education: The Case of Jordan. *Journal of Education and Practice*, 6(2), 15–21. https://files.eric.ed.gov/fulltext/EJ1083789.pdf

Baker, W. (2015). Culture and complexity through English as a lingua franca: rethinking competences and pedagogy in ELT. *Journal of English as a Lingua Franca*, 4(1), 9–30. https://doi.org/10.1515/jelf-2015-0005

Baron-Epel, O., Bord, S., Elias, W., Zarecki, C., Shiftan, Y., & Gesser-Edelsburg, A. (2014). Alcohol consumption among Arabs in Israel: A qualitative study. *Substance Use & Misuse*, 50(2), 268–273. https://doi.org/10.3109/10826084.2014.962051

Bataineh, R., & Reshidi, A. E. (2017). The cultural gap in EFL secondary stage curricula and instructional practices as perceived by Saudi students, teachers and supervisors. *International Journal of Teaching and Education*, V(2), 1–21. ahttps://doi.org/10.20472/te.2017.5.2.001

Berry, J. W. (1997). Immigration, acculturation, and Adaptation. *Applied Psychology*, 46(1), 5–34. https://doi.org/10.1111/j.1464-0597.1997.tb01087.x

Bove, V., & Gokmen, G. (2016). Cultural distance and interstate conflicts. *British Journal of Political Science*, 47(4), 939–949. https://doi.org/10.1017/s0007123415000551

Brown, H. D. (2000). *Principles of language learning and teaching* (4th ed.). Longman.

Brown, H. D. (2007). *Principles of language learning and teaching* (5th ed.). Pearson Education.

Byram, M. (2021). Teaching and assessing intercultural communicative competence. In *Multilingual matters ebooks*. https://doi.org/10.21832/9781800410251

Cormoş, V. C. (2022). The Processes of adaptation, assimilation and integration in the country of migration: A psychosocial perspective on place identity changes. *Sustainability*, 14(16), 10296. https://doi.org/10.3390/su141610296

Crystal, D. (2003). *English as a global language* (2nd ed.). Cambridge University Press. https://doi.org/10.1017/cbo9780511486999

Damen, L. (1987). *Culture learning: The fifth dimension in the language classroom* (4th ed.). Addison-Wesley Longman.

Diallo, I. (2014). Emirati students encounter Western teachers tensions and identity resistance. *Learning and Teaching in Higher Education Gulf Perspectives*, 11(2), 46–59. https://doi.org/10.18538/lthe.v11.n2.158

Education at a Glance. (2021). In *Education at a glance. OECD indicators/Education at a glance.* https://doi.org/10.1787/b35a14e5-en

Ellis, R. (1994). *The study of second language acquisition* (illustrated ed., reprint). Oxford University Press.

Elshenawy, A. A. (2017). Globalization's effect on Qatari culture. *IAFOR Journal of Cultural Studies*, 2(1), 6–17. https://doi.org/10.22492/ijcs.2.1.01

Ferguson, Y. L., Ferguson, K. T., & Ferguson, G. M. (2015). I am AmeriBritSouthAfricanZambian: Multidimensional remote acculturation and well-being among urban Zambian adolescents. *International Journal of Psychology*, 52(1), 67–76. https://doi.org/10.1002/ijop.12191

Gardner, R. C. (1985). *Social psychology in second language learning*. Edward Arnold Ltd.

Gardner, R. C., & Lambert, W. E. (1959). Motivational variables in second language acquisition. *Canadian Journal of Psychology*, 13, 266–272.

Gardner, R. C., & Lambert, W.E. (1972). *Attitudes and motivation in second language learning*. Newbury.

Gardner, R., Lalonde, R., & Moorcroft, R. (1985). The role of attitudes and motivation in second language learning: Correlational and experimental considerations. *Language Learning*, 35(2), 207–227. https://doi.org/10.1111/j.1467-1770.1985.tb01025.x

Genc, B., & Bada, E. (2005). Culture in language learning and teaching. *The Reading Matrix*, 5(1), 73–84. http://www.readingmatrix.com/articles/genc_bada/article.pdf

Getie, A. S. (2020). Factors affecting the attitudes of students towards learning English as a foreign language. *Cogent Education*, 7(1). https://doi.org/10.1080/2331186X.2020.1738184

Grimm, P. (2010). Social desirability bias. *Wiley International Encyclopedia of Marketing*. https://doi.org/10.1002/9781444316568.wiem02057

Hofstede, G. (2011). Dimensionalizing cultures: The Hofstede model in context. *Online Readings in Psychology and Culture*, 2(1), 3–26. https://doi.org/10.9707/2307-0919.1014.

Jiang, W. (2000). The relationship between culture and language. *ELT Journal*, 54(4), 328–334. https://doi.org/10.1093/elt/54.4.328

Khuwaileh, A. A. (2000). Cultural Barriers of Language teaching: A case study of classroom cultural obstacles. *Computer Assisted Language Learning*, 13(3), 281–290. https://doi.org/10.1076/0958-8221(200007)13:3;1-3;ft281

Kramsch, C. (1998). *Language and culture* (reprint). Oxford University Press.

Kuang, J. F. (2007). Developing students' cultural awareness through foreign language teaching. *Sino-US English Teaching*, 4(12), 74–81. https://www.davidpublisher.com/index.php/Home/Article/Index?id=20673.html

Lanucha, K. (2018). Developing cultural competence for global engineers: How "soft" skills have become the new "hard" skills. *Journal of Teaching English for Specific and Academic Purposes*, 6(2), 297–303. https://doi.org/10.22190/jtesap1802297l

Lukmani, Y. (1972). Motivation to learn and language proficiency. *Language Learning*, 22, 261–273.

Lustig, M. W., & Koester, J. (1999). *Intercultural competence: Interpersonal communication across cultures* (3rd ed.). Addison Wesley Longman.

Miller, A. L. (2012). Investigating social desirability bias in student self-report surveys. *Educational Research Quarterly, 36*(1), 30–47. http://cpr.indiana.edu/uploads/SDB.pdf

Muir, P. (2007). Toward culture: Some basic elements of cultural-based instruction in China's high schools. *Sino-US English Teaching, 4*(4), 38–43.

Pauls, E. (2008). assimilation. Entry in *Encyclopedia Britannica*. https://www.britannica.com/topic/assimilation-society

Raphael, K. (1987). Recall bias: A proposal for assessment and control. *International Journal of Epidemiology, 16*(2), 167–170. https://doi.org/10.1093/ije/16.2.167

Roman Jr., R., & Nunez, A. M. (2020). Motivational factors that influence English as a foreign language learners at Quality Leadership University, Panama City, Panama. *Journal of Language Teaching and Research, 11*(4), 543–554. https://doi.org/10.17507/jltr.1104.03

Sadek, G. (2007). *Arab students' attitudes toward Western culture and motivation to learn English* [Unpublished master's thesis]. American University of Sharjah. Academia. https://www.academia.edu/67797131/Arab_Students_Attitudes_Toward_Western_Culture_and_Motivation_to_Learn_English

Suliman, W., Charles, T., & Sawalha, O. (2024). Students' integrative and instrumental motivation for learning English as a second language. *Revista De Gestão Social E Ambiental, 18*(8), e06092. https://doi.org/10.24857/rgsa.v18n8-040

Tang, R. (1999). The place of "culture" in the foreign language classroom: A reflection. *The Internet TESL Journal, 5*(8). http://iteslj.org/Articles/Tang-Culture.html

Uddin, N. (2017). Culture in teaching EFL in Saudi Arabia from learners' perspective. *Journal of Arts and Humanities, 6*(3), 8–17. https://doi.org/10.18533/journal.v6i3.1120

Wadell, E., & Shandor, A. (2012). Changing views on motivation in a globalizing world. *The Language Teacher, 36*(6), 32–36. https://doi.org/10.37546/jalttlt36.6-3

Zaid, M. A. (1999). Cultural confrontation and cultural acquisition in the EFL classroom. *IRAL—International Review of Applied Linguistics in Language Teaching, 37*(2), 111–126. https://doi.org/10.1515/iral.1999.37.2.111

Appendix A
Selected Survey Items

Note: The survey consisted of both Likert-scale statements and multiple-choice questions. For statements 1-16 (unless otherwise specified), participants were asked to choose from the following options: strongly agree, agree, disagree, strongly disagree.

Statement 1. "I think English is necessary for my success (work, social status, family)."

Statement 1a. "Please justify your answer."

Statement 2. "I enjoy listening to Western music."

Statement 2a. "Please justify your answer."

Statement 4. "I enjoy learning about Western culture while learning English."

Statement 4a. "Please justify your answer."

Statement 7. "I feel as though English is dominating the world."

Statement 7a. "Please justify your answer."

Statement 14. "I feel that learning about Western culture interferes with my culture."

Statement 14a. "Please justify your answer."

Statement 15. "I think Western people: (a) Have extremely different values that do not overlap with Arab values; (b) Have almost the same values as Arabs; (c) Other."

Statement 16. "I think Arabs should learn more about their own traditions instead of adopting Western traditions."

Statement 16a. "Please justify your answer."

Question 21. "What motivates you to learn English? (a) Communicating with native English speakers; (b) Better job opportunities and success in life; (c) Studies; (d) Other."

Question 22. "What would hinder your motivation to learn English? (a) Being taught primarily about Western Culture while learning English; (b) Not being taught about the Western culture while learning English; (c) Other."

CHAPTER SEVENTEEN | **MONIKA ZASOWSKA**

Difficult Neighborhoods
Consensus and Conflict in Academic Book Reviews

Abstract

The contemporary classification of linguistics as a humanities field and psychology as a social science discipline has not always been universally agreed upon, and over the centuries, many different representations have abounded. Regardless of the taxonomy adopted, both disciplines deal with the human subject in one way or another and may therefore be regarded as neighboring areas of knowledge. However, the two fields frequently blend, overlap, and diverge, creating a conceptual territory that defies clear interpretations. From this perspective, the notion of *difficult neighborhoods* becomes particularly relevant. This article sees the notion of difficult neighborhoods in a dual way. First, in terms of the intrinsic polarity of evaluative meanings, pertaining to either positive or negative assessments, formulated in all manner of ways and carried across the pages of an academic book review. Second, in terms of the very status of the two disciplines from which the book reviews have been retrieved, namely, linguistics and psychology. This paper offers an exploration of the management and distribution of positive and negative evaluations in the two corpora of 240 book reviews. The analysis was conducted with the UAMCT software (O'Donnell, 2019), short for Universidad Autonoma de Madrid Corpus Tools. The study makes use of part of a structured annotation scheme comprising two overarching classifications: EVALUTION-TYPE and EVALUATION-OBJECT (Zasowska, 2023). As part of a more extensive analysis, this paper takes as its prime focus the parameter of STYLE as an EVALUATION-OBJECT and its 12 subcategories. Upon a detailed examination of the evaluative expressions within two interrelated yet independent academic disciplines, several observations regarding the writing style in each corpus have been identified. The findings conclude that what is crucially important is the extent to which the evaluative parameters are represented in the two corpora. Specifically, the parameter of ATTRACTIVENESS emerges as a distinctive feature of psychology reviews, while the parameter of CLARITY is highlighted as emblematic of the linguistics corpus.

Keywords: evaluation, book review, linguistics, psychology, consensus, conflict, difficult neighborhoods

Introduction

Although most academic texts are not structured to evoke explicit evaluative assessments, more often than not, they carry a significant amount of personal judgement. It is particularly evident in the realm of the review genres, which generally aim to assess the work of other scholars. Among these, the book review stands out as a form where opinion-related language becomes visibly expressive and potentially confrontational.

While conveying an opinion means many things, consensus and conflict seem to be its most prominent driving forces. It may be argued that consensus is reflected through attributions of credit to the volume under review or the author of the work, demonstrating solidarity of reviewers with their colleagues in shared communities, and acknowledging the reputation and credibility of the authors. On the other hand, expressions of criticism and complaints, which may give rise to conflict, are frequently mitigated and softened in a variety of ways so as not to undermine a person's face or threaten their professional standing. These intentions and actions manifest in the book review genre, where consensus and conflict are closely intertwined and molded by the expectations of disciplinary communities.

Over the last three decades, numerous investigations into the evaluative language of the book review have offered an extensive body of research conducted mainly within the field of linguistics, often juxtaposed with one or more academic disciplines (e.g., Hyland, 2000; Nicolaisen, 2002; Römer, 2005; Shaw, 2009; Giannoni, 2010; D'Angelo, 2012). A number of studies have demonstrated that the analysis of positive and negative meanings should concentrate not only on single lexical items such as adjectives or nouns, but also take a much broader look at the syntactic signals of evaluation (see, e.g., Hunston & Francis, 1996; Hunston & Sinclair, 2000; Hoey, 2005; Römer, 2010). This is to say that some language patterns exhibit an evaluative meaning, without being overly explicit about it (see e.g., Bednarek, 2009, on language patterns and meaning or Hunston, 2011, in her study on modal-like expressions). Furthermore, there are situations in which the lexicogrammatical environment is indicative of a specific evaluation, not readily accessible through intuition or introspection (see the discussion of semantic prosody by Channell, 2000; Sinclair, 2004; Hunston, 2008; Partington, 2015; or Malory, 2024).

While explicit and implicit expressions of praise and criticism have been the subject of numerous corpus analyses, the latter sparked more academic curiosity. Literature shows a significant amount of studies that have been devoted to investigating the various ways in which academic book reviews make negative evaluations, often in terms of a third variable, for example, gender (e.g., Römer, 2006; Tse & Hyland, 2006), authorship (e.g., Zasowska, 2019), academic identity (e.g., Giannoni, 2010), or language of the book (e.g., Itakura & Tsui, 2011; Junqueira & Cortes, 2014).

Despite considerable research on evaluation in the academic book review, relatively scant attention has been paid to exploring the mechanisms of evaluation in a detailed quantitative and qualitative analysis of only two disciplines at hand, especially in the context of the writing style of the author(s) of the reviewed book, which appears to be crucially important in disseminating knowledge claims to the reading public. The rationale behind this study stems from the author's desire to challenge a somewhat unwritten expectation that encourages researchers to select two or more fields of knowledge from opposite sides of the scientific spectrum, such as linguistics and chemistry, sociology and biology and engineering, and so on. Having two or more contrasting disciplines may provide more opportunities to find a wide range of differences, and, as mentioned earlier, numerous scholars have elaborated on the nature of such differences so far. This study aims to compare and contrast two fields that come from similar spheres of knowledge and, as such, present a challenging avenue of research. While it is true that linguistics, as the study of the human language, and psychology, as the study of the human psyche, are inexorably connected, the two disciplines follow divergent paths regarding their research methods, theoretical frameworks, and practical implementations. Therefore, although interrelated, linguistics and psychology remain distinct fields within the contemporary scientific neighborhoods. How they interact across disciplinary boundaries makes their relationship worthy of exploration and further discussion.

This article investigates the management of positive and negative evaluations in book reviews of linguistics and psychology, with the aim of exploring similarities and differences in how the author's writing style is assessed in the review. The corpora selected for the analysis were obtained from the *Science Direct Elsevier* database and consist of 120 book reviews from each field, spanning the years 2008 to 2018. The investigation has been carried out with the help of the UAMCT corpus software (O'Donnell, 2019). First, the author created her multilayered annotation scheme, and subsequently, the UAMCT software was used to annotate instances of evaluation in the two corpora. To a degree, the multiparameter annotation scheme represents an advancement over "the categories of evaluation" introduced by Hyland (2000, p. 47) and "evaluative constructions" offered by Shaw (2009). However, the complete annotation scheme pays more attention to the unexplored or, at the very least, underexplored parameter of "the syntax of evaluation" and develops more nuanced parameters of evaluation. The scheme consists of two basic classifications: EVALUATION-TYPE, which looks at the polarity of the evaluative expressions at a syntactic level, and EVALUATION-OBJECT, which is concerned with the target of the evaluation. The two overarching types are further divided into their lower-level categories; however, for reasons of space and relevance, these are not fully presented and discussed in this paper (for details, see Zasowska, 2023). This study brings into focus positive and negative evaluations within the parameter of STYLE (one of the seven categories of EVALUATION-OBJECT) and its 12 sub-parameters. The parameter of STYLE corresponds to the manner in which the book's author communicates knowledge claims in the two fields under investigation, which is subsequently evaluated in the review.

Throughout this paper, *italics* are used for emphasis, CAPITALS indicate parameters of evaluation as originally outlined in the annotation scheme, and a standard font is used when referring to terms in a general sense.

1. Difficult Neighborhoods: Linguistics and Psychology on the Map of Disciplines

Given the richness of the numerous divisions of sciences throughout the history of human knowledge-making, it should come as no surprise that this section cannot discuss them in detail. It is worth remembering, however, that the classification of linguistics as a humanities discipline and psychology as a social science has never been set in stone. In fact, only in the last century have the various taxonomies of disciplines placed linguistics and psychology either in the same subject domain (see e.g., Beth, 1959; Kedrov, 1965), or in a completely separate area (see e.g., Hooper, 1906; Strumilin, 1954).

Currently, the Web of Science classifies research areas into five broad categories, in which both linguistics and psychology are placed within the domain of social sciences. In the Scopus Database, linguistics is classified under *"Language and Linguistics" and placed in the Arts and Humanities, as well as under "Linguistics and Language" within the Social Sciences*. Psychology, conversely, constitutes a separate subject area in Scopus and is subdivided into several other subcategories, such as applied psychology, clinical psychology, experimental and cognitive psychology, and social psychology.

In the context of the Polish higher education system, there have been notable transformations regarding the classification of linguistics as a humanities discipline and psychology as a social science over the last two decades. It is crucial to acknowledge that the official categorization of scientific fields and disciplines in Poland between 2005 and 2011, as outlined in the Resolution of the Central Commission for Academic Degrees and Titles on December 10, 2008 (originally in Polish: *Uchwała Centralnej Komisji do Spraw Stopni i Tytułów z dnia 10 grudnia 2008 r.* [Journal of Laws of 2008, No.97, item 843]) initially positioned linguistics and psychology under the same category of humanities. However, a significant shift occurred with the promulgation of the Ministry of Science and Higher Education's regulation on August 8, 2011, regarding the domains of knowledge, scientific, and artistic disciplines (Journal of Laws of 2011 r. No. 179, p. 1065). This decree led to the reassignment of linguistics and psychology to distinct academic fields, specifically the humanities and social sciences.

1.1. Points of Connection and Areas of Divergence

Taking a bird's-eye view of the disciplinary territory of linguistics and psychology, it should be noted that any similarity or difference outlined below is only a broad generalization and may vary significantly for individual theoreticians and researchers in pursuit of their own research objectives.

Linguistics studies human language, specifically its structure and form, historical development, and relationship with culture and society. As a humanities discipline, linguistics emphasizes the study of language as a system of communication and focuses strongly on form and meaning. Furthermore, linguistics is distinguished by its interpretative and analytical approach to studying language usage. These methods are associated with the humanities disciplines and their emphasis on critical thinking, interpretation, and hermeneutics. Finally, linguistics, probably unlike psychology, resorts to historical and comparative analysis by frequently examining the historical development and the evolution of languages, as well as performing comparative studies of different languages and language families. The historical and comparative approach resonates with the focus of the humanities disciplines on understanding the historical context and cultural evolution (see, e.g., Risager, 2005, on language and culture in applied linguistics, or Sharifian, 2017, on the notion of cultural linguistics).

Psychology as a social science is concerned with human behavior and cognition. It investigates emotions and mental processes and explores how individuals think, feel, and behave in all manner of situational contexts, be it cognitive, emotional, or institutional. Furthermore, psychology can be distinguished from other sciences on the basis of its empirical and scientific methods. The discipline puts emphasis on empirical research, employing systematic observation, experimentation, and statistical analysis to investigate human behavior and cognitive processes (see, e.g. Myers, 2008; Hergenhahn, 2009; Goodwin & Goodwin, 2016). Consequently, this empirical approach aligns with the scientific methods commonly associated with social sciences (e.g., Schinka et al., 2003). Among these, there are at least two worth mentioning. The first can be referred to as interaction and influence within social contexts, which involves how individuals interact, form relationships, and are influenced by social, cultural, and environmental factors (e.g., Grzyb & Dolinski, 2022). One important characteristic of the social sciences perspective is its strong focus on social interactions and the examination of how a social context shapes individuals. The second method, often highlighted by theoreticians, points out the aspect that could be described as applied research and intervention (e.g., Brawley, 1993). This applied "dimension" of psychology is visible because the discipline often seeks to apply research findings to understand and improve human well-being, mental health, or education. The emphasis on practical applications is consistent with the focus of social sciences on addressing social issues and positive change for the betterment of society (e.g., Goodwin & Goodwin, 2016).

Based on the discussion so far, it can be argued that linguistics and psychology are related disciplines. Their respective domains share several features in at least five aspects. First, both fields exhibit strong interdisciplinary connections. With varying levels of commitment, linguistics and psychology overlap with disciplines such as anthropology, computer science, neurology, history, and sociology (e.g., Bolshakov & Gelbukh, 2004). A second point of connection is the shared interest in studying language and communication, although the intensity of this interest varies. While linguistics focuses on the structure and form of language and its use, psychology explores how language is processed, acquired, and used cognitively in social interactions. The two fields also share a range of research methods, including experimental studies, surveys, observations, corpus analysis, and other empirical methods to gather data and test hypotheses. A fourth area of agreement is the reliance on statistical analysis and data interpretation in the research process. Finally, as much as psychology, linguistics also deals with the understanding of human behavior. While linguists mainly focus on analyzing language-related behavior, psychologists concentrate on a broader spectrum of mental processes, including cognition, emotion, development, personality, and social interaction.

The existence of similarities between the two disciplines should not obscure the fact that there are differences between them, although they may not be immediately apparent. Paradoxically, what serves as a mutual area of interest is, at the same time, a point where the two disciplines diverge. A crucial difference between linguistics and psychology lies in the focus and scope of research each field exhibits. Linguistics might be considered a narrower field of study as it primarily investigates language structure, synchronically and diachronically, with its many forms and variations, both spoken and written. Conversely, psychology examines a much broader selection of topics, including cognition, perception, memory, personality, developmental processes, psychopathology, and social behavior, to name but a few. For linguists, social aspects of behavior are important *additions* to language study. While these may significantly facilitate the understanding of language, they are not typically the primary motivators of investigation. For psychologists, however, the social aspect comes to the forefront of a research inquiry, with language considered as *one* of *several* behavior-related elements and often given secondary importance.

A similar observation can be made about methods and data. Again, it is the *scope* and the *extent* of these approaches that differentiate linguistics from psychology. Linguistic research often focuses on analyzing language patterns and features through manual and computerized analysis, surveys, and interviews. However, it is also open to exchange methods with other fields, incorporating experiments or statistical analysis where appropriate (e.g., Levon, 2013; Johnson, 2013; Paltridge & Phakiti, 2015). In testing hypotheses and refining theories, psychologists employ all manner of methods, including descriptive, correlational, and experimental approaches. These are applied in case studies, surveys, clinical assessments, naturalistic observations, experimentation, neuroimaging, or behavioral observations (e.g., Myers, 2008; Schinka et al., 2013).

A final point of divergence lies in the applicability of research in both fields. Psychology is often characterized by its strong emphasis on application and intervention, as seen in areas such as clinical psychology, counselling, educational psychology, industrial-organizational psychology, and forensic psychology. Linguistics, by contrast, tends to focus more on theoretical and descriptive aspects of language.

In summary, it may be metaphorically argued that linguists and psychologists do not necessarily look in the very same direction, as each scholar attaches different levels of importance to aspects that may lie on the periphery of interest for the other. As previously mentioned, linguistics and psychology occupy neighboring areas of knowledge, and their intellectual territories offer challenging and potentially fruitful directions for research. The evaluative repertoires used by reviewers in these disciplines, particularly as far as the author's writing style is concerned, reflect the value systems of each field and provide further textual evidence on their disciplinary differences.

2. Materials and Methods

The book reviews collected for this study were obtained from the *Science Direct Elsevier* database as PDF files, spanning the years 2008 to 2018. As already mentioned, there were 240 book review files in total, with the linguistics and psychology databases consisting of 222,700 and 180,59 running words, respectively.

The database representing linguistics was compiled from nine academic journals from the *Science Direct Elsevier* database, such as *Discourse and Communication, English for Specific Purposes, Journal of English Linguistics, Journal of English for Academic Purposes, Lingua, Language Teaching Research, Journal of Sociolinguistics, Journal of Linguistics*, and *World Englishes*. For ease of identification, the full journal names have been shortened to acronyms. For example, *Discourse and Communication* becomes DAC, *Lingua* becomes LNG, while *Journal of Linguistics* is abbreviated as JOL. The psychology corpus also comprises book reviews from nine journals, and these are *Archives of Clinical Neuropsychology, Applied Psychological Measurement, Brain, Behaviour, and Immunity, Cognitive and Behavioural Practice, Evolution and Human Behaviour, Intelligence, Journal of Economic Psychology, Personality, Individual Differences*, and *Psychosomatics*. Similarly, as with the first database, the journal titles have been abbreviated as acronyms.

Due to the requirements set by the UAMCT software, it was necessary to convert the PDF files into plain text format. Then, irrelevant data such as the title of the journal, the bibliographical information, the name and the affiliation of the reviewer were removed. The texts were subsequently annotated using UAMCT with the author's structured annotation scheme. The scheme consists of the two highest-level categories: EVALUATION-TYPE and EVALUATION-OBJECT (Zasowska, 2023). The former involves two main categories, POSITIVE-TYPE and NEGATIVE-TYPE, which were used to classify positive and negative instances of evaluation at their syntactic level. The latter, EVALUATION-OBJECT, consists of seven main categories (types): CONTENT, STYLE, READERSHIP, TEXT, AUTHOR, PRODUCTION STANDARDS, and GENERAL-TYPE. The presented article is concerned with evaluations of STYLE and its 12 parameters, which correspond to the writing style of the author of the book under review. The analysis comprises quantitative and qualitative data and identifies the parameters that were found to be statistically significant in both corpora.

2.1. The Parameters of EVALUATION-TYPE: POSITIVE and NEGATIVE Polarity

As has been previously outlined, EVALUATION-TYPE is concerned with how an evaluative act is structured syntactically, whereas the EVALUATION-OBJECT addresses the target of the evaluation. Figure 1 shows EVALUATION-TYPE comprising two obvious parameters: POSITIVE-TYPE and NEGATIVE-TYPE, which are further divided into subcategories, each focusing on a different syntactic structure of an evaluative act. As noted earlier, for reasons of space and relevance, the complete annotation scheme will not be replicated here. Suffice it to say that POSITIVE-TYPE and NEGATIVE-TYPE are divided into SIMPLE-TYPE and CHAINED-TYPE, each breaking down into several categories. In short, SIMPLE-TYPE for both polarities involves evaluations classified as –ALONE (i.e., occurring singly in a syntactic unit and left without a further comment within the same segment), –REASON (receiving an explanation within the same or an adjacent unit), and –PLUS-OTHER (receiving a comment different from an explanation, such as a paraphrase or an example). The CHAINED-TYPE refers to evaluations that occur within the same clause (INTRACLAUSAL) or involve two or more clauses within the same sentence (INTERCLAUSAL), which then subdivide into DOUBLETS and MULTIPLES.

When addressing the parameter of STYLE, the presented article references the basic division of positive and negative meanings, as indicated by broken lines in Figure 1.

2.2. The Parameters OF EVALUATION-OBJECT: STYLE-TYPE

The parameter of STYLE has been defined and exemplified with the help of relevant literature sources. In the *Longman dictionary of language teaching and applied linguistics* (2002, p. 575), "style" is defined as "a person's speech or writing," while for Crystal

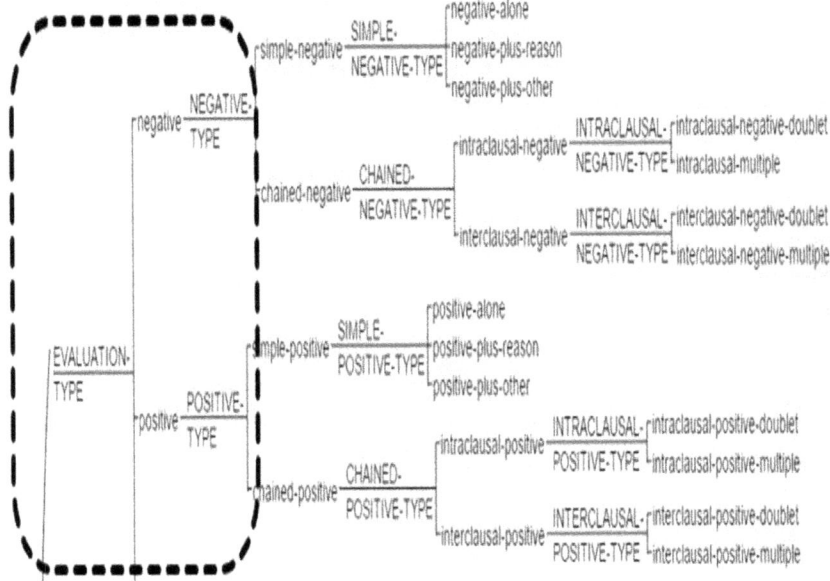

Fig 1. The categories of EVALUATION-TYPE (Zasowska, 2023)

(2008), it relates to situationally distinctive linguistic features. For the purpose of this analysis, a particularly useful definition of "style" comes from *Collins Dictionary*, where it is defined as "the manner in which something is expressed or performed, considered as separate from its intrinsic content, meaning, etc." This definition highlights the uniqueness of the expression and performance, drawing a line between style, content, and meaning. Figure 2 presents the parameters of STYLE and its 12 categories.

CLARITY, as a feature of an academic book, pertains to the quality of writing and presentation, which allows readers to grasp and understand the content easily. CLARITY can be assessed based on how well it communicates ideas: a book that demonstrates clarity conveys its arguments and ideas to its target audience. ORGANIZATION refers to how ideas are presented. Ideally, the book or a book chapter should exhibit a logical flow of ideas with a well-designed arrangement of content to contribute to its coherence and readability effectively. CONCISENESS is instrumental in conveying ideas and information in a clear and brief manner, avoiding verbosity. A concise style is about brevity while ensuring the content remains clear and understandable.

Another parameter involves DIFFICULTY, which has been found to be problematic, as it potentially overlaps with CLARITY. While both parameters bear interrelated qualities, it is crucial to recognize their distinctiveness and non-mutually exclusive nature. It is proposed here that DIFFICULTY refers to how challenging it is for readers to comprehend and integrate the connection proposed by the book's author(s).

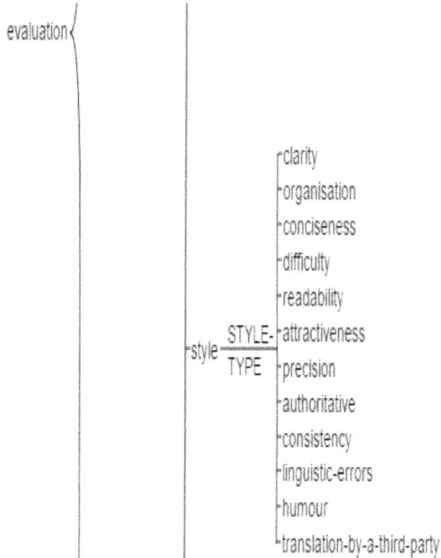

Fig 2. The parameter of STYLE-TYPE and its categories (Zasowska, 2023)

READABILITY refers to the assessment of how challenging a text is to read based on its complexity. In other words, this parameter is considered a subjective value measured in terms of language suited to the intended audience. A book that is praised for its readability engages and informs its readers.

ATTRACTIVENESS is a parameter that refers to a book or a book section characterized by a well-crafted and engaging writing style that clearly captivates the reader or, at the very least, the reviewers themselves. It is ATTRACTIVENESS that draws readers in, encouraging them to explore the text further.

The parameter of AUTHORITATIVE (STYLE) describes a writing style in which the author shows their confidence, expertise, and mentorship. When evaluated positively, AUTHORITATIVE (STYLE) refers to a style free from absolute claims or unsupported generalizations yet presenting the author's credibility.

Yet another parameter is CONSISTENCY, through which the author strives to maintain uniformity in style, concepts, and methods in order to ensure a logical and unified presentation of ideas. LINGUISTIC ERRORS is a self-explanatory parameter aimed at identifying language inconsistencies by the book authors that may hinder overall comprehension or affect the reception of the text. When registered by reviewers, linguistic errors highlight flaws in the language of the text.

The last two parameters are HUMOR and TRANSLATION-BY-A-THIRD PARTY. However marginal role humor plays in the context of the book review, it has been hypothesized that some academic authors may incorporate it to capture the

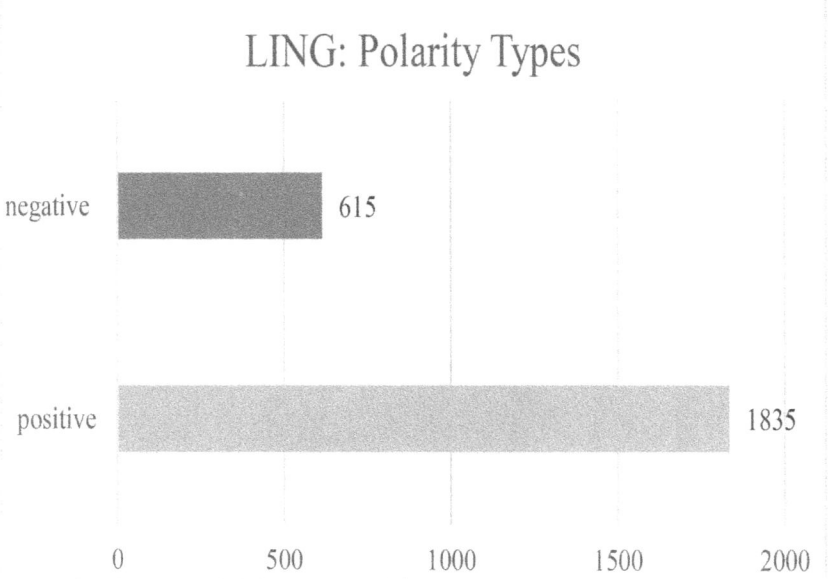

Fig 3. The division of polarity types in the LING corpus

reader's attention and add a touch of levity to otherwise complex and serious subjects. TRANSLATION-BY-A-THIRD PARTY is a parameter designed to evaluate the accuracy of translations of originally non-English books or chapters into the English language.

3. Results

The following section aims to present the research findings obtained from the analysis of the evaluative acts centered around the category of STYLE. In discussing the results of the study in the two disciplines under investigation, this article uses a one-at-a-time approach, starting with the linguistics book reviews, short for LING, and then moving on to the psychology database, short for PSYCH.

3.1. EVALUATION-TYPE: POSITIVE and NEGATIVE Polarity in the LING Corpus

In the linguistics database there have been found 2,450 evaluative acts in total, which comprise 615 negative comments and 1835 instances of positive assessments, as shown in Figure 3.

Examples 1–2 below come from the original database that illustrate these evaluations. The bold type is used to indicate where exactly the evaluation has been identified.

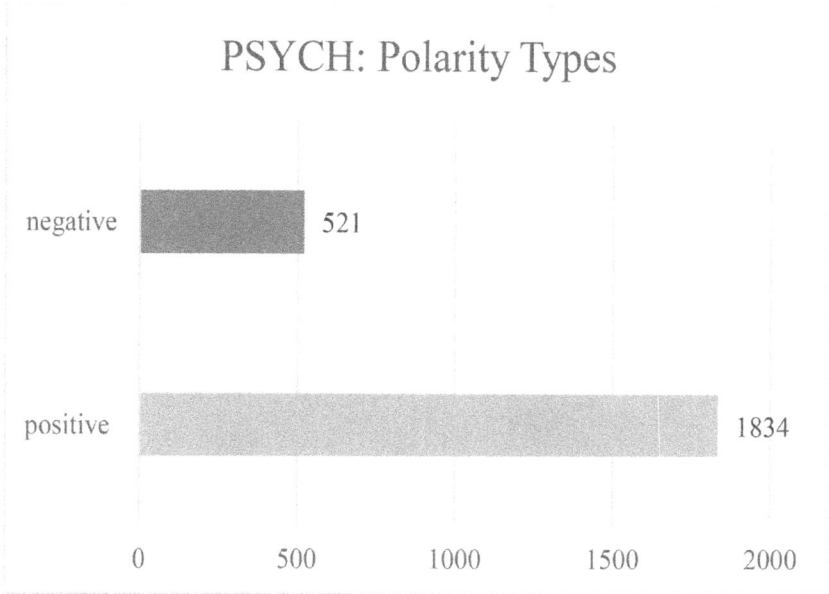

Fig 4. The division of polarity types in the PSYCH corpus

POSITIVE-TYPE

(1) The editors have **successfully organized these chapters into five thematically-distinct blocks** which, if desired, may be read as separate units [Linguistics/DAN_008_2011.txt].

NEGATIVE-TYPE

(2) I noticed only **one missing contact type** on the list of contact phenomena: the multilingual urban varieties that are spoken largely by the youth in some major African cities, and surely elsewhere in the urban world, are not mentioned [Linguistics/JEL_001_2012.txt]

A similar situation has been observed in the corpus of psychology book reviews, in which 2,355 evaluative assessments have been identified. The numerical data are presented in Figure 4.

As could be seen, positive evaluations constitute the dominant polarity type, having been identified 1,834 times. Negative assessments have been recorded in 512 evaluations. The two polarities are shown in examples 3–4.

Table 1. The categories of EVALUATION-OBJECT in terms of polarity in the LING corpus

EVALUATION-OBJECT	POSITIVE		NEGATIVE		Comparison			
	N	%	N	%	ChiSqu	P	Signif	Effect Size
CONTENT	956	52.0	417	67.8	46.46	0.0000	+++	0.323
STYLE	180	9.8	97	15.8	16.41	0.0000	+++	**0.180**
READERSHIP	181	9.9	11	1.8	41.52	0.0000	+++	0.370
TEXT	117	6.4	31	5.0	1.43	0.2312		0.057
AUTHOR	44	2.4	3	0.5	8.92	0.0028	+++	0.171
PUBLISHING STANDARDS	10	0.5	25	4.1	40.59	0.0000	+++	0.258
GENERAL	63	3.4	1	0.2	19.34	0.0000	+++	0.292

POSITIVE-TYPE

(3) For instance, Babikian and Boone **exhaustively review** both simulated and known-group feigning of intellectual deficits (mainly on the WAIS-R and WAIS-III) [Psychology/ACN_002_2008.txt]

NEGATIVE-TYPE

(4) For example, some chapters are **very long** and contain **more information than one would want to really know** about certain diagnoses. [Psychology/ACN_010_2012.txt]

3.2. EVALUATION-OBJECT: STYLE-TYPE in the LING Corpus

For STYLE-TYPE as EVALUATION-OBJECT, the results obtained from the UAMCT analysis reveal that there are 277 instances of evaluations, out of which 180 are identified as POSITIVE and 97 as negative assessments. Table 1 shows the data gathered for all seven parameters of the EVALUATION-OBJECT, with STYLE being the second most frequently addressed parameter. It is vital to note that the parameter of STYLE has been identified as statistically significant.

The detailed results for STYLE-TYPE and its twelve parameters are shown in Table 2.

It is worth highlighting that not all parameters are found in positive and negative evaluations. While the negative polarity of evaluations of LINGUISTIC ERRORS could

Table 2. STYLE-TYPE in terms of polarity: general and descriptive statistics in the LING corpus

STYLE-TYPE	POSITIVE		NEGATIVE		Comparison			
	N	%	N	%	ChiSqu	P	Signif	Effect Size
CLARITY	57	3.1	26	4.2	1.76	0.1842		0.060
ORGANISATION	50	2.7	32	5.2	8.73	0.0031	+++	0.129
CONCISENESS	6	0.3	12	2.0	16.65	0.0000	+++	0.166
DIFFICULTY	2	0.1	3	0.5	3.24	0.0717	+	0.074
READABILITY	32	1.7	14	2.3	0.71	0.4007		0.038
ATTRACTIVENESS	10	0.5	4	0.7	0.09	0.7647		0.014
PRECISION	14	0.8	0	0.0	4.72	0.0298	++	0.175
AUTHORITATIVE STYLE	5	0.3	1	0.2	0.23	0.6329		0.024
CONSISTENCY	3	0.2	2	0.3	0.59	0.4422		0.033
LINGUISTIC ERRORS	0	0.0	3	0.5	8.96	0.0028	+++	0.140
HUMOUR	1	0.1	0	0.0	0.34	0.5625		0.047
TRANSLATION-BY-A-THIRD-PARTY	0	0.0	0	0.0	0.00	1.0000		
TOTAL:	**180**	**9.8%**	**97**	**15.8%**				

be well expected, it is interesting to note that the parameter of PRECISION appears exclusively in positive terms. Furthermore, ChiSqu statistics show that negative evaluations are also likely to refer to ORGANIZATION and CONCISENESS. Examples 5–13 illustrate bolded instances where evaluation has been identified.

(5) Another strength of this volume is that all articles are **written in a clear, accessible** and **engaging style** [Linguistics/DAN_005_2010.txt] CLARITY

(6) The resulting **imbalance is visible in the basic organization** of the book [Linguistics/JOL_002_2008.txt] ORGANIZATION

(7) The survey of the common basis of the phonology of the individual Semitic languages (pp. 64–80) is **commendable for its brevity** [Linguistics/LNG_013_2015.txt] CONCISENESS

(8) Only the sections dedicated to phonetics **may be difficult for readers** with **no background** in linguistics [Linguistics/WEN_011_2015.txt] DIFFICULTY

(9) Yet, while the introductory chapters are **very accessible**, the later chapters constitute **heavier reading** [Linguistics/JOL_003_2010.txt] READABILITY

(10) All of the volume's 10 chapters, which range in topic from language politics and ideology in Indonesia to the question of indigenous cultural education in Brazil, are **engaging** [Linguistics/JOS_003_2011.txt] ATTRACTIVENESS

(11) It has **an "authoritative" feel** to it [Linguistics/WEN_002_2010.txt] AUTHORITATIVE (STYLE)

(12) This is where Shohamy and Gorter's skills as editors to **utilize the topics and space in this volume** to **demonstrate the strengths and weaknesses** of LL lead to support the possibility of more stringent LL methodologies [Linguistics/JOS_005_2012.txt] CONSISTENCY

(13) Perhaps the **main weaknesses** of this volume are formal: several chapters display **stylistic problems** or even **syntactic errors**, a problem that might have been addressed with more rigorous peer review and editing [Linguistics/LTR_008_2011.txt] LINGUISTIC ERRORS

3.3. EVALUATION-OBJECT: STYLE-TYPE in the PSYCH Corpus

The findings show that the psychology corpus contains more evaluation of STYLE-TYPE, with 250 positive assessments and 82 instances of negative instances. However, the differences in STYLE were not identified as statistically significant in the psychology database. Table 3 presents the parameters of EVALUATION-OBJECT in the PSYCH corpus, with STYLE being the second most frequently reported.

The 12 parameters of STYLE are shown in Table 4.

As said, STYLE is the second most frequently employed category in the PSYCH corpus in terms of both positive and negative evaluations. As in the previously discussed case, positive evaluations numerically outnumber negative ones. However, the percentage of STYLE evaluations in both polarity groups is roughly equal, around 15%. Among the most frequently positively evaluated features of STYLE are CLARITY, READABILITY, and ATTRACTIVENESS. Parameters such as CONCISENESS or CONSISTENCY are evaluated positively and negatively with a roughly similar frequency. Negative assessments of ORGANIZATION occur more often, though in absolute terms, the number of positive and negative evaluations remains around 45 occurrences. There are statistically significant differences for a few parameters, such as CLARITY, ORGANIZATION, READABILITY, ATTRACTIVENESS and CONSISTENCY.

Examples 14–18 provide excerpts illustrating the psychological database.

(14) The chapter **does well in explaining the strengths and weaknesses of each method** so that the practitioner may make the best decision for their own test [Psychology/APM_011_2015.txt]. CLARITY

(15) When they do, they will find that these chapters are **laid out logically**. [Psychology/ACN_011_2013.txt]. ORGANIZATION

Table 3. The categories of EVALUATION-OBJECT in terms of polarity in the PSYCH corpus

EVALUATION-OBJECT	POSITIVE		NEGATIVE		Comparison			
	N	%	N	%	ChiSqu	P	Signif	Effect Size
CONTENT	903	49.2	347	66.6	49.13	0.0000	+++	0.354
STYLE	250	13.6	82	15.7	1.49	0.2225		0.060
READERSHIP	151	8.2	14	2.7	19.16	0.0000	+++	0.253
TEXT	103	5.6	21	4.0	2.04	0.1528		0.074
AUTHOR	52	2.8	7	1.3	3.70	0.0545	+	0.106
PUBLISHING STANDARDS	14	0.8	13	2.5	10.74	0.0010	+++	0.142
GENERAL	82	4.5	0	0.0	24.13	0.0000	+++	0.426

Table 4. STYLE-TYPE in terms of polarity: general and descriptive statistics in the PSYCH corpus

STYLE-TYPE	POSITIVE		NEGATIVE		Comparison			
	N	%	N	%	ChiSqu	P	Signif	Effect Size
CLARITY	61	3.3	5	1.0	8.34	0.0039	+++	0.171
ORGANISATION	46	2.5	45	8.6	41.03	0.0000	+++	0.279
CONCISENESS	28	1.5	10	1.9	0.39	0.5302		0.030
DIFFICULTY	3	0.2	3	0.6	2.71	0.0995	+	0.071
READABILITY	65	3.5	5	1.0	9.40	0.0022	+++	0.183
ATTRACTIVENESS	25	1.4	1	0.2	5.10	0.0240	++	0.146
PRECISION	9	0.5	1	0.2	0.86	0.3547		0.053
AUTHORITATIVE	2	0.1	2	0.4	1.81	0.1788		0.058
CONSISTENCY	7	0.4	8	1.5	8.54	0.0035	+++	0.125
LINGUISTIC ERRORS	1	0.1	1	0.2	0.90	0.3420		0.041
HUMOUR	2	0.1	1	0.2	0.22	0.6397		0.022
TRANSLATION-BY-A-THIRD-PARTY	1	0.1	0	0.0	0.28	0.5940		0.047

(16) This **highly readable account** uses the conceptual framework of inclusive fitness theory [Psychology/EHR_009_2012.txt] READABILITY

(17) What makes the **book unappealing as a read** is its general antagonism: these authors are angry at not being taken more seriously by economists and others [Psychology/JEP_004_2013.txt] ATTRACTIVENESS

(18) One is a **lack of consistency** [Psychology/ACN_010_2012.txt]. CONSISTENCY

1. Discussion

At its heart, the genre of the book review is about providing a critique of a book or a book chapter. Gea-Valor (2000, p. 86) observes that the genre is also a "highly threatening act since it basically involves the assessment of the work of a fellow researcher." In a similar vein, Hyland (2000, p. 41) argues that it is precisely in the book review genre where "the interpersonal stakes are much higher," and elsewhere, he notes that the genre is an open and more direct encounter with a particular text and with a particular author than any other academic genre. While not disputing the validity of such claims, it should be noted that such observations have not been offered in the present study. On the contrary, evaluative meanings concerning the writing style of the author in the selection of the book reviews in linguistics and psychology have proven to be less threatening to the author's face than might have initially been expected.

The analysis of the collected corpora from two neighboring fields reveals that book reviewing practices regarding the writing style of the author differ, which points to disciplinary distinctions between linguistics and psychology. While the prevailing polarity of evaluative acts is positive, clearly reflecting the reviewer's intention or preference for consensus over conflict, the two disciplines express praise in different ways, accentuating different aspects of the author's research. Criticism, though less frequent than positive comments, targets specific features of the writing style of the author, prioritizing clarity of thought in the linguistics corpus and underscoring the importance of organization of the text. However, at the level of individual parameters of STYLE, the list of similarities between the two corpora is quite short. It should be emphasized that it is the *extent* to which these are represented in the two corpora that plays a crucial role here.

As mentioned previously, this paper is part of a larger project where all seven EVALUATION-OBJECTS have been examined. Among these, evaluative expressions pertaining to STYLE account for 29.3% of all evaluations in the PSYCH corpus and 25.4% in the LING database. In the case of the PSYCH corpus, the difference between positive and negative is not statistically significant, with only a 2.1% advantage in favor of negative evaluations. In the LING corpus, however, a substantial discrepancy can be observed, as negative evaluations (15.7%) are nearly twice as numerous as positive ones, which aligns with a certain stereotype suggesting that linguistics should display more sensitivity to issues of linguistic correctness.

The category of STYLE as an EVALUATION-OBJECT comprises twelve parameters, of which CLARITY and ORGANIZATION are unquestionable leaders with regard to the quantitative data, yet not in the same order in the two corpora. The evaluations pertaining to CLARITY are present in 83 segments in the LING corpus and in 66 in the PSYCH one, which represent 7.3% and 4.3% of all evaluations, respectively. Although the number of positive evaluations is roughly the same in both corpora, the issue of clarity is more frequently raised and questioned in the linguistics book reviews, accounting for 4.2% and contrasted with as little as 1% of such assessments in the PSYCH corpus. This difference has been shown to be statistically significant and demonstrates that the issue of smooth communication with a target audience, as well as a coherent order of ideas, is particularly important for linguists.

The parameter of ORGANIZATION has been addressed in 82 instances in the LING corpus and 91 in the PSYCH corpus. However, while the total number of evaluations remains similar, their distribution differs between the two corpora. In the PSYCH corpus, positive and negative evaluations are almost equal and amount to 46 and 45 cases, respectively. Due to the relatively lower number of negative evaluations, the share of ORGANIZATION-related evaluations makes up 8.6%, which contrasts sharply with the share of positive evaluations of 2.5%. In contrast, the LING corpus shows a different pattern, with positive evaluations at 2.7% and negative evaluations, which are less frequent than in the PSYCH corpus, at 5.2%. Overall, these findings suggest that the issue of a well-designed arrangement of content plays a greater role in the case of psychology book reviews.

READABILITY is another prominent parameter of STYLE. In the LING corpus, evaluations concerning READABILITY appear in 4.1% of all evaluations. As far as the PSYCH corpus is concerned, its overall share is slightly higher and stands at 4.5%. The stark contrast between the distribution of positive and negative evaluations is the most significant feature of this parameter. While in the LING corpus, the share of critical assessments exceeds positive ones, in the case of the PSYCH, we are confronted almost exclusively with positive evaluations of the readability of the book under review (65 positive assessments vs. five negative ones). In this regard, the reviews in the LING corpus show a much higher degree of criticism, which may be related, yet again, to the greater emphasis on language itself on the part of the linguists, if not to the higher degree of abstractness of the theories presented in linguistics and more technical description of linguistic mechanisms. However, the latter explanation is not supported by the conceptually similar parameter of DIFFICULTY, as for both LING and PSYCH databases, there are only about six evaluations regarding it, with a balanced distribution of positive and negative assessments.

CONCISENESS is among the few parameters whose contribution to the two corpora exceeds 2% of all evaluative comments. It is higher in the PSYCH corpus, where evaluations related to CONCISENESS account for 3.4% of all evaluations, compared to 2.2% in the LING corpus. Again, as with the previously mentioned parameters of STYLE, linguistics book reviewers are more critical when assessing CONCISENESS. They highlight issues such as excessive verbosity or, on the contrary, unsuccessful attempts to condense large amounts of material. In contrast, PSYCH reviewers praise authors for their ability to write concise yet sufficiently informative texts.

CONSISTENCY as a parameter representing uniformity in terms of the writing style falls into the category of parameters with a very low frequency in the two corpora. The frequency is higher for the PSYCH corpus, and this parameter is present in 1.9% of all evaluations, of which 1.5% are negative. In contrast, reviewers in the LING corpus take remarkably little interest in this parameter, as it appears in only five evaluations of both polarities. One possible explanation for such a situation may lie in the prevalence of multiauthored psychology books under review, where the expectation for a consistent style is more prominent in the PSYCH corpus.

No significant difference was observed in the two corpora with regard to the parameter of PRECISION. Whenever there is an evaluation concerning this parameter, it is invariably used in positive contexts, which makes for 14 instances in the LING and 9 in the PSYCH corpora. However, the share of this parameter in the total evaluations does not exceed 1% and, as such, cannot form the basis for any claims about differences in the creation of book reviews.

The parameters of AUTHORITATIVE STYLE, LINGUISTIC ERRORS, HUMOR, and TRANSLATION-BY-A-THIRD-PARTY can be omitted due to their very low level of occurrence in both corpora. Their combined contribution to the total of evaluations is 1.2% in PSYCH and 1.1% in LING.

Conversely, it is impossible to ignore the parameter that plays a special role in the PSYCH corpus, namely, ATTRACTIVENESS, which denotes an engaging writing style that captivates the reader. Phrases such as "enjoyable style," "enjoyable read," "engaging prose," or "a pleasure to read" appear in as many as 25 positive assessments in the psychology book reviews. In the case of the linguistics corpus, the number is considerably lower, breaking down into 9 positive evaluations and 4 negative ones. Undoubtedly, ATTRACTIVENESS may, therefore, be regarded as a parameter characteristic of psychology book reviews only, which values not only the aforementioned readability, usually assessed positively, but also expects that reading a book, apart from its undoubted cognitive worth, should also contribute to the reader's well-being. It also seems that the tone of the positive evaluations in the LING is somewhat subdued, as phrases such as "manages to avoid a dry style" or "manages to give a flavour" can be found alongside phrases such as "enjoyable read" or "enjoyable compilation."

Table 5. Similarities and differences in STYLE-related evaluations in the LING and PSYCH corpora

	LING	PSYCH
STYLE-TYPE	more negative evaluations of STYLE in general more emphasis laid on **CLARITY** more negative evaluations of CLARITY more critical evaluations of CONCISENESS	more emphasis laid on **ORGANIZATION** READABILITY evaluated almost *always* positively CONCISENESS evaluated almost always positively more emphasis on **CONSISTENCY** more emphasis on ATTRACTIVENESS, evaluated almost always positively

For ease of reference, the findings from the analysis are presented in Table 5, with positive and negative evaluations marked in green and red, respectively. The bold type signifies that more emphasis was placed on individual parameters in the quantitative analysis.

In view of what has been said and what becomes evident from the data above, the LING corpus shows more negative evaluations within the parameter of STYLE. The two corpora differ in the emphasis laid on specific parameters, assessed by the reviewers either almost exclusively positively, such as ATTRACTIVENESS, READABILITY, and CONCISENESS in the PSYCH corpus, or negatively, as is the case with CLARITY or CONCISENESS in the LING reviews. It also becomes evident that certain parameters are absent from this general comparison, specifically, there are no significant differences concerning parameters of DIFFICULTY, LINGUISTIC ERRORS, HUMOR, and TRANSLATION-BY-THE-THIRD-PARTY, all of which have been rather scarce in the corpora. This does not necessarily indicate that elements of humor are non-existent in the book review genre or that certain difficulties in grasping the content of the book never occur. Rather, it is reasonable to assume that the reason why these parameters were largely absent in the collected corpora is perhaps due to the size of the corpora themselves.

5. Concluding Remarks

The analysis has offered an exploration of the STYLE-related evaluations in book reviews from the fields of linguistics and psychology. By comparing the frequency and distribution of the selected parameters of STYLE, as outlined in the author's annotation scheme, the study aimed to identify the objectives and priorities of reviewers in each of the two neighboring disciplines, which may have shaped their evaluative choices. In doing so, the findings provide an opportunity to examine the mechanisms of evaluations and offer insights into the territories occupied by linguistics and psychology.

Once again, it is worth emphasizing that the parameters of STYLE vary in the extent to which they are considered by reviewers in each discipline. Notably, the parameter of ATTRACTIVENESS appears to be a unique feature of psychology book reviews, suggesting a greater emphasis on how ideas are communicated to the reading public and how they should be received by professionals in the field. In contrast, this parameter is largely absent in the corpus of linguistics book reviews, which may reflect a more theoretical orientation among linguists toward their readership, where the expectation for a book to be "enjoyable" or "pleasant" is not high on the list of priorities.

A reverse situation is observed in the communication of ideas in the text, as represented by the parameter of CLARITY. While CLARITY is represented in both corpora, it is more frequently evaluated, both positively and negatively, in the LING corpus. In contrast, although CLARITY is also noted by reviewers in the PSYCH corpus, it tends to receive more positive evaluations. Such evaluative choices may be linked with the reviewer's tendency to underscore the language aspect of the reviewed book in linguistics, a preference that is clearly less pronounced in the field of psychology. Similarly, assessments of the author's ability to avoid unnecessary verbosity, reflected in the parameter of CONCISENESS, are more critical in the LING corpus than in the PSYCH corpus, where they are predominantly positive. It is worth noting, however, that CONCISENESS is mentioned more frequently in the psychological database. How these parameters have been approached by the reviewers structures our perception of the nature of the book review in each field and points to the significance of the writing style in general.

Overall, while the theme of "difficult neighborhoods" is far from exhausted, it is the hope of the author that this paper has provided insights into the language of consensus and conflict expressed through praise and criticism in the book review genre. The selected parameters of STYLE encompassing a range of stylistic aspects of a book text serve as a useful reminder of academic review practices in these fields. As noted previously, while linguistics and psychology are interrelated, mainly due to their shared interest in the human subject, the two fields exhibit a number of unique characteristics unraveled only when looking closely at the intricacies of their nature. This certainly includes the writing style of the book authors, in particular how they communicate their ideas and research objectives, engage with the reading public, or use the creative potential of language to convey their message and align with their disciplinary community. In other words, throughout the pages of the book, the author's writing style helps to ensure that both authors and readers are on the same page. This role becomes even more significant in reviews, where reviewers offer their critical assessment of the book's contents to vouch for the author, raise objections to their work, or sometimes do both. Therefore, the author's writing style, defined in the *Collins Dictionary* as "the uniqueness of expression and performance" applauded or criticized but ultimately validated by the reviewer in their public text, appears to play a critical role in the communicative intentions of the book review genre.

Finally, it is important to acknowledge the limitations of the study. Given the size of the two corpora, comprising 120 texts in each field, the analysis has offered valuable observations into the nature of evaluation in these two neighboring disciplines, while also accentuating the need for further research. Hopefully, the obtained findings contribute to a better understanding of how writing style and evaluative practices in the book review differ between linguistics and psychology. The investigation is also a vital step toward understanding the academic landscape and the difficult neighborhoods that are often part of it.

References

Bednarek, M. (2009). Language patterns and attitude. *Functions of language, 16*(2), 165–192.

Beth, E.W. (1959). Science and classification. *Synthese, 11*(3), 231–244. [Selected fragments retrieved at https://atlas-disciplines.unige.ch/].

Bliss, H. E. (1929). *The organization of knowledge and the system of sciences*. Holt. [Selected fragments retrieved at https://atlas-disciplines.unige.ch/].

Bolshakov, I., & Gelbukh, A. (2004). *Computational Linguistics. Models, Resources, Applications*. Ciencia de la Computación, Mexico.

Brawley, L. R. (1993). The practicality of using social psychological theories for exercise and health research and intervention. *Journal of Applied Sport Psychology, 5*(2), 99–115.

Collins Dictionary. (n.d.). *Style*. In *Collins English Dictionary*. Retrieved May 15, 2023, from https://www.collinsdictionary.com/dictionary/english/style

Crystal, D. (2008). *The Cambridge encyclopedia of the English language* (3rd ed.).

D'Angelo, L. (2012). Identity conflicts in book reviews. A cross-disciplinary comparison. In M. Gotti (Ed.), *Academic identity traits* (pp. 70–94). Linguistics Insights, Vol. 150, Peter Lang.

Gea Valor, L. (2000). *A pragmatic approach to politeness and modality in the book review*. Studies in English Language and Linguistics, Lengua Inglesa, Universitat de Valéncia.

Giannoni, D. (2010). *Mapping academic values across disciplines. A corpus-based approach*. Linguistics Insights, Volume 124. Peter Lang.

Goodwin, K., & Goodwin, J. (2016). *Research in psychology*. Methods and Design. Wiley.

Grzyb, T., & Dolinski. D. (2022). *The field study in social psychology: How to conduct research outside of a laboratory setting?* Routledge.

Hergenhahn, B. R. (2009). *An introduction to the history of psychology*. Cengage Learning.

Hoey, M. (2005). *Lexical priming: A new theory of words and language*. Routledge.
Hooper, C. (1906). *The anatomy of knowledge: An essay in objective logic*. Watts. https://atlas-disciplines.unige.ch/
Hyland, K. (2000). *Disciplinary discourses: Social interactions in academic writing*. Longman.
Itakura, H., & Tsui, A. (2011). Evaluation in academic discourse. Managing criticism in Japanese and English book reviews. *Journal of Pragmatics*, 43(5), 1366–1379. https://doi.org/10.1016/j.pragma.2010.10.023
Johnson, D. (2013) Descriptive statistics. In R. Podesva & D. Sharma (Eds.), *Research methods in linguistics* (pp. 288–315). Cambridge University Press.
Junqueira, L., & Cortes, V. (2014). Metadiscourse in book reviews in English and Brazilian Portuguese: A corpus-based analysis. *Journal of Rhetoric, Professional Communication, and Globalization*, 6(1), 87–109.
Levon, E. (2013). Ethnography and recording interaction. In R. Podesva & D. Sharma (Eds.), *Research methods in linguistics* (pp. 195–215). Cambridge University Press.
Lindholm-Romantschuk, Y. (1998). *Scholarly book reviewing in the social sciences and humanities: The flow of ideas within and among disciplines*. Greenwood Press.
Malory, B. (2024). Polarized discourses of abortion in English: A corpus-based study of semantic prosody and discursive salience. *Applied Linguistics*, 45, 481–497.
Myers, D. (2008). *Exploring Psychology*. Hope College, Michigan, USA.
Nicolaisen, J. (2002). The scholarliness of published peer reviews: A bibliometric study of book reviews in selected social science fields. *Research Evaluation*, 11(3), 129–140.
O'Donnell, M. (2019). UAM CorpusTool (version 6.2j). Retrieved February 28, 2023, from http://www.corpustool.com/download.html
Paltridge, B., & Phakiti, A. (2015). *Research methods in applied linguistics*. Bloomsbury.
Richards, J. C., & Richard S. (2002). *Longman: Dictionary of language teaching and applied linguistics*. Pearson Education Limited.
Risager, K. (2005). Languaculture as a key concept in language and culture teaching. In B. Preisler, A. Fabricius, H. Haberland, S. Kjærbeck, & K. Risager (Eds.), *The Consequences of Mobility* (pp. 185–196). Roskilde University, Department of Language and Culture.
Römer, U. (2005). This seems somewhat counterintuitive, though… Negative evaluation in linguistic book reviews by male and female authors. In E. Tognini-Bonelli & G. Del Lungo Camiciotti (Eds.), *Strategies in Academic Discourse* (pp. 97–115). John Benjamins Publishing Company.
Römer, U. (2010). Establishing the phraseological profile of a text type. The construction of meaning in academic book reviews. *English Text Construction*, 3(1), 95–119.
Sandoz, R. *Interactive historical atlas of the disciplines*. University of Geneva. Retrieved at https://atlas-disciplines.unige.ch/
Schinka, J. A., Velicer, W. F., & Weiner, I. B. (Eds.). (2013). *Handbook of psychology: Research methods in psychology*. John Wiley & Sons, Inc.
Sharifian, F. (2017). *Cultural linguistics. Cultural conceptualizations and language*. John Benjamins Publishing Company.
Shaw, P. (2009). The lexis and grammar of explicit evaluation in academic book reviews, 1913 and 1993. In K. Hyland & G. Diani (Eds.), *Academic evaluation. Review genres in university settings* (pp. 217–235). Palgrave, Macmillan.

Strumilin, S. G. (1954). Science and development of productive sources. In *Questions of Philosophy*, 3, pp. 46–61. [Selected fragments retrieved at https://atlas-disciplines.unige.ch/]

Tse, P., & Hyland, K. (2009). Discipline and gender: Constructing rhetorical identity in book reviews. In K. Hyland & G. Diani (Eds.), *Academic evaluation. Review genres in university settings* (pp. 105–121). Palgrave, Macmillan.

Zasowska, M. (2019). Reviews of single-authored versus multiple-authored academic books. Is two *less* than one? *Studia Linguistica Universitatis Iagellonicae Cracoviensis*, 136(4), 327–351. https://doi.org/10.4467/20834624SL.19.025.11318

Zasowska, M. (2023). *Evaluation in academic discourse: An analysis of book reviews in linguistics and psychology* [Unpublished doctoral dissertation]. University of Silesia.

LIST OF CONTRIBUTORS

Yousif Al-Naddaf is a PhD candidate in linguistics at the University of Warsaw, where he also lectures in the Institute of English Studies. He has taught undergraduate courses including *English Across Academic Domains, Writing for Practical Purposes*, and *Grammar*. His research focuses on culture-sensitive English language teaching (ELT), second language acquisition in Arab contexts, learner motivation and attitudes, linguistic relativity, and cross-cultural communication. He earned his MA in Literature and Linguistics from the University of Warsaw, graduating *summa cum laude*, with a thesis that explored the role of culture in the motivation and attitudes of Arab learners. He has presented at international academic conferences, including *Beyond Language 2025* and the *10th International Students' Corner*. He also serves as an editor and proofreader for *Second Thoughts*, an award-winning student-led academic magazine.

Dorota Brzozowska is a professor at the Institute of Linguistics of the Opole University, Poland. Her scholarly research interests comprise research on intercultural communication, humor studies, language and identity, stylistics, discourse analysis, pragmatics, and semiotics. She has authored three books and many papers on jokes as a genre, humor, identity and cultural stereotypes. She is a coeditor of *Culture's Software: Communication Styles* (Cambridge Scholars, 2015) and *Humorous Discourse* (De Gruyter, 2017). She is an editor of *The European Journal of Humour Research* and *Tertium Linguistic Journal*.

Anita Buczek-Zawiła is an assistant professor in the Department of English Linguistics at the University of the National Education Commission, Kraków, where she teaches courses on English phonetics and phonology, nonverbal communication, and varieties of English in both the undergraduate and graduate programs, in face-to-face and hybrid modes. Her research interests cover CAPT, sound systems interactions, language prosody as well as emoji and other graphic elements contribution to communication. She authored several book chapters and articles in numerous Polish journals (*Prace Językoznawcze, Roczniki Humanistyczne, Świat i Słowo, Anglica, Linguistica Silesiana, SLING*) and co-edited the volume *CALL for Background* (with Anna Turula).

Władysław Chłopicki is a professor of linguistics and translation at the Institute of English Studies, Jagiellonian University, Kraków, Poland, as well as at the Academy of Applied Sciences in Krosno, Poland. His research focuses on humor studies, his first book *O humorze poważnie* (*Humor taken seriously*) was published in 1995 by the Polish Academy of Sciences. He is a coeditor of *Culture's Software: Communication Styles* (Cambridge Scholars, 2015), *Humorous Discourse* (De Gruyter, 2017), and the *De Gruyter Handbook of Humor Studies* (De Gruyter, 2024). Most recently, his main focus has been humor in the public sphere, and he coordinates the large international Horizon grant on humor literacy acronymed HUMLIT (2025–2028). He is also an editor of *The European Journal of Humour Research* and *Tertium Linguistic Journal*.

Monika Coghen is a faculty member at the Institute of English Studies of the Jagiellonian University in Kraków, where she teaches courses on English Literature. In 2001–2002, she was a visiting professor at Troy State University, Alabama. She has published numerous articles on British Romantics and the Gothic and contributed two chapters to the British Academy Project, The Reception of British and Irish Authors in Europe. She is also the author of a chapter on Polish Romanticism in *The Oxford Handbook of European* Romanticism. She has coedited two volumes on Romantic literature: *Romantic Dialogues and Afterlives* (Jagiellonian University Press, 2020) and *Nowe oblicza romantyzmu: Eseje na dwusetlecie* [*British Romanticism: Bicentenary Essays*] (Wydawnictwa Uniwersytetu Warszawskiego, 2021).

Giordano Durante is a bilingual poet and translator from Gibraltar. He was born in 1981 and studied in London. His first book of poems *West* was published in 2017. A second collection, the pamphlet *Machotes*, came out in 2020 and satirically examines notions of masculinity. In 2022, his third collection *Nostalgia Elsewhere* was released.

Dan Elliot is a graphic designer and educator whose work exists at the intersection of typography, materiality, and experimentation. His research and teaching engage with both the historical and formal dimensions of design, examining typographic traditions while exploring new methods of making. Through these investigations, his work considers how process shapes not only form but also meaning.

Todd Fraley is dean of the Honors College at ECU and is an associate professor in the School of Communication. He has taught classes on media and culture, research methods, and media writing. His research interests focus on the politics of representation, media and sport, and media and democracy. He holds a bachelor degree in political science and sociology from James Madison University and earned his MA and PhD in journalism and mass communication from the University of Georgia, Athens.

Romuald Gozdawa-Gołębiowski is an associate professor of linguistics at the Institute of English Studies, University of Warsaw, where he earned his PhD in 1991. His teaching and research center on applied linguistics, second language acquisition, pedagogical grammar, contrastive Polish–English syntax, CLIL, and language testing. He has published extensively on formulaic language use, grammatical components in university-level English testing, and corpus-informed pedagogical approaches. He coordinated the international Erasmus+ project TE-CON3 (Teaching English as Content), which developed a modular, content-based approach to English language instruction in higher education. At the University of Warsaw, he also oversees English language course programs within the Institute and is active in initiatives supporting educational innovation. His recent work includes survey-based studies on English-medium instruction (EMI) in Polish universities. Professor Gozdawa-Gołębiowski continues to mentor graduate researchers and contribute to interdisciplinary projects in linguistics and higher education pedagogy.

Daiki Horiguchi is an associate professor at the Graduate School of Human and Environmental Studies, Kyoto University. He has taught courses in Russian, Latvian, Slavic, and Baltic linguistics, as well as court interpretation. His research interests include word formation, verbal aspect, sociolinguistics, language identity, and the relationship between language and sports. His work has been published in *Russian Linguistics*, *Valoda: Nozīme un forma*, *Półrocznik*

Językoznawczy Tertium, among others. He is the author of *New Express Plus Latvian* (2018, Hakusuisha), a Latvian textbook designed for Japanese speakers.

Krzysztof Idczak has a BA in English studies, UKEN Kraków, and is pursuing his MA in English (communication and linguistics). His research interests center around the evolution and the potential of internet memes, as well as word building mechanisms in the lexicon of video games. He has copresented papers at international conferences: "The growing problem of children's lack of desire and satisfaction derived from learning English and possible solutions in the form of visual novels" at *PL-CALL 2023* (Kraków); "GIFs in a conflict—A conflict with GIFs" at *Across Borders X* (Krosno), and "The educator's approach to the use of AI by students at academia in Poland and foreign countries: Rules, restrictions and concerns" at *AILLT2025* (UKEN, online).

Kumi Ishii is a professor in the School of Media and Communication at Western Kentucky University. She teaches both the undergraduate and graduate levels of communication courses primarily in the area of organizational communication including communication in multinational/global organizations and communication with technologies in face-to-face and online formats. Her research interests are communication issues in the workplace and the use of emerging technologies in communication. These studies have been presented at international conferences and published in a variety of international journals.

Emilia Januś has a BA in English studies, UKEN Kraków, and is pursuing her MA in English (communication and linguistics). Her research focuses on the relationship of music and language, or music as language, as well the communicative potential of silence in Stephen King's *Pet Sematary*. She has copresented papers international conferences: "The growing problem of children's lack of desire and satisfaction derived from learning English and possible solutions in the form of visual novels" at *PL-CALL 2023* (Kraków); "GIFs in a conflict—A conflict with GIFs" at *Across Borders X* (Krosno), and "AI at academia: English Department students' perspective" at *AILLT2025* (UKEN, online).

Linda Godbold Kean holds both a master's degree and a PhD from the University of Wisconsin–Madison. Her academic research focuses on media content and its effects, with particular emphasis on the representations of race and health. She currently serves as the dean of the College of Fine Arts and Communication at East Carolina University, where she leads initiatives that bridge creative practice, scholarship, and public engagement. Dr. Kean is also a dedicated advocate for international educational exchange. She maintains active collaborations with several universities abroad, with a sustained focus on building academic partnerships in Poland.

Eryk Kowalczyk has a BA in English studies, UKEN Kraków, and is pursuing his MA in media content and creative writing programs. His research interests lie in small communities' communicative systems, like Polari, the language of queer community in London, as well as the formation of narrative structures in tabletop role-playing games. He is also a soon-to-be-published author of a horror short story titled *Rybie Oko* ("Fish eye"). He copresented papers at international conferences: *GIFs in a conflict* –A conflict with GIFs at *Across Borders X* (Krosno), and "The educator's approach to the use of AI by students at academia in Poland and foreign countries: Rules, restrictions and concerns" at *AILLT2025* (UKEN, online).

Michał Kowalski is a professor of international law at Jagiellonian University. He is vice dean of the Jagiellonian University Faculty of Law and Administration for International Relations and head of the doctoral program in law in the Jagiellonian University Doctoral School of Social Sciences. He is conciliator at the OSCE Court of Conciliation and Arbitration in Geneva (terms 2019–2025 and 2025–2031), independent expert for the OSCE Human Dimension Mechanism (term 2023–2029), member of the Legal Advisory Committee to the Minister of Foreign Affairs of the Republic of Poland (2014–2021 and since 2024), former judge ad hoc in the European Court of Human Rights (2018–2024) and former adjudicating member of the Polish Refugee Board (terms 2009–2014 and 2014–2019). He is a member of the International Law Association's International Committee "Use of Force: Military Assistance on Request (Military Action with Consent)." He was also fellow of Alexander von Humboldt Stiftung, Max-Planck-Gesellschaft, and the Tokyo Foundation.

Wiktoria Kozieł has a BA in English Studies, UKEN Kraków, and is pursuing her MA in English (communication and linguistics). She researches intertextuality and narrative structures, and their communicative potential, in creative arts (Goya's *Saturn Devouring His Son*) and film (Elena Ferrante's *My Brilliant Friend*). She has copresented papers at international conferences: "The growing problem of children's lack of desire and satisfaction derived from learning English and possible solutions in the form of visual novels" at *PL-CALL 2023* (Kraków); GIFs in a conflict—A conflict with GIFs at *Across Borders X* (Krosno), and "AI at academia: English Department students' perspective" at *AILLT2025* (UKEN, online).

Elena Kurant is an assistant professor at the Institute of East Slavic Philology, Jagiellonian University in Kraków. A philologist and translator by training, she teaches courses in specialized translation, the history of Russian theater, and film. Her scholarly interests include contemporary theater and drama, anti-war Russian dramaturgy, protest art, and socially engaged performance. She has presented her work at numerous national and international conferences. She is the author of the monograph *Театр Чудес. Авторские стратегии в драматургии Ивана Вырыпаева* (*Theatre of Wonders: Authorial Strategies in the Drama of Ivan Vyrypaev*, 2020).

Liisi Laineste is a researcher and professor in the Department of Folkloristics at the Estonian Literary Museum, where she leads the working group of humor research. Her main research object is folk humor and its online manifestations. She has published articles and edited books and journal issues on ethnic humor, internet folklore and online communication, many of which represent an interdisciplinary angle and combine folkloristics with linguistics, psychology, sociology, or communication studies. She has a standing interest in digital humanities.

Carrie Meadows is an associate professor in the School of Communication at East Carolina University. Dr. Meadows received her PhD in mass communication at the University of Alabama. Her research focuses on public relations, health communication, and intercultural communication. Her publications have been featured in *Public Relations Review*, the *International Journal of Communication*, *Communication and Sport*, *Corporate Reputation Review*, *Communication Studies*, *Chinese Journal of Communication*, *Journal of International and Intercultural Communication*. She has presented in conferences including the International Communication Association, the Association for Education in Journalism and Mass Communication, the Broadcast Education Association, and the National Communication Association.

Charles Meadows is an associate professor in the School of Communication at the College of Fine Arts and Communication of East Carolina University. Dr. Meadows' research areas focus on the intersection of public relations, social media, and innovative technologies. He has presented at conferences such as the International Communication Association, The Association for Education in Journalism and Mass Communication, the Broadcast Education Association, and the National Communication Association. His publications have been featured in *Public Relations Review*, the *International Journal of Communication*, *Communication and Sport*, *Corporate Reputation Review*, *Communication Studies*, and *Journal of the American Society for Information Science and Technology*.

Gerard McCann is a professor of international studies and principal lecturer at St Mary's University College, a college of Queen's University Belfast, UK. He is the College's head of international programs and a visiting professor at Jagiellonian University, Kraków, and the European University of Rome. He has authored or coedited a dozen books, including three volumes of *From the Local to the Global*; *COVID-19, the Global South, and the Pandemic's Developmental Impact*; *Global Education in Ireland*; *International Human Rights: Social Policy and Global Development*; *Ireland's Economic History*; *Lustration*; *Theory and History: The Political Thought of E. P. Thompson*; and *Globalisation: Policy, Values, Critique*. He coordinates the UK Government-funded "Beyond Borders" intensive program, which is held in a different European country each year and is the UK/Ireland lead on the Education Development in Ukraine (EDUWAP) program.

Olga E. O'Toole is a lecturer at the Institute of English Studies, Jagiellonian University in Kraków, where she teaches courses in language and sociolinguistics. Some of the courses she has taught include "Language, Gender, and Sexuality," "Analyzing Discourse: Linguistic and Social Perspectives," and "Ethnographic Approaches in (Micro-)Sociolinguistics." Her research interests range from critical discourse studies, linguistic anthropology, language, gender and sexuality, gender studies, and the sociology of sexuality. She has authored several academic publications in sociolinguistics and sociology.

Agnieszka Romanowska is a literary historian and translation scholar, professor in the Institute of English Studies, Jagiellonian University in Kraków, Poland. She teaches courses on Shakespeare and other British literature and leads BA and MA seminars on Shakespeare and adaptation. Her research interests include literary and theatrical reception of Shakespeare, drama translation, and adaptation. She has published on the theatrical potential of Shakespeare's dramatic text in translation, Polish poet-translators and the history of Shakespeare's reception in Poland. She is author of two monographs: *Hamlet po polsku. Teatralność szekspirowskiego tekstu dramatycznego jako zagadnienie przekładoznawcze* [*Hamlet in Polish. Theatricality of Shakespeare's Dramatic Text in Translation*] (Kraków 2005) and *Za głosem tłumacza. Szekspir Iwaszkiewicza, Miłosza i Gałczyńskiego* [*Following the Translator's Voice. Shakespeare of Iwaszkiewicz, Miłosz, and Gałczyński*] (Kraków 2017) and articles in Journal of Adaptation in Film and Performance, Litteraria Pragensia, Multicultural Shakespeare and other journals. She is a member of the European Shakespeare Research Association.

Dorota Rygiel, PhD, is a faculty member in the Department of English at the State University of Applied Sciences in Krosno, Poland. She has taught courses such as "English Literature," "History of Great Britain," and "British Studies," and supervised numerous BA-level dissertations on British culture and literature. Her research interests focus on British Asian postcolonial literature, intercultural communication, and migration. She has authored several articles and book chapters on topics including immigrant narratives in Britain, identity and belonging, and the role of food in immigrant contexts. She coedited *Culture, Language, and Literature in European and World Border Regions*, Vol. 27 (2007), and has been a reviewer for various academic publications. As a guest lecturer, she has collaborated with several universities across Europe.

Orest Semotiuk is an associate professor at the Institute of Slavic Studies in Warsaw (Polish Academy of Sciences) and a MAXQDA Professional Trainer (computer-aided content analysis). His research interests cover political humor, the medialization of armed conflicts, hybrid warfare, and the weaponization of media culture. Recent publications include "Crime and punishment: Prigozhin's mutiny and Putin's revenge in Ukrainian and Russian cartoons and memes" (2024), "Impartial humor in war times: Global and national cartoons on Russian full-scale aggression in Ukraine" (2025). His papers have been published in *Visual Communication, European Journal of Humor Research, Cognitive Studies, and Geopolitica*. He is the author of the monograph *Russian-Ukrainian War in Modern Political Cartoons. Mediatization of Modern Military Conflicts* (2021, in Ukrainian).

Sachiyo M. Shearman is a professor in the School of Communication at East Carolina University. She has taught in both the undergraduate and graduate programs in the School of Communication as well as in the master's program in international studies. She has taught courses such as "Conflict and Communication," "Intercultural Communication," and "Research Methods" in both traditional face-to-face classes and distance education formats. Her research interest lies in the analysis of culture, conflict, and communication, focusing on the examination of cultural impact, individual differences, and cognitive processing in conflict resolution and intercultural communication. She has written an electronic textbook, *Communication Across Cultures*, and authored several book chapters. Her research studies have been published in *Communication Teacher, Communication Quarterly, Human Communication Research, The International Journal of Human Resources Management, Journal of Family Communication, Journal of Family Research,* and the *Howard Journal of Communication*.

Jaylin Thompson is a graduate student in the MA program at the School of Arts and Design at East Carolina University. She is originally from upstate New York and moved to North Carolina in his/her preteen years. Her father was a graphic designer, so naturally, that influenced her love for art and his/her decision to enroll at ECU for her BFA. In her designs, she takes great pride in helping people find their voice and spread their message through art, as she believes that helping one another is the only way forward.

Rafael Vélez Núñez is a professor in the English department at the Universidad de Cádiz (Spain), where he teaches Early Modern English literature and culture. His early research deals mostly with Early Modern drama, especially courtly productions, and gender studies. In the last few years, he has collaborated in various research projects on Restoration comedy (databases and catalogues) and prose fiction. His main publications focus on this period, especially on historical novels and translations. Recently, he has shown a growing interest in the burgeoning field of Gibraltarian literature. He has delivered talks and attended international conferences on this topic in universities in Spain and Poland and some related research work will be published this year.

Władysław Witalisz is a professor at the Institute of English Studies, Jagiellonian University in Kraków. His research interests include medieval drama and theater, chivalric romance and its political meanings, the depiction of the Trojan War in the Middle Ages, medieval religious literature, English medieval mysticism, the reception of Boethius in literature, William Shakespeare, and medievalism in contemporary literature. He has edited and coedited over twenty books and published numerous articles on Middle English romance, medieval drama, and medieval mysticism. His book *The Trojan Mirror: Middle English Narratives of Troy as Books of Princely Advice* (2011) is widely quoted in literature on medieval Trojan romance. Witalisz is the founder and general editor of the series "TEXT-MEANING-CONTEXT" published by Peter Lang. He has a long history of working in university administration. He is currently head of the Department of British Literature and Culture and dean of the Faculty of Philology at Jagiellonian University.

Monika Zasowska is an assistant professor at the Institute of Linguistics, University of Silesia in Katowice, Poland. She is an academic teacher in the undergraduate English Philology programs at the Faculty of Humanities, where she teaches both practical English subjects and academic courses. Her research focuses on the phenomenon of evaluation, review genres, and corpus approaches to studying academic discourse. Her research studies have been published in *Linguistica Silesiana* and *Studia Linguistica Universitatis Iagellonicae Cracoviensis*. Most recently, she has authored a monograph entitled *Evaluation in Academic Discourse: Book Reviews in Linguistics and Psychology* (University of Silesia Press, 2025). She has also contributed a chapter entitled "Semantic prosody in academic book reviews" to the edited volume *Engaged Languages and Literatures. Critical Views* (V&R Unipress Publishers, 2025).

www.ingramcontent.com/pod-product-compliance
Lightning Source LLC
Chambersburg PA
CBHW071619170426
43195CB00038B/1448